JUSTICE IN EXTREME CASES

In *Justice in Extreme Cases*, Darryl Robinson argues that the encounter between criminal law theory and international criminal law (ICL) can be illuminating in two directions: criminal law theory can challenge and improve ICL, and conversely, ICL's novel puzzles can challenge and improve mainstream criminal law theory. Robinson recommends a 'coherentist' method for discussions of principles, justice and justification. Coherentism recognizes that prevailing understandings are fallible, contingent human constructs. This book will be a valuable resource to scholars and jurists in ICL, as well as scholars of criminal law theory and legal philosophy.

Darryl Robinson is professor of law at Queen's University (Canada). He has helped shape international criminal law as a negotiator of the ICC Statute, a legal adviser at the Court, and as an influential scholar. He received the Antonio Cassese Prize for International Criminal Legal Studies for his work on moral coherence of criminal law.

T0371260

Justice in Extreme Cases

CRIMINAL LAW THEORY MEETS INTERNATIONAL CRIMINAL LAW

DARRYL ROBINSON

Queen's University

CAMBRIDGE
UNIVERSITY PRESS

CAMBRIDGE
UNIVERSITY PRESS

University Printing House, Cambridge CB2 8BS, United Kingdom

One Liberty Plaza, 20th Floor, New York, NY 10006, USA

477 Williamstown Road, Port Melbourne, VIC 3207, Australia

314-321, 3rd Floor, Plot 3, Splendor Forum, Jasola District Centre, New Delhi - 110025, India

103 Penang Road, #05-06/07, Visioncrest Commercial, Singapore 238467

Cambridge University Press is part of the University of Cambridge.

It furthers the University's mission by disseminating knowledge in the pursuit of education, learning and research at the highest international levels of excellence.

www.cambridge.org
Information on this title: www.cambridge.org/9781009318556
DOI: 10.1017/9781107300422

First published 2020
First paperback edition 2022

A catalogue record for this publication is available from the British Library

ISBN 978-1-107-04161-5 Hardback
ISBN 978-1-009-31855-6 Paperback

Cambridge University Press has no responsibility for the persistence or accuracy of URLs for external or third-party internet websites referred to in this publication, and does not guarantee that any content on such websites is, or will remain, accurate or appropriate.

Contents

Acknowledgements

It has taken me years – many more years than I anticipated – to complete this book. It was over twelve years ago that I first wrote about (i) the need for a method to explore deontic constraints in international criminal law and (ii) how such an effort could produce insights not only for international criminal law, but also for criminal law theory. This project brings together international criminal law scholarship, criminal law theory, and moral philosophy. The investigation in turn took me into other fields, such as cosmopolitanism, and ultimately into deeper epistemological theory, which led me to coherentism.

I have benefited immensely from discussions with a great number of colleagues and scholars. Among these scholars in the field of international criminal law are Diane Marie Amann, Kai Ambos, Ilias Bantekas, Elena Baylis, Alejandro Chehtman, Nancy Combs, Robert Cryer, Caroline Davidson, Randle DeFalco, Margaret (Meg) deGuzman, Mark Drumbl, Markus Dubber, Jean Galbraith, Alexander (Sasha) Greenawalt, Adil Haque, Kevin Heller, Neha Jain, Mark Kersten, Frédéric Mégret, Sarah Nouwen, Jens Ohlin, Leila Sadat, Elies van Sliedregt, Carsten Stahn, Cassandra Steer, Milena Sterio, James Stewart, François Tanguay-Renaud, Jenia Turner, and Harmen van der Wilt. In addition, I have received helpful feedback at various conferences and workshops, including particularly from colleagues at Queen's University (Canada) and the University of Toronto, among whom I would especially thank Chris Essert, Michael Pratt, Jacob Weinrib, Vincent Chiao, Markus Dubber, Karen Knop and Malcolm Thorburn. I am particularly grateful to Meg deGuzman, who organized a workshop at Temple University to further discuss and refine the ideas in this book, and to all participants in that workshop. I apologize to those scholars whom I have inevitably overlooked in this list; my ideas have been shaped by many minds.

The ideas in this book were also developed in a doctoral thesis at Leiden University under Carsten Stahn. I thank Carsten and the other most excellent members of the supervisory and doctoral committees – including Giulia Pinzauti,

Joseph Powderly, William Schabas, Elies van Sliedregt, Harmen van der Wilt, Robert Heinsch and Letitzia Lo Gaccio – for their insights and comments.

I spent a very fruitful term in 2014 at the Centre for Ethics at the University of Toronto, where I was inspired by conversations with political and moral philosophers. It was there that I found the path that led me to the coherentist method.

I published provisional findings as I progressed, in order to benefit from online symposia and scholarly engagement. Accordingly, this book draws on and develops material previously presented in "The Identity Crisis of International Criminal Law"[1] (Chapter 2), "A Cosmopolitan Liberal Account of International Criminal Law"[2] (Chapter 3), "International Criminal Law as Justice"[3] (Chapters 1 and 5), "How Command Responsibility Got So Complicated: A Culpability Contradiction, Its Obfuscation, and a Simple Solution"[4] (Chapters 6 and 7), "A Justification of Command Responsibility"[5] (Chapter 8), and a draft "The Humanity of Criminal Justice: Five Themes."[6] Many of my earlier ideas are significantly refined here.

Many students at Queen's University Faculty of Law have provided excellent research assistance, including Deborah Bayley, Marion Blight, Ted Brook, Logan Crowell, Kathleen Davis, Avene Derwa, Jennifer Dumoulin, Stephanie Ford, Anne Marie Heenan, Andrew Hills, Zoe Knes-Gray, Gillian MacNeil, Clara Milde, Rachel Oster, Steve Taylor, and Eric Znotins. I extend to them all my heartfelt thanks.

Finally, I am very grateful to have received funding from the Social Sciences and Humanities Research Council of Canada. I was also honoured to receive the Antonio Cassese Prize for International Criminal Legal Studies to enable this research.

Antonio Cassese's writing always had heart. My work with fundamental principles has brought me into areas of criminal law theory that can often be very analytical, abstract, and categorical. My research so far has underscored the Cassese wisdom that we must not lose touch with our compassion. My experience has pushed me toward a realization that the exploration of justice is not just a series of cerebral deductions from abstract principles but rather a conversation. Wisdom requires not only reason but also empathy and humanity. Heart plays a role – a big role – in our deepest principles.

---

[1] (2008) 21 Leiden Journal of International Law 925.
[2] (2013) 26 Leiden Journal of International Law 127.
[3] (2013) 11 Journal of International Criminal Justice 499.
[4] (2012) 13 Melbourne Journal of International Law 1.
[5] (2017) 28 Criminal Law Forum 633.
[6] Expected to be published with *Brill Research Perspectives in International Legal Theory and Practice*.

Cases, Statutes, and Other Authorities

INTERNATIONAL AND SUPRANATIONAL CASES

European Court of Human Rights (ECtHR)

East African Asians v United Kingdom App Nos 4403–4419/70, 4422/70, 4423.70, 4434/70, 4443/70, 4476–4478/70, 4486/70, 4501/70 and 4526–4530/70 (joined) [1973] 3 EHRR 76.
Golder v United Kingdom App No 4451/70 [1975] 1 EHRR 524.

Extraordinary Chambers in the Courts of Cambodia (ECCC)

Prosecutor v Chea, Sary, Thirith and Samphan, Decision on the Applicability of Joint Criminal Enterprise, ECCC T.Ch, Case No 002/19-09-2007-ECCC-TC, 12 September 2011.

Inter-American Court of Human Rights (IACHR)

Compulsory Membership in an Association Prescribed by Law for the Practice of Journalism (1985), Advisory Opinion OC-5/85, Inter-Am Ct HR 2.
Prosecutor v Bámaca Velásquez – Series C No 70 [2000] IACHR 7.

International Court of Justice (ICJ)

Case Concerning United States Diplomatic and Consular Staff in Tehran (United States of America v. Iran) [1980] ICJ Rep 3.

International Criminal Court (ICC)

Prosecutor v Jean-Pierre Bemba Gombo, Decision Pursuant to Article 61(7) (a) and (b) of the Rome Statute on the Charges of the Prosecutor

International Criminal Tribunal for Rwanda (ICTR)

Prosecutor v Seromba, Judgment, ICTR A.Ch, ICTR-2001-66-A, 12 March 2008.

International Criminal Tribunal for the former Yugoslavia (ICTY)

Prosecutor v Aleksovski, Judgment, ICTY T.Ch, IT-95-14/1-T, 25 June 1999.
Prosecutor v Aleksovski, Judgment, ICTY A.Ch, IT-95-14/1-A, 24 March 2000.
Prosecutor v Blagojević and Jokić, Judgment, ICT T.Ch, IT-02-60-T, 17 January 2005.
Prosecutor v Blagojević and Jokić, Judgment, ICTY A.Ch, IT-02-60-A, 9 May 2007.
Prosecutor v Blaškić, Judgment, ICTY T.Ch, IT-95-14-T, 3 March 2000.
Prosecutor v Blaškić, Judgment, ICTY A.Ch, IT-95-14-A, 29 July 2004.
Prosecutor v Brđanin, Decision on Interlocutory Appeal, ICTY A.Ch, IT-99-36-A, 19 March 2004.
Prosecutor v Brđanin, Judgment, ICTY T.Ch, IT-99-36-T, 1 September 2004.
Prosecutor v Brđanin, Judgment, ICTY A.Ch, IT-99-36-A, 3 April 2007.
Prosecutor v Delalić et al (Čelebići), Judgment, ICTY T.Ch, IT-96-21-T, 16 November 1998.
Prosecutor v Delalić et al (Čelebići), Judgment, ICTY A.Ch, IT-96-21-A, 20 February 2001.
Prosecutor v Đordevic, Judgment, ICTY A.Ch, IT-05-87/1-A, 27 January 2014.
Prosecutor v Erdemović, Judgment, ICTY A.Ch, IT-96-22-A, 7 October 1997.
Prosecutor v Furundžija, Judgment, ICTY T.Ch, IT-95-17/1-T, 10 December 1998.
Prosecutor v Hadžihasanović, Decision on Interlocutory Appeal Challenging Jurisdiction in Relation to Command Responsibility, ICTY A.Ch, IT-01-47-AR72, 16 July 2003.
Prosecutor v Halilović, Judgment, ICTY T.Ch, IT-01-48-T, 16 November 2005.
Prosecutor v Kordić and Čerkez, Judgment, ICTY A.Ch, IT-95-14/2-A, 17 December 2004.
Prosecutor v Krajišnik, Judgment, ICTY A.Ch, IT-05-87/1-A, 27 January 2014.
Prosecutor v Krnojelać, Third Amended Indictment, ICTY, IT-27-95-I, 25 June 2001.
Prosecutor v Krnojelać, Judgment, ICTY A.Ch, IT-97-25-A, 17 September 2003.
Prosecutor v Krstić, Judgment, ICTY A.Ch, IT-98-33-A, 19 April 2004.
Prosecutor v Kvočka, Judgment, ICTY T.Ch, IT-98-30/1-T, 2 November 2001.
Prosecutor v Kvočka, Judgment, ICTY A.Ch, IT-98-30/1-A, 28 February 2005.
Prosecutor v Milutinović, Decision on Dragoljub Ojdanić's Motion Challenging Jurisdiction – Joint Criminal Enterprise, ICTY A.Ch, IT-99-37-AR72, 21 May 2003.
Prosecutor v Mladić, Judgment, ICTY T.Ch, IT-09-92-T, 22 November 2017.
Prosecutor v Mrkšić et al, Judgment, ICTY A.Ch, IT-95-13/1-A, 5 May 2009.
Prosecutor v Orić, Judgment, ICTY T.Ch, IT-03-68-T, 30 June 2006.
Prosecutor v Orić, Judgment, ICTY A.Ch, IT-03-68-A, 3 July 2008.
Prosecutor v Perišić, Judgment, ICTY A.Ch, IT-04-81-A, IT-05-87-A, 28 February 2013.
Prosecutor v Popović, Judgment, ICTY A.Ch, IT-05-88-A, 30 January 2015.
Prosecutor v Prlić, Judgment, ICTY A.Ch, IT-04-74-A, 29 November 2017.

International Military Tribunals (Nuremberg and Tokyo)

Special Court for Sierra Leone (SCSL)

Prosecutor v Sesay, Kallon and Gbao (RUF Case), Judgment, SCSL T.Ch, SCSL-04-15-T, 2 March 2009.

Special Tribunal for Lebanon (STL)

Prosecutor v Ayyash, Interlocutory Decision on the Applicable Law: Terrorism, Conspiracy, Homicide, Perpetration, Cumulative Charging, STL A.Ch, Case No. STL-11-01/I, 16 February 2011.

United Nations Human Rights Committee

A v Australia, Communication No 560/1993, Views 3 April 1997, A/52/40 (Vol II), Annex VI, sect L.

Keith Cox v Canada, Communication No 539/1993, Views 31 October 1994, A/50/40, Vol. II, Annex X, sect M, reproduced in (1994) HRLJ 410.

DOMESTIC CASES

Canada

R v Beatty [2008] 1 SCR 49.
R v Finta [1994] 1 SCR 701.
R v Gladue [1999] 1 SCR 688.
R v Hasselwander [1993] 2 SCR 398.

United Kingdom

R v Bateman (1925) 19 Cr App R 8 (CCA).

United States

State v Tally, 102 Ala. 25, 15 So. (1894).
United States v Medina, CM 427 162 (ACMR 1971).
United States v Reese, 92 U.S. 214 (1875).
United States v RLC, 503 U.S. 291 (1992).
Re Yamashita, 327 U.S. 1 (1946).

STATUTES

Canada

Criminal Code RSC, 1985, c C-46.

Germany

Gesetz zur Einführung des Völkerstrafgesetzbuches [*Act to Introduce the Code of Crimes against International Law*], 26 June 2002, Bundesgesetzblatt Jahrgang 2002 Teil II, Nr 42, 2254, online: www.mpicc.de/shared/data/pdf/vstgbleng2.pdf.

OTHER AUTHORITIES

Basic Instruments of International Courts and Tribunals

Elements of Crimes, ICC-ASP/1/3 (2002).

Statute of the International Criminal Tribunal for Rwanda, 8 November 1994, appended to UNSC Res 955 (1994), UN Doc S/RES/955 (1994), as amended up to UNSC Res 1901 (2009).

Statute of the International Criminal Tribunal for the Former Yugoslavia, 25 May 1993, appended to UNSC Res 827 (1993), UN Doc S/RES/827 (1993), as amended up to UNSC Res 1877 (2009).

Statute of the Special Court for Sierra Leone, 16 January 2002, UN Doc S/2002/246, 2178 UNTS 138.

Treaties

Charter of the United Nations, 26 June 1945, 1 UNTS XVI.

Convention on the Prevention and Punishment of the Crime of Genocide, 9 December 1948, 8 UNTS 277.

Geneva Convention for the Amelioration of the Condition of the Wounded and Sick in Armed Forces in the Field (First Geneva Convention), 12 August 1949, 75 UNTS 31.

Geneva Convention for the Amelioration of the Condition of Wounded, Sick and Shipwrecked Members of Armed Forces at Sea (Second Geneva Convention), 12 August 1949, 75 UNTS 85.

Geneva Convention Relative to the Treatment of Prisoners of War (Third Geneva Convention), 12 August 1949, 75 UNTS 135.

Geneva Convention Relative to the Protection of Civilian Persons in Time of War (Fourth Geneva Convention), 12 August 1949, 75 UNTS 287.

Protocol Additional to the Geneva Conventions of 12 August 1949, and relating to the Protection of Victims of International Armed Conflicts (Protocol I), 8 June 1977, 1125 UNTS 3.

Rome Statute of the International Criminal Court, 17 July 1998 (last amended 2010), 2187 UNTS 3.

Vienna Convention on the Law of Treaties, 23 May 1969, 1155 UNTS 331.

Other UN Documents

International Commission of Inquiry on Darfur, *Report to the United Nations Secretary-General Pursuant to Security Council Resolution 1564 of 18 September 2004* (25 January 2005), online: www.un.org/ruleoflaw/files/com_inq_darfur.pdf.

United Nations General Assembly, *Basic Principles and Guidelines on the Right to a Remedy and Reparations for Victims of Gross Violations of International Human Rights Law and Serious Violations of International Humanitarian Law*, GA Res 60/147, UNGAOR, 60th Sess, UN Doc A/RES/60/147 (2005).

United Nations General Assembly, *Draft Articles on Responsibility of States for Internationally Wrongful Acts*, Annex to GA Res 58/83, UNGAOR, 58th Sess, UN Doc A/56/49(Vol I)/Corr.4 (2001).

United Nations Secretary General, *Report of the Secretary-General Pursuant to Paragraph 2 of Security Council Resolution 808*, UN Doc S/25704 (1993).

Abbreviations

A.Ch	Appeals Chamber
AJIL	*American Journal of International Law*
Am J Comp L	*American Journal of Comparative Law*
AP I	Additional Protocol I to the Geneva Conventions
ASIL Proc	*American Society of International Law Proceedings*
Calif L Rev	*California Law Review*
Canadian J Phil	*Canadian Journal of Philosophy*
Can JL & Jur	*Canadian Journal of Law and Jurisprudence*
Can J L & Soc	*Canadian Journal of Law and Society*
Cardozo J of Int'l & Comp L	*Cardozo Journal of International and Comparative Law*
Case W Res L Rev	*Case Western Reserve Law Review*
CCA	Court of Criminal Appeals (England & Wales)
Columbia J Transn'l L	*Columbia Journal of Transnational Law*
Crim L & Phil	*Criminal Law and Philosophy*
Crim L Forum	*Criminal Law Forum*
Denver J Int L & Pol'y	*Denver Journal of International Law and Policy*
Duke J Comp & Int'l L	*Duke Journal of Comparative and International Law*
ECCC	Extraordinary Chambers in the Courts of Cambodia
ECHR	European Convention on Human Rights
ECtHR	European Court of Human Rights
EJIL	*European Journal of International Law*
Eur J Crime Cr L Cr J	*European Journal of Crime, Criminal Law and Criminal Justice*
Eur J Int'l Rel	*European Journal of International Relations*
Eur J Oper Res	*European Journal of Operational Research*
Fletcher F World Aff	*Fletcher Forum of World Affairs*

Geo J Legal Ethics	*Georgetown Journal of Legal Ethics*
Harvard HRJ	*Harvard Human Rights Journal*
HRLJ	*Human Rights Law Journal*
HRQ	*Human Rights Quarterly*
HRTK	had reason to know
ICC	International Criminal Court
ICJ	International Court of Justice
ICL	international criminal law
ICRC	International Committee of the Red Cross
ICTR	International Criminal Tribunal for Rwanda
ICTY	International Criminal Tribunal for the former Yugoslavia
IJCACJ	*International Journal of Comparative and Applied Criminal Justice*
Indian J Const L	*Indian Journal of Constitutional Law*
Inter Am Ct HR	Inter-American Court of Human Rights
Int'l & Comp LQ	*International and Comparative Law Quarterly*
Int'l Crim L Rev	*International Criminal Law Review*
Int'l LJ	*International Law Journal*
Int'l LQ	*International Law Quarterly*
J Appl	*Journal of Applied Social Psychology*
JBS	*Journal of British Studies*
JCE	joint criminal enterprise
JCLC	*Journal of Criminal Law and Criminology*
J Conflict & Sec L	*Journal of Conflict and Security Law*
J Contemp Legal Iss	*Journal of Contemporary Legal Issues*
Jerusalem Phil Q	*Jerusalem Philosophical Quarterly*
J Ethics Soc Philos	*Journal of Ethics and Social Philosophy*
JICJ	*Journal of International Criminal Justice*
J Int'l L	*Journal of International Law*
J Phil	*Journal of Philosophy*
Justice Q	*Justice Quarterly*
L&C	*Law and Critique*
L & Contemp Probs	*Law and Contemporary Problems*
L & Phil	*Law and Philosophy*
Law & Hist Rev	*Law and History Review*
LDR	*Law and Development Review*
LHR	*Law and History Review*
LJ	*Law Journal*
LJIL	*Leiden Journal of International Law*
Loy U Chi LJ	*Loyola University of Chicago Law Journal*
LQR	*Law Quarterly Review*

L Rev	*Law Review*
Melbourne U L Rev	*Melbourne University Law Review*
NC J Int'l L & Comm Reg	*North Carolina Journal of International Law and Commercial Regulation*
Neth Q Hum Rights	*Netherlands Quarterly of Human Rights*
NGO	non-governmental organization
Nw U L Rev	*Northwestern University Law Review*
NYIL	*Netherlands Yearbook of International Law*
NYU J Int'l L & Pol	*New York University Journal of International Law and Politics*
Ohio St J on Disp Resol	*Ohio State Journal on Dispute Resolution*
Oxf J L Stud	*Oxford Journal of Legal Studies*
Phil & Pub Aff	*Philosophy and Public Affairs*
PPR	*Philosophy and Phenomenological Research*
PTC	Pre-Trial Chamber
S Cal Interdisc LJ	*Southern California Interdisciplinary Law Journal*
SCER	*Supreme Court Economic Review*
SCR	Supreme Court Reports (Canada)
SCSL	Special Court for Sierra Leone
SHK	should have known
Soc Psychol Q	*Social Psychology Quarterly*
Southern J Phil	*Southern Journal of Philosophy*
STL	Special Tribunal for Lebanon
T.Ch	Trial Chamber
Theor Inq L	*Theoretical Inquiries in Law*
Transnat'l L & Contemp Probs	*Transnational Law and Contemporary Problems*
Transnat'l L & Pol'y	*Transnational Law and Policy*
U C Davis J Intl L & Pol'y	*UC Davis Journal of International Law and Policy*
U Cincinnati L Rev	*University of Cincinnati Law Review*
U Illinois L Rev	*University of Illinois Law Review*
U Miami L Rev	*University of Miami Law Review*
UN	United Nations
UNGA	United Nations General Assembly
UNSC	United Nations Security Council
U Pa J Int'l L	*University of Pennsylvania Journal of International Law*
U Pittsburgh L Rev	*University of Pittsburgh Law Review*
U Toronto LJ	*University of Toronto Law Journal*
Wis Int'l LJ	*Wisconsin International Law Journal*
Wm & Mary Bill Rts J	*William & Mary Bill of Rights Journal*
Yale J L & HR	*Yale Journal of Law and Human Rights*

PART I

Introduction and Problem

1

Introduction

OVERVIEW

This book is about the encounter between criminal law theory and international criminal law (ICL).[1] I argue that the encounter can be illuminating in both directions. Criminal law theory can challenge and improve ICL, and in turn ICL can challenge and improve criminal law theory. To manage the scope of the inquiry, I focus on one subset of criminal law theory: exploring the deontic[2] constraints of a system of justice, such as the fundamental principles of culpability and legality. ICL often addresses extraordinary circumstances and mass atrocities, which can pose special difficulties for this type of inquiry; however, these difficulties also present opportunities for insight.

I urge a "mid-level principles" and "coherentist" approach to identifying and delineating deontic principles. This approach differs from some common academic instincts, for example that we must seek certainty by grounding propositions in firm bedrock, or that we must ground normative claims in one of the main comprehensive ethical theories. Coherentism recognizes that, in the human condition, the best we can do is to work with all available clues. Prevailing understandings are fallible, contingent, human constructs; nonetheless, we use those understandings as the best guide we have, while also trying to improve them. Furthermore, I argue that principles of criminal justice are neither abstract and metaphysical, nor vengeful and backward-looking; they are thoroughly humanistic. Empathy, intuition, and experience are recurring touchstones in this book.

The study of deontic constraints is important for several reasons. One is to ensure that persons are treated justly. Another is that clarifying the constraints can produce more effective law that avoids excessively rigid conceptions that are not normatively supported. Yet another is that the study of ICL's novel problems can advance criminal law theory by revealing that many commonplace assumptions are

---

[1] In this book, "international criminal law" refers to the law for the investigation and prosecution of persons responsible for genocide, crimes against humanity, and war crimes, as well with attendant principles such as command responsibility, superior orders, and so on. This law was developed and applied primarily by international criminal tribunals and courts, but also by domestic courts.

[2] I explain this term more carefully in §1.1.3 and Chapters 3 and 4.

predicated on the "normal" context. As an analogy, the study of physics near a black hole, or at velocities near the speed of light, or at the subatomic scale, may lead us to notice that concepts we have used in everyday experience are actually more subtle than we thought. The study of special cases is necessary for a truly general theory of criminal justice.

To illustrate the proposed approach, I unpack specific controversies in command responsibility. Command responsibility is currently contested, confused, and convoluted. I trace how an inadvertent culpability contribution caused the present entanglement. I also argue that the "should have known" standard, which seems problematic at first glance, reveals on closer inspection a sound insight about justice. I offer prescriptions for a morally justified and practical law to address gross derelictions that unleash deadly forces.

1.1 CONTEXT: WHY PRINCIPLES MATTER

1.1.1 Rapid Construction of a New Body of Criminal Law

Domestic criminal law has existed in most regions for many centuries,[3] and yet the practices and principles of domestic criminal law are still contested. In comparison, ICL is still a nascent innovation. After some sporadic historic forerunners and a brief surge after World War II, ICL has really taken root only in the last two decades, following the creation of the International Criminal Tribunal for the former Yugoslavia (ICTY) and the International Criminal Tribunal for Rwanda (ICTR) (known collectively as "the Tribunals").[4] Despite initial skepticism in the 1990s, the field has demonstrated its feasibility in securing the arrests and trials of major figures, and it has become relatively established far more quickly than anyone anticipated.

The field has also seen major stumbles and setbacks, and currently ICL is awash with controversies and criticisms from every direction. Projecting criminal law onto the international plane to respond to the worst crimes is still very much a new and uncertain experiment in human history. The International Criminal Court (ICC) in particular has been struggling, and, at the time of writing, several major ICC cases have collapsed or ended in highly controversial acquittals.

Contemporary ICL was produced by means of a rapid transnational conversation involving thousands of jurists, drawing on diverse sources and legal systems. The elaboration of ICL began in earnest in the mid-1990s, with the creation of international criminal tribunals. While there were some important international and national precedents, those precedents were often sparse and inconsistent. As a result,

---

[3] See, e.g., G MacCormack, *Traditional Chinese Penal Law* (Edinburgh University Press, 1990); P Olivelle (trans and ed), *Dharmasutras: The Law Codes of Apastamba, Gautama, Baudhayana, and Vasistha* (Motilal Banarsidass, 2003); J Tyldesley, *Judgement of the Pharaoh: Crime and Punishment in Ancient Egypt* (Weidenfeld & Nicolson, 2000).

[4] D Robinson & G MacNeil, "The Tribunals and the Renaissance of International Criminal Law: Three Themes" (2016) 110 AJIL 191.

jurists had to make significant choices in shaping the doctrines. They made those choices under severe time pressures; there was not time to ponder rarefied points. Later choices in turn built on those initial choices at increasingly fine levels of granularity. Thus many hands have hastily woven together the elaborate tapestry of definitions and principles that we recognize today.

While it is an achievement that a body of criminal law was fashioned so quickly, it is inevitable that there will be oversights, contradictions or incoherencies in the resulting patchwork of doctrines. Now, as the need to articulate a common set of rules has become less urgent, the time is ripe for a more systematic analytical and normative examination of the fabric of rules that has been stitched together. It is an opportune moment for an invigorated criminal law theory of ICL.

1.1.2 The Liberal Critique and Possible Overcorrection

Scholarship about ICL has recently flourished and diversified, with scholars scrutinizing ICL from a multiplicity of perspectives, including interdisciplinary, critical, and theoretical approaches.[5] One prominent strand of this new scholarship has been the liberal critique of ICL, which brings criminal law theory to bear on ICL problems, with particular emphasis on the fundamental constraints of a liberal justice system. Scholars have pointed out that ICL, despite proclaiming its adherence to fundamental principles, often seems to contravene those principles.[6] Concerns initially tended to focus on "joint criminal enterprise," but critical attention quickly spread to other doctrines, such as command responsibility and duress. Many scholars are now doing thoughtful work in this vein.

But things move quickly in ICL. In the last decade, ICL has already demonstrated its adaptability by embracing the liberal critique. Scholarly literature and judicial reasoning has already evinced much more careful grappling with fundamental principles. Recent judicial decisions are particularly mindful of personal culpability and conversant with concepts from criminal law theory.[7]

---

[5] For impressive canvassing of the literature, see C Kreß, *Towards a Truly Universal Invisible College of International Criminal Lawyers* (Torkel Opsahl Academic, 2014); S Vasiliev, "On Trajectories and Destinations of International Criminal Law Scholarship" (2015) 28 LJIL 701; S Nouwen, "International Criminal Law: Theory All over the Place," in A Orford & F Hoffman, eds, *Oxford Handbook of the Theory of International Law* (Oxford University Press, 2016); C Stahn, *A Critical Introduction to International Criminal Law* (Cambridge University Press, 2018).

[6] Among the first pioneers in this respect were G P Fletcher and J D Ohlin: G P Fletcher & J D Ohlin, "Reclaiming Fundamental Principles of Criminal Law in the *Darfur Case*" (2005) 3 JICJ 539; A M Danner & J S Martinez, "Guilty Associations: Joint Criminal Enterprise, Command Responsibility, and the Development of International Criminal Law" (2005) 93 Calif L Rev 75; K Ambos, "Remarks on the General Part of International Criminal Law" (2006) 4 JICJ 660; M Damaška, "The Shadow Side of Command Responsibility" (2001) 49 Am J Comp L 455.

[7] As just two examples, see *Prosecutor v Lubanga Dyilo*, Judgment pursuant to Article 74 of the Statute, ICC T.Ch, ICC-01/04–01/06, 14 March 2012, at paras 917–1018 (co-perpetration and culpability); *Prosecutor v Bemba Gombo*, Judgment pursuant to Article 74 of the Statute, ICC T.Ch, ICC-01/05–01/08, 21 March 2016 (command responsibility and culpability). Other examples are discussed

Indeed, there is a very real danger that the system may even *over*correct. It is entirely understandable that judges, in response to sustained academic criticism that their approaches are too expansive, might swing to the opposite extreme, adopting approaches that are excessively conservative, demanding, and rarefied, all in the name of rigour. It has become arguable that judges – particularly at the ICC – may be falling at times into the opposite pitfall of *Überdogmatisierung* – that is, excessively rigid over-theorizing that loses sight of the purposes and practicalities of criminal law adjudication in non-ideal earthly conditions.[8] Taking the broadest interpretation at every turn is overly simplistic, but so is always taking the narrowest. "Just Convict Everyone"[9] was rightly criticized as the problematic extension of one tendency, but "Just Acquit Everyone" is the problematic overextension of the opposite tendency.[10]

Whereas the Tribunals have, at times, been (unfairly) criticized by some commentators as "conviction machines," the ICC is, if anything, in danger of emerging as an "acquittal machine," given that the majority of cases so far have ended in acquittals, collapses at trial, and even failures at the charge confirmation stage. This trend has culminated in the controversial acquittals of Jean-Pierre Bemba in 2018 and then Charles Gbagbo in 2019.[11] Currently, the reflex narrative among many commentators is to ascribe every failed case at the ICC to faulty investigations by the Office of the Prosecutor. While investigative shortcomings are undoubtedly part of the problem, observers appear to be waking to the fact that judicial standards are also part of the equation and that some ICC judges may be applying abnormally exacting procedural requirements, evidentiary expectations, standards of review, narrow definitions, and conceptions of the culpability principle.[12]

---

elsewhere in the book, esp at §2.5. This laudable trend in judicial reasoning is noted in J D Ohlin, "Co-perpetration: German *Dogmatik* or German Invasion?," in C Stahn, ed, *The Law and Practice of the International Criminal Court: A Critical Account of Challenges and Achievements* (Oxford University Press, 2015).

[8]   M Bergsmo, E J Buis & N H Bergsmo, "Setting a Discourse Space: Correlational Analysis, Foundational Concepts, and Legally Protected Interests in International Criminal Law," in M Bergsmo & E J Buis, eds, *Philosophical Foundations of International Criminal Law: Correlating Thinkers* (Torkel Opshal Academic, 2018) at 3–5; E van Sliedregt, "International Criminal Law: Over-Studied and Underachieving?" (2016) 29 LJIL 1; see also §2.5.

[9]   M E Badar, "Just Convict Everyone! Joint Perpetration from *Tadić* to *Stakić* and Back Again" (2006) 6 Int'l Crim L Rev 293.

[10] See §2.5.

[11] *Prosecutor v Jean-Pierre Bemba Gombo*, Judgment on the appeal of Mr Jean-Pierre Bemba Gombo against Trial Chamber III's Judgment pursuant to Article 74 of the Statute, ICC A.Ch, ICC-01/05–01/08 A, 8 June 2018; *Prosecutor v Gbagbo and Goudé*, Dissenting Opinion to the Chamber's Oral Decision of 15 January 2019, ICC T.Ch I, ICC-02/11–01/15–1234, 15 January 2019 (Judge Carbuccia).

[12] I explore the possibility of "overcorrection" in the *Bemba* case in Annex 4; see also D Robinson, "The Other Poisoned Chalice: Unprecedented Evidentiary Standards in the *Gbagbo* Case?" (5 November 2019) EJIL Talk (blog); see also D M Amann, "In *Bemba* and Beyond, Crimes Adjudged to Commit Themselves" (13 June 2018) EJIL Talk (blog); L N Sadat, "Fiddling While Rome Burns? The Appeals Chamber's Curious Decision in *Prosecutor v Jean-Pierre Bemba Gombo*" (12 June 2018) EJIL Talk (blog); M Jackson, "Commanders' Motivations in *Bemba*" (15 June 2018) EJIL Talk (blog); S SáCouto, "The Impact of the Appeals Chamber Decision in *Bemba*: Impunity for

The inclination toward higher standards is commendable, but if barriers to conviction are increased out of misguided enthusiasm beyond what is required by deontic principles, then one sacrifices the system's impact and purpose for no deontic or consequentialist reason. A convergence of inappropriately rigid standards will, at best, increase the time and resources required for each investigation and prosecution; at worst, it will lead to the continued collapsing of cases. Either outcome entails unnecessary expenditure of social resources and a diminishment of the intended expressive message and beneficial impact of ICL. Thus it is all the more important to delineate soundly the fundamental principles appropriate to the system.

1.1.3 Two Reasons to Clarify Principles

Scholars sometimes suggest that the way out of this quandary is to "balance" utilitarian and deontological considerations.[13] But "balance," while sound as an aspiration, is still a bit too vague. It does not provide us with a conceptual framework of how and why these considerations would be "balanced," nor does it provide a methodology for doing so.

A helpful first step was famously suggested by H L A Hart, who helped to clarify the interplay of consequentialist and deontological considerations.[14] Purely deontological accounts of criminal law are generally unconvincing, because the objective

Sexual and Gender-Based Crimes?" (22 June 2018) IJ Monitor (blog); J Trahan, "*Bemba* Acquittal Rests on Erroneous Application of Appellate Review Standard" (25 June 2018) Opinio Juris (blog); J Powderly & N Hayes, "The *Bemba* Appeal: A Fragmented Appeals Chamber Destabilises the Law and Practice of the ICC" (26 June 2018) Human Rights Doctorate (blog); B Kahombo, "Bemba's Acquittal by the Appeals Chamber of the International Criminal Court: Why Is It So Controversial?" (9 July 2018) ICJ Africa (blog); F Foka Taffo, "Analysis of Jean-Pierre Bemba's Acquittal by the International Criminal Court" (13 December 2018) Conflict Trends (blog); B Hyland, "The Impact of the *Bemba* Appellate Judgment on Future Prosecution of Crimes of Sexual and Gender-Based Violence at the ICC" (25 May 2019) ICC Forum (blog); L Sadat, "Judicial Speculation Made Law: More Thoughts about the Acquittal of Jean-Pierre Bemba Gomba by the ICC Appeals Chamber and the Question of Superior Responsibility under the Rome Statute" (27 May 2019) ICC Forum (blog); D Guilfoyle, "Of Babies, Bathwater, and List B Judges at the International Criminal Court" (13 November 2019) EJIL Talk (blog).

[13] To give just one example, see B Womack, "The Development and Recent Applications of the Doctrine of Command Responsibility: With Particular Reference to the *Mens Rea* Requirement," in S Yee, ed, *International Crime and Punishment: Selected Issues, Vol 1* (University Press of America, 2003). The aspiration is correct, but I will elaborate in this book on the roles of deontic and consequentialist reasoning.

[14] H L A Hart, *Punishment and Responsibility: Essays in the Philosophy of Law,* 2nd ed (Oxford University Press, 2008) at 3–12 and 74–82. See also J Rawls, "Two Concepts of Rules" (1955) 64 Philosophical Review 3. The proposal that the general justifying aim may be entirely utilitarian has been questioned by other scholars. For example, John Gardner notes that retributive considerations may be not only a constraint on punishment, but also a part of the aim and indeed the essence of punishment: J Gardner, "Introduction," in Hart, *supra,* at xii–xxxi. The point for now is that *even if* the justification for the system is consequentialist (reducing crime), deontological considerations at least constrain the pursuit of those aims.

of "righting the cosmic balance" by meting out deserved punishment does not seem to justify the expense and hardships flowing from criminal law. Conversely, purely consequentialist accounts of criminal law are also inadequate, because they fail to capture our abhorrence at punishing the innocent. If punishment of an individual could be decided solely on utilitarian grounds, there would be no inherent limits precluding punishing the innocent. Presumably, we object to punishing the innocent not only because it is inefficient or because it erodes long-term confidence in the system, but also and more importantly because it is unjust.[15] Hart helpfully distinguished between the justification of the *system* as a whole and the justification of the *punishment of a particular individual*. Thus it may be that the system as a whole is justified by its social benefits, but punishment of a particular person still requires individual desert. There have been many discussions and developments since then, questioning whether the justifications are quite so separate.[16] Nonetheless, this basic model is sufficient for now to illuminate the importance of constraints. The point is that, regardless of the basis of justification of the system as a whole, it is important to respect constraints of justice. In this book, I will use the term "deontic" to refer to these constraints, which arise from respect for the individual. I will set aside until Chapter 4 the question of the more precise philosophical underpinnings of those constraints.[17]

Hart's clarification helps us to see what is at stake in formulating and respecting fundamental principles. Where we breach a deontic commitment to the individual by understating or neglecting a fundamental principle, we are treating that individual *unjustly*. Conversely, where we *overstate* a fundamental principle – that is, when we are too conservative because we construe a principle unsupportably broadly – we sacrifice beneficial impact for no normative reason. It is "bad policy." We are failing to fulfill the aim of the system for no countervailing reason.

Thus clarifying the fundamental principles of justice that constrain the system will assist ICL in two ways. Most obviously, it delineates what we must not do because it would be unjust. Conversely and less obviously, it also delineates the zone

---

[15]   Utilitarian arguments could be advanced to respond to this challenge, for example by highlighting the disutility if society learned that innocents were liable to punishment. However, such counter-arguments are unsatisfactory because they are contingent on empirical facts and thus still leave open the possibility of punishing innocents if doings so benefits society. Hart, *supra* note 14, at 77.

[16]   It is possible, for example, that there are both consequentialist and deontological considerations at play in the justification of the system and in the justification of the application of punishment, and there could be connections between the aims of the system and its constraints, rather than a system of purely consequentialist aims and deontological "side constraints." See, e.g., Gardner, "Introduction," at xii–xxxi; K Ambos & C Steiner, "On the Rationale of Punishment at the Domestic and International Level," in M Henzelin & R Roth, eds, *Le Droit Pénale à l'Éprouve de l'Internationalisation* (LGDJ, 2002); M Dubber, "Theories of Crime and Punishment in German Criminal Law" (2005) 53 Am J Comp L 679.

[17]   In Chapter 4, I will argue that concern for deontic principles does not necessarily commit one to any single deontological theory; on the contrary, there are multiple philosophical accounts that could converge in agreeing on these constraints.

of *permission*, where there is no deontic constraint limiting the pursuit of sound policy (for example promoting general welfare or human flourishing).

In this book, when referring to "fundamental principles" or "deontic principles," I am provisionally[18] referring to the following three principles.

(1) The first is the principle of *personal culpability* – namely, that persons are held responsible only for their own conduct. ICL recognizes as "the foundation of criminal responsibility" that "nobody may be held criminally responsible for acts or transactions in which [they have] not personally engaged or in some other way participated."[19] The principle also requires sufficient knowledge and intent in relation to the conduct[20] such that we may find the person "personally reproachable."[21]

(2) A second is the principle of *legality* (*nullum crimen sine lege*, "no crime without law"), which requires that definitions not be applied retroactively and that they be strictly construed (*in dubio pro reo*, "when in doubt, for the accused," also known as the rule of lenity), to provide fair notice to individual actors and to constrain arbitrary exercise of coercive power.[22] This principle is a "solid pillar" without which "no criminalization process can be accomplished and recognized."[23]

(3) At times I will refer to a possible third principle, the principle of *fair labelling*, which requires that the label of the offence should fairly express and signal the wrongdoing of the accused, so that the stigma of conviction corresponds to the wrongfulness of the act.[24]

---

[18] See Chapter 4.

[19] *Prosecutor v Tadić*, Judgment, ICTY A.Ch, IT-94-1-A, 15 July 1999, at para 186; see also *Judgment of the International Military Tribunal (Nuremberg)*, reproduced in (1947) 41 (supplement) AJIL 172 at 251 ("[C]riminal guilt is personal").

[20] See e.g. *Prosecutor v Delalić et al (Čelebići)*, Judgment, ICTY T.Ch, IT-96-21-T, 16 November 1998 ("*Čelebići* Trial Judgment") at para 424; A Cassese, *International Criminal Law* (Oxford University Press, 2003) at 136–37; ICC Statute, Arts 30–33; G Werle & F Jessberger, " 'Unless Otherwise Provided': Article 30 of the ICC Statute and the Mental Element of Crimes under International Criminal Law" (2005) 3 JICJ 35.

[21] H-H Jescheck, "The General Principles of International Criminal Law Set out in Nuremberg, as Mirrored in the ICC Statute" (2004) 2 JICJ 38 at 44. As will be discussed in the next section, ICL jurisprudence has also required blameworthy moral choice: see e.g. *United States v Otto Ohlendorf et al (Einsatzgruppen case)*, 4 *Trials of War Criminals before the Nuremberg Military Tribunals under Control Council Law No 10*, Case No 9.

[22] ICC Statute, Art 22; Čelebići Trial Judgment, supra note 20, at paras 415–18; B Broomhall, "Article 22, Nullum Crimen Sine Lege," in O Triffterer, ed, *Commentary on the Rome Statute of the International Criminal Court: Observer's Notes, Article by Article*, 2nd ed (Beck, 2008) at 450–51.

[23] Čelebići Trial Judgment, *supra* note 20, at para 402. The principle has also been described by the Sierra Leone Special Court as an "essential element of all legal systems": *Prosecutor v Sesay, Kallon and Gbao*, Judgment, SCSL T.Ch, SCSL-04-15-T, 2 March 2009, at para 48. See also *Prosecutor v Vasiljević*, Judgment, ICTY T.Ch, IT-98-32-T, 29 November 2002, at paras 193–96 (fair notice, specificity).

[24] See, e.g., *Prosecutor v Kvočka*, Judgment, ICTY A.Ch, IT-98-30/1-A, 28 February 2005, at para 92, emphasizing the difference between two forms of participation (commission versus accessory), "both

1.1.4 Special Challenges in ICL

Scholars have advanced numerous thoughtful criticisms questioning whether famil-iar principles even apply in ICL. Are we simply transplanting principles that may be inappropriate in extraordinary contexts of mass criminality? Are fundamental prin-ciples simply "Western" constructs that should not be imposed in other settings?[25]

Even if we had provisional answers to those questions, what method would we use to discuss the parameters of fundamental principles, especially in the new contexts of ICL? The legality principle is often said to require prior legislation, but what does this principle entail in a system that does not have a legislature? The culpability principle requires a degree of "fault" (mental aspect) and a degree of involvement in a crime (material aspect) for liability, but how much fault and how much involve-ment? Unusual contexts and extremes require and enable us to explore the param-eters of the principles.

Where can we look to identify and clarify the appropriate principles? Scholars in the liberal tradition in ICL sometimes invoke principles as declared in ICL itself, principles appearing in national systems, or principles deduced from normative argument. But each of these potential sources of reference are problematic and vulnerable to critique.[26] We need a method to even embark upon criminal law theory in ICL.

1.2 OBJECTIVES

In this book, I have three main objectives. First, I demonstrate the *problem* – that is, the need for more careful deontic reasoning. Second, I outline a *solution* – a method for deontic analysis, especially in new contexts such as ICL. Third, I *apply* the methodology to some specific problems to demonstrate and clarify its application and to illustrate the themes I have identified.

---

to accurately describe the crime and to fix an appropriate sentence." See also *R v Finta* [1994] 1 SCR 701 at para 188:

> [T]here are certain crimes where, because of the special nature of the available penalties or of the stigma attached to a conviction, the principles of fundamental justice require a mental blameworthiness or a mens rea reflecting the particular nature of that crime. It follows that the question which must be answered is not simply whether the accused is morally innocent, but rather, whether the conduct is sufficiently blameworthy to merit the punishment and stigma that will ensue upon conviction for that particular offence.

See generally A Ashworth, "The Elasticity of *Mens Rea*," in C F H Tapper, ed, *Crime, Proof and Punishment: Essays in Memory of Sir Rupert Cross* (Butterworths, 1981); G Williams, "Conviction and Fair Labelling" (1983) 42 Cambridge LJ 85; D Guilfoyle, "Responsibility for Collective Atrocities: Fair Labelling and Approaches to Commission in International Criminal Law" (2011) 64 Current Legal Problems 255.

[25] M Drumbl, *Atrocity, Punishment, and International Law* (Cambridge University Press, 2007) at 8, 24, 38, 123–24.
[26] See Chapter 4.

1.2.1 The Problem: The Need for More Careful Deontic Analysis

First, I demonstrate the problem to which this project responds – namely, the need for more careful deontic reasoning in ICL. One of the recurring themes in this book is the importance of attending to reasoning. While most scholarship understandably focuses on the *outcomes* reached by an analysis (for example the rule adopted), I argue that we must also attend carefully to the *reasoning* employed. Law is a reasoning enterprise, and if there are systematic distortions in reasoning, then sooner or later that reasoning will lead to errors and problems.

To better isolate what I mean by "deontic" reasoning, I will contrast it with two other types of reasoning: source-based reasoning, and teleological reasoning.

- *Source-based* reasoning involves parsing legal instruments and precedents to determine what the legal authorities permit or require.
- *Teleological* reasoning examines purposes and consequences.

I argue that criminal law also requires a third kind of reasoning: deontic reasoning.

"Deontic" reasoning is normative reasoning that focuses on our duties and obligations to others. Deontic reasoning focuses not on what the texts and precedents allow or how to maximize beneficial impact, but on the principled constraints arising from respect for the personhood or agency of accused persons as moral agents. This type of reasoning requires us to consider the limits of personal fault and punishability.

I propose the term "deontic" as a useful addition to the lexicon of ICL jurisprudence and literature. Even in criminal law theory literature, we have struggled with various wordy or imperfect terms (e.g. "mindful of constraints of justice," "justice-oriented," "desert-based," "culpability-based," "tracking moral responsibility," "principled," "liberal") to convey this type of reasoning. The term "deontic" succinctly and elegantly captures this distinct and necessary form of reasoning, and handily distinguishes it from, for example, precedential or teleological reasoning. I will explain this type of reasoning in much more detail in Chapters 3 and 4. As I will explain in Chapter 4, what I call "deontic" reasoning does not necessarily have to be grounded in the leading deontological ethical theories; there are multiple ethical theories that could support principled constraints such as the legality and culpability principles.[27]

As I will show throughout this book, ICL jurisprudence and scholarship have always been proficient in source-based and teleological reasoning, but have often trailed in the deontic dimension, at least in the earlier days.[28] Of course, ICL has always declared its commitment to fundamental principles of justice, but the early tendency was often to engage with those principles as if they were mere "legal" or "doctrinal" rules. As a result, the principles were often downplayed or circumvented

---

[27] See esp §3.3 and §4.3.
[28] See Chapter 2 and see further illustrations in Chapter 6.

using the familiar doctrinal legal arguments that one would use to evade any inconvenient rule.[29] In early ICL jurisprudence and scholarship, the word "justice" was often used in an overly simplistic way in which "justice" was simply the antonym of "impunity." "Impunity" is the failure to punish persons for serious atrocities; "justice," by contrast, meant punishment. Early literature often fretted about interpretations that might allow accused persons to "escape justice" without first establishing that it would even be fair to consider the accused culpable in the circumstances.[30] A richer conception of "justice" includes facilitating prosecutions, but only where the deontic question of fairness of punishment has been answered affirmatively.

Because reasoning matters, I believe it is also important to be on the lookout for possible distortions in our reasoning. Accordingly, in Chapter 2, I provide some illustrations of how some additional challenges arising in ICL may affect reasoning in a way that undermines compliance with deontic principles. The ICL discourse has, at times, drawn on the interpretive, structural, and ideological assumptions of human rights law without adequately bearing in mind the context shift to criminal law. In a coherentist account, one seeks to be autocritical and vigilant for possible distortions in reasoning.

Mainstream ICL thought has evolved rapidly in the last ten years, and we now see thoughtful engagement with deontic constraints. It is even arguable that, in some instances, the field may even have overcorrected. It is all the more urgent to refine the tools for the new invigorated conversation about the appropriate deontic constraints of ICL.

1.2.2 Proposed Solution: A Coherentist Approach

My more central and ambitious objective is to develop some of the methodological and conceptual groundwork for the criminal law theory of ICL. The main prescription of the foregoing section was that we need thoughtful deontic analysis. But that prescription is not easy to implement in any system, and ICL in particular often raises additional uncertainties and difficulties (see §1.1). I highlight five central points of my framework, as follows.

---

[29] One such technique is to question whether a principle is formally legally applicable. For example, in *Nuremberg* it was said that the legality principle is merely a "principle of justice" and not a "limitation of sovereignty," i.e. a legally binding rule in international law. That argument may be credible in a source-based, legalistic analysis. However, if a system aspires to be a system of justice, it should not lightly dismiss a principle on the ground that it is "merely" a principle of justice.
    Similarly, in Chapter 6, I examine the Tribunals' early attempts to respond to a fundamental culpability objection by invoking fairly superficial source-based arguments, such as textual interpretation or invoking lack of precedent. Those arguments did not even attempt to engage with the deontic problem of lack of personal culpability.
[30] See examples in Chapter 2.

(1) **Liberal** Some thoughtful scholars have raised important questions about whether fundamental principles from national systems should apply at all in the extraordinary contexts in which ICL operates. I argue that fundamental principles do and must apply because they are not merely artifacts of positive law; they reflect important commitments to the individual. The term "liberal" is used to mean many different things and is often used pejoratively. I use the term in the minimal sense in which it is often used in criminal law theory: it means that one recognizes at least some deontic constraints on punishment.[31]

(2) **Open-minded and reconstructivist** However, we do not necessarily have to transplant the formulations from national systems; instead, we can examine what the underlying deontic commitment to the individual entails in the new context. In doing so, we may discern that familiar formulations are actually contingent expressions of deeper principles that have previously unnoticed preconditions or limits.[32]

(3) **Humanistic and cosmopolitan** I argue that many of the best insights of both the liberal critique and the critique of the liberal critique can be absorbed and reconciled in a humanistic and cosmopolitan account of fundamental principles. My account is *humanistic* in that is rooted in compassion and respect for humanity. Thus it regards even perpetrators of horrible crimes as moral subjects, not as objects for an object lesson to others. Such an account need not entail the unsound individualistic views that are sometimes ascribed to liberal theories. For example, a sensible account of human behaviour can consider group dynamics, community, social construction, and social roles.[33] The account is *cosmopolitan* in that it is not simply a matter of parochial replication, but rather an open-minded, cross-cultural conversation. Another cosmopolitan feature is that the account is not necessarily fixated on states; rather, it is prepared to contemplate other structures of governance, including international courts and tribunals.[34]

(4) **Coherentist** A core recommendation of this book is that I advocate a "coherentist" method for identifying fundamental principles. A common academic instinct is that, to be rigorous and grounded, all of our propositions must be supported by more basic propositions until we can trace down to some basic foundation. The problem with the "foundationalist" approach is that it would mean we cannot make headway on culpability and legality issues in ICL until we determine the correct foundation (which, on most accounts, would require us to determine the ultimately correct comprehensive moral theory).[35] The main rival to the foundationalist approach is coherentism.

---

[31] This is developed further in Chapter 3.
[32] See Chapter 3.
[33] See Chapter 3.
[34] See Chapter 3.
[35] Different foundational accounts, including "modest foundationalism," are discussed in Chapter 4.

Coherentism accepts that we can work on problems of the middle range, trying to develop models that best reconcile all available clues, without first solving all of the ultimate questions about underpinnings. Indeed, as human beings in an uncertain world, the very best we can do is work with the clues that are available to us. Coherentism acknowledges that it works with contingent human constructs and that its hypotheses are revisable and fallible, but argues that we can nonetheless do valuable work. I believe that coherentism is already the implicit method many scholars and judges use when they debate deontic principles and other constructs. However, by making the method explicit, I can show its justification, its limits, and its requirements for rigour and substantiation, which can refine and sharpen argumentation.

The most common misunderstanding of coherentism is that it merely aims at internal consistency and hence cannot be very radical or profound. However, coherentism is far more ambitious. We draw not only on patterns of practice, but also on the entire range of clues available to us: normative arguments, practical reason, and casuistic testing of our considered judgements. We use all of our critical reasoning tools to test past understandings for bias and inapt assumptions. With a coherentist approach, we can take common formulations of fundamental principles as starting hypotheses, then continue to test and refine them. We can develop constructs ("mid-level principles"), test whether those constructs are analytically useful and normatively convincing, and then use our findings to reform our practice.[36]

(5) **A two-way exchange** The application of general criminal law theory to ICL is not necessarily a one-way process. Criminal law theory has much to offer ICL; conversely, ICL has much to offer general criminal law theory. Contemporary criminal law theory developed around what is the "normal" case in today's world: humans inhabiting a relatively orderly society in a Westphalian state. Accordingly, many of the commonplaces of criminal law theory may implicitly assume preconditions that do not universally apply. The extreme cases and novel problems of ICL may reveal that seemingly elementary principles contain unnoticed conditions and parameters. As discussed in Chapter 5, ICL cases can raise new questions about legality without a legislature, about culpability in collective behaviour, about duress and social roles, and about why state authority matters in criminal law theory.

1.2.3 Illustration: Exploring Culpability in Command Responsibility

To demonstrate and clarify this method, as well its questions, its themes, and its usefulness, I carefully dissect some controversies in command responsibility.

---

[36] J Coleman, *The Practice of Principle: In Defence of a Pragmatist Approach to Legal Theory* (Oxford University Press, 2003).

Command responsibility offers fertile territory for theoretical and deontic investigation. Other modes of liability have been subjected to centuries of scrutiny; command responsibility is comparatively novel. The doctrine also warrants study
because it is important in ICL, and it has become intensely controversial. The
debate has become so convoluted that even the very nature of command responsibility (whether it is a mode of liability, a separate offence, or something *sui generis*) is
now shrouded in uncertainty. I will look at two controversies: causal contribution,
and the special fault element.

Demonstrating my themes about reasoning, I show that early Tribunal jurisprudence approached command responsibility with somewhat hasty source-based and
consequentialist reasoning. As a result, early cases rejected a requirement of causal
contribution, even though it is a recognized requirement for personal culpability. In
doing so, the jurisprudence created a latent contradiction between the doctrine and
the culpability principle, as expressly recognized by the system itself. I argue that
subsequent efforts to deny, evade, or resolve that basic contradiction led the doctrine
to become incredibly convoluted and opaque.[37] The inquiry will show how sensitivity to the deontic dimension can help to clarify controversies. I argue that the most
elegant solution is to repair the underlying problem that caused the subsequent
problems.

My proposed solution is to recognize command responsibility as a mode of
accessory liability, as it was in World War II jurisprudence, in early Tribunal
jurisprudence, and in the ICC Statute. I will deal with a host of counter-
arguments, including the "separate offence" characterization, to show that acknowledging accessory liability is the most elegant and coherent solution.[38] Accordingly,
I argue that the commander's dereliction must at least encourage, facilitate, or have
an effect on subordinate crimes. I hope this inquiry will clarify the operation of
coherentist deontic analysis and its value.[39]

As a second illustration, I examine the controversy over the modified fault
standards, such as the "should have known" test. Many scholars have rightly raised
concerns about a criminal negligence standard. That caution is commendable
because it shows concern for personal culpability. However, I argue that, on
a more careful account, the "should have known" standard is deontically justified
and that, in fact, it is the unique insight and value added of the command responsibility doctrine. Whereas early Tribunal cases incorrectly conflated criminal negligence with strict liability, I show that criminal negligence, properly understood,
reflects significant personal culpability. I also argue that many criticisms of command responsibility have overlooked the important distinction between principal
and accessory liability: an accessory need not have the same *mens rea* required of
a principal. Finally, I argue that, in the special context of command responsibility,

[37] See Chapter 6.
[38] See Chapter 6.
[39] See Chapters 6 and 7.

a criminal negligence standard is deontically justifiable and valuable. Indeed the "should have known" standard is the "genius" of command responsibility: it reflects an astute insight into the culpability of the commander. As a result, whereas the ICC "should have known" standard is often condemned for departing from Tribunal jurisprudence, I would defend and rehabilitate it as the more appropriate and justifiable standard.[40]

1.3 THE SCOPE OF THIS WORK

1.3.1 Other Important Theoretical and Moral Questions

This book falls within the field of criminal law theory – a field that applies philosophical inquiry to criminal law. More specifically, this book focuses on one of the main preoccupations within that field: the moral justification of doctrines and the deontic constraints appropriate in a system of justice.[41] There are numerous other important questions criminal law theory could ask about ICL, and I believe a coherentist method would be a fruitful approach to such questions, even though they are outside the more specific topic selected for this particular book.

Justification of criminal law

A lot of interesting criminal law theory now focuses not on the deontic justification of specific doctrines, but rather on the *political* theory of criminal law[42] and on the justification of the system as a whole. One cluster of issues examines the purpose of criminal law and whether and how criminal law in general is justified. Is the practice of criminal law justified, and what is that justification? How should that justification influence the content and constraints of the law? What gives a state the authority to punish on behalf of a community? Should criminal law take the form that it currently typically does, or are there other more organic forms of justice that would be better? International criminal law adds another layer to such inquiries, requiring us to consider, among other things, the additional justifications needed for extraterritorial jurisdiction, how those justifications influence the content of ICL,

---

[40] See Chapter 8.
[41] As a few exemplars, see: Fletcher & Ohlin, *supra* note 6; Danner & Martinez, *supra* note 6; G Fletcher, *The Grammar of Criminal Law: American, Comparative and International* (Oxford University Press, 2007); J D Ohlin, "Second-Order Linking Principles: Combining Vertical and Horizontal Modes of Liability" (2012) 25 LJIL 771; E van Sliedregt, *Individual Criminal Responsibility in International Law* (Oxford University Press, 2012); J G Stewart, "Overdetermined Atrocities" (2012) 10 JICJ 1189; N Jain, *Principals and Accessories in International Criminal Law* (Hart, 2014); A K A Greenawalt, "International Criminal Law for Retributivists" (2014) 35 U Pa J Intl L 969; M Jackson, *Complicity in International Law* (Oxford University Press, 2015); C Steer, *Translating Guilt: Identifying Leadership Liability for Mass Atrocity Crimes* (TMC Asser Press, 2017).
[42] See, e.g., M Thorburn, "The Criminal Law as Public Law," in R A Duff & S Green, eds, *The Philosophical Foundations of Criminal Law* (Oxford University Press, 2011); V Chiao, "What Is the Criminal Law for?" (2016) 35 L & Phil 137.

and the possibilities of criminal law outside the state context.[43] To some extent, those questions of general justification are logically prior to the issues I address here. After all, if the system as a whole is not justified and should not exist, then we need not worry about the appropriate constraints.[44] I believe a coherentist methodology would be appropriate and helpful for these general questions; however, the topic is so distinct and massive that I must set it aside for a future work.[45] To manage the scope of this book, I focus here on deontic constraints, which is by itself an enormous and important topic.[46] Accordingly, in this book, I provisionally treat deontic constraints as "side constraints," meaning that, irrespective of the justification of the system as a whole (i.e. even if the justification is consequentialist), the deontic constraints should be respected, out of regard for the affected individuals.

Selectivity and distribution of justice

At present, the loudest, most prominent, and most urgent controversies concern selectivity and how ICL distributes its attention. As I write these words, the ICL project is under intense criticism from opposing directions. Both powerful and less powerful states have accused ICL of unfairly targeting them. Each line of attack is selective in what it highlights and ignores.[47] These questions are outside my current

---

[43] See, e.g., L May, *Crimes against Humanity: A Normative Account* (Cambridge University Press, 2005); K Ambos, "Punishment without a Sovereign? The *Ius Puniendi* Issue of International Criminal Law: A First Contribution towards a Consistent Theory of International Criminal Law" (2013) 33 Oxf J L Stud 293; R Liss, "Crimes against the Sovereign Order: Rethinking International Criminal Justice" (2019) 113 AJIL 727; C Stahn, *Justice as Message: Expressivist Foundations of International Criminal Justice* (Oxford University Press, 2020). These questions matter not only because they address whether the system is justified, but also because they have different prescriptive implications for the doctrines and practices of ICL.

[44] Furthermore, identifying the justification of a system also sheds light on its constraints. For example, if a system is justified in accordance with consequentialist desiderata, then a particular practice contradicting those desiderata should be avoided.

[45] In particular, I hope to address those criticisms voiced in transitional justice literature that portray criminal law as simply about vengeance or about replicating domestic practices out of habit; I believe that such portrayals understate the prosocial purposes of criminal law. The "sense of justice" appears to be widely shared among human beings, and measured responses to violators appear to have benefits in building social trust. For some foreshadowing, see §3.1.2 and §3.3.3, and see A Walsh, "Evolutionary Psychology and the Origins of Justice" (200) 17 Justice Quarterly 841; P S Churchland, *Braintrust: What Neuroscience Tells Us about Morality* (Princeton University Press, 2011); P H Robinson, *Intuitions of Justice and the Utility of Desert* (Oxford University Press, 2013) at 35–62.

[46] See §1.1.3 and §3.2.1; see also, e.g., Hart, *supra* note 14.

[47] The critique that ICL is a neocolonialist project directed against the weak has gained traction since the ICC, a central institution, has predominantly selected situations in Africa for scrutiny. (At the time of writing, nine out of twelve territories selected for investigation are in Africa; the three exceptions are Georgia, Bangladesh/Myanmar, and Afghanistan. At the time of writing, the ICC Office of the Prosecutor has requested authorization to investigate crimes in Palestinian territories.) The ICC Office of the Prosecutor responds that it is applying its legal criteria, that the gravest admissible situations in its jurisdiction have mostly been in Africa, and that most of its interventions in Africa were specifically requested by African governments. Critics tend to dismiss the ICC arguments without addressing the factual and legal questions. For an effort to independently assess

inquiry (deontic constraints), but I can note some questions that would benefit from critical and coherentist analysis. First, while popular caricatures that present ICL as a pernicious plot are overstated, there are questions worth investigating about implicit biases and about the difficulties of prosecuting the powerful. Second, assuming that the ICC is applying reasonable interpretations of the existing selection criteria, there may be plausible arguments to add diverse geographic distribution as a criterion. Third, one could tap into thinking on distributive justice, but what does the ICC "distribute"?[48] Does it distribute something negative (condemnation), as most criticisms assume, or something positive (acting as a backstopping rule of law for the security and affirmation of victims), as supporters assume, or both?

Other constraints

To further clarify the focus of my field of inquiry, my topic is not about *all* constraints on criminal law. For example, ICL should likely also be sensitive to consequentialist constraints,[49] as well as constraints reflecting the optimal division of labour between national systems and ICL. However, this book explores only those constraints rooted in the fair treatment of persons (such as the principles of legality, culpability, and fair labelling), which I will call "deontic" constraints.

1.3.2 A Preliminary Sketch of a Vast and Intricate Topic

The remaining topic – exploring the deontic constraints of ICL – is nonetheless enormous. In many respects, I have developed the groundwork with more detail and care than was the case in the existing literature. Yet I am acutely aware that, in the interests of conciseness and accessibility, I am at many points skimming the surface of many intricate debates. There are many points that I have dealt with in a few pages that could easily warrant treatment in vastly greater granularity.[50]

To offer this framework, the book brings together a vast range of materials: ICL jurisprudence, scholarship on ICL and scholarship on criminal law theory, moral philosophy, coherentism, and cosmopolitanism. I cannot possibly do justice to each of those components. This book is an initial foray, drawing heavily on works written in English. The conversation will have to be broadened and diversified with a far greater range of perspectives and arguments. As will be discussed, a broadened conversation is an aspect of the coherentist method. This book is by no means

---

   situation selection, see A Smeulers, M Weerdesteijn & B Hola, "The Selection of Situations by the ICC: An Empirically Based Evaluation of the OTP's Performance" (2015) 15 Int'l Crim L Rev 1.

[48] F Mégret, "What Sort of Justice Is 'International Criminal Justice'?" (2015) 13 JICJ 7.

[49] If a particular practice (e.g. prohibiting a particular activity) appears to do more harm than good in the long run, then that at least furnishes a significant reason for not continuing that practice.

[50] For example, one could easily expand on: the historical and cultural context of familiar principles and the extent to which they are empirically "Western" (Chapter 3); the implications of criminal law outside the construct of the modern "state" (Chapter 5); and the identified problems raised by ICL that might illuminate criminal law theory (Chapter 5).

intended to be a final word, but rather an early contribution in an ongoing broader conversation.

I illustrate my framework with specific case studies from command responsibility. There are numerous other controversies that could be fruitfully investigated. In Chapter 5, I outline some the other issues ripe for inquiry: the legality principle and the role of customary law; the parameters of the duress defence in extreme situations; and the possible normative foundations of the superior orders defence. Even my command responsibility illustrations, which I believe offer a more careful and detailed deontic account than currently exists, are each only the tip of an iceberg. There are many controversies even in command responsibility that I could have delved into for even more granular investigation.[51] I have condensed my arguments to exemplify an analysis that is rigorous, yet hopefully brisk enough to maintain general interest.

I am speaking to different audiences with different interests and priorities. Readers who are most interested in black letter implications for ICL may prefer less of the theory, whereas readers with a more philosophical bent may wish that I had delved into some issues in even more depth. Similarly, readers have opposing preferences on command responsibility: Some are more interested in the general approach I outline (Chapters 2–5) and could do with less discussion of command responsibility; other readers wish to see particular issues unpacked in even more detail. Please recall that I am striking a middle path and that it is impossible to satisfy the conflicting preferences. To accommodate various perspectives, I have included some "annexes" that delve a little further into issues that may be of particular interest to one audience or another.

Criminal law theory of ICL is a relatively new field. We are still in the pioneering stages of a new field of law (ICL) that raises new problems, and of a new discipline (ICL theory) that tries to understand, systematize, evaluate, and critique that field. I hope that my efforts here will be understood as a first introduction to a method. We are still making the early broad brushstrokes on a canvas. I hope and expect that there will be many corrections and refinements from other hands yet to come.

---

[51] Further work could expand upon: alternatives to causal contribution for culpability; a more cosmopolitan account of criminal negligence drawing on a broader range of legal systems; the proper scope of liability of civilian superiors; and how my account of command responsibility would inform the "effective control" test.

2

The Identity Crisis of International Criminal Law

OVERVIEW

In this chapter, I demonstrate the problem to which the rest of this book proposes a solution – namely, the need for more careful deontic reasoning. I will focus on certain distinctive habits of reasoning that have often recurred in ICL, which have a tendency to undermine compliance with deontic principles.

All legal systems sometimes generate doctrines that appear to conflict with stated principles. However, in national systems, the clash tends to be openly between liberal principles and "law and order" considerations. I argue that ICL discourse often features an additional and interesting dynamic. In ICL, the distortions often result from habits of reasoning that are progressive and appropriate in human rights law and humanitarian law, but which become problematic when transplanted without adequate reflection to a criminal law system. I highlight three kinds of such reasoning: interpretive assumptions, substantive and structural assumptions, and ideological assumptions. These habits of reasoning were more prevalent in the early days of the renaissance of ICL than they are today. It is still valuable to discern and dissect these habits of reasoning, because their legacy continues, because they still recur today, and because they help to show the value of attending to reasoning.

2.1 CONTEXT AND ARGUMENT

2.1.1 Context: Internal Contradictions with Proclaimed Principles

This chapter is based on a previously published article, "The Identity Crisis of International Criminal Law."[1] I wrote that article in 2007, at a time when scholars were starting to notice contradictions between ICL doctrines and fundamental principles. My focus was different from those works, however, because my focus was not on evaluating the contradictions, but on *reasoning*: on structures of argument that culminated in the controverted doctrines.

ICL has always proclaimed its exemplary commitment to fundamental principles of criminal justice, both in its earlier stages after World War II and again in its

[1] D Robinson, "The Identity Crisis of International Criminal Law" (2008) 21 LJIJ 925.

renaissance following the creation of the Tribunals in the mid-1990s.[2] By "fundamental principles," I am referring to principles such as the culpability principle, the
legality principle, and the principle of fair labelling, as recognized by ICL.[3] These
fundamental principles distinguish a liberal system of criminal justice from an
authoritarian system.[4] A liberal system embraces restraints on its pursuit of societal
aims, out of respect for the autonomy of the individuals who may be subject to the
system. Thus, while the purpose of the criminal law system as a whole may be to
protect society, some further deontic justification is still required for punishment to
be justly applied to a particular individual.[5] Treating individuals as subjects rather
than objects for an object lesson – that is, as more than just means to an end –
imposes principled restraints on the infliction of punishment.[6]

In the mid-2000s, thoughtful scholarship began to question ICL's compliance
with those principles. Early literature focused particularly on the doctrine of "joint
criminal enterprise" (JCE),[7] but scholars also raised concerns about many other
doctrines, including sweeping modes of liability, expanding definitions of crimes,
and reticence toward defences. How did a liberal system of criminal justice – one
that strives to serve as a model for liberal systems – come to embrace apparently
illiberal doctrines?

Faced with evidence of frequent departures, one might be tempted to conclude
that ICL is indifferent to liberal principles and is simply harsher than many national
criminal law systems.[8] While that is one possible conclusion, I propose that we first
try taking ICL's proclamations seriously. After all, mainstream ICL does not *reject*
fundamental principles, but rather sees itself as fully compliant.

---

[2] See, e.g., *Judgment of the International Military Tribunal (Nuremberg)* ("Nuremberg Judgment"),
reproduced in (1947) 41 (supplement) AJIL 172 at 251; *Prosecutor v Tadić*, Judgment, ICTY A.Ch,
IT-94-1-A, 15 July 1999 ("*Tadić* Appeal Judgment") at para 186; *Prosecutor v Delalić et al (Čelebići)*,
Judgment, ICTY T.Ch, IT-96-21-T, 16 November 1998 ("*Čelebići* Trial Judgment") at para 424;
Prosecutor v Vasiljević, Judgment, ICTY T.Ch, IT-98-32-T, 29 November 2002 ("*Vasiljević* Trial
Judgment") at paras 193–96; *Prosecutor v Sesay, Kallon and Gbao*, Judgment, SCSL T.Ch,
SCSL-04-15-T, 2 March 2009, at para 48; *Prosecutor v Ayyash*, Interlocutory Decision on the
Applicable Law: Terrorism, Conspiracy, Homicide, Perpetration, Cumulative Charging, STL A.Ch,
Case No. STL-11-01/I, 16 February 2011, at para 76; ICC Statute, Arts 22–24 and 30–32; United Nations
Press Office, "Rome Statute of the International Criminal Court: Some Questions and Answers" (no
longer available online, on file with author); T Meron, "Revival of Customary Humanitarian Law"
(2005) 99 AJIL 817 at 821–29.
[3] See §1.1.3 for more detailed description of the principles and examples of their support in ICL.
[4] I refer to "liberal" and "authoritarian" only as conceptual archetypes; in Chapter 3, I will explain the
minimalist sense in which I use the term "liberal."
[5] See, e.g., H L A Hart, *Punishment and Responsibility* (Oxford University Press, 1968), esp at 3–12 and
74–82.
[6] See, e.g., G Fletcher, *Basic Concepts of Criminal Law* (Oxford University Press, 1998) at 43.
[7] See §2.2.3.
[8] See, e.g., A T O'Reilly, "Command Responsibility: A Call to Realign the Doctrine with Principles of
Individual Accountability and Retributive Justice" (2004–05) 40 Gonzaga L Rev 127 at 154. And see,
developing this possibility in more detail, M Dubber, "Common Civility: The Culture of Alegality in
International Criminal Law" (2011) 24 LJIL 923.

2.1.2 The Identity Crisis Theory

I suggest that *part* of the problem lies in habits of reasoning and argumentation that were transplanted from human rights and humanitarian law without adequate recognition that the new context – criminal law – requires different thinking. In creating ICL, jurists drew on criminal law, as well as international human rights and humanitarian law. Human rights and humanitarian law provided both substantive content and a familiar framework for internationalized oversight. I argue that, in combining criminal law with human rights and humanitarian law, ICL initially absorbed some contradictory assumptions and methods of reasoning. Insightful glimpses into some specific elements of this phenomenon have previously been offered by George Fletcher and Jens David Ohlin,[9] and by Allison Marston Danner and Jenny Martinez.[10] I build upon those insights to place them within a broader account and explanation of some observable tendencies in ICL discourse.

The explosive growth of ICL in the mid-1990s – a boom in institution-building and norm-articulation – led to a sudden need for international criminal lawyers. Because few such creatures existed, the vacuum was filled – at least at the outset – primarily by international lawyers with training in the fields of human rights and humanitarian law.[11] Indeed, ICL was perceived and heralded as a major advance in human rights and humanitarian law, offering a valuable remedy and means of enforcement by punishing violators. Emerging ICL professionals eagerly adopted and sought to respect the forms and principles of criminal law; however, they also brought with them the habits of reasoning of their native domains of expertise.

These early influences have shaped the areas of myopia in ICL. ICL jurists affirmed principles such as culpability and legality, but often engaged with them as if they were mere "doctrinal" rules, narrowing or circumventing them with standard interpretive moves. I will argue in this book that criminal justice requires

---

[9]   G Fletcher & J D Ohlin, "Reclaiming Fundamental Principles of Criminal Law in the *Darfur* Case" (2005) 3 JICJ 539 at 541, have convincingly suggested that ICL's weaknesses in respecting legality and culpability are a product of "an under-theorized shift" from public international law (which focuses on states or groups) to criminal law (which focuses on the individual). In this chapter, I suggest that the shift in focus from *systems* to *individuals* is only one example of the different approaches, consequences, and philosophical underpinnings of these areas of law. Moreover, by considering the transition not only from general international law, but also more specifically from international human rights and humanitarian law, one discerns an additional range of interpretive, structural, and ideological assumptions in play.

[10] A M Danner & J S Martinez, "Guilty Associations: Joint Criminal Enterprise, Command Responsibility and the Development of International Criminal Law" (2005) 93 Calif L Rev 75 at 81–89, have suggested that a human rights approach to interpretation, favouring large and liberal constructions, is inapposite to ICL. I agree with that observation, and I supplement it by pointing out other modes – including substantive, structural, and ideological assumptions – by which habits of thought in human rights law, with liberal aims, can actually undermine liberal principles if applied in a criminal law context without considering the context shift.

[11] J Wessel, "Judicial Policy-Making at the International Criminal Court: An Institutional Guide to Analyzing International Adjudication" (2006) 44 Columbia J Transn'l L 377, esp at 449; M Damaška, "The Shadow Side of Command Responsibility" (2001) 49 Am J Comp L 455 at 495.

an additional and special type of reasoning – deontic reasoning – which directly and normatively explores the principled moral limitations on blame and punishment. Even more interestingly, the problem is not only one of inadequate deontic analysis, but also that habits of human rights and humanitarian law reasoning can actively work at *cross-purposes* to fundamental principles if they are uncritically and inappropriately transplanted into a penal system.

In this chapter, I present three of the "modes" by which this distortion occurs. One mode is the influence of *interpretive approaches* from human rights and humanitarian law, such as victim-focused teleological reasoning. Such reasoning not only undermines strict construction, but also fosters sweeping interpretations that may run afoul of culpability and fair labelling.

The second mode is *substantive and structural conflation* – that is, the assumption that criminal norms must be coextensive with similar norms in human rights or humanitarian law. Such assumptions overlook the different structure and consequences of these areas of law, and thus they neglect the additional deontic principles that constrain punishment of individual human beings.

A third mode is *ideological assumptions*, for example about "progress" and "sovereignty." These assumptions can lead to an overly hasty embrace of expansive doctrines and rejection of narrower, but principled, doctrines. Each of these assumptions can distort analysis against fundamental principles when applied without sensitivity to the context shift in criminal law.

I do not suggest that human rights and humanitarian law assumptions are the sole *cause* of departures from fundamental principles. They are not. Other influences are undoubtedly in play. For example, ICL deals with violations of exceptional magnitude and severity, and studies indicate that the more severe the crime, the greater the perceived pressure to convict and the greater the likelihood of perceiving an accused person to be responsible for the crime.[12] Another possible influence could be the incentive of judges and professionals in an emerging field to demonstrate the efficacy of their field and to increase their influence and prestige by expanding the scope and role of ICL.[13] Reputational incentives may also have a subtle impact. For example, at least in the early days of the renaissance of ICL, the judge or jurist who espoused conviction-friendly interpretations could reliably expect to be applauded as progressive and compassionate by esteem-granting communities.[14] In addition,

---

[12] J K Robbennolt, "Outcome Severity and Judgments of 'Responsibility': A Meta-analytical Review" (2000) 30 J Appl 2575; J Lucas, C Graif & M Lovaglia, "Misconduct in the Prosecution of Severe Crimes: Theory and Experimental Test" (2006) 69 Soc Psychol Q 97.

[13] S Estreicher & P B Stephan, "Foreword: Taking International Law Seriously" (2003) 44 Virginia J Int L 1 at 1; M Osiel, "The Banality of Good: Aligning Incentives against Mass Atrocity" (2005) 105 Columbia L Rev 1751 at 1823; K Rittich, "Enchantments of Reason/Coercions of Law" (2003) 57 U Miami L Rev 727 at 729; Wessel, *supra* note 11, at 420–21.

[14] See, e.g., F Schauer, "Incentives, Reputation and the Inglorious Determinants of Judicial Behavior" (1999–2000) 68 U Cincinnati L Rev 615; R Posner, "What Do Judges and Justices Maximize? (The Same Thing Everyone Else Does)" (1993) 3 SCER 1; D Kennedy, "Strategizing Legal Behavior in

consequentialist "law and order" aspirations emerge in any system and can lead to apparent contraventions of principles. Current efforts to respond to terrorism and organized crime have led to many doctrines that appear problematic.

However, my topic here is the *reasoning*, and what is important for present purposes is that the *reasoning* in ICL is often different, in interesting ways, from the national law discourse. Particularly in the first decade of the renaissance of ICL (roughly 1995–2005), there was relatively little awareness of any incongruity with fundamental principles; indeed, the system prided itself on being an exemplary liberal system. The interesting and distinctive feature of these distortions in ICL reasoning is that the participants are often applying what they believe to be sound legal methods *with appropriately liberal aims*.

Thus, even if other factors may be in play, the impact of human rights and humanitarian assumptions is of special interest because it offers not only a *why*, but also a *how*. Reliance on these assumptions and methods of argumentation furnishes the *analytical steps* by which such departures are effected and provides the plausibility that allows the departures to pass unnoticed. Our favoured reasoning methods may contain distortions, and hence we need to *think about the way we think*.

The identity crisis theory helps to explain why an overwhelmingly liberal-minded profession may have endorsed illiberal doctrines and developments. In a typical criminal law context, liberal sensitivities focus on protecting individuals from inappropriate coercive power of the state. In ICL, however, prosecution and conviction are often conceptualized as the fulfilment of the victims' human right to a remedy.[15] Indeed, an appropriate criminal law response can be part of the victims' right to a remedy, but we have to be wary of simply transplanting human rights methodology and norms into a penal system. The criminalization of human rights and humanitarian law has at times shifted the preoccupation of thinkers.[16] Many traditionally liberal actors (such as non-governmental organizations or academics), who in a national system would vigilantly protect defendants and potential

---

Legal Interpretation" (1996) 3 Utah L Rev 785; R Graham, "Politics and Prices: Judicial Utility Maximization and Construction" (2007) 1 Indian J Const L 57. Conversely, there was little incentive within the profession to disagree with expansionist arguments, at least during the early resurgence of ICL, in the light of what Henry Kissinger has described as the "intimidating passion of [ICL] advocates": H Kissinger, "The Pitfalls of Universal Jurisdiction" (2001) 80 Foreign Affairs 86 at 86. As I will note in §2.5, some of these tendencies have now subsided.

[15]   See, e.g., United Nations General Assembly, *Basic Principles and Guidelines on the Right to a Remedy and Reparations for Victims of Gross Violations of International Human Rights Law and Serious Violations of International Humanitarian Law*, GA Res 60/147, UNGAOR, 60th Sess, UN Doc A/RES/60/147 (2005); J M van Dyke, "The Fundamental Human Right to Prosecution and Compensation" (2001) 29 Denver J Int L & Pol'y 77.

[16]   Even in a national system, the rhetoric of justice for victims can increase pressure within the system to overlook fairness to the accused: K Roach, "Four Models of the Criminal Process" (1999) 89 JCLC 671. What is distinct about ICL is not only that there is an increased sensitivity to victims, but also that we import an entire set of argumentative assumptions from international human rights and humanitarian law.

defendants, have often been among the most strident pro-prosecution voices, arguing for broader crimes and modes of liability and against defences, in order to secure
convictions and thereby fulfil the victims' right to justice.[17] In a national system, one
may hear that it is preferable to let ten guilty persons go free rather than to convict
one innocent person. The ICL literature, especially in earlier days, was instead
replete with fears that defendants might "escape conviction" or "escape accountability" unless inculpating principles were broadened further and exculpatory principles
narrowed.[18]

Thus a distinctive feature of ICL reasoning is that illiberal doctrines often arrive in
a *liberal* garb rather than in a typical authoritarian garb.[19] In both human rights law
and criminal law, liberal principles aim to protect human beings from the state. But
if we are operating a criminal law institution, it is now *we* who are wielding power
over individuals, and thus the liberal principles now engage to restrain *us*. Advocates
accustomed to championing victims and restraining governments must reconsider
some habits of thought when applying ICL. For example, confidently maximizing
the protection of victims may culminate in punishing human beings without fair
warning, culpability, or fair labelling. Furthermore, human rights law and humanitarian law are addressed to collective entities (e.g. states) and thus are not directly
constrained by principles such as culpability or fair labelling. Thus copying rules
and assumptions from human rights law can corrode liberal protective principles if
one fails to fully consider the context shift to criminal law.

The following sections will look at three modes by which assumptions that are
appropriate in human rights can distort ICL discourse: interpretive assumptions

---

[17] W Schabas, "Sentencing by International Tribunals: A Human Rights Approach" (1997) 7 Duke
J Comp & Int'l L 461 at 515, observes this shift with respect to human rights non-governmental
organizations (NGOs). More subtly, human rights NGOs generally retain their affinity for procedural
rights, but on substantive principles they tend to favour broad inculpatory principles and to resist
exculpatory principles. On NGO hostility to defences, see R J Wilson, "Defences in Contemporary
International Criminal Law" (2002) 96 AJIL 517 at 518. Boot reports on NGO proposals "to give several
definitions of crimes an open-ended character or to broaden existing definitions" in order to avoid
rigid formulations "that could lead to acquitting an accused": M Boot, *Genocide, Crimes against
Humanity and War Crimes:* Nullum Crimen Sine Lege *and the Subject Matter Jurisdiction of the
International Criminal Court* (Intersentia, 2002) at 614.

[18] See, e.g., C Bassiouni, "The Normative Framework of International Humanitarian Law: Overlaps,
Gaps and Ambiguities" (1998) 8 Transnat'l L & Contemp Probs 199 at 200 ("escape accountability");
G Vetter, "Command Responsibility of Non-military Superiors in the International Criminal Court"
(2000) 25 Yale J Int L 89 at 95 ("escape conviction"); B Womack, "The Development and Recent
Application of the Doctrine of Command Responsibility, with Particular Reference to the *Mens Rea*
Requirement," in S Yee, ed, *International Criminal Law and Punishment* (University Press of
America, 2003) at 168 ("escape justice"); S L Russell-Brown, "The Last Line of Defense: The
Doctrine of Command Responsibility and Gender Crimes in Armed Conflict" (2004) 22 Wisconsin
Int'l LJ 125 at 158 ("escape criminal responsibility"); C T Fox, "Closing a Loophole in Accountability
for War Crimes: Successor Commanders' Duty to Punish Known Past Offenses" (2004) 55 Case
W Res L Rev 443 at 444 ("gap will allow certain atrocities to go unpunished").

[19] By "arriving in a liberal garb," I mean they are rooted in assumptions (interpretative, structural, and
ideological) that are appropriate and liberal (human-oriented) in a human rights context.

(§2.2), substantive and structural assumptions (§2.3), and ideological assumptions (§2.4). I will use the doctrine of command responsibility as a recurring example under all three modes.

My examples in this chapter draw heavily from the early days of the renaissance of ICL – that is, following the creation of the Tribunals and their jurisprudence (roughly 1995–2005). After that period, there was an interesting shift in ICL discourse: the "deontic turn." In the final section of this chapter (§2.5), I will discuss that shift and how it intensifies the need for a thoughtful method for deontic inquiry.

2.1.3 Clarifications

As the following analysis may at times seem rather critical, some important qualifications are in order. First, I by no means suggest that ICL jurisprudence is always flawed. In this chapter, I provide examples to demonstrate some *tendencies* that are common in ICL discourse. I do not suggest that the tendencies amount to an iron rule. They definitely do not.[20] The observations are offered in the spirit of improving a discipline that is still relatively new. Through critical awareness of these tendencies, we may consciously determine the values and principles of the system and apply them consistently.

Second, the contradictions identified here are a contingent phenomenon and not an immutable fatal flaw in the ICL project. Tensions in reasoning habits can be addressed by exposing them to scrutiny and developing ICL's distinct philosophical underpinnings. Doctrinal contradictions can be unearthed and resolved by reforms that bring doctrines and principles into alignment. Indeed, my original article on this topic observed that the "identity crisis" phenomenon was potentially diminishing even at that time.[21] I speculated on the possible reasons for this progress, such as the changing composition or the intellectual maturation of the field.[22] As I will discuss in §2.5, that positive trend has continued, with an invigorated critical scholarship mindful of fundamental principles of justice.[23] It is still important to be aware of the reasoning techniques discussed here, because they still frequently recur in ICL argumentation, they have left a legacy in existing doctrines, and they show the importance of attending to reasoning.

Third, and most crucially, where I highlight a problematic structure of argumentation in a case, it does not necessarily mean I disagree with the *outcome* reached in

---

[20]   Even in early Tribunal jurisprudence, there were examples of judges taking a stance in favour of liberal principles. See, e.g., *Vasiljević* Trial Judgment, *supra* note 2, at paras 193–204 (a rather strict stand on the requirement of precision); *Prosecutor v Simić*, Judgment, ICTY T.Ch, IT-95-9-T, 17 October 2003, at paras 1–5, Dissenting Opinion of Judge Lindholm (dissenting judge distancing and disassociating from the JCE doctrine).

[21]   Robinson, *supra* note 1, at 932.

[22]   *Ibid.*

[23]   See §2.5 and see Chapter 3.

that case.[24] A judge or scholar might advance a problematic argument, and yet the conclusion might still be defensible on other grounds.[25] Nonetheless, it is worth being aware of faulty recurring arguments, because facile and flawed reasoning will sooner or later lead to error. Furthermore, where I discuss an internal contradiction, it should not be assumed that I believe that the doctrine is wrong and that the articulation of the principle is necessarily correct. To evaluate how best to resolve any given contradiction would require a careful philosophical analysis of the merits of particular principles. That is a very complex task, and the remainder of this book aims at developing a method for that task.

To keep the focus in this chapter on problematic reasoning habits, I am working with the internal contradictions with principles as articulated by ICL itself,[26] thus setting aside for now substantive normative evaluation of the principles. That substantive evaluation will be the focus of the remaining chapters of this book. My goal here is simply to demonstrate some pitfalls in reasoning, to establish the need for more careful deontic analysis.[27]

2.2 INTERPRETIVE ASSUMPTIONS

2.2.1 Victim-Focused Teleological Reasoning

ICL jurisprudence proclaims that it follows particularly stringent standards in interpreting definitions of crimes and inculpatory rules, applying only norms that are "clearly" and "beyond doubt" customary law.[28] It emphasizes its faithful adherence to the principle of strict construction, which provides that ambiguities are to be resolved in favour of the accused.[29] As the ICTY has held:

> [P]enal statutes must be strictly construed, this being a general rule which has stood the test of time ... A criminal statute is one in which the legislature intends to have the final result of inflicting suffering upon, or encroaching upon the liberty of, the individual ... [T]he intention to do so shall be clearly expressed and without ambiguity. The legislature will not allow such intention to be gathered from doubtful inferences from the words used ... [I]f the legislature has not used words

[24] A judgment could, for example, engage in faulty reasoning, but still reach a result that is justified under more careful reasoning.
[25] As I have noted elsewhere, a decision may "reach the right result with the wrong reasoning." To disagree with the outcome, we would need a substantive account of what the principles, properly understood, truly require: D Robinson, "Legality and Our Contradictory Commitments: Some Thoughts about the Way We Think" (2009) 103 ASIL Proc 104 at 105.
[26] In Chapter 4, I will discuss the "internal account" of principles, as well as other possible approaches (comparative, normative, and the proposed coherentist approach).
[27] In Annex 1, I address reactions to and questions about "the identity crisis," and I thereby provide additional clarifications for any readers who are interested.
[28] See, e.g., *Tadić* Appeal Judgment, *supra* note 2, at para 662; *Prosecutor v Blaškić*, Judgment, ICTY A. Ch, IT-95-14-A, 29 July 2004 (*"Blaškić* Appeal Judgment") at para 114; *Čelebići* Trial Judgment, *supra* note 2, at paras 415–18.
[29] ICC Statute, Art 22(2).

sufficiently comprehensive to include within its prohibition all the cases which should naturally fall within the mischief intended to be prevented, the interpreter is not competent to extend them.[30]

Similarly, Article 22(2) of the ICC Statute affirms that "the definition of a crime shall be strictly construed and shall not be extended by analogy. In case of ambiguity, the definition shall be interpreted in favour of the person being investigated, prosecuted or convicted."

Notwithstanding these proclamations of principle, ICL thinking has frequently been influenced by the distinctively "liberal," "broad," "progressive," and "dynamic" approach to interpretation that is a hallmark of human rights law.[31] Purposive interpretation may be found in any area of law, but human rights law features a distinctively progressive brand on the grounds that it aims at increasing the protection of human dignity rather than reciprocal obligations undertaken by states.[32] Given that ICL norms are often drawn from human rights or humanitarian law, it is entirely understandable for practitioners to draw not only on the norms, but also on these familiar interpretive approaches. ICL discourse has frequently borne the fingerprints of the distinct interpretive approach from human rights law. As just one example, the Darfur Commission, in interpreting genocide, invoked the principle of effectiveness and giving maximal effect.[33] That approach is familiar from general international law and human rights in particular. Maximal construction is, however, the diametric opposite of strict construction.

---

[30] *Čelebići* Trial Judgment, *supra* note 2, at paras 408–10.

[31] A v *Australia*, Communication No. 560/1993, Views 3 April 1997, A/52/40, Vol II, Annex VI, sect L (at 125–46) ("broadly and expansively"). In the inter-American system, see, e.g., *Compulsory Membership in an Association Prescribed by Law for the Practice of Journalism* (1985), Advisory Opinion OC-5/85 Inter Am Ct HR 2, Judge Rodolfo Piza, paras 6 and 12 ("necessity of a broad interpretation of the norms that it guarantees and a restrictive interpretation of those that allow them to be limited"); *Prosecutor v Bámaca Velásquez* – Series C No 70 [2000] IACHR 7, Judgment of Judge Sergio Garcia Marquez, para 3 ("progressive interpretation," "guiding momentum of international human rights law, which strives to take the real protection of human rights increasingly further"). Similarly, the European Convention on Human Rights (ECHR) is not to be narrowly interpreted having regard to the sovereignty of states but rather given a broad interpretation to protect rights effectively: *Golder v United Kingdom* [1975] 1 EHRR 524 at para 9; *East African Asians v United Kingdom* [1973] 3 EHRR 76 at paras 192–95.

[32] "[S]ince the primary beneficiaries of human rights treaties are not States or governments but human beings, the protection of human rights calls for a more liberal approach than that normally applicable in the case of ambiguous provisions of multilateral treaties": *Keith Cox v Canada*, Communication No 539/1993, Views 31 October 1994, A/50/40, Vol II, Annex X, sect M, at 105–29, reproduced in (1994) HRLJ 410; CCPR/C/57/1, at 117–47; see also the European and Inter-American authorities, *supra* note 31.

[33] See, e.g., International Commission of Inquiry on Darfur, *Report to the United Nations Secretary-General Pursuant to Security Council Resolution 1564 of 18 September 2004* (25 January 2005) at para 494: "[T]he principle of interpretation of international rules whereby one should give such rules their maximum effect (principle of effectiveness, also expressed by the Latin maxim *ut res magis valeat quam pereat*) suggests that the rules on genocide should be construed in such a manner as to give them their maximum legal effects."

A reasoning technique commonly used in ICL is (i) to adopt a purposive interpretive approach, (ii) to assume that the exclusive object and purpose of an ICL
enactment is to maximize victim protection, and (iii) to allow this presumed object
and purpose to dominate over other considerations – including, if necessary, the text
itself. The principle of strict construction fails to constrain this technique because, as
in many national systems, this principle is applied only as a final resort, *after* other
canons of construction have failed to solve the question.[34] If we apply, at a prior
stage, a single-value teleological approach that simply maximizes victim protection,
then there is never an ambiguity left for strict construction to resolve.[35] All ambiguities will have already been resolved *against* the accused. As a result, the promise of
in dubio pro reo ("when in doubt, for the accused"), which ICL holds out to accused
and which bolsters ICL's legitimacy, is easily inverted, and the rule faced by the
accused is closer to *in dubio **contra** reum* ("when in doubt, against the accused").

Notice carefully that I do not object to teleological reasoning or consideration of
object and purpose per se. My concern is the *reductive* and *aggressive* form of
teleological reasoning that has all too often driven ICL analyses (particularly in
earlier stages of the field). It is "reductive" because it assumes one single purpose
(maximizing victim protection), ignoring that every enactment delineates
a boundary between multiple competing purposes. It is "aggressive" because it
uses that (presumed) single purpose to override other tools of construction, such as
the text and context.

Here is an example of the *"reductive"* or blinkered approach – that is, presuming
a single purpose. The jurisprudence of the ICTY has often asserted that the purpose
of the Geneva Conventions is to "ensure the protection of civilians to the maximum
extent possible,"[36] using this proposition to prefer a "less rigorous standard" in
interpretation of its provisions.[37] However, it is doubtful that the Geneva
Conventions can credibly be said to reflect a singular purpose.[38] If the Geneva
Conventions really had one sole purpose of *"maximizing"* the protection of civilians,
then they would contain only a single article, forbidding any use of force or violence

---

[34] *Čelebići* Trial Judgment, *supra* note 2, at para 413. For examples from the common law system, see
G Williams, *Textbook of Criminal Law* (Stevens & Sons, 1983) 12; Note, "The New Rule of Lenity"
(2006) 119 Harvard L Rev 2420 at 2435–41; A P Simester & W J Brookbanks, *Principles of Criminal Law*
(Brookers, 2002) at 35–36; *United States v RLC*, 503 U.S. 291 (1992) at 305–06; *R v Hasselwander* [1993]
2 SCR 398 (Canada).

[35] W Schabas, "Interpreting the Statutes of the Ad Hoc Tribunals," in L C Vohrah et al, eds, *Man's
Inhumanity to Man* (Kluwer Law International, 2003) at 886, finds that the principle has found
"virtually no place" in Tribunal jurisprudence.

[36] See, e.g., *Prosecutor v Aleksovski*, Judgment, ICTY A.Ch, IT-95-14/1-A, 24 March 2000 ("*Aleksovski*
Appeal Judgment") para 146; *Tadić* Appeal Judgment, *supra* note 2, at para 168.

[37] *Aleksovski* Appeal Judgment, *supra* note 36, at para 146.

[38] See A M Danner, "When Courts Make Law: How the International Criminal Tribunals Recast the
Laws of War" (2006) 59 Vanderbilt L Rev 1 at 32: "The records of the 1949 Diplomatic Conference,
however, reveal that most states did not, in fact, seek to protect civilians 'to the maximum extent
possible' ... [T]hose guarantees are relatively weak ... Geneva Convention IV balances the needs of
individual and state security."

that could affect civilians. Instead, the Geneva Conventions contain complex provisions, evincing a much more nuanced matrix of purposes: improving civilian protection, while also balancing military effectiveness and state security.[39] Thus interpretations that focus only on one purpose will systematically distort the balances struck in the law. An intelligent teleological analysis would note that the purpose of creating those conventions was to improve (not "maximize") protection for human beings, and it would also consider the *competing* goals and purposes underlying the various provisions.

Here is an example of the *"aggressive"* version of such reasoning – that is, allowing the one presumed purpose to eclipse all other considerations. In *Čelebići* the Appeals Chamber held that "to maintain a distinction between the two legal regimes [international and internal armed conflicts] and their criminal consequences in respect of similarly egregious acts because of the difference in nature of the conflicts would ignore the very purpose of the Geneva Conventions, which is to protect the dignity of the human person."[40]

I welcome the regulation of internal conflicts, but nonetheless this particular *argument* warrants skepticism. The Geneva Conventions contain more than 300 articles regulating international armed conflict and only one short article on internal conflicts, which was adopted only after acrimonious debate.[41] The Conventions criminalize some violations in international conflicts, but – pointedly – do not do so in internal conflicts. It strains credibility to suggest that the "very purpose" of the Conventions logically compels an outcome so deeply contradicted by the actual terms of the Conventions.[42]

The problem with reductive victim-focused teleological reasoning is that it conflates the "general justifying aim" of the criminal law system as a whole – which may indeed be a consequentialist aim of protecting society – with the question of whether it is justified to punish a particular individual for a particular crime.[43] George Fletcher has drawn an analogy to a tax regime to demonstrate the problem: while the primary function of an income tax regime is to raise revenue, it does not follow that each decision to allow or disallow a given deduction should be

---

[39] *Ibid*; L C Green, *The Contemporary Law of Armed Conflict* (Manchester University Press, 2000) at 348.

[40] *Prosecutor v Delalić et al (Čelebići)*, Judgment, ICTY A.Ch, IT-96-21-A, 20 February 2001 ("*Čelebići* Appeal Judgment") at para 172.

[41] O Uhler & H Coursier, *Commentary on the Geneva Conventions of 12 August 1949*, Vol IV (International Committee of the Red Cross, 1958) at 26–34.

[42] In a similar vein, Joseph Powderly discusses examples of judges invoking drafters' intent to advance propositions contrary to the discernable drafters' intent: J C Powderly, "Judicial Interpretation at the Ad Hoc Tribunals: Method from Chaos?," in J C Powderly & S Darcy, eds, *Judicial Creativity at the International Criminal Tribunals* (Oxford University Press, 2010) at 41.

[43] Hart, *supra* note 5, at 77–78. The latter question cannot be determined by utilitarian concerns alone, because otherwise there would be no principled limitations on liability. As Hart has shown, utilitarian responses to this objection – e.g. the disutility if it were learned that the innocent were punished – are contingent on outcomes and fail to capture our abhorrence.

resolved by reference to this overarching goal.[44] In a criminal justice system adhering to liberal principles, "society has no warrant to treat persons unjustly in its pursuit of utilitarian gains."[45] Thus the aim of criminal law may be to protect society from individuals, but the pursuit of that goal is qualified by principled restraints to protect the individual from society.[46]

My previous works have been at times understood, even in ICC jurisprudence,[47] as suggesting that teleological reasoning is per se inappropriate in criminal law, despite my attempts to explicitly affirm the contrary.[48] Accordingly, I reiterate: teleological reasoning is an appropriate part of legal reasoning. Law is a purpose-laden endeavour. My objection is to the recurring reductive and aggressive form of teleological reasoning, because is overly simplistic and problematic.[49]

2.2.2 Illustration: Command Responsibility

In this chapter, I will use command responsibility as a recurring example for all three "modes" of reasoning. Reductive victim-focused teleological reasoning is prominent in the discourse on command responsibility. Even the origins of the doctrine lie in such reasoning. The doctrine was judicially created and applied in war crimes trials after World War II, despite the absence of a provision in the Nuremberg and Tokyo Charters, after the *Yamashita* decision deduced the doc-

---

[44]   G Fletcher, *Rethinking Criminal Law*, 3rd ed (Oxford University Press, 2000) at 419.

[45]   D Husak, *Philosophy of Criminal Law: Selected Essays* (Oxford University Press, 1987) at 51; Fletcher, *supra* note 44, at 511.

[46]   Hart, *supra* note 5, at 81.

[47]   See, e.g., *Prosecutor v Ruto and Sang*, Decision on Defence Applications for Judgments of Acquittal, ICC T.Ch, ICC-01/09-01-11, 5 April 2016, at para 328 (Judge Chile Eboe-Osuji), citing Robinson, *supra* note 1, for this narrow proposition. Judge Eboe-Osuji responds that teleological interpretation can be accompanied by insistence on the procedural rights of the accused. I agree – and I assume he meant of course to include not only procedural rights, but also fundamental principles. My objection, however, was to the reductive and aggressive form of teleological interpretation seen in cases and literature as cited for example in this section, which reduces analysis to a one-dimensional question and can lead to contradictions with fundamental principles.

   I think that the discussion in *Prosecutor v Katanga*, Judgment Pursuant to Article 74 of the Statute, ICC T.Ch, ICC-01/04-01-07, 7 March 2014, at para 54 conveys my concern accurately, since the passage referred the use of teleological reasoning in a "determinative" way (which would accurately reflect my concern with "aggressive" and reductive teleological reasoning). I agree entirely with the interpretive approach in the judgment: teleological analysis matters, but should not be used reductively or aggressively.

[48]   Robinson, *supra* note 1, esp at 935 and 938.

[49]   It is also sometimes thought that, in objecting to maximal construction, I must be supporting strict construction. However, my point is simply that there is a contradiction between declaring strict construction and applying maximal construction. I am exploring the habits of reasoning that make this lapse seem natural, so that the contradiction goes unnoticed. To engage in substantive evaluation first requires the methodology that I develop in the remainder of this book. For tentative discussion of strict construction, see §5.2.1.

trine from the need to curb violations of the laws of war.[50] Their consequentialist observations make a compelling case for the *desirability* of command responsibility liability, but they did not necessarily demonstrate that such a rule was in fact established in ICL.[51]

An example from Tribunal jurisprudence appears in the opinion of Judge Shahabuddeen in *Hadžihasanović*, on command responsibility.[52] He argued that strict construction is applied only at the final stage, after other methods have been applied,[53] that the provision must first be interpreted by reference to object and purpose,[54] and that the purpose is to ensure that crimes do not go unpunished.[55] The third step of this argument is an example of reductive ("single issue") teleological reasoning. He also applied the "aggressive" version, because he noted that even if the actual textual provisions did not support his conclusion, then "they do not prevail."[56] This is an example of how diverse purposes and conflicting interpretive clues can disappear under the steamroller of a reductive teleological approach.[57] As I will argue in Chapter 6, more attention to the interpretive clues would have suggested a path conforming to the culpability principle.

---

[50]   In *Re Yamashita*, 327 U.S. 1 (1946) at 15, the majority derived the doctrine from the purpose of the laws of war – namely, to protect civilians:

> It is evident that the conduct of military operations by troops whose excesses are unrestrained by the orders or efforts of their commander would almost certainly result in violations which it is the purpose of the law of war to prevent. Its purpose to protect civilian populations and prisoners of war from brutality would largely be defeated if the commander of an invading army could with impunity neglect to take reasonable measures for their protection.

[51]   The dissents of Justices Murphy and Rutledge argued that the majority, in its pursuit of its teleological aims, had contravened the principles of legality and culpability:

> In all this needless and unseemly haste there was no serious attempt to charge or to prove that he committed a recognized violation of the laws of war. He was not charged with personally participating in the acts of atrocity or with ordering or condoning their commission. Not even knowledge of these crimes was attributed to him ... The recorded annals of warfare and the established principles of international law afford not the slightest precedent for such a charge.

   Ibid at 28.

[52]   *Prosecutor v Hadžihasanović*, Decision on Interlocutory Appeal Challenging Jurisdiction in Relation to Command Responsibility, ICTY A.Ch, IT-01-47-AR72, 16 July 2003 ("*Hadžihasanović* Command Responsibility Decision").

[53]   Partially Dissenting Opinion of Judge Shahabuddeen *ibid* at para 12.

[54]   *Ibid* at paras 11, 13, 23.

[55]   *Ibid* at para 24.

[56]   *Ibid* at para 18.

[57]   For a careful dissection of the jurisprudence on legality and problems of elasticity, see G Vanocore, "Legality, Culpability and *Dogmatik*: A Dialogue between the ECtHR, Comparative and International Criminal Law" (2015) 15 Int'l Crim L Rev 823. For discussion of other examples of problematic reasoning, see A Zahar, "Civilizing Civil War: Writing Morality as Law at the ICTY," in B Swart, G Sluiter & A Zahar, eds, *The Legacy of the International Criminal Tribunal for the Former Yugoslavia* (Oxford University Press, 2011).

The same reasoning is common in ICL scholarship. To offer an example (and this example is representative rather than intended to single out any author), an argument by Greg Vetter illustrates a typical syllogism.[58]

(1) To deter human rights abuses, potential perpetrators must perceive prosecution as a possible consequence of their actions.[59]

(2) Some features of the command responsibility doctrine in the Rome Statute are "less strict" than other instruments,[60] because they set "an easier standard for the accused to exonerate himself or herself."[61]

(3) Therefore, the weaker standard is plainly "undesirable," because it will not deter to the same extent;[62] it reduces the efficacy of the ICC because superiors will "not be as fearful" of being convicted.[63]

As you may see from this syllogism, if we look exclusively at maximizing protection of victims, then analysis of doctrines becomes a simple, one-dimensional task. The broadest articulation is the best. But our analysis should not be one-dimensional; we also have to consider important constraints, such as legality and culpability. It is not enough to show that conviction would be more difficult; we also have to ask whether conviction would be appropriate. In this example, Vetter demonstrated his concerns with the ICC Statute provisions by showing that persons who were convicted in the Tokyo tribunals might get acquitted under the ICC standard. He showed that a superior might get acquitted if crimes were committed by persons not under her authority and control,[64] or that a civilian manager might be acquitted for crimes committed by civilian employees while off-duty and without her knowledge.[65] However, what he does not show is that persons *ought* to be convicted in such circumstances. In the two examples given, conviction would seem contrary to the principle of personal culpability.[66] If so, then the ICC formulation is actually preferable. It is this

---

[58] Vetter, *supra* note 18. His article examined the bifurcation in the Rome Statute, which applies a stricter constructive knowledge standard for military commanders and a more generous standard for civilian superiors. The article concluded that the more generous standard leaves more room for exoneration of the accused and is therefore undesirable.

[59] *Ibid* at 92.

[60] *Ibid* at 93 and 103. Similarly, Womack, *supra* note 18, at 167–68, concluded that a restrained provision is "undesirable" because commanders "would not need to be as fearful of prosecution" and hence would monitor subordinates less closely, increasing the likelihood of crimes and thereby "removing the utility" of the doctrine. This may be true, but it leaves unanswered whether such a departure complies with fundamental principles.

[61] Vetter, *supra* note 18, at 120.

[62] *Ibid* at 94.

[63] *Ibid* at 103.

[64] *Ibid* at 126.

[65] *Ibid* at 127.

[66] See §2.3.2 and Chapter 6.

deontic dimension that was frequently missing in early ICL discourse and is still sometimes missing in arguments today.

A common type of argument in the literature is that "the scope of liability is formally over-inclusive, but only in order to make up for severe practical dangers of under-inclusiveness."[67] Thus "the hope is that the threat of serious criminal liability for 'mere' negligence will lead even the most reluctant commander (in order to protect himself) to take all reasonable measures to prevent war crimes by subordinates."[68] The problem with such arguments is that they consider only the consequentialist aims (e.g. maximizing deterrence) without considering the deontic constraints of justice. (I emphasize again that my objection here is to these forms of *argument* and not necessarily to the outcome advocated; it may be that, with a careful deontic analysis, the outcome could be justified.[69])

2.2.3 Illustration: Joint Criminal Enterprise

Another illustration is the emergence of the "joint criminal enterprise" (JCE) doctrine in Tribunal jurisprudence. The problems with JCE are now so well known throughout the ICL field, and have been so thoroughly discussed, that I propose not to rehearse this particular example at any length here. In the interests of brevity, I will simply provide a summary recounting here, but I offer more detailed explanation and demonstration in Annex 2 for any readers who may wish to hear more about the doctrine, the controversies, and the reasoning that produced it.

In a nutshell, JCE was developed by Tribunal judges, and it is far broader than any of the modes of liability actually listed in the Tribunal Statutes. It amalgamates the most sweeping inculpatory features of various national doctrines into a single doctrine of unusual breadth. Under JCE, a relatively minor contribution to a criminal enterprise, including a reluctant contribution, can render a person liable as a *principal* for *every* crime committed in the criminal enterprise, which can involve thousands of crimes, nationwide, structurally and geographically remote from the accused.[70] As

---

[67] M Osiel, *Obeying Orders: Atrocity, Military Discipline and the Law of War* (Routledge, 2002) at 193.

[68] *Ibid.*

[69] In Chapter 8, I advance a deontic justification for a criminal negligence standard.

[70] See, e.g., Danner & Martinez, *supra* note 10; Osiel, *supra* note 13; V Haan, "The Development of the Concept of Joint Criminal Enterprise at the International Criminal Tribunal for the Former Yugoslavia" (2005) 5 Int'l Crim L Rev 167; D Nersessian, "Whoops, I Committed Genocide! The Anomaly of Constructive Liability for Serious International Crimes" (2006) 30 Fletcher F World Aff 81; J D Ohlin, "Three Conceptual Problems with the Doctrine of Joint Criminal Enterprise" (2006) 5 JICJ 69; K Ambos, "Joint Criminal Enterprise and Command Responsibility" (2007) 5 JICJ 159; N Jain, *Perpetrators and Accessories in International Criminal Law* (Hart, 2014) at 29–65. For jurisprudence outlining these features, see, e.g., *Prosecutor v Vasiljević*, Judgment, ICTY A.Ch, IT-98-32-A, 25 February 2004, at paras 99–102; *Prosecutor v Brđanin*, Judgment, ICTY A.Ch, IT-99-36-A, 3 April 2007 ("*Brđanin* Appeal Judgment") at paras 422–27; *Tadić* Appeal Judgment, *supra* note 2, at paras 202–28; *Prosecutor v Karemera*,

a result of these features, the doctrine has been wryly referred to as "Just Convict Everybody."[71]

My interest here is not to assess the doctrine (many others have meticulously done so),[72] but to look at the *reasoning* that engendered it. The doctrine emerged in the *Tadić* decision. The judges were confronted with a fact pattern that would not allow a conviction under the modes of liability listed in the Tribunal Statute (Article 7). The judges filled that gap, and enabled conviction, by reasoning teleologically:

> An interpretation of the Statute based on its object and purpose leads to the conclusion that the Statute intends to extend the jurisdiction of the International Tribunal to *all* those "responsible for serious violations of international humanitarian law" committed in the former Yugoslavia (Article 1) . . . If this is so, it is fair to conclude that the Statute does not confine itself to providing for jurisdiction over those persons who plan, instigate, order, physically perpetrate a crime or otherwise aid and abet in its planning, preparation or execution. The Statute does not stop there.[73]

The reasoning employed in this passage is single-issue teleological reasoning (it focuses on maximizing reach and does not consider other possible aims, such as restricting jurisdiction to persons with significant responsibility for crimes). The reasoning was employed to the exclusion of other interpretive considerations, including the text itself ("the Statute does not stop there"). As a result, the judges read in a mode of liability far broader than any of the listed modes (which conflicts with the *esjudem generis* principle). The applied approach contrasts sharply with the declared approach of strict construction, reliance on unambiguous terms, and rejection of doubtful inferences.[74] Furthermore, the JCE doctrine continued to expand in subsequent cases as, at each interpretive juncture, chambers opted for the more progressive option.[75] For any who are interested, these arguments are developed in more detail in Annex 2. In short, the exuberant reasoning seems to have produced conflicts with the principles of legality, culpability, and fair labelling.[76]

Decision on Jurisdictional Appeals, ICTR A.Ch, ICTR-98–44-AR72.5, 12 April 2006, at paras 11–18. See also Annex 1.

[71] See, e.g., M E Badar, "Just Convict Everyone! Joint Perpetration from *Tadić* to *Stakić* and Back Again" (2006) 6 Int'l Crim L Rev 293.

[72] See Annex 2 for a survey of principled criticisms of JCE.

[73] *Tadić* Appeal Judgment, *supra* note 2, at paras 189–90 (emphasis in original).

[74] See §2.2.1.

[75] *Prosecutor v Krnojelać*, Judgment, ICTY A.Ch, IT-97–25-A, 17 September 2003, at para 97 (no agreement needed); *Brđanin* Appeal Judgment, *supra* note 70, at para 410 (physical perpetrators need not be part of the JCE); *Prosecutor v Kvočka*, Judgment, ICTY A.Ch, IT-98–30/1-A, 28 February 2005, at paras 105–06 (*dolus eventualis* suffices); *Prosecutor v Brđanin*, Decision on Interlocutory Appeal, ICTY A.Ch, IT-99–36-A, 19 March 2004, at paras 5–10 (JCE-III can circumvent the special intent requirement of genocide); *Prosecutor v Đordevic*, Judgment, ICTY A.Ch, IT-05–87/1-A, 27 January 2014, at paras 906–07 (JCE-III does not require awareness of probability but mere "possibility").

[76] See literature cited at §2.2.3.

2.2.4 Victim-Focused Teleological Reasoning Aggravated by Utopian Aspirations

The problem of victim-focused teleological reasoning is aggravated where ICL also becomes imbued with utopian aspirations.[77] For example, whereas national criminal law seeks to *manage* crime – by reducing, or at least visibly responding to, crimes – ICL at times appears to aim, more ambitiously, to *end* the crimes. For example, the United Nations Security Council resolutions creating the ICTY and ICTR refer to the determination "to put an end to such crimes" and express confidence that the creation of tribunals "would enable this aim to be achieved."[78] This more urgent aspiration arguably creates greater pressure to be aggressive in the articulation of norms.

The problem may be compounded further still by the grave disparity between the utopian aspirations and the dystopian realities faced by ICL. In other words, the severity and scale of the crimes and the extreme difficulty of securing arrests means that, once an accused is at trial, the desire may be stronger to make a clear object lesson, and to serve the didactic function of ICL, in the desperate hope of trying to have a preventive impact in such chaotic situations.[79] At times, it seems that ICL seeks to offset its weakness on the ground through more draconian rules – or, in other words, to overcompensate for *material weakness* through *normative harshness.*[80]

To give an example from the literature, Professor Sherrie Russell-Brown starts from the "foundational precept . . . that the continuing commission of gender crimes in war must end."[81] It is perhaps unsurprising that, from a foundational precept of *ending* such crimes, she concludes that the already controversial doctrine of command responsibility must be rendered harsher still: "[I]t is unacceptable to allow commanders to escape criminal responsibility for their subordinates' gender crimes on the basis that the commanders lacked 'knowledge.' "[82] Her proposal is to deem the knowledge requirement to be satisfied automatically by virtue of the historic frequency of sexual offences by troops. Such an approach would certainly facilitate

---

[77] See, e.g., J R Morss, "Saving Human Rights from Its Friends: A Critique of the Imaginary Justice of Costas Douzinas" (2003) 27 Melbourne U L Rev 889 at 899 ("the future-oriented and utopian character of human rights aspirations"); see also, e.g., J W Nickel, "Are Human Rights Utopian?" (1982) 11 Phil & Pub Aff 246; C Douzinas, "Human Rights and Postmodern Utopia" (2000) 11 L&C 219.

[78] See, e.g., UN Security Council Resolution 827 (1993), preamble at paras 5 and 6; UN Security Council Resolution 955 (1994) at paras 6 and 7.

[79] To be clear, didactic and preventive impact are proper concerns, provided that the deontic constraints are convincingly addressed.

[80] In a similar vein, Immi Tallgren has argued that, given the enormity of crimes and the improbability of punishment, a purely utilitarian theory would require punishment so severe that the system would face difficulties in making the treatment compatible with its generally enlightened ideas: I Tallgren, "The Sensibility and Sense of International Criminal Law" (2002) 13 EJIL 561 at 576. Wessel argues that, when confronted with such severe crimes, "the 'imperious immediacy of interest' in conviction can exclude considerations of more systemic consequences." Wessel, *supra* note 11, at 441.

[81] Russell-Brown, *supra* note 18, at 158.

[82] *Ibid.*

convictions, but it would create vicarious absolute liability for serious international crimes, which conflicts with the culpability principle. Admirable, but utopian, objectives such as eliminating crimes, which no criminal law system can achieve, are likely to generate calls for ever harsher rules and thus promote a tendency away from principled restraints. (In Chapter 8, I offer an account that considers the historic context of crimes to build a deontic justification for a "should have known" standard. However, my account does not dispense with fault by appealing to urgency; instead, it explores fault.)

For an example from case law, consider the *Erdemović* case. In *Erdemović*, a young soldier in a non-combat unit was told to participate in a firing squad. He objected to the order and was given the alternative of being shot alongside the victims. Faced with the harsh alternative of losing his life for no gain in saved lives, and concerned for his wife and infant son, he complied.[83] The majority concluded that duress may never be raised as a defence in relation to the killing of civilians.[84] The decision has been criticized by some commentators for lacking sensitivity to fundamental principles,[85] for departing from previous ICL pronouncements on the role of moral choice,[86] and for disregarding the fact that the only way for Erdemović to be innocent was to be dead.[87] For present purposes, my interest is not whether the decision was correct or incorrect,[88] but rather the reasoning – that is, how the majority framed the issue and hence sidestepped the deontic dimension.

The majority decision reasoned teleologically from the mandate granted by the Security Council, which was to " 'halt and effectively redress' the widespread and flagrant violations of international humanitarian law occurring in the territory of the former Yugoslavia and to contribute thereby to the restoration and maintenance of peace."[89] By focusing on this onerous responsibility of "halting" violations, the majority could only favour sending a strong message:

---

[83] *Prosecutor v Erdemović*, Judgment, ICTY A.Ch, IT-96–22-A, 7 October 1997 ("*Erdemović* Appeals Judgment").

[84] *Ibid* at para 19. Judges Cassese and Stephens dissented.

[85] R E Brooks, "Law in the Heart of Darkness: Atrocity and Duress" (2003) Virginia J Int L 861; I R Wall, "Duress, International Criminal Law and Literature" (2006) 4 JICJ 724; A Fichtelberg, "Liberal Values in International Criminal Law: A Critique of *Erdemović*" (2008) 6 JICJ 3; V Epps, "The Soldier's Obligation to Die When Ordered to Shoot Civilians or Face Death Himself" (2003) 37 New England L Rev 987.

[86] See, e.g., *United States v Otto Ohlendorf et al* (*The Einsatzgruppen Case*), 4 Trials of War Criminals before the Nuremberg Military Tribunals under Control Council Law No 9, at 470: "[T]here is no law which requires that an innocent man must forfeit his life or suffer serious harm in order to avoid committing a crime which he condemns." See also *Nuremberg* Judgment, *supra* note 2, at 251 (moral choice test).

[87] Brooks, *supra* note 85, at 868.

[88] While the reasoning was superficial, a careful deontic account might still support higher expectations of firmness based on a person's role. See §5.2.3.

[89] *Erdemović* Appeals Judgment, *supra* note 83, Separate Opinion of Judges McDonald and Vohrah, at para 75. The majority held that where there is ambiguity or uncertainty, a policy-directed choice can be made (*ibid* at para 78) to serve the "broader normative purposes" of ICL, which means "the protection of the weak and vulnerable" (*ibid* at para 75).

We would assert an absolute moral postulate which is clear and unmistakable for the implementation of international humanitarian law ... We do so having regard to our mandated obligation under the Statute to ensure that international humanitarian law, which is concerned with the protection of humankind, is not in any way undermined.[90]

The adopted aim of "halting" crime was one that only the harshest measures could hope to satisfy. The majority dismissed deontic concerns about personal culpability as "intellectual hair-splitting" and "metaphysics,"[91] and instead emphasized the "normative purposes" of law, highlighting the scale of crimes, the protection of the weak and vulnerable, and the need to ensure the effectiveness of humanitarian law and to deter crimes.[92] Hence the Chamber focused on the need to send a clear message, but did not consider whether the system's principles allowed it to use Dražen Erdemović to send that message. Ironically, although the majority purported to reject "utilitarian logic,"[93] its reasoning was entirely utilitarian, because it was focused on future deterrence.[94] It was through this process of reasoning that a system that aims to deal only with the persons *most responsible* for the most serious crimes was instead transformed into a "criminal law that could be obeyed only by exceptional individuals."[95] (Again, my concern here is with this overly simplistic form of reasoning and not with assessing the outcome; I outline a nuanced deontic assessment in Chapter 5.[96])

In conclusion, ICL – at least in its early resurgence – showed a contradictory allegiance to interpretive assumptions from two different regimes. For example, at the same time as the ICTY insisted that it scrupulously applies only rules that are "beyond any doubt customary international law,"[97] it also took credit for having "expanded the boundaries of international humanitarian and international criminal law."[98] This is an overt contradiction: the Tribunal cannot both apply the law strictly as it is *and* expand it. Such contradictions are the products of the conflicting normative assumptions simultaneously permeating ICL. While criminal law principles forbid the judicial expansion of norms, human rights and humanitarian law assumptions lead us to celebrate that very expansion. Contradictorily, we both *laud* and *deny* the expansions – a product of incompatible allegiances in the heritages of

---

[90] *Ibid* at paras 84 and 88. Similarly, Judge Li, concurring on this point, held that (i) the aim of humanitarian law is to protect innocent civilians, (ii) admitting duress would encourage subordinates to kill instead of deter them, and (iii) therefore such an "anti-human policy" cannot be adopted. *Ibid*, Separate and Partially Dissenting Opinion of Judge Li, at para 8.
[91] *Ibid* at paras 74 and 75.
[92] *Ibid* at para 75.
[93] *Ibid* at para 80.
[94] Fichtelberg, *supra* note 85, at 4.
[95] Tallgren, *supra* note 80, at 573.
[96] See §5.2.2.
[97] See, e.g., *Tadić* Appeal Judgment, *supra* note 2, para 662; *Blaškić* Appeal Judgment, *supra* note 28, at para 114; *Čelebići* Trial Judgment, *supra* note 2, at paras 415–18.
[98] ICTY, "Achievements," online: www.icty.org/en/about/tribunal/achievements.

ICL. A more careful and coherent ICL would parse out those commitments with more care.

2.3 SUBSTANTIVE AND STRUCTURAL CONFLATION

2.3.1 Substantive and Structural Conflation in ICL Discourse

Another way in which the assumptions of human rights and humanitarian lawyers may distort ICL reasoning is through what I call "substantive and structural conflation." Many of the prohibitions of ICL are drawn from prohibitions in human rights and humanitarian law. Faced with familiar-looking provisions, ICL practitioners often assume that the ICL prohibitions are, or ought to be, coextensive with the human rights or humanitarian law provisions. The problem arises when one assumes coextensiveness of content without considering that these bodies of law have different purposes and different consequences and thus entail different normative constraints.

Human rights law and humanitarian law apply to *collective entities* – states or parties to conflict. They focus on *systems*, seeking to improve the practices of collective entities, to advance protection of and respect for identified beneficiaries. The *remedies* are civil remedies, such as a cessation of the conduct, an apology, an undertaking of non-repetition, and possibly compensation or other efforts to restore the *status quo ante*.[99]

The primary focus of ICL, however, is on the culpability of *individuals*. Its scope is meant to be limited to the *most serious crimes* of concern to the international community as a whole.[100] Thus it is not primarily a vehicle for instilling "best practices"; it is considered with criminal conduct. ICL is enforced through the arrest, stigmatization, punishment, and imprisonment of individual human beings found responsible for crimes. As a result, ICL features several additional restraining principles. Thus, when transplanting rules, one must pause to consider deontic principles as well as the narrower scope of ICL.

By "*substantive conflation*," I mean the assumption that the norms must have the same substantive content when transplanting them from other domains. By "*structural conflation*," I mean reliance on structural assumptions of human rights and humanitarian law when reasoning about the norms, for example, focusing on improving systems rather than on the culpability of accused individuals.

A simple form of substantive conflation is the assumption that because a prohibition is recognized in human rights or humanitarian law, it must be (or ought to be) criminalized in ICL as well. An example of this is the frequently voiced

---

[99] As has previously been observed by Danner and Martinez, human rights law uses comparatively gentle methods of enforcement or persuasion, addresses broad social phenomena, and includes aspirational norms: Danner & Martinez, *supra* note 10, at 86–89.

[100] ICC Statute, Art 1.

view that "there is widespread recognition that every violation of the law of war is a war crime."[101] Given that the laws of war contain detailed regulations concerning, for example, the waterproofing of identity cards, it is implausible that every violation of the law of war constitutes a war crime. Other examples of conflation assume that conduct violating human rights law is also a crime against humanity, without considering the additional constraints relevant to ICL.[102] The additional constraints include not only fundamental principles (such as legality and personal culpability), but also the question of whether criminal law (and indeed ICL) is the appropriate tool to deal with the problem.[103]

A more interesting, and more subtle, form of conflation arises with respect to those norms that are indeed criminalized in ICL. Where an ICL prohibition is drawn from another area of law, it is understandable to assume that the norms have the same scope as they have in their original domain. As a result, jurists may transplant related rules from human rights or humanitarian law into criminal law, without pausing to reflect that those rules were not originally penal provisions and hence that they need to be scrutinized for compliance with the principles peculiar to criminal law.

As an illustration, consider Common Article 3 to the Geneva Conventions. Common Article 3 requires that, before any sentencing of protected persons, a party must provide a trial affording "all indispensable judicial guarantees."[104] A significant number of guarantees have been identified as "indispensable."[105]

---

[101]   J J Paust, "Content and Contours of Genocide, Crimes against Humanity, and War Crimes," in S Yee & W Tieya, eds, *International Law in the Post-Cold War World: Essays in Memory of Li Haopei* (Routledge, 2001).

[102]   See, e.g., E Davidsson, "Economic Oppression as an International Wrong and a Crime against Humanity" (2005) 23 Neth Q Hum Rights 173, arguing for the use of crimes against humanity to punish those responsible for IMF structural adjustment programmes, UN-mandated economic sanctions, failure to offer humanitarian assistance, and for "gross negligence in eradicating extreme poverty." I agree that such decisions violate economic and social rights. However, the analysis also requires us to demonstrate that criminal law is an appropriate and permissible manner in which to bring about UN or IMF reform. Similarly, M Møllmann, "Who Can Be Held Responsible for the Consequences of Aid and Loan Conditionalities? The Global Gag Rule in Peru and Its Criminal Consequences," Michigan State University's Women and International Development Program, Working Paper #29 (2004) at 12, describes the hardships imposed by the US policy of not contributing to organizations that condone abortion and argues for criminalization. Møllmann persuasively demonstrates that the US policy is unwise and deplorable, and probably a violation of health and autonomy rights, but it does not necessarily follow that one can criminalize the choices of the United States as to whom it gives its money, nor is it clear how to localize personal guilt.

[103]   See discussion *ibid*.

[104]   Common Art 3 to the Geneva Conventions: International Committee of the Red Cross (ICRC), *Geneva Convention for the Amelioration of the Condition of the Wounded and Sick in Armed Forces in the Field (First Geneva Convention)*, 12 August 1949, 75 UNTS 31.

[105]   See, e.g., W Fenrick, "Article 8, War Crimes," in O Triffterer, ed, *Commentary on the Rome Statute of the International Criminal Court: Observers' Notes, Article by Article*, 2nd ed (Beck, 2008) at 184; International Committee of the Red Cross (ICRC), *Commentary on the Additional Protocols of 8 June 1977 to the Geneva Conventions of 12 August 1949* (International Committee of the Red Cross, 1987) at 861–90.

Assume that a judge has made a ruling that an accused was too disruptive to remain in the courtroom, but in hindsight the judge is found to have applied the standard erroneously. It would follow that (i) the error breached the guarantee of the right to be present, (ii) the breach, although it may be minor and inadvertent, is nonetheless a breach, (iii) a breach of even one guarantee constitutes a failure to provide "all" guarantees, and therefore (iv) the error would violate Common Article 3. Thus it would, quite rightly, require an appropriate *humanitarian law* remedy, which might include a new trial, a reform, an apology, and compensation.[106]

Notice the problem that arises if we follow the same type of reasoning in the corresponding war crime. It is well established that Common Article 3 also gives rise to individual criminal responsibility for war crimes.[107] However, if an identical standard were applied in ICL, as authorities assume,[108] then – by the chain of reasoning just discussed – it would follow that the breach of *even one* guarantee not only requires a civil remedy, but also constitutes a war crime. On a literal application of the provision, the *actus reus* and *mens rea* would easily be established. (You might be thinking that the judge would not have *mens rea* if the legal error was inadvertent, but recall that, in general, a mistake of law is no excuse.[109]) Thus the judge would be liable to imprisonment as a war criminal, based on that single error, for sentencing a protected person without a trial that respected *all* guarantees.

That outcome would be unjust and overreaching. In all systems of the world, trial judges make errors and breach trial rights. As a result, new trials are granted; we do not automatically imprison the erring judge. Thus, although Common Article 3 has been incorporated directly into ICL, it surely requires some thoughtful *translation* so that it is correctly focused on criminally blameworthy conduct rather than judicial errors. In my view, the criminal law provision must work differently from the humanitarian law provision: The latter is violated by even one minor error, but the former surely requires something more egregious.

ICL discourse furnishes many examples of the "assumption of coextensiveness." For an example from literature, a thoughtful scholar in a leading commentary on the ICC Statute has voiced concern about a *mens rea* requirement inserted into the ICC

---

[106] See, e.g., Additional Protocol I to the Geneva Conventions of 12 August 1949 ("AP I"), Arts 89–91 on remedies.

[107] ICC Statute, Art 8(2)(c); ICTR Statute Art 4; SCSL Statute, Art 3; *Prosecutor v Tadić*, Decision on the Defence Motion for Interlocutory Appeal on Jurisdiction, ICTY A.Ch, IT-94-1-A, 2 October 1995 ("*Tadić* Decision on Jurisdiction") at para 134.

[108] Common Art 3 is recognized as so fundamental that "violations of . . . Common Article 3 are by definition serious violations of international humanitarian law within the meaning of the Statute": see, e.g., *Prosecutor v Blaškić*, Judgment, ICTY T.Ch, IT-95–14-T, 3 March 2000, at para 176.

[109] ICC Statute, Art 30. The judge's failure to realize that he was depriving a person of a right would arguably provide no excuse, since "a mistake of law as to whether a particular type of conduct is a crime within the jurisdiction of the Court shall not be a ground for excluding criminal responsibility": ICC Statute, Art 32(2). There are different ways of solving this problem; one option would be to find that mistake of law can preclude *mens rea* for this particular offence.

Elements of Crimes for the crime of enforced disappearance.[110] The Elements
indicate that a person denying the fact of detentions also commits enforced disappearance, but require that the person must have awareness of such detentions.[111]
The criticism was that the Elements were too restrictive, because human rights law
does not require that personal *mens rea*. However, this criticism overlooks the
structural difference. In human rights law, the knowledge of the individual denying
the detention is irrelevant, because the focus is on the *system* and its impact on the
victim. In ICL, however, the focus is on the criminal culpability of the accused
individual, and thus personal fault matters. When we assume that norms from other
domains should be replicated exactly as found, we may overlook the necessary
adaptations to convert rules for civil responsibility of collective systems into rules
appropriate for criminal punishment of individual human beings.

2.3.2 Illustration: Conflation and Command Responsibility

Many examples of this conflation appear in ICL reasoning on command responsibility. Jurists have copied command responsibility provisions from humanitarian law
into ICL without adequately reflecting on the context shift (civil liability to criminal
punishment). Confident that they were simply following "precedents," jurists did
not always adequately ponder the additional constraints, such as personal culpability, which are applicable for criminal prohibitions addressed to individuals.

To show why the conflation was problematic, I must briefly outline an internal
contradiction with the culpability principle. Tribunal jurisprudence recognizes the
principle of culpability as the "foundation of criminal responsibility."[112] The jurisprudence declares it "firmly established" that "for the accused to be criminally
culpable his conduct must have … contributed to, or have had an effect on, the
commission of the crime."[113] Nonetheless, Tribunal jurisprudence allows the commander to be held liable as a party to offences of subordinates[114] even when there was
no possible contribution to or effect on the crimes.[115] This is a stark contradiction,
and it initially went unnoticed. I demonstrate this contradiction, and its origins and
consequences, with more care in Chapter 6.

[110] L N Sadat, *The ICC and the Transformation of International Law: Justice for the New Millennium* (Transnational Press, 2002) at 140–41.
[111] Elements of Crimes (ICC-ASP/1/3 (2002)), Art 7(1)(i).
[112] *Tadić* Appeal Judgment, *supra* note 2.
[113] *Prosecutor v Kayishema*, Judgment, ICTR T.Ch, ICTR-95-1T, 21 May 1999, at para 199. The contribution can be simply making the crime more likely or at least easier: see also *Prosecutor v Orić*, Judgment, ICTY T.Ch, IT-03–68-T, 30 June 2006, at paras 280–82.
[114] Some suggest that command responsibility is a "separate offence," but this characterization is rejected in Tribunal jurisprudence and, in any event, is contrary to the actual charges and convictions issued by the Tribunals. See §6.6.
[115] *Čelebići* Trial Judgment, *supra* note 2, at paras 396–400; *Blaškić* Appeal Judgment, *supra* note 28, at paras 73–77.

For now, I point out that the contradiction was produced in part[116] by conflation. Interestingly, the *Čelebići* case acknowledged the "central place assumed by the principle of causation in criminal law," but then neglected it without qualms on the grounds that past cases and instruments seemed not to require it.[117] However, those past cases and instruments concerned the civil duty under humanitarian law, not individual criminal liability for the underlying crimes.

While humanitarian law quite reasonably imposes a civil duty to punish past violations, this is not the same as saying that the commander becomes personally *guilty* of those past crimes if she fails to punish them. Additional Protocol I to the Geneva Conventions (AP I) rightly distinguished between the commander's general duty under humanitarian law and the commander's personal criminal liability.[118] Article 87 of AP I recognizes a humanitarian law duty on commanders to prevent breaches by their subordinates, to report breaches to competent authorities, and to initiate disciplinary or penal actions against violations.[119] This civil duty is enforceable by international law remedies (e.g. reparations from that party to the conflict).[120] Article 86(2) supports that general civil duty with a narrow, *criminal* law provision:

> The fact that a breach of the Conventions or of this Protocol was committed by a subordinate does not absolve his superiors from penal or disciplinary responsibility, as the case may be, if they knew, or had information which should have enabled them to conclude in the circumstances at the time, that he was committing or was about to commit such a breach and if they did not take all feasible measures with in their power to prevent or repress the breach.

The penal provision of Article 86(2) refers only to *ongoing or imminent* crimes ("was committing or about to commit"). The penal provision requires contemporaneity, meaning that there is a possibility of the commander's acts or omissions influencing the subordinate's behaviour.

---

[116] In Chapter 6, I will dissect other aspects of the reasoning, including uncertainty about how to deal with the "failure to punish" branch of command responsibility.

[117] *Čelebići* Trial Judgment, *supra* note 2, at para 398.

[118] I will argue in the next section (§2.4) that instruments negotiated by parties, not knowing if the rules will be invoked *by* them or *against* them, may be more sensitive to principles of justice than instruments that are unilaterally imposed on others.

[119] AP I, Art 87. Article 87(3) provides:

> The High Contracting Parties and Parties to the conflict shall require any commander who is aware that subordinates or other persons under his control are going to commit or have committed a breach of the Conventions or this Protocol, to initiate such steps as are necessary to prevent such violations of the Conventions or this Protocol, and, where appropriate, to initiate disciplinary or penal action against violators thereof.

[120] Such remedies are applied against the state or the party to the conflict and include the payment of reparations (Art 91), as well as exposure to fact-finding (Art 90) and to Security Council action (Art 89). States are internationally liable for breaches by their commanders (Art 91).

These differences rightly reflect *structural differences* between criminal law and humanitarian law. The humanitarian law duty quite reasonably does not require any causal contribution by the commander to the crimes. The purpose of the humanitarian law provision is to create better *systems* and thus to improve compliance by requiring a system of prevention and repression.[121] But, before copying and pasting humanitarian law provisions into criminal law, we have to pause to consider the different focus and consequences of criminal law, and hence the additional constraints.

Nonetheless, ICL discourse – both jurisprudence and literature – has frequently assumed the co-extensiveness of the humanitarian law norm and the criminal law norm, without reflecting on the different structures and consequences, and hence the different principles in play.[122] For example, the drafters of the ICTY and ICTR Statutes – declaring rules to be applied to others[123] – blithely combined Articles 86(2) and 87(3) into a single criminal provision, encompassing both pending crimes and past crimes, and both failure to prevent and failure to punish.[124] In doing so, they overlooked the differences between the criminal and non-criminal provisions of the Additional Protocols, and they effaced the causal contribution required by the culpability principle.

Rather than detecting the problem, Tribunal jurisprudence followed the same pattern of blurring the humanitarian law duty and personal criminal liability. In *Blaškić*, defence counsel argued – pursuant to the culpability principle – that some contribution to the crimes is necessary in any mode of liability; hence a commander's failure to punish should create liability only if that failure encouraged or facilitated later crimes.[125] In rejecting the defence argument, the Appeals Chamber relied on Article 87(3) of the Protocol, noting that it imposes a duty to punish persons responsible for past crimes.[126] However, the Chamber's argument overlooks that Article 87(3) deals with a duty in *humanitarian* law (collective civil responsibility), not the assignment of personal *criminal* liability. Had the Chamber studied the precedents with more attention to the structural differences between

---

[121] ICRC, *supra* note 106, at 1018.

[122] Such conflation appeared in *Yamashita, supra* note 50. The *Yamashita* decision illustrates victim-focused teleological reasoning (§2.2) and also substantive conflation, because it derived the command responsibility principle from the purposes of the laws of war. The majority decision converted a humanitarian law duty into a criminal law norm, and because of its assertion that it was simply applying existing law, it did not engage in reflection on compliance with fundamental principles. As Justice Murphy argued in dissent, the majority approach overlooked the difference between civil claims and "charging an individual with a crime against the laws of war": *ibid* at 36–37.

[123] See §2.4 on the tendency of drafters to favour more sweeping rules when the rules are applied to others.

[124] ICTY Statute, Art 7(3); ICTR Statute, Art. 6(3). The report of the drafters indicates no intention to change the law: *Report of the Secretary-General Pursuant to Paragraph 2 of Security Council Resolution 808* (1993), UN Doc. S/25704 (1993) at para 56; the premise was to apply only "rules … which are beyond any doubt part of customary law" (*ibid* at para 34).

[125] *Blaškić* Appeal Judgment, *supra* note 28, paras 73 and 78.

[126] *Ibid* at para 83.

international humanitarian law and ICL, it might have noticed that AP I specifically separated the broader humanitarian law duty from the narrower criminal law provision in Article 86(2) and that the separation mapped onto the limits of personal culpability.[127]

Substantive conflation allows judges and jurists to proceed in complacent confidence that they are simply following "precedents," overlooking the fact that the "precedents" are actually from non-criminal areas of law. As a result, broader norms are absorbed into ICL without first triggering alarms as to the need to scrutinize the proposed norm for compliance with fundamental principles.

This tendency of substantive conflation may also be seen in literature, where it is frequently assumed that any differences in scope between the humanitarian law duty and the imposition of criminal liability are obviously "gaps," "lacunae," or "steps backward" that will "allow atrocities to go unpunished."[128] But, actually, there may be sound reasons of principle for the criminal prohibition to be narrower, in order to comply with principles of justice.

2.4 IDEOLOGICAL ASSUMPTIONS (SOVEREIGNTY AND PROGRESS)

2.4.1 The "Sovereignty versus Progress" Dichotomy

The third set of transplanted assumptions is what I will call "ideological" assumptions. These include common narratives and heuristics around concepts such as "progress" or "sovereignty." Such assumptions, familiar in human rights and humanitarian law discourse, also appear in ICL reasoning. Uncritical recourse to such assumptions can lead to an embrace of illiberal doctrines.

In a human rights instrument, there is a fairly straightforward inverse relationship between the obligations undertaken and the freedom of action retained by the state. The more sovereign freedom of action retained, the narrower the human rights obligations. As a result, human rights and humanitarian law discourse routinely casts

---

[127] A minor theme of this book is that sensitivity to deontic considerations may at times improve even our doctrinal, precedential analysis, by making us more alert to nuances in the precedents that reflect fundamental principles. Other examples appear in Chapter 6.

[128] See, e.g., Fox, *supra* note 18, at 443, arguing that an interpretation not encompassing all of Art 87(3) would be "erroneous," "illogical," and "contradicted by the plain language of the Protocol" (at 466), and would mean a "gap [that will] allow certain atrocities to go unpunished" (at 444) and "a troubling drift toward allowing impunity" (at 494). See also G Mettraux, *International Crimes and the Ad Hoc Tribunals* (Oxford University Press, 2005) at 301 ("gaping hole," "highly questionable from a legal and practical point of view"). Similarly, van Schaack argues that the causal requirement in the ICC Statute (which, as argued in §2.2, is essential for compliance with the principle of culpability) is a "step backward" that "significantly truncates" the doctrine, and the resulting "lacuna" or "loophole" "sends a message" that it is acceptable not to punish: B van Schaack, "Command Responsibility: A Step Backwards" (17 July 1998) *On the Record – International Criminal Court* (blog). Paust, *supra* note 102, at 305, sees the causal contribution requirement as a "problem" and hopes that a creative interpretation, in the light of "customary international law," can fill in such "needless limitations."

"sovereignty" in elemental opposition to "progress." Sovereignty is the "traditional enemy,"[129] the "stumbling block in the advance of civil rights,"[130] the irksome vestige of "divine right," "which human rights law is still in the process of extirpating."[131] Sovereignty is often portrayed as the obstacle raised by short-sighted lawyers, diplomats, and bureaucrats,[132] and a constant threat to the project of international law.[133] This inverse relationship underlies the progress narrative of human rights, wherein a darker age of "sacrosanct and unassailable" sovereignty has recently "suffered progressive erosion at the hands of the more liberal forces at work in the democratic societies, particularly in the field of human rights."[134]

These assumptions about sovereignty and progress are often carried over into ICL discourse. Sovereignty is a "contradiction" to human rights and justice[135] and an "enduring obstacle" in advancing ICL;[136] the "movement for global justice has been a struggle against sovereignty,"[137] such that human rights and justice must "trump" state sovereignty,[138] since for sovereignty to prevail would be a "travesty of law and a betrayal of the human need for justice."[139] As Robert Cryer wryly observes, "[w]hen sovereignty appears in [ICL] scholarship, it commonly comes clothed in hat and cape. A whiff of sulphur permeates the air."[140]

---

[129]   G Robertson, *Crimes against Humanity: The Struggle for Global Justice* (The New Press, 2006) at 624.

[130]   *Ibid* at 176 (emphasis omitted).

[131]   *Ibid* at 2.

[132]   "Sovereignty appears in the arguments of lawyers, the commitments of diplomats and the reassurances of international bureaucrats as a barrier to the over-ambitious extension of ICL": G Simpson, "Politics, Sovereignty, Remembrance," in D McGoldrick, P Rowe & E Donnelly, eds, *The Permanent International Criminal Court: Legal and Policy Issues* (Hart, 2004) at 53.

[133]   "[W]henever state sovereignty explodes onto the scene, it may demolish the very bricks and mortar on which the Law of Nations Is Built": A Cassese, "Current Trends towards Criminal Prosecution," in N Passas, ed, *International Crimes* (Ashgate/Dartmouth, 2003) at 587.

[134]   See, e.g., *Tadić* Decision on Jurisdiction, *supra* note 108, at para 55.

[135]   "The contradiction between the principle of national sovereignty and the universal nature of human rights reaches its apogee faced with crimes against humanity. Humanitarian law – and universal conscience – dictate that these crimes must not go unpunished. But State sovereignty subjects this demand for justice to the contingencies of political choices": R Badinter, "International Criminal Justice: From Darkness to Light," in A Cassese, P Gaeta & J R W D Jones, eds, *The Rome Statute of the International Criminal Court: A Commentary* (Oxford University Press, 2002) at 1932.

[136]   "Throughout the twentieth century, state sovereignty has provided one of the most enduring obstacles for advancing ICL": S C Roach, *Politicizing the ICC: The Convergence of Ethics, Politics and Law* (Rowman & Littlefield, 2006) at 19.

[137]   Robertson, *supra* note 130, at xxx.

[138]   "[The ICC is] the primary reference for those who believe that borders, state sovereignty and political expediency cannot shield the perpetrators of massive human rights violations from prosecution . . . .It is widely acknowledged that the moral commitment to protect the most fundamental human rights at a global scale trumps state sovereignty and the legal pillars that sustained classic international law": P C Diaz, "The ICC in Northern Uganda: Peace First, Justice Later" (2005) 2 Eyes on the ICC 17.

[139]   "It would be a travesty of law and a betrayal of the human need for justice, should the concept of State sovereignty be allowed to be raised successfully against human rights": *Tadić* Decision on Jurisdiction, *supra* note 108, at para 58.

[140]   R Cryer, "International Criminal Law vs. State Sovereignty: Another Round?" (2005) 16 EJIL 979 at 980; see also F Mégret, "Politics of International Criminal Justice" (2002) 13 EJIL 1261 at 1261.

The common narrative about sovereignty in human rights is in part correct and in part overstated. The demonization of sovereignty is at least somewhat overstated, because "sovereignty" may often reflect other legitimate pro-human objective,[141] and is not always a matter of elites "jealously clinging" to their prerogatives. Nonetheless, in human rights or humanitarian law, it is at least usually accurate to ascribe limitations in instruments to states' wishes to preserve governmental freedom of action (sovereignty), since the treaties limit state action.

In ICL, however, there is an *additional variable* in play: the instruments not only circumscribe state freedom of action, but also allow *punishment of human individuals*. Thus restrictive provisions in ICL might not be only about protecting sovereignty; they may also reflect principled constraints of justice that respect individuals. In ICL discourse, it is common to overlook this important shift and to make the same assumption as in human rights discourse: any limitations are ascribed to "sovereignty" or "compromise," – that is, the usual business of short-sighted states failing to reflect the full scope of human rights because they cling to outdated prerogatives.[142]

Such reasoning can foster an uncritical reception of expansive interpretations as a victory of humanity over sovereignty, as well as a knee-jerk rejection of provisions that comply with liberal principles. These hasty assumptions can lead jurists and scholars to overlook important deontic concerns.[143]

---

[141] See, e.g., Mégret, *supra* note 141, at 1261 and 1279–80, referring to these "clichés" about sovereignty that may overlook sovereignty's "emancipatory potential" and its role in self-determination. I would add that "safeguarding sovereignty" is not always short-sighted and problematic. When we further parse the underlying purpose, we might see that it is to protect other social goods (national security), or to recognize that states diverge in their views (the conduct is not generally condemned, so latitude is left for variations), or to delineate the proper boundaries between ICL and matters for domestic jurisdiction.

[142] For examples, see Fox, *supra* note 18, at 480 (requirement of causal contribution is one of the "weaknesses and limitations" of the Rome Statute), overlooking the possible significance of the culpability principle. See also Boot, *supra* note 17, at 606 and 640 (interpretation of war crimes narrower than *Tadić* and not including political groups in genocide "manifestly show to what extent States have sought to protect their sovereignty, which prevailed over human rights concerns"), overlooking the possibility that states felt constrained by the current state of the law (principle of legality). For further examples drawing from a variety of authors and issues, see G Mettraux, "Crimes against Humanity in the Jurisprudence of the ICTY and ICTR" (2002) 43 Harvard Int'l LJ 237 at 279 (dismissing a codification of crimes against humanity on the grounds that it was a "highly political affair"); A Pellet, "Applicable Law," in Cassese, Gaeta & Jones, *supra* note 136, at 1056 ("pretext"); D Hunt, "High Hopes, 'Creative Ambiguity' and an Unfortunate Mistrust in International Judges" (2004) 2 JICJ 56 at 57–58, 68 and 70 ("compromise and expediency"; "powers of judges were strongly curtailed to assuage the fears ... that the court could infringe upon sovereignty"); Sadat, *supra* note 111, at 152 and 267 ("compromises"); Bassiouni, *supra* note 18, at 202 ("mostly for political reasons"), each of which fails to contemplate fundamental principles (such as the principle of legality) as a possible consideration.

[143] See, e.g., Boot, *supra* note 17, at 434: "By expanding the protection of specifically mentioned groups to all permanent and stable groups in the definition of genocide, as well as expanding the boundaries of 'racial groups', the Tribunals also tend to let humanitarian gains prevail over arguments of State sovereignty." This binary conflict between "humanitarian gains" versus "state sovereignty" overlooks what should be another important constraint: the principle of legality.

Robert Cryer has convincingly demonstrated the deplorable double standards of states – namely, states tend to take a wider view of definitions of crimes and principles when they are imposing them on others than when their own officials and nationals may be scrutinized.[144] In such cases, we are still left with the question of whether the broader or narrower version of the doctrine is the more appropriate one. Confronted with such discrepancies, ICL jurists routinely adopt the same "progress versus sovereignty" assumption seen in human rights discourse: that the broader version is the truer, better articulation, and that the narrower is a tragic retrenchment caused by compromise and self-interest.[145]

However, before reaching such conclusions in ICL, we have to take the additional step of considering deontic constraints that respect individuals as persons. Doubtlessly, many conservative aspects of codification efforts may indeed be traced to unprincipled self-interest. However, it is also possible that a deliberative codification process involving diverse participants, such as the Rome Conference to adopt the ICC Statute, may identify legitimate issues of principle. Self-interest may even play a *productive* role: participants have more incentive to engage in thoughtful examination of principles than if they were applying rules only to others. Potential exposure seems to have a marvellous effect for many people in sharpening their sensitivity to fairness. Conversely, drafters or judges articulating rules for "others" do not always have the same direct incentive to scrutinize compliance with fundamental principles.[146]

Thus the simplistic "progress versus sovereignty" dichotomy can lead jurists to dismiss more principled formulations all too quickly. Ironically, as a result, ICL practitioners can embrace the more illiberal doctrines as the more "progressive." As Mirjam Damaška notes, many ICL jurists uncritically embrace Nuremberg jurisprudence as the true and enlightened standard,[147] without considering its origins in punitive victors' justice. As one example, Jordan Paust has argued that definitions of crimes against humanity subsequent to the Nuremberg definition "are severely limited in their reach, and do not reflect customary international law as evidenced in earlier instruments."[148] However, the definition of crimes against humanity in Nuremberg was vague and open-ended, and did not delineate its thresholds at all, so it is not necessarily a principled model that we should be lauding or replicating.

Other examples appear in the debate over the defence of superior orders. The Nuremberg and Tokyo Charters, announcing rules to apply to vanquished foes,

---

[144]   R Cryer, *Prosecuting International Crimes* (Cambridge, 2005).

[145]   See examples *supra* note 140.

[146]   They may have incentives to favour expansive rules, particularly in the earlier heyday of ICL. Such incentives may include the wish to send a deterrent message, to demonstrate righteousness, or to gain reputational esteem mentioned at §2.1.3.

[147]   Damaška, *supra* note 11, at 489 observes that many practitioners take "a rather uncritical stance" toward Nuremberg and related jurisprudence: "[T]hey stop deferentially before each decision as if it were a station in a pilgrimage."

[148]   Paust, *supra* note 102.

declared that there would be no defence of superior orders.[149] In the ICC Statute, negotiated multilaterally, states reinstated a limited version of the defence.[150] The ICC provision has been extensively criticized as a betrayal of the Nuremberg standard and has been assumed to be a retrogressive concession to self-protection by states.[151] In Chapter 5, I will show that these assumptions may be too hasty and that the arguments do not engage with the deontic dimension. If we consider constraints of justice and if we look at teleological aims other than maximal deterrence, then a more nuanced conversation awaits about the normative justifications of a partial defence.[152]

Additional examples of the "sovereignty versus progress" assumption appear in the debate about open-ended versus closed definitions. The Nuremberg and Tokyo Charters and the ICTY and ICTR Statutes – which were unidirectionally applied to "others" – included broad, open-ended definitions of crimes, with formulas such as "shall include but not be limited to," leaving extensive room for judges to expand the definitions of crimes.[153] Conversely, the drafters of the Rome Statute, who could not know whether the provisions would be applied to their foes, to strangers, to friends, or to themselves, opted for a more careful codification with a closed list of defined crimes. As a matter of fundamental principle, codification is generally welcomed in a system of criminal justice to provide fair warning to individuals.[154] Nonetheless, respected scholars and jurists in ICL, such as Alain Pellet and David Hunt, have reacted with concern that states have "sought to codify the law" to be applied by the judges, which in their view demonstrates a "deep suspicion" and "unfortunate mistrust for the judges."[155] Their analyses adopt the "progress versus sovereignty" assumption, focusing only on the benefits of expansive norms – benefits they perceive to be frustrated by the unfortunate myopia of governmental officials. Hunt's concern is that codification will "preclude significantly the necessary judicial development of the law," and he attributes such provisions to "fear," "political compromise," and "diplomatic expediency."[156] Pellet assumes that the cause was "ceding to American pressure" and "not trusting the judges," with the result that "the

---

[149] Nuremberg Charter, Art 8; Tokyo Charter, Art 6.

[150] ICC Statute, Art 33.

[151] As examples, see P Gaeta, "Defence of Superior Orders: The Statute of the International Criminal Court versus Customary International Law" (1999) 10 EJIL 172; M Frulli, "Are Crimes against Humanity More Serious than War Crimes?" (2001) 12 EJIL 329; C Fournet, "When the Child Surpasses the Father: Admissible Defences in International Criminal Law" (2008) 8 Int'l Crim L Rev 509.

[152] See §5.2.3.

[153] For example, the Nuremberg Charter in Art 6 included an illustrative list of war crimes, with an open-ended "shall include, but not be limited to" introduction; the Tokyo Charter in Art 5 did away with the illustrative list and left it entirely to the judges; the ICTY Statute in Art 3 included a "shall include, but not be limited to" illustrative list, as did the ICTR Statute in Art 4.

[154] See, e.g., P Robinson, "Fair Notice and Fair Adjudication: Two Kinds of Legality" (2005) 154 U Pa J Intl L 335 at 340, 344.

[155] See Hunt, *supra* note 143, esp at 56–59; see Pellet, *supra* note 143, esp at 1056.

[156] Hunt, *supra* note 143, at 56–59.

authors of the Statute have limited the chances of making the Court an efficient instrument in the struggle against the crimes it is supposed to repress."[157]

These illustrations show how even the leading minds in the field can assume that the broadest approach is automatically the best approach and that narrower approaches must be the result of myopic, sovereignty-driven concerns. Such analyses neglect that open-ended criminal norms originated in victors' justice, and they fail to ask whether that is a pattern we wish to replicate. Is an illustrative, open-ended list of crimes really the benchmark to which ICL should aspire? The "progress versus sovereignty" assumption can short-circuit adequate reflection on the third variable: deontic constraints owed to the individual. In this way, ideological assumptions that are liberal and appropriate in a human rights context can lead to hasty preference for expansive doctrines that were unilaterally imposed, but which may depart from fundamental principles.

2.4.2 Illustration: Ideological Assumptions and Command Responsibility

For another illustration, I return to my recurring example of command responsibility. If we review the legal history of command responsibility, a clear pattern emerges: states tend to adopt a broad approach when announcing rules for others and a narrower approach when it might apply to themselves.

(1) In the Nuremberg and Tokyo trials, where rules were being applied to vanquished foes, command responsibility was loosely defined and did not expressly require a causal contribution.[158]

(2) Conversely, when a US court applied command responsibility to its own forces in Vietnam, the doctrine was tightly defined, requiring a causal contribution for personal liability.[159]

(3) In the negotiation of AP I, states were in a position more akin to a "veil of ignorance," because they did not know whether they would be the beneficiaries or the accused. In this more neutral situation, they required causal contribution.[160]

(4) The drafters of the ICTY and ICTR Statutes, applying rules unidirectionally to others, wiped out the requirement of causal contribution, perhaps inadvertently, by blending criminal and non-criminal provisions of AP I.[161]

(5) The drafters of the ICC Statute, once again in a position somewhat akin to the "veil of ignorance," reinstated causal contribution.[162]

---

[157] Pellet, *supra* note 143, at 1058.
[158] See *Yamashita, supra* note 50, and *Trial of Wilhelm List and Others (The Hostages Case)* (1949) 8 Law Reports of Trials of War Crimes 1.
[159] *United States v Medina*, CM 427162 (ACMR, 1971) 8.
[160] AP I, Art 86(2); cf AP I, Art 87.
[161] ICTY Statute, Art 7(3); ICTR Statute, Art 6(3).
[162] ICC Statute, Art 28.

This double standard is objectionable, but we are still left with the question of whether the narrower or broader approach is the more appropriate. I have outlined the argument (and will develop the argument in much more detail in Chapter 6) that fundamental principles require a person to have causally contributed to crimes if that person is to be convicted for those crimes.[163] If that is so, then this appears to be one of the examples of where potential exposure enhanced the sensitivity of rule-articulators to justice and fairness.

Nonetheless, the assumptions about progress and sovereignty have often fostered a simplistic heuristic whereby ICL participants consider only the "unprincipled self-protection" possibility, and thus they condemn the narrower provision without analysis. For example, Judge Hunt, in a partially dissenting opinion, was confronted with the Rome Statute's requirement of causal contribution for command responsibility and the fact that Tribunal jurisprudence accords the Rome Statute "significant legal value."[164] The reinstatement of causal contribution in the Rome Statute could have served as an opportunity to detect that a deontic principle was in play. Instead, Judge Hunt simply observed that the Statute provision was the result of "negotiation and compromise," as was "patent ... from the vast differences between ... those provisions and existing instruments such as the Statutes of the ad hoc Tribunals," and hence he dismissed the Statute provision as "of very limited value."[165] Among the suppressed premises in such arguments are that "negotiation and compromise" invalidate an outcome, and that departure from the broader (unilaterally imposed) instrument shows that the narrower (multilaterally negotiated) instrument is incorrect. This analysis overlooks the deontic dimension, and it overlooks the possibility that a deliberative process might have been more sensitive to principles. Similarly, several scholars have not hesitated to dismiss the causal requirement in the Rome Statute provision as a tragic concession to self-interest and, as a result, have not explored the possibility that it has a principled basis.[166]

Thus assumptions about progress and sovereignty can lead ICL participants not only to look with suspicion upon the processes most likely to generate liberal doctrines, but also to favour broad but illiberal doctrines born in selective justice. These easy conclusions lead ICL participants to miss opportunities to detect contradictions between ICL jurisprudence and fundamental principles.

---

[163] See §2.3.2.
[164] Separate and Partially Dissenting Opinion of Judge David Hunt, in *Hadžihasanović* Command Responsibility Decision, *supra* note 52, at paras 29–30. As a simultaneous statement by 120 states, the Rome Statute offers significant evidence of customary law: *Prosecutor v Furundžija*, Judgment, ICTY T.Ch, IT-95-17/1-T, 10 December 1998, at para 227.
[165] Separate and Partially Dissenting Opinion of Judge David Hunt, in *Hadžihasanović* Command Responsibility Decision, *supra* note 52, at paras 30–32.
[166] See, e.g., Vetter, *supra* note 18 ("weakness"); Paust, *supra* note 102 ("needless limitation"); Fox, *supra* note 18 ("gap," "troubling drift toward allowing impunity").

2.5 AFTER THE IDENTITY CRISIS: THE DEONTIC TURN

The reasoning habits I have just described were relatively commonplace when I began work on this book, in the early days of the renaissance of ICL. These structures of argument are still often seen in ICL discourse today, but they are now much less common. In recent years, mainstream ICL analysis has become far more attentive to deontic constraints of criminal liability.

Of course, ICL has always declared its fidelity to fundamental principles such as culpability and legality, but the problem was with the reasoning. The tendency has been to engage with those principles as if they were mere doctrinal rules – "artifacts of legal positivism" – and hence jurists have used the same technical doctrinal arguments that they would use to minimize any inconvenient doctrinal rule.[167] I will argue in Chapter 3 that criminal justice requires an additional type of analysis – *deontic* analysis – in addition to source-based and teleological reasoning.[168] Deontic analysis engages directly with the principled limits of the system's licence to punish, in light of duties owed to the individual.

More recent jurisprudence has engaged much more carefully with the deontic dimensions (e.g. the limits of personal culpability).[169] We can only speculate as to *why* ICL has shifted in this way. Part of the reason could be that practitioners have heeded the liberal critique, including the works of scholars such as Kai Ambos, Mirjan Damaška, George Fletcher, Sasha Greenawalt, Neha Jain, Guénaël Mettraux, Jens Ohlin, Elies van Sliedregt, and James Stewart, among many others. Other possible factors include the changing composition of the field (greater emphasis on criminal law experience), as well as the ongoing maturation and systemic conceptualization of the field of ICL. These developments are welcome and consistent with my stated hope that these distortions can be detected and reduced with critical awareness and more attention to reasoning.[170]

It is entirely understandable that some judges and scholars, after sustained academic criticism for being too loose and liberal, might move to the opposite extreme by adopting approaches that are extremely demanding and rarefied. This

---

[167] See B Roth, "Coming to Terms with Ruthlessness: Sovereign Equality, Global Pluralism, and the Limits of International Criminal Justice" (2010) 8 Santa Clara J Int'l L 231; see also discussion in §3.2.1.

[168] Source-based reasoning parses legal authorities and sifts precedents, whereas teleological reasoning considers aims and consequences.

[169] See, e.g., *Prosecutor v Lubanga Dyilo*, Decision on Confirmation of Charges, ICC PTC, ICC-01/04-01/06, 29 January 2007 (dissecting co-perpetration and culpability); *Prosecutor v Bemba Gombo*, Judgment Pursuant to Article 74 of the Statute, ICC T.Ch, ICC-01/05-01/08, 21 March 2016 (carefully discussing mental and physical aspects of culpability in command responsibility); *Prosecutor v Perišić*, Judgment, ICTY A.Ch, IT-04-81-A, IT-05-87-A, 28 February 2013; *Prosecutor v Šainović*, Judgment, ICTY A.Ch, IT-05-87-A, 23 January 2016 (debating outer limits of culpability in aiding and abetting). These cases are in contrast to earlier cases that emphasized consequentialist and precedentialist analysis.

[170] See, e.g., §2.1.4 and §2.5. I also noted in Chapter 2, and in Robinson, *supra* note 1, that these tendencies were not immutable characteristics of ICL and that they seemed to be diminishing.

would present the opposite pitfall of *Überdogmatisierung* or "hypergarantismo" – that is, excessively fastidious theorizing and overstating the deontic constraints.[171] There is a danger that judges, aiming to show that they are setting the highest standards, may adopt incorrectly rarefied conceptions of deontic constraints, as well as evidentiary and procedural requirements beyond what transnational practice and underlying principles require.[172] A confluence of such standards, divorced from practice and underlying normative considerations, can create unnecessary or even insurmountable barriers. Such overcorrections would contribute (and may already have contributed) to the collapse of cases that cost millions of euros to investigate and prosecute, dashing the hopes of victims, witnesses, and affected communities, and undermining the aims of the system.

I gave two potential[173] examples in Chapter 1, noting the controversies over reasoning in the acquittals in *Bemba* and in *Gbagbo*.[174] (In Annex 4, I outline some ways in which the *Bemba* Appeal Judgment may include examples of this "pendulum swing.") A less-discussed possible additional example is the *Mbarushima* case at the ICC. In that case, a majority of the Pre-Trial Chamber declined to confirm charges; the reasons included the majority's conclusion that the requirements for personal culpability under the relevant mode of liability were not met. I would suggest that the Chamber had good grounds to conclude that the relevant requirement is that the accused make a "significant" contribution, but Judge Monageng in dissent makes a very convincing case that the majority misapplied that standard, given the evidence.[175] Unfortunately, that question was not addressed on appeal.[176]

These problems help to show the stakes. If we contravene fundamental principles (properly understood), then we treat persons unjustly. However, if we are unnecessarily conservative because of an unsupported and inflated understanding of the

---

[171] See, e.g., E van Sliedregt, "International Criminal Law: Over-Studied and Underachieving?" (2016) 29 LJIL 1; see also *Prosecutor v Lubanga Dyilo*, Judgment Pursuant to Article 74 of the Statute, ICC T. Ch, ICC-01/04-01/06-2842, 14 March 2012, Separate Opinion of Judge Adrian Fulford at paras 10–17; D M Amann, "In *Bemba* and beyond, Crimes Adjudged to Commit Themselves" (13 June 2018) EJIL Talk! (blog).

[172] See, e.g., D Robinson, "The Other Poisoned Chalice: Unprecedented Evidentiary Standards in the *Gbagbo* Case?" (5 November 2019) EJIL Talk! (blog), and §1.1.2.

[173] I say "potential" examples because, to conclude that any of these decisions were indeed problematic examples of this tendency, I would first need to analyze each one more closely. The aim of this book is to develop the methodology for such analyses. I reference these potential examples to show how serious the stakes may be.

[174] See §1.1.2.

[175] *Prosecutor v Callixte Mbarushima*, Decision on Confirmation of Charges, ICC PTC, ICC-01/04-01/10-465-Red, 16 December 2011, esp Dissenting Opinion of Judge Monageng appended thereto at paras 65–112. The dissent argues that the majority applied incorrect standards for the extent of contribution required for liability, as well as the requirement of a group with common purpose.

[176] *Prosecutor v Callixte Mbarushima*, Judgment on the Appeal of the Prosecutor against the Decision of Pre-Trial Chamber I of 16 December 2011 entitled "Decision on the Confirmation of Charges," ICC AC, ICC-01/04-01/10-514, 30 May 2012, at paras 50–69.

principles, then we undermine the beneficial impact of the system without good reason. Thus it is all the more important to delineate, as best we can,[177] the fundamental principles appropriate to the system.

2.6 IMPLICATIONS

My purpose in highlighting these problems is to pave the way for more sophisticated reasoning. Law is an enterprise of reasoning, and thus I believe that we must pay careful attention not only to the legal conclusions reached, but also to the structure of arguments employed. A judgment might employ problematic reasoning and still reach a defensible result. Nonetheless, the reasoning matters, because replication of faulty structure of arguments will eventually produce faulty outcomes. Our reasoning is our "math," and systemic distortions in our math will eventually throw off our calculations in significant ways.

There are many possible reasons why a criminal justice system might adopt a doctrine departing from fundamental principles: preoccupation with law and order, revulsion at particular crimes, hasty analyses, authoritarian systems unmindful of principled constraints, or legitimate differences of understanding about the principles. In this chapter, I have sought to reveal some additional dynamics distinctive to ICL. I have given numerous examples to demonstrate how the interpretive, substantive, structural, and ideological assumptions and reflexes of human rights and humanitarian lawyers have often been absorbed into ICL discourse. I have sought to show, with concrete examples, how the transposition of such assumptions without adequate reflection on the context shift can create subtle distortions in favour of broad provisions that may not comply with fundamental principles. (For readers who are interested, in Annex 1 I address reactions to and questions about my arguments here, with the aim of clarifying some key points.)

The research project that emerges is not only to unearth contradictions and to identify the tendencies that engender them, but also – and most importantly – to develop a more refined account of the fundamental principles appropriate for ICL.

In this chapter, to keep a spotlight on the topic of reasoning, I used an "internal" account, working with the principles as recognized by ICL itself. Thus, where I identify a seeming conflict between a doctrine and a principle, it should not be assumed that I necessarily believe that the formulation of the principle is correct. From a purely internal perspective, contradictions between a doctrine and principle could be resolved by correcting the doctrine or by refining the principle. To decide on the correct resolution, we would need considerable groundwork to help us to

---

[177] As I will argue in Chapter 4, there is no formula to articulate the parameters of fundamental principles with confident precision, and thus I do not argue that judges and jurists need to identify the single "correct" articulation. The method I advocate merely allows us to narrow in on a set of the most defensible articulations and to dismiss the most incongruous and problematic understandings. In my view, this is the best that humans operating a system of justice can be expected to do.

discuss the appropriate formulations of principles. This is what I attempt in the remainder of this book.

In Chapter 3, I will put forward the normative case for compliance with fundamental principles. However, this does not necessarily consign ICL to mimicking the principles exactly as they are known in national law.[178] Although, in this chapter, I have emphasized the need to be critical of ICL's human rights and humanitarian law inheritance, there is also scope to reconsider the criminal law inheritance – namely, the specific articulations of those fundamental principles as found in national law.[179] The special contexts of ICL may pose philosophical questions not previously considered in mainstream criminal theory and hence help us to unearth new insights into the fundamental principles. Thus the project is to discover not only how criminal theory may illuminate ICL, but also how ICL may illuminate criminal theory.

---

[178] Some scholars have suggested steps in such a direction, noting e.g. that the paradigm of individual culpability may be altered in contexts in which atrocities are not a product of individual deviance, but rather of compliance with deviant societal norms. However, even these revised theories do not absolve the need to grapple with principled limits on the punishment of autonomous individuals. See, e.g., M Reisman, "Legal Responses to Genocide and Other Massive Violations of Human Rights" (1996) 59 L & Contemp Probs 75 at 77. Special challenges of organizational behaviour and diffusion of responsibility, the meaning of "fair warning" in a decentralized criminalization system, or the need to tap into non-Western cultural traditions could conceivably be elements of a revamped and tailored theoretical justification. See, e.g., D Luban, A Strudler & D Wasserman, "Moral Responsibility in the Age of Bureaucracy" (1992) 90 Michigan L Rev 2348, on diffusion of responsibility in organizational structures; M Drumbl, "Toward a Criminology of International Crime" (2003) 19 Ohio St J on Disp Resol 263; M Drumbl, *Atrocity, Punishment and International Law* (Cambridge University Press, 2007); M Damaška, *supra* note 11, at 457 and 475–58; Osiel, *supra* note 13; G Fletcher, "Collective Guilt and Collective Punishment" (2004) 5 Theor Inq L 163, esp at 168–69 and 173–74; L Fletcher, "From Indifference to Engagement: Bystanders and International Criminal Justice" (2005) 26 Michigan J Int'l L 1013.

[179] See Chapters 3–6.

PART II

Proposed Solution: A Humanist, Coherentist, Deontic Account

The next three chapters develop a framework or method for exploring deontic[1] constraints in the special contexts raised by ICL. To this end, I will overcome a series of methodological hurdles, each of which presents us with an opportunity for discovery.

My prescriptive argument in Chapter 2 was quite modest: that ICL should avoid *self-contradiction* – that is, promising compliance with certain principles and then contravening them.[2] I now advance a stronger, substantive claim: that such contradictions should be resolved in favour of fundamental principles. However, this substantive position must be accompanied by a careful methodology to identify and formulate the fundamental principles properly applicable in ICL.

In Chapter 3, I advance two main points. First, I respond to arguments questioning whether fundamental principles are even appropriate in the extraordinary contexts encountered by ICL. I argue that, even in extreme contexts of collective action and social pressure, we must still consider deontic constraints such as culpability. Second, I argue that this does not necessarily mean replicating formulations of principles as known in national systems. We can re-examine what the underlying commitment to the individual entails in the given context.

In Chapter 4, I consider how we might go about such a discussion of principles. I argue for a "coherentist" method, which means that we do not have to trace our views down to bedrock, for example by identifying the "correct" comprehensive moral theory. Instead, we work with all available clues, including patterns of practice and normative arguments, to build the most coherent and convincing picture that we can. This process accepts that we will never have "certainty" about principles of

---

[1] By "deontic" I mean constraints rooted in respect for the individual – constraints such as the legality principle and the culpability principle, which allow the system to be described as a system of "justice." I leave aside until Chapter 4 the question of the precise underpinnings of those principles. In that chapter, I will argue that they might be rooted in classical deontological theories or various other normative theories. The common kernel is simply that there are some constraints on how we treat individuals even in pursuit of good consequentialist aims.

[2] I worked with principles as recognized by ICL itself, because I wanted to maintain focus on reasoning and not get bogged down in substantive normative evaluation of principles.

justice. It is a human conversation about human ideas. Nonetheless, the conversation is valuable: We must try to ensure that our institutions and practices are justified, and the justice conversation is our best and only method to advance that goal.

Chapter 5 gives some examples of new criminal law problems that arise given the special challenges of ICL. Thus the solution is not simply a matter of applying general criminal law theory to ICL problems: ICL problems can raise new questions for criminal law theory, and hence exploring these problems might provide new insights for both ICL and mainstream criminal law theory.

3

The Humanity of Criminal Justice

OVERVIEW

In this chapter, I address important preliminary challenges to any discussion of deontic principles in ICL. Addressing those challenges produces a more nuanced framework.

Thoughtful scholars have raised concerns that familiar liberal principles may be entirely out of place in ICL. Are the principles simply being transplanted out of a reflexive legalistic habit? Are principles rooted in individual agency unsuited to mass criminality? Do such principles entail unsound individualistic ideologies? Are such principles simply Western constructs being imposed in other settings?

In this chapter, I will argue as follows.:

(1) For any system that chooses to punish individuals, deontic principles do matter, and thus they should constrain ICL.
(2) This does not necessarily mean replicating formulations of fundamental principles familiar from national systems; instead, we can return to our underlying deontic commitments and see what they entail in these new contexts.
(3) We can learn from common critiques of liberal accounts, to build a sensitive, humanistic account of deontic principles.

In response to various criticisms of criminal justice and liberal principles, I emphasize the "humanity" of criminal justice. Criminal justice and its restraining principles are sometimes portrayed as abstract, metaphysical, retributive, vengeful, Western, or ideologically unmoored from experience. But criminal law serves prosocial aims. Its constraints are rooted in compassion, empathy, and regard for humanity. An intelligent liberal account considers all facets of human experience, including social context, social roles, and collective endeavours. Principles reflect broadly shared human concerns and can be refined through human conversation.

3.1 CONTEXT AND ARGUMENT

3.1.1 Context: The Critique of the Liberal Critique

In this chapter, I propose a framework that builds on previous approaches. The simplest way to introduce this framework is to outline, in general terms, three significant ways of approaching ICL doctrines so far. (I am not saying that any particular scholars are committed to any one of these ways of thinking, nor am I saying that these approaches emerged in perfect chronological sequence. I am highlighting them as discernible movements in a dialectic.[3] It is helpful to notice and label these ways of thinking in order to clarify the options and to illuminate a way forward.)

The first approach was the *doctrinal* approach. The doctrinal approach primarily focuses on interpreting *sources* (authorities, precedents)[4] and also often includes *teleological* reasoning. I am using the word "doctrinal" as it used in the common law system, to refer to relatively standard legal reasoning. (Unfortunately, the word has a near-opposite meaning in other legal traditions, but there is a dearth of alternative words to describe this basic legal reasoning.[5]) The doctrinal approach was particularly dominant during the first decade of the renaissance of ICL (see Chapter 2). It is not a criticism when I say that reasoning in this phase often had a necessarily rushed character. Jurists were rightly preoccupied with the urgent task of constructing a new legal system; there was not time for prolonged rumination upon every subtle question.

The second movement was the *liberal critique* of ICL. As I explained in Chapter 2,[6] the liberal critique emphasizes that doctrinal (source-based and teleological) reasoning is not sufficient; one must also consider deontic constraints such

---

[3]   I am indebted to Jens Ohlin's extremely helpful restatement of my survey of the debate so far, in an online symposium: J D Ohlin, "MJIL Symposium: A Response to Darryl Robinson by Jens Ohlin" (15 November 2012) Opinio Juris (blog).

[4]   "Source-based" analysis applies basic tools of interpretation to determine what the enactments, precedents, and authorities allow. For succinctness, I will at times call this "precedential" or "formalist" analysis.

[5]   The common law usage therefore seems to be nearly the opposite of the German usage, where "doctrine" refers to deep systematization and working with underlying unifying concepts. The doctrinal approach, as I use the term here, works in a relatively piecemeal way, determining what the legal sources permit, without deep conceptualization or deontic considerations. To reduce confusion with the opposite German usage, I will refer to "source-based," "black letter," "formalist," or "precedential" analysis where those terms apply.

[6]   Among the first pioneers in this respect were George Fletcher, Jens Ohlin, Allison Danner, Jenny Martinez, Kai Ambos, and Mirjan Damaška. As the corpus of ICL took shape, scholars began to point out that, although contemporary ICL proclaims its exemplary compliance with fundamental liberal principles, it often seems to contravene these principles – at times, rather dramatically. Concerns initially tended to focus on the doctrine of "joint criminal enterprise," but critical attention quickly spread to other doctrines, such as the Tribunals' approach to command responsibility and duress. See, e.g., G P Fletcher & J D Ohlin, "Reclaiming Fundamental Principles of Criminal Law in the Darfur Case" (2005) 3 JICJ 539; A M Danner & J S Martinez, "Guilty Associations: Joint Criminal Enterprise, Command Responsibility, and the Development of International Criminal Law" (2005) 93 Calif

as the limits of personal culpability. This genre of scholarship revitalized the debate, bringing questions of criminal law theory, normative theory, coherence, and fairness in the discussions, and critiquing many doctrines of ICL.[7] The liberal critique has also entered mainstream judicial thinking, which today is much more mindful of deontic constraints and the rights of the accused (see §2.5).

The third movement is the *critique of the liberal critique*. Scholars such as Mark Drumbl, Mark Osiel, and others have pointed out that the assumptions and principles of ordinary criminal law may not even be applicable or appropriate in the context of international crimes and thus should not be extended automatically to the international plane.[8] For example, ICL crimes involve extraordinary collective dimensions and extensive communal engagement in which participation is not so self-evidently "deviant," frustrating classic assumptions about "moral choice" and individual agency.[9] Western principles should not be imposed on others – particularly principles that assume the individual as the central unit of action and attempt to shoehorn collective activities into individualist paradigms.[10] Thus it is argued that objections to departures from orthodox principles are "exaggeratedly heated," that departures from principles of individual responsibility may be necessary to deal with collective violence, and that it is possible that the principle of culpability may need to be modified or abandoned.[11]

L Rev 75; K Ambos, "Remarks on the General Part of International Criminal Law" (2006) 4 JICJ 660; M Damaška, "The Shadow Side of Command Responsibility" (2001) 49 Am J Comp L 455.

[7] For surveys of the field, see C Kreß, *Towards a Truly Universal Invisible College of International Criminal Lawyers* (Torkel Opsahl Academic, 2014); S Vasiliev, "On Trajectories and Destinations of International Criminal Law Scholarship" (2015) 28 LJIL 701; S Nouwen, "International Criminal Law: Theory All over the Place," in A Orford & F Hoffman, eds, *Oxford Handbook of the Theory of International Law* (Oxford University Press, 2016).

[8] M Drumbl, *Atrocity, Punishment, and International Law* (Cambridge University Press, 2007) at 8, 24, 38, 123–24; M Drumbl, "Collective Violence and Individual Punishment: The Criminality of Mass Atrocity" (2005) 99 Nw U L Rev 539 at 545; M Osiel, "The Banality of Good: Aligning Incentives against Mass Atrocity" (2005) 105 Columbia L Rev 1751 at 1753; M Osiel, *Making Sense of Mass Atrocity* (Cambridge University Press, 2009) at 8.

[9] Drumbl, *Atrocity, supra* note 6, at 24–32; Osiel, "Banality," *supra* note 6, at 1752–55; Osiel, *Making Sense, supra* note 6, at x–xi; L Fletcher & H Weinstein, "Violence and Social Repair: Rethinking the Contribution of Justice to Reconciliation" (2002) 24 HRQ 573 at 604–05; L Fletcher, "From Indifference to Engagement: Bystanders and International Criminal Justice" (2005) 26 Michigan J Int'l L 1013 at 1076; W M Reisman, "Legal Responses to Genocide and Other Massive Violations of Human Rights" (1996) 4 L & Contemp Probs 75 at 77; M J Aukerman, "Extraordinary Evil, Extraordinary Crime: A Framework for Understanding Transitional Justice" (2002) 15 Harvard HRJ 39 at 41 and 59; A Sepinwall, "Citizen Responsibility and the Reactive Attitudes: Blaming Americans for War Crimes in Iraq," in T Isaacs & R Vernon, eds, *Accountability for Collective Wrongdoing* (Cambridge University Press, 2011) at 233.

[10] Osiel, *Making Sense, supra* note 6, at 8 (extending Western doctrines); Aukerman, *supra* note 7, at 41 (Western); M Drumbl, "Collective Responsibility and Postconflict Justice," in Isaacs & Vernon, *supra* note 7, at 29 (central unit of action); Drumbl, "Collective Violence," *supra* note 6, at 542 (central unit); Drumbl, *Atrocity, supra* note 6, at 39 (shoehorn collective agency into individual guilt); Sepinwall, *supra* note 7, at 233 (Western individualist paradigm versus collective nature).

[11] Drumbl, *Atrocity, supra* note 6, at 38–39 (criticisms exaggeratedly heated; departures may be necessary); Osiel, "Banality," *supra* note 6, at 1765 and 1768.

3.1.2 My Argument: The Humanity of Criminal Justice

My objective in this chapter is to show the possibility of a fourth step in this dialectic. Although the liberal critique and the critique of the liberal critique appear to be in opposition, my aim is to show that a new account can draw from the best features and overcome the most plausible objections to each of the two prior approaches. To do so, we have to introduce some important clarifications and refinements to the prior approaches.

The result is a more careful liberal account: a humanistic, open-minded (or reconstructive), cosmopolitan, and coherentist account.[12] I embrace the critique that we cannot simply project familiar national principles onto ICL; rather, we must inspect and rearticulate those principles to take into account the special contexts encountered by ICL, which include massively collective action, state criminality and non-legislative forms of law creation. However – and this is the crucial caveat – the special contexts do not mean that we are free to discard our underlying deontic commitment to our fellow human beings. Thus my account remains a liberal account, in that it still respects principled constraints rooted in respect for the moral agency of individuals. I suggest that we have a responsibility and an opportunity to explore how our deontic commitment may manifest differently in different circumstances.

Engaging with the main criticisms of liberal accounts of criminal justice has led me to a set of intertwined ideas, all of which emphasize the "humanity" of justice. Several diverse concerns can be answered by highlighting that justice is "human," in these diverse senses.

(1) **Human aims (not abstract retribution)** Many criticisms question the aim or purpose of criminal law, stating that it is about backward-looking vengeance or abstract retribution (balancing the scales of cosmic justice), or that it is a symptom of a "liberal legal disorder" that mindlessly reproduces a familiar system out of habit. However, while criminal law looks back at past events, the purpose of the system is forward-looking, meliorative, and prosocial: it seeks to advance valuable human aims. While criminal law is punitive, its aims are beneficent. Evidence suggests that systems of accountability are an adaptive, prosocial trait widely shared in human societies and that systems of accountability enable higher levels of social trust, cooperation, and stability.[13]

---

[12]　I explain each of these terms in this chapter and the next.
[13]　See, e.g., P S Churchland, *Braintrust: What Neuroscience Tells Us about Morality* (Princeton University Press, 2011); P H Robinson, *Intuitions of Justice and the Utility of Desert* (Oxford University Press, 2013); M D Hauser, *Moral Minds* (Harper Collins, 2006); A Walsh, "Evolutionary Psychology and the Origins of Justice" (2000) 17 Justice Q 841; E Fruehwald, "A Biological Basis of Rights" (2009) 19 S Cal Interdisc LJ 195; J Tooby & L Cosmides, "The Psychological Foundations of Culture," in J H Barkow, L Cosmides & J Tooby, eds, *The Adapted Mind: Evolutionary Psychology and the Generation of Culture* (Oxford University Press, 1992); D Kochenov, "The Just World," in D Kochenov, G de Búrca & A Williams, *Europe's Justice Deficit?* (Hart, 2015); A Calnan, "Beyond Jurisprudence" (2017) 27 S Cal Interdisc LJ 1.

(2) **Human constraints (not artifacts of positive law)** A criticism of fundamental principles is that they are artifacts of national positive law, which are being unreflectingly transplanted into ICL. I will argue, however, that the constraints of criminal law are recognized for humanistic reasons: they are rooted in empathy and respect for the moral personhood of affected individuals.

(3) **Human experience (not individualistic ideology)** A criticism of liberal principles is that they assume an unrealistic worldview that treats humans as isolated individuals abstracted from their social environment. However, a sound account of principles is sensible and grounded, and it can consider the full richness of human experience, including its social and collective dimensions.

(4) **Human concerns (not Western)** Another common criticism is that familiar liberal principles reflect Western preoccupations. A brief survey of different histories of legal traditions, as well as cross-cultural empirical surveys, gives strong reason to doubt those claims. Indeed, those criticisms themselves may have Eurocentric premises. The best understandings of principles will reflect widely shared human concerns articulated in a cosmopolitan conversation.

(5) **Human constructs (not metaphysical)** Another criticism rightly questions any claims that deontic principles are timeless and abstract laws deduced from *a priori* metaphysical premises. However, I argue instead for a "coherentist" conception (see Chapter 4), which acknowledges that principles of justice are human constructs that can be explored through human debates.

(6) **Human activity (not Westphalian states)** It is sometimes thought that criminal law can be carried out only by states, which makes ICL a problematic anomaly. I argue, however, that criminal law is an activity carried about by human beings. A more general theory can contemplate criminal law carried out not only by states, but also by other structures of human governance. Doing so may expose assumptions in mainstream criminal law theory and raise new questions.

In these brief summaries, I am deliberately using the term "humanity" in different senses; each usage has to be understood within the context of the debate to which it responds. In a nutshell, in contrast to portrayals of criminal law and deontic principles as abstract and inhumane, I respond that criminal law, properly done, has pro-social aims. Its constraining principles should be rooted in respect and empathy, grounded in experience, and built on widely shared values. I am not using the word "humanity" in a speciesist sense,[14] but as a helpful placeholder to convey these ideas.

---

[14] As I explain in Chapter 5, deontic constraints respect some quality of individuals, but it has not generally been necessary to specify what quality or qualities give rise to personal accountability or to deontic duties (e.g. agency, autonomy, capacity for reason-directed behaviour, innate Buddha-nature). It has not been necessary to specify further because we agree that humans have these qualities. However, if a problem were to arise that required further disambiguation – e.g. encountering other beings that could plausibly be subjects of criminal law – then we would need to unpack the relevant qualities with more precision. We would have to clarify these ideas that I am currently clumping in the term "humanity." See, e.g., T M Scanlon, *What We Owe to Each Other* (Harvard University Press, 1998) at 179.

The first of these topics – the purpose and justification of criminal law – is an enormous topic in its own right. Thus, as explained in Chapter 1, I set it aside for a future work, so that I can focus here on the topic of this book: the deontic constraints of ICL.[15] This chapter will elaborate on the second, third, and fourth ideas (deontic constraints respect humanity, are informed by human experience, and reflect widely shared human concerns). Chapter 5 will explain the fifth idea (human constructs, not metaphysical essences). Chapter 6 will touch on the sixth (criminal law is a human activity and not necessarily only a "state" activity).

3.1.3 Outline and Terminology

In §3.2, I look at why constraints matter, rooting them in respect for humanity. We can, however, engage in a deontic analysis to see what the underlying commitment to individuals requires in new and unusual contexts. In §3.3, I argue that a thoughtful account can absorb common criticisms of liberal accounts. I show how a humanistic account can be subtle, taking into account collectivity, community, and culture.

In this chapter and in this book, I use the following terms in the following ways.

- A *doctrine* is a rule, posited in the legal system, stating, for example, the elements of crimes against humanity or the requirements of command responsibility.
- A *fundamental principle* presumably includes (subject to further work in Chapter 4) principles of culpability, legality, and possibly fair labelling.
- A *formulation of a fundamental principle* is a certain understanding of the concrete features of a fundamental principle, for example the proposition that the principle of legality requires prior published legislation.
- Finally, the *underlying deontic commitment* refers to the basic commitment from which these fundamental principles are derived. I leave aside the question of the philosophical underpinnings of that commitment until Chapter 4, where we will see that there are different possible understandings and underpinnings. For now, we can simply say that it is the commitment to treat persons as moral agents, possessed of dignity and capable of directing their behavior by reason.

I am using the term *liberal* in a specific and minimalist sense. The term "liberal" is prone to be misunderstood, because it is used by different people in different contexts to mean very different things.[16] Here, I am using the term as it is often used in criminal law theory: to convey that the system is constrained by respect for the autonomy, dignity, or agency of the individual. A liberal system, in this narrow sense, is one that entails *some* principled (non-consequentialist) constraints on the

---

[15] See §1.3.1.
[16] As has been noted previously, including by G Fletcher, *The Grammar of Criminal Law: American, Comparative and International*, Vol 1 (Oxford University Press, 2007) at 167.

pursuit of societal protection. As I will explain in Chapter 4, the minimalist sense in which I am using the term here is compatible with more than one political philosophy, moral philosophy, economic outlook, or vision of society or of individuals.[17]

3.2 WHY ENGAGE WITH CONSTRAINTS: A HUMAN COMMITMENT

In this part, I address why constraints matter. First, in response to doctrinal arguments that treat principles as black letter rules that might be sidestepped, I lay out the deeper normative basis for compliance. Second, I address arguments that persons accused of serious atrocities have "forfeited" their rights. Third, I deal with the best of the arguments, which is that familiar principles are inapposite in the special contexts of ICL. The result is an account that combines the strengths of previous accounts and which can raise new questions for ICL and criminal law theory.

3.2.1 The Doctrinal Challenge to Principles and the Normative Response

In ICL literature and jurisprudence, fundamental principles such as the principles of legality and culpability have often been treated as mere doctrinal rules – that is, as "artifacts of legal positivism" and "inconvenient obstacles to be circumvented."[18] Indeed, if one sees the principles as simply black letter rules in national systems, then the obvious initial positivist question is whether those rules *legally* apply in ICL at all.[19] For example, in the post-World War II era, it was common to sidestep the principle of legality with the positivistic argument that legal sources did not formally recognize the principle in ICL.[20] Furthermore, even where the principles were

---

[17]   As long as one agrees to constraints in criminal law to preclude treatment that is not fair to the individual, that is a "liberal" account in the minimalist sense here. Thus one could agree to these constraints even if one were not a "liberal" in other senses of the word. For example, as shown in Chapter 4, one could be a "communitarian" and still recognize some constraints on how individual members of the community can be treated. Of course, that leaves enormous room to debate what the constraints are; that is discussed in Chapter 4.

[18]   B Roth, "Coming to Terms with Ruthlessness: Sovereign Equality, Global Pluralism, and the Limits of International Criminal Justice" (2010) 8 Santa Clara J Int'l L 231 at 252 and 287, discussing this tendency. This tendency was more commonplace in earlier days of ICL, but with the emergence of the liberal critique, ICL jurisprudence has come to show more thoughtful, deontic engagement with fundamental principles.

[19]   In §3.2, I examine a more subtle *normative* question of whether adjustments to familiar formulations can be deontically justified.

[20]   A Cassese, *International Criminal Law*, 2nd ed (Oxford University Press, 2008) at 38–41; H Kelsen, "Will the Judgement in the Nuremberg Trial Constitute a Precedent in International Law?" (1947) 1 Int'l LQ 153 at 164; *United States of America et al v Hermann Göring et al*, 1 Trial of the Major War Criminals before the International Military Tribunal, 14 November 1945–1 October 1946 (Nuremberg: International Military Tribunal, 1947) 171 at 219; see also argument of Judge Röling in *United States of America et al v Araki et al*, in N Boister & R Cryer, eds, *Documents on the Tokyo International Military Tribunal; Charter, Indictment and Judgments* (Oxford University Press, 2008) at 700.

recognized as legally applicable, doctrinal arguments were often made to minimize or sidestep them.[21] If one sees the principles as mere stipulations of positive law and one observes them hindering successful prosecutions, it is entirely understandable that one would employ the same clever doctrinal techniques that are used to avoid or minimize any problematic rule.

Accordingly, it is worth highlighting some of the reasons why ICL should comply with fundamental principles. There are at least four reasons; I will note first the two less important ones and then proceed to the two more important ones. The first reason is to maintain the *internal coherence* of ICL: ICL should conform to fundamental principles because it proclaims that it does so. This reason is less important, because coherence could be achieved by disavowing the principles; nonetheless, for as long as the principles are proclaimed, violations should be unearthed and resolved.[22]

A second reason – possibly a counter-intuitive reason – is *consequentialist*. As Paul Robinson and John Darley have sought to demonstrate, "desert" may have "utility"[23]: Conforming to broadly shared notions of justice strengthens law's influence on norm-internalization (which may be more important to prevention than rational calculations of deterrence), and it may also strengthen the legal system's legitimacy and support (and hence its effectiveness).[24] These consequentialist considerations are not a central basis for a liberal account, because a liberal account would respect principled constraints even if it were to entail disutility,[25] but the consequentialist support is worth noting.

The third and most important reason to comply with principles is *deontic* – that is, we accept that there is something about people (personhood, dignity, moral agency) that warrants respect and recognition; as a result, we can punish persons only in accordance with what they *deserve*. A system that neglects the constraint of desert is arguably not a system of "justice"[26] and, in some sense, might not even be a system of "criminal law," but rather an exercise of "police" power.[27] Thus, even if the aim of

---

[21]   Some illustrations are discussed in Chapter 6 (command responsibility).

[22]   Of course, in a dynamic legal system, some internal contradictions may be inevitable as doctrines and principles evolve. Nonetheless, coherence is an aspiration of the system.

[23]   P H Robinson & J M Darley, "The Utility of Desert" (1997) 91 Nw U L Rev 453, cite research showing that (i) the impact of criminal law depends more on the internalization of norms by individuals and social groups than on the rational calculations of deterrent threats (*ibid* at 468–71), and (ii) criminal law's influence on norm-internalization depends on its moral credibility and conformity to broadly shared conceptions of justice (*ibid* at 471–88).

[24]   It can also be argued that a criminal law system will produce the desired benefits only if it adopts a requirement of compliance with constraints matching those of a deontic account. See J Rawls, "Two Concepts of Rules" (1955) 64 Philosophical Review 3.

[25]   Otherwise it would be a utilitarian account, upholding certain principles only as long as they had long-term consequentialist value.

[26]   H L A Hart, *Punishment and Responsibility*, 2nd ed (Oxford University Press, 2008) at 22; D N Husak, *The Philosophy of Criminal Law* (Oxford University Press, 1987) at 30.

[27]   Markus Dubber contrasts "criminal law" with the exercise of "police." The former involves top-down "management of the household" by a *pater familias* figure. Criminal law applies in a political community of free and equal persons, and thus the governor and the governed stand in

criminal law is to protect society from individuals, the pursuit of that goal is qualified by principled restraints to protect individuals from society.[28]

The fourth reason is the deeper *conceptual* coherence of the system.[29] ICL is a project aimed at upholding human dignity and autonomy. If ICL, in its eagerness to protect human dignity and autonomy, abandons principles that are themselves based on respect for human dignity and autonomy, then the system may contradict its own values.[30] It is true that fundamental principles may, at times, seem to inhibit the pursuit of maximal victim protection. However, the alternative – to create a punitive system for the "administrative elimination of wrongdoers"[31] in the name of advancing human rights – seems philosophically incoherent.[32]

To sum up, if ICL wishes to instill the value that human beings must be treated as moral agents possessed of dignity, it must in turn treat persons as moral agents possessed of dignity.[33] To treat persons as objects in order to send a message that persons may not be used as objects is to embark on a project riven with self-contradiction.

I wish to emphasize a point that may seem counter-intuitive: compassion, empathy, and humanity are important in criminal justice. This seems counter-intuitive, because criminal law is obviously punitive. Moreover, criminal law theory can often be very cerebral and analytical. Nonetheless, I think that the kernel of justice is empathy. As Markus Dubber notes, the "sense of justice" requires imaginative role-taking, or an empathetic thought experiment, to identify with the adjudged person at least as a fellow moral person.[34] As I reflect on instances in national and

a relationship of equality. It requires not only prudential considerations by the punisher (i.e. effectiveness), but also consistency with a moral ideal of the punished. It is a power to do justice rather than only a power to regulate. M D Dubber, "A Political Theory of Criminal Law: Autonomy and the Legitimacy of State Punishment" (15 March 2004), online: http://papers.ssrn.com/sol3/papers .cfm?abstract_id=529522, esp at 6–7, 13, 19. See also M D Dubber, "Common Civility: The Culture of Alegality in International Criminal Law" (2011) 24 LJIL 923.

[28] Hart, *supra* note 24, at 81; Husak, *supra* note 24, at 51.

[29] Here, I am talking not simply about the simple formal coherence mentioned in the first reason (complying because the principles are declared); rather, I am talking about a deeper coherence with the values of the system. In Chapter 4, I will expand upon deontic constraints and coherence: I will argue that coherentism in its broadest sense is the only guide we have to debating and articulating the deontic constraints.

[30] Similarly, Damaška, *supra* note 4, at 456 asks whether it is appropriate for ICL, with its humanitarian orientation, to disregard culpability principles that are rooted in humanitarian concerns.

[31] Dissenting opinion of Justice Robertson in *Prosecutor v Norman*, Decision on Preliminary Motion Based on Lack of Jurisdiction, SCSL A.Ch, SCSL-2004-14-AR72(E), 31 May 2004, at para 14.

[32] To give one example, see L L Fuller, *The Morality of Law*, 2nd ed (Yale University Press, 1969) at 162, arguing that a concept of persons as responsible agents is inherent in the enterprise of law, so that every "departure from the principles of law's inner morality is an affront to man's dignity as a responsible agent." See also R A Duff, *Answering for Crime: Responsibility and Liability in the Criminal Law* (Hart, 2007) at 45–46.

[33] See Fuller, *supra* note 30; see also K Rundle, *Forms Liberate: Reclaiming the Jurisprudence of Lon L Fuller* (Oxford University Press, 2012).

[34] M D Dubber, *The Sense of Justice: Empathy in Law and Punishment* (Universal Law, 2006), esp at 7–8, 24, 52, 71, 75 and 83.

international criminal law in which legal reasoning has lost sight of deontic constraints, it usually is accompanied by a fixation on societal protection and a failure to truly consider the situation of the accused or potential accused, often because the accused is looked upon as a criminal or as the "other." Deontic reasoning requires us to at least briefly inhabit the situation of Dražen Erdemović, father of a young child, given a "choice" either to participate in a firing squad or to die alongside the victims.[35] Or the situation of a soldier given an order to relocate a village population away from the front, who is unsure of the legality of the order.[36] Or the situation of a military commander taking over a unit with defective procedures or severed lines of communication. Of course, we also cerebrally apply our analytical constructs, and we also have compassion for society at large and for persons affected by crimes. But this modicum of empathy – our humanity and our respect for the humanity of others – is part of the deontic reasoning process and part of our reasoning about justice.

3.2.2 The Humanity of the "Enemy of Humanity"

A potentially tempting argument to sidestep principles is that complicity in major atrocities leads the accused to *forfeit* some of the protection of fundamental principles. This sentiment arguably underlies some older legal practices. For example, it may underlie the historic claim that legal rules may be relaxed in relation to atrocious crimes (*in delictis atrocissimis jura transgredi liceat*).[37] It may underlie historic conceptions of an "outlaw," which stipulated that persons could flout the law to such an extent that they were outside the law and no longer protected by it.[38] It also might draw support from international legal doctrines that describe the transgressor as *hostis humanis generis* – the enemy of humanity.[39] That label – which, in my view, arose only as an explanation of universal jurisdiction – could instead be used to more dramatic effect, to imply that the enemy of humanity is in some way opposed to and outside of the human family.[40] The argument would be that, by acting inhumanely to others, the accused loses some of the protections of humanity.

---

[35] See §5.2.2.

[36] See §5.2.3.

[37] Some problems with the argument *in delictis atrocissimis jura transgredi liceat* are discussed by Damaška, *supra* note 4, at 482 and M Bohlander, "Commentary," in A Klip & G Sluiter, eds, *The International Criminal Tribunal for the former Yugoslavia 2000–2001* (Intersentia, 2003) at 909.

[38] For discussion of *hostis humani generis*, outlaw and outsider, and the "trend toward the moralizing clarity of good and evil," see G Simpson, *Law, War and Crime: War Crimes Trials and the Reinvention of International Law* (Polity, 2007) at 159–77. See also Duff, *supra* note 30, at 212–13; L May, "Collective Punishment and Mass Confinement," in Isaacs & Vernon, *supra* note 7, at 179.

[39] See Simpson, *supra* note 36; Duff, *supra* note 30; May, *supra* note 36.

[40] C Schmitt, *The Concept of the Political* (Duncker & Humblot, 1932; trans and reprinted University of Chicago Press, 2006) at 54, albeit writing about war, raises a pertinent concern: "The concept of humanity is an especially useful ideological instrument" because "denying the enemy the quality of being human and declaring him to be an outlaw of humanity" allows the most extreme inhumanity.

The "forfeiture" argument may have initial appeal, because it at least refers to the individual's own actions and choices. Nonetheless, it should be rejected for at least two reasons. The first is that the argument is circular. The argument invokes the person's responsibility for core crimes to allow harsher principles, and then uses those harsher principles to allow a finding of responsibility. Such an argument is either unnecessary (if the person already was responsible under normal principles) or else it is invalid (*petitio principii*, boot-strapping).

Second, the argument would contradict values that are probably central to the enterprise of criminal law and ICL. ICL aims to affirm and protect dignity of persons even in circumstances of great social pressures. Critics of criminal law (and ICL) sometimes suggest that criminal law (and ICL) seeks to portray violators as the "other," dehumanizing them.[41] That claim may be partially true of criminal law *done badly* – that is, criminal law in which privileged authorities punish others, possibly from very different and disempowered backgrounds, without adequately pondering the accused person's circumstances and available choices.[42] The forms of criminal law can indeed be misemployed as a tool of repression and stigmatization.

But criminal law as a system of *justice* requires a recognition of accused persons as persons, including an empathetic assessment of their circumstances and choices. As Markus Dubber notes, it may be tempting to deny our sense of justice to those who have denied justice to others, but justice still requires some identification with the person judged: we must see them as a fellow moral person.[43] Criminal law is unlike other responses, such as war, which treats persons as adversaries. Criminal law recognizes that we are, in some sense, part of the same community or polity, such that we can be called to answer for our actions.[44] Moreover, criminal law differs from our responses to harms not caused by responsible agents, and it also differs from other legal responses, such as quarantine, which acts for public safety without regard to "fault." Criminal law recognizes and honours the accused as *persons* – as agents responsible and answerable for their actions.[45] Criminal law is predicated precisely on that personhood and responsibility; its task is assessing the extent of accused persons' criminal responsibility based on their actions. Criminal law is not employed against sharks, or bears, or rocks, or machines; it is premised on the acknowledgement of the accused as a responsible human agent who could have chosen otherwise. Thus criminal law does the *opposite* of portraying persons as outside

---

[41] See discussion in Simpson, *supra* note 36, at 159–77.
[42] For an example from my country (Canada) and the treatment of Indigenous accused and the need to better consider systemic background conditions, see *R v Gladue* [1999] 1 SCR 688.
[43] Dubber, *supra* note 32, esp at 2, 6 and 52.
[44] The ICC, for example, applies its criminal law within a community of states parties (and other states accepting jurisdiction of the Court).
[45] See, e.g., G H W Hegel, *Elements of the Philosophy of Right*, A Wood, ed, (Cambridge University Press, 1991) at 125–27 (§§99–100), asserting that criminal law does not comprise only threats and coercion to alter behaviour (as when one punishes a dog or renders a dangerous animal harmless); it also recognizes the accused as a rational being.

the human family. The essence of criminal law is that it recognizes the accused as a fellow member of a community of accountable moral agents.

There are many reasons why ICL must recognize the humanity even of the so-called *hostis humanis generis*.[46] Indeed, the label *hostis humanis generis* is no longer often invoked and should likely be abandoned, given that it focuses on the actor rather than the act. We have to justify our treatment of persons in a way that recognizes their humanity. We cannot skip that justification on the grounds that all persons accused of ICL crimes are, as a class, persons for whom no compassion or respect is warranted.

3.2.3 Toward a More General Theory of Criminal Law

Finally, we arrive at the best of the arguments for skepticism about fundamental principles. The most important challenge is the normative argument that familiar principles are simply not appropriate in the unusual contexts of ICL crimes. Mark Drumbl, Mark Osiel, and others have convincingly argued against the automatic replication of the assumptions, methods, and principles of national doctrinal frameworks in ICL.[47] Drumbl argues, for example, that the paradigm of individual culpability, created for deviant isolated crimes, is not suited to mass crimes, which involve organic group dimensions.[48] Many scholars rightly emphasize that whereas ordinary crime involves "deviance" from societal expectations, ICL faces situations of "inverted morality" in which there is strong social pressure to participate in crimes.[49] In ICL contexts, it is often *abstention* from crime that would be "deviant." Scholars also warn against extending "Western doctrines onto the transnational plane without considering the implications for societies not sharing similar assumptions."[50] For these and other reasons (see also §3.3), it is argued that principles such as culpability may have to be adapted, modified, or even abandoned.[51]

---

[46] Reasons to adhere to principles include: an other-regarding (deontic) reason that the accused, as a person, is inherently entitled to this minimum degree of respect; a systemic reason that the coherence (inner morality) of law entails treating persons as agents; a didactic reason of encouraging respect for dignity; and a self-constituting reason that the law-applying community chooses not to violate certain principles.

[47] Drumbl, *Atrocity, supra* note 6, at 5–9, 23, 38–39; Osiel, *Making Sense, supra* note 6, at 8; Osiel, "Banality," *supra* note 6, at 1753 and 1768; Drumbl, "Collective Violence," *supra* note 6, at 545.

[48] Drumbl, *Atrocity, supra* note 6, at 24; see also Sepinwall, *supra* note 7, at 233 ("the collective nature of crimes of war escapes the bounds of the individualist paradigm of Western criminal law").

[49] Reisman, *supra* note 7, at 77 (inverted morality); Drumbl, *Atrocity, supra* note 6, at 24–35; Fletcher & Weinstein, *supra* note 7, at 605; D Luban, "State Criminality and the Ambition of International Criminal Law," in Isaacs & Vernon, *supra* note 7, at 62–63; Aukerman, *supra* note 7, at 59.

[50] Osiel, *Making Sense, supra* note 6, at 8; see also Aukerman, *supra* note 7, at 59; Sepinwall, *supra* note 7, at 233.

[51] M Drumbl, "Pluralizing International Criminal Justice" (2005) 103 Michigan L Rev 1295, at 1309; Osiel, "Banality," *supra* note 6, at 1765 and 1768; Osiel, *Making Sense, supra* note 6, at 25.

I agree that ICL need not replicate familiar formulations of fundamental principles merely because they appear in national systems.[52] We may and must critically inspect formulations of fundamental principles to assess their relevance and soundness in new contexts. However, I would add a crucial caveat to these observations. Namely, this latitude for reinspection does not entail that we are free to abandon the underlying deontic commitment to treat humans justly as moral agents. Thus we must still grapple with the question of desert. Common formulations of principles may be re-evaluated and rearticulated, but the revised formulations require a plausible deontic justification.

What are some of the ways in which we may have to reconsider familiar national formulations? Mainstream criminal law theory is understandably predicated on the "normal" case: a generally orderly society, in which a single overarching state is the law-giver, law-adjudicator, and law-enforcer. A host of implicit assumptions about that context are unproblematic for the normal case. However, examining desert in the abnormal contexts of ICL can lead us at times into new and largely unexplored territory. These abnormal features compel us to explore a more general account of criminal justice that includes very different conditions.

For example, in the normal context of criminal law theory, it is understandable to assert that the legality principle requires prior written legislation. But ICL has often encountered violent atrocities for which there was no national prohibition, leading to more complex queries into other forms of "fair warning." ICL, a system with no formal "legislature" per se, challenges us to consider the outer parameters of the legality principle more carefully. It can also help us to explore the limits of personal culpability. ICL addresses collective criminal enterprises involving thousands of perpetrators playing very different roles, which invites us to clarify culpability in complex mass endeavours. Causally overdetermined crimes raise questions about causation and blame.[53] Crimes of obedience challenge some normal thinking about deviance, conformity, and wrongdoing. Criminal governments overturn the normal role of state as law-provider. Competing authority structures invite us to reflect on the significance of legal "authorization" of acts. As I will discuss in Chapter 5, the tools of thought that help us in criminal law theory, including community, citizenship, or authority, may at times require further reflection in a more general theory of criminal law.

3.2.4 Combining Liberal and Critical Insights

My aspiration is that this modified account will be convincing both to "liberal" theorists and to those who have critiqued liberal accounts. I expect that most scholars

---

[52] A position foreshadowed in D Robinson, "The Identity Crisis of International Criminal Law" (2008) 21 LJIL 925 at 932, 93, and 962–63; D Robinson "The Two Liberalisms of International Criminal Law," in C Stahn & L van den Herik, eds, *Future Perspectives on International Criminal Justice* (TMC Asser, 2010) at 118 n 9 and 160.

[53] J Stewart, "Overdetermined Atrocities" (2012) 10 JICL 1189.

adopting a "liberal" approach to ICL would agree with the proposed approach, because their preoccupation is presumably not with replicating national formulations of principles, but rather with respecting the underlying deontic commitment.[54] Similarly, it is my hope that those scholars who emphasize the distinctiveness of ICL would agree that any refashioned rules must still comport with a credible account of just treatment of individuals.

Insofar as scholars such as Drumbl and Osiel are simply calling for thoughtful inspection of liberal principles,[55] the position I outline is compatible with theirs. There are only a few passages in Drumbl's work that seem to suggest a fundamentally different approach, in which case my caveat would be significant. For example, Drumbl observes that the Tribunals' "recourse to generous – and at times somewhat vicarious – liability theories become eminently understandable" in light of the collective and organic sources of violence.[56] I agree that the pressure to expand liability doctrines is *understandable* in a psychological sense. My caveat is that if vicarious liability refers to liability without culpability, it does not seem *justifiable* in a system of criminal law. Responsibility short of personal culpability should be addressed through other mechanisms. I suspect, based on other passages of Drumbl's work, that he would likely agree with this caveat.[57]

I believe my proposed approach is also reconcilable with that of Mark Osiel.[58] Osiel seems to express slightly different ideas at different points on the need to comply with the culpability principle. (i) At times, he emphasizes the need to comply with fundamental principles,[59] while arguing that there is scope to adapt those principles.[60] (ii) At times, he contemplates some degree of non-compliance,

---

54   Indeed, leading criminal law theorists, bringing liberal principles to bear on ICL problems, have made some very compatible suggestions. For example, George Fletcher calls for comparative study, a thoughtful inquiry into individual culpability in collective contexts, and systematic philosophical reflection on concepts: Fletcher, *supra* note 14, at vii–xi, 94, 265, 340. Similarly, Kai Ambos advocates an approach that is comparative rather than rooted in any one tradition, gives philosophical consideration to individual responsibility in collective contexts, avoids "flat legal thinking," and adheres to deontological restraints: K Ambos, "Toward a Universal System of Crime: Comments on George Fletcher's *Grammar of Criminal Law*" (2010) 28 Cardozo L Rev 2647. The framework I suggest in this chapter and the next is in line with such calls; I develop in more detail a humanistic, coherentist, and cosmopolitan approach to address such challenges (Chapters 3–5).

55   Drumbl, *supra* note 49, at 1310; Drumbl, "Collective Violence," *supra* note 6, at 567; Osiel, "Banality," *supra* note 6, at 1765.

56   Drumbl, *supra* note 49, at 1309.

57   Drumbl, *Atrocity, supra* note 6, at 40, noting that the availability of other mechanisms may reduce the pressures for an expansive doctrine of joint criminal enterprise.

58   Some readers of Osiel's thoughtful work, *Making Sense of Mass Atrocity*, may find this optimism surprising, because in that work he presents my approach as being in opposition to his own. However, the approach he ascribes to me appears to miss the nuances of the programme that I foreshadowed in early works (see, e.g., Robinson, "Identity Crisis," *supra* note 50, esp at 932 and 962–63). I clarify the points of seeming disagreement in Annex 1.

59   Osiel, *Making Sense, supra* note 6, at 129, 202, and 245 (noting consistency with personal culpability).

60   *Ibid* at xi–xiii and 245 (liberal approach, but can adapt to novel changes). There is some ambiguity here, because Osiel includes utilitarianism within liberalism, which is perfectly sound, but it is quite different from its typical use in criminal law theory. In criminal law theory, the term "liberal" is used

suggesting that ICL should *"ideally"* comply,[61] that it should not *"unduly"* depart,[62] and that incompatibility should be kept to a "morally acceptable minimum."[63] (iii) At other times, he seems more skeptical, lamenting the prevalence of deontological thinking in criminal theory and the "reverential status accorded to the culpability principle in current criminal theory."[64]

The first suggestion is entirely compatible with the approach I advance here. The second suggestion *could* be compatible with my general framework if a "moderate" deontological approach were developed and were to prove convincing.[65] The third position is likely incompatible, unless its skepticism is directed toward historically contingent *formulations* of the culpability principle or to the "punctilious"[66] manner in which it is sometimes applied. I would argue that criminal law should carefully respect the culpability and legality principles once they are properly delineated.[67] Thus I could agree with "modification," but not "abandonment,"[68] of the culpability principle. For reasons outlined in §3.2.1, if we punish without culpability, we are arguably no longer engaged in criminal law, but rather – to use Markus Dubber's term – an "ethical-administrative enterprise."[69]

Osiel raises a valuable point when he argues that public policy decisions cannot be based on "philosophical 'principle' or metaphysics," because "normative questions are ... at stake here, not metaphysical ones."[70] I agree that the questions are normative, but that still leaves the crucial question: are we speaking of a normativity of the *good* or of the *right*? In other words, are we simply maximizing general public welfare (the good),[71] or are we also respecting the autonomy, rights, and agency of others (the right)? Consequentialist considerations can play an important role in criminal law analysis, but we also have to respect deontic constraints of justice.[72] The

---

for a system that embraces deontic constraints, and thus the term is in deliberate contrast to a purely utilitarian approach.

[61] *Ibid* at 21.

[62] *Ibid.*

[63] *Ibid* at 199.

[64] Osiel, "Banality," *supra* note 6, at 1845.

[65] See §3.2.2 and §4.4 for brief discussions of "moderate" deontology. A moderate deontological account would recognize some "thresholds" or limitations by which duties to individuals could be overridden by extreme necessity. None of the issues in this book require me to take a position on the feasibility or desirability of such an account. Such an account, if adopted, could provide an explicit higher-order theory allowing assessment of "morally acceptable" departures.

[66] Osiel, *Making Sense, supra* note 6, at 8.

[67] For examples of exploring the parameters of the culpability principle, see Chapters 7 and 8.

[68] Osiel, "Banality," *supra* note 6, at 1768.

[69] Dubber, "Common Civility," *supra* note 25, at 923.

[70] Osiel, *Making Sense, supra* note 6, at 127–28, 129.

[71] Or any other desideratum that one argues should be maximized, such as human flourishing.

[72] Osiel, "Banality," *supra* note 6, at 1845 describes the "unfortunate equation of liberal morality with its Kantian variant, banishing its consequentialist cousin to undeserved obscurity." As I will explain in Chapter 4, in my view, the deontic constraints do not necessarily have to be Kantian. However, they cannot be simple consequentialism: the point of the constraints is that they restrain untrammelled consequentialist reasoning. Consequentialist considerations have not been "banished" in criminal

question of culpability *is* a normative question – an urgent one – delineating some important limits of a system of justice.

3.3 ABSORBING COMMON CRITICISMS: A HUMANISTIC ACCOUNT

In this part, I discuss some specific objections to liberal approaches. I argue that a sensitive, humanistic liberal account can embrace these critiques and be strengthened by them. The most common objections to liberal accounts include that (i) they are fixated on the individual and cannot cope with the collective dimensions of atrocity, (ii) they conceive of persons as socially unencumbered individuals and fail to account for communitarian values and social meaning, and (iii) they impose Western constructs. On each issue, my answer emphasizes the "humanity" of justice. We can develop a humanistic account that takes in the full richness of human life, including its social dimensions, and seek principles that reflect widely shared human concerns.

3.3.1 Grappling with Collective Action

As was discussed in §3.2, many scholars have emphasized that the collective dimensions of mass atrocity and the attendant social pressures create severe challenges for orthodox ideas about crime and "conformity," "deviance," "agency," and "moral choice."[73] I agree that these collective and societal dimensions call for a fresh inquiry. We may find that familiar conceptions are no longer convincing in these new contexts, and thus we may need to reflect more about what the deeper underlying commitments entail. Nonetheless, I would insist we must still inquire into individual agency, choice, and desert even where crimes have a collective context. The reason is that, once one chooses to employ criminal law and thereby to blame, punish, and stigmatize *individuals* for crimes, one has no choice but to grapple with *individual* agency, choice, and desert.

A common criticism of liberal criminal theory is that it fixates on the individual as the central "unit of action."[74] This is often portrayed as a product of myopia or

---

law doctrine or theory; they rightly remain commonplace. However, non-consequentialist constraints are also needed. For example, as H L A Hart has shown, a consequentialist theory would condone punishing the innocent if it were shown to have optimal consequences; to describe punishing the innocent as "inefficient" fails to capture our repugnance of it: Hart, *supra* note 24, at 77.

[73] See examples cited in §3.2; see also Drumbl, *Atrocity, supra* note 6, at 21 (drained collective nature to fit comforting frameworks) and 23–35 (conformity and deviance); Drumbl, "Collective Responsibility," *supra* note 8, at 24; Osiel, "Banality," *supra* note 6, at 1752–55; Osiel, *Making Sense, supra* note 6, at 2–3 and 187–89; Simpson, *supra* note 36, at 73–74; G Fletcher, "Liberals and Romantics at War: The Problem of Collective Guilt" (2002) 111 Yale LJ 1499 at 1513 and 1541; Sepinwall, *supra* note 7.

[74] Drumbl, "Collective Responsibility," *supra* note 8, at 29 (central unit of action); G Fletcher, *supra* note 71, at 1504 (ultimate unit of action); Drumbl, "Collective Violence," *supra* note 6, at 539 and 542.

a distortion of liberal thought. However, I think this criticism slightly misses the reason for the focus on the individual. I think that the focus on the individual arises because, once criminal law is employed, the individual is the *unit of punishment*. Once we decide to punish and stigmatize individuals for crimes, we are obliged to determine what we are punishing them *for*. This inevitably raises questions of individual agency – to identify the actions and contributions for which that individual is to be held responsible.

The "unit of action" criticism sometimes claims that the choice to employ criminal law (i.e. to punish individuals) arises because of a supposed liberal myopia that sees a world of isolated individual actors. But that is not how ICL (or criminal law) came about. There are numerous other legal and social mechanisms that respond in diverse ways to harms, wrongdoings, and systemic failures. These mechanisms include legal responses such as state responsibility, human rights law, civil liability, administrative law, and constitutional law, as well as an enormous array of social and political mechanisms (commissions of inquiry, reforms, etc.). What ICL does is *add* a mechanism to those other existing mechanisms, which have historically proven inadequate in preventing mass atrocities. Criminal law focuses on individual wrongdoing not because of some myopic defect, but because that is the distinctive lens it is asked to offer to supplement other mechanisms. The hope is that assessment, stigmatization, and punishment of individual wrongdoing might eventually create additional disincentives and help to instantiate new norms of behaviour. But other mechanisms continue to examine other dynamics (such as the collective liability of a state, the civil responsibility of individual or collective actors, the roots of conflict, or preventative reforms), and efforts to improve and strengthen those mechanisms are ongoing. Thus ICL focuses on individual crimes not because of an ideological blind spot, but because that is the facet of the problem it is tasked to address, as part of a holistic social response.

Furthermore, contrary to common claims, a liberal account is not so obsessively individualistic that we have to parcel out each contribution so that each harm is attributed to one, and only one, individual.[75] A liberal account can easily recognize that when individuals pool their efforts together, they can share in various forms of responsibility for their collective doings.[76] On a sophisticated liberal account of mass crimes, we would contend with the challenge that collective action can both *expand* agency, by allowing attainment of aims that could not be attained alone, and also *diminish* agency and moral choice in situations of social pressure, propaganda, or demands of authority.[77]

---

[75] Objecting to such a finely individuated approach, see May, *supra* note 36, at 170; T Erskine, "Kicking Bodies and Damning Souls: The Danger of Harming Innocent Individuals While Punishing Delinquent States," in Isaacs & Vernon, *supra* note 7, at 265.

[76] May, *supra* note 36; Erskine, supra note 73.

[77] K J Fisher, *Moral Accountability and International Criminal Law: Holding the Agents of Atrocity Accountable to the World* (Routledge, 2012) at 68–82; see generally T Isaacs, "Individual Responsibility

We must also avoid the tendency to overstate the myopias of criminal law. The argument is often made that "criminal law sees a world of separate persons, whereas mass atrocity entails collective behavior,"[78] or that "the collective nature of crimes of war escapes the bounds of the individualist paradigm of Western criminal law."[79] It would be a mistake to suggest that criminal law or liberal criminal law theory is so fixated on individuals that it is completely unequipped to cope with collective action. Collective action is not a new phenomenon. Individuals have been working together to commit crime since "crime" was first conceived. Criminal law doctrine and theory draws on centuries of thought and experience concerning individuals pooling their efforts to produce crimes. This has generated tools such as joint commission, commission through an organization, complicity, and the distinction between principals and accessories. In the context of macro-criminality, much interesting thought has been given, for example, to how to address the *Hintermann* – the "man in the background" – who is not present at the crime scene, but who masterminds the crime.[80]

It is true that collective action may figure more routinely and on a larger scale in ICL cases, making it an even more central problem. Because ICL can involve much larger groups of perpetrators, coordinating in diverse ways, we may need to specify more thoughtfully the outer limits of complicity doctrines. But it is premature to say that criminal law is unable to do so.

Problems of diminished agency are not unique to ICL. National legal systems also confront puzzles of diminished agency, such as gang violence, fetal alcohol syndrome, children raised in contexts of organized crime, and communities in states of anomie in which criminality is normalized. The agency issues faced by ICL may be different in some respects, but they are not exclusive to ICL.

3.3.2 Acknowledging Social Context

A related critique is that liberal accounts are so individualistic and abstract that they miss out on the social significance and context of actions.[81] The concern is that

for Collective Wrongs," in J Harrington, M Milde & R Vernon, eds, *Bringing Power to Justice?: The Prospects of the International Criminal Court* (McGill-Queen's University, 2006).

[78] Osiel, *Making Sense*, *supra* note 6, at x eloquently articulates such positions, without necessarily endorsing them. And see *ibid* at 2: "With its focus on discrete deeds and isolated intentions, legal analysis risks missing the collaborative character of genocidal massacre, the vast extent of unintended consequences, and the ways in which 'the whole' conflagration is often quite different from the sum of its parts."

[79] Sepinwall, *supra* note 7, at 233.

[80] See, e.g., Ambos, *supra* note 4, esp at 663–64; J Stewart, "The End of 'Modes of Liability' for International Crimes" (2012) 25 LJIL 165; J D Ohlin, "Second-Order Linking Principles: Combining Vertical and Horizontal Modes of Liability" (2012) 25 LJIL 771; A Nollkaemper & H van der Wilt, eds, *System Criminality in International Law* (Cambridge University Press, 2009).

[81] For a helpful review of communitarian critiques of liberal, individualistic accounts, see N Lacey, *State Punishment: Political Principles and Community Values* (Routledge, 1988) at 143–68; P W Kahn, *Putting Liberalism in Its Place* (Princeton University Press, 2005) at 38–50; L Green, *The Authority of the State* (Clarendon Press, 1988) at 188–206.

liberal theory misconceives of the individual as completely separate from society and must disaggregate complex events into "socially unencumbered individuals independently interacting," producing distorted understandings.[82] Certainly, some political theories, such as classical liberal contractarian theories, might be vulnerable to such a critique. However, we can advance a liberal criminal law theory without necessarily subscribing to an empirically untenable worldview in which we are all atomistic, self-created individuals who enter into a social contract to advance our personal aims. As Alan Brudner notes, "[c]ontrary to a common belief, a liberal theory of penal justice is not necessarily one that conceives the individual as an abstract subject or person uprooted from its social and ethical environment."[83] A humanistic, intelligent liberal theory can acknowledge that we are social and political animals, that we were born in society, and that our identities and our realities are richly socially constructed.

Indeed, in a careful liberal theory, social context and social roles may play a powerful role.[84] The acknowledgement of community and of social roles may bear fruit (as we will see in Chapter 5 in the discussion on duress) by bringing into question some easy conclusions of more atomistic theories.

An intelligent, humanistic approach to criminal law theory also draws from empirical studies – in particular, from criminology – to refine its understandings. After all, normative arguments often entail empirical suppositions (for example about the extent to which capacity for choice is undermined in particular social contexts). Intriguing criminological and sociolegal literature is exploring the ways in which the commission of ICL crimes differs from the commission of crimes in a normal domestic context.[85] For example, atrocities in ICL are most often not committed by psychopaths or sadists, as casual observers might suppose; the crimes seem to largely be committed by "ordinary" people in

---

[82] Osiel, "Banality," *supra* note 6, at 1837, articulating without endorsing the viewpoint.

[83] A Brudner, *Punishment and Freedom: A Liberal Theory of Penal Justice* (Oxford University Press, 2009) at ix. See also Fletcher, *supra* note 14, at 169 (challenging the "oft-repeated charge" that liberals regard individuals as abstracted from history and culture).

[84] See, e.g., Duff, *supra* note 30, at 23–30.

[85] P Roberts & N MacMillan, "For Criminology in International Criminal Justice" (2003) 1 JICJ 315; A Smeulers, "What Transforms Ordinary People into Gross Human Rights Violators?," in S C Carey & S C Poe, eds, *Understanding Human Rights Violations: New Systematic Studies* (Ashgate, 2004); P Zimbardo, *The Lucifer Effect: Understanding How Good People Turn Evil* (Random House, 2007); A Smeulers & R Haveman, eds, *Supranational Criminology: Towards a Criminology of International Crimes* (Intersentia, 2008); D L Rothe & C W Mullins, "Toward a Criminology of International Criminal Law: An Integrated Theory of International Criminal Violations" (2009) 33 IJCACJ 97; D Maier-Katkin, D P Mears & T J Bernard, "Towards a Criminology of Crimes against Humanity" (2009) 13 Theoretical Criminology 227; A Chouliaras, "Bridging the Gap between Criminological Theory and Penal Theory within the International Criminal Justice System" (2014) 22 Eur J Crime Cr L Cr J 249; A Bandura, *Moral Disengagement: How People Do Harm and Live with Themselves* (Worth, 2016); A Smeulers, M Weerdesteijn & B Hola, *Perpetrators of International Crimes: Theories, Methods, and Evidence* (Oxford University Press, 2019); M Aksenova, E van Sliedregt & S Parmentier, eds, *Breaking the Cycle of Mass Atrocities: Criminological and Socio-legal Approaches in International Criminal Law* (Hart, 2019).

extraordinary contexts.[86] Criminological inquiry can inform our understanding of the conditions in which ICL crimes occur and the resulting constraints on capacity and culpability. Thus empirical inquiry can shape normative prescriptions on many topics, such as how we delineate between principals and accessories,[87] or how we assess culpability in contexts of superior orders.[88]

In conclusion, a liberal criminal law theory in no way entails ignoring the importance of society and social dynamics. It merely requires that we *justify* our actions against the individual on behalf of society. We may indeed be social animals, but we are not drones in a hive, to be used without concern as instruments for the collective good. A liberal account recognizes that there is some attribute of persons (whether it be labelled autonomy, or dignity, or capacity for reason[89]) that requires us to justify our punishment and treatment of them.

3.3.3 Western Constructs or Shared Concerns?

Finally, I come to the most difficult challenge for a humanistic liberal account. A frequently advanced objection to liberal principles is that they are a "Western" construct.[90] Such warnings rightly alert us to the historical and cultural contingency of familiar formulations of principles. They alert us to the inappropriateness, or even neocolonialism, of extending such principles in other contexts.

In a humanistic, cosmopolitan, and coherentist account, we want to do the best we can to identify principles reflecting broadly shared human concerns. In Chapter 4, I explain the "coherentist" method: we try to draw on all possible clues, which includes practices and perspectives from diverse regions and traditions. In Chapter 5 I discuss "cosmopolitanism," which also strives for a conversation drawing inspiration from diverse legal systems and traditions.[91]

---

[86] S Mohamed, "Of Monsters and Men: Perpetrator Trauma and Mass Atrocity" (2015) 115 Columbia L Rev 1157; A Smeulers & F Grünfeld, *International Crimes and Other Gross Human Rights Violations: A Multi- and Interdisciplinary Textbook* (Martinus Nijhoff, 2011).

[87] S Mohamed, "Leadership Crimes" (2017) 105 Calif L Rev 777 argues for a focus not only on coercive control, but also on those who create "moral inversions" through persuasive power. A Smeulers, "A Criminological Approach to the ICC's Control Theory," in K J Heller at al, eds, *Oxford Handbook on International Criminal Law* (Oxford University Press, 2020), notes the special responsibility of those persons who create the conditions in which ordinary law-abiding persons commit mass atrocities.

[88] A Smeulers, "Why International Crimes Might Not Seem 'Manifestly Unlawful' to Low-Level Perpetrators" (2019) 17 JICJ 1.

[89] In Chapter 4, I discuss the multiple possible underpinnings of principles.

[90] Drumbl, *Atrocity*, *supra* note 6, at 5, 19, 23, 123, 198; Osiel, *Making Sense*, *supra* note 6, at 8; Aukerman, *supra* note 7, at 41; Sepinwall, *supra* note 7, at 233.

[91] K Appiah, *Cosmopolitanism: Ethics in a World of Strangers* (WW Norton & Co, 2006) at 151 and see also 57–71 (cosmopolitanism is not universalism; it merely requires sufficient overlaps in vocabularies for a conversation, and it is possible to agree on a practice even if not agreeing on justifications). In the same inclusive spirit, see Ambos, *supra* note 52, at 2653–54.

There is a potentially powerful objection to this aspiration. Some will argue that fundamental principles (liberal principles, deontic constraints) are irreducibly "Western" and hence that a cosmopolitan account based on widely shared human concerns is impossible. Many entire volumes have been written on the "universalism versus relativism" debate in the human rights context; I cannot purport to resolve the similar question around fundamental principles here. Instead, I aim merely to sketch out what I believe would be the two main lines of response to this challenge.[92]

The first line of response is empirical: it would question the premise of the "provenance" argument. Is it really true that concerns about fair warning and personal culpability are preoccupations only of the West? Or are such concerns sufficiently basic and plausible as to be widely shared? For example, in the negotiation of the Rome Statute, delegates from all regions and legal traditions exhibited a shared commitment to principles such as legality and personal culpability.[93] The standard counter-argument is that the delegates may have reflected a Westernized elite. The response in turn is to point to a survey of domestic systems, which indicates that the principles seem to have recognition and support across traditions. The counter-argument is that liberal principles of criminal justice are still Western in origin and were imposed and exported during waves of colonization. It is normally around here that the debate bogs down into an unresolved stalemate.

What I wish to point out is that the provenance objection is on shakier ground than is commonly assumed. Historical evidence indicates that criminal law and its restraining deontic principles developed in multiple regions and cultures long before they emerged in Europe. Thus these practices and principles may reflect more widely shared human ideas about justice than is commonly assumed.

For example, Egypt had a system of criminal law as early as 3000BC, which featured written prohibitions, as well as an act requirement and a fault requirement for personal culpability.[94] The Egyptian system also had procedural safeguards

---

[92] In particular, I am not attempting to prove that fundamental principles are "universal." Proving an empirical universal is, in any event, impossible. I am advancing two lines of thought that should be considered in further conversation on these issues.

[93] See, e.g., P Saland, "International Criminal Law Principles," in R S Lee, ed, *The International Criminal: The Making of the Rome Statute* (Kluwer, 1999) at 194–95 ("never a contentious issue"); B Broomhall, "Article 22, *Nullum Crimen Sine Lege*," in O Trifterrer, ed, *Commentary on the Rome Statute of the International Criminal: Observers' Notes, Article by Article*, 2nd ed (Beck, 2008) at 715 ("widespread agreement" on need for clarity, precision, and specificity in accordance with principle of legality and that fundamental principles of criminal law should be clearly set out in the Statute); D Piragoff & D Robinson, "Article 30," in K Ambos, ed, *Commentary on the Rome Statute of the International Criminal: Observers' Notes, Article by Article*, 4th ed (Beck, 2020) (general view that no criminal responsibility without *mens rea*); S Lamb, "*Nullum Crimen, Nullum Poena Sine Lege*," in A Cassese et al, eds, *Rome Statute of the International Criminal: A Commentary* (Oxford University Press, 2002) at 734 (viewed by most delegates as self-evident) and 735 (relatively little controversy).

[94] R VerSteeg. "The Machinery of Law in Pharaonic Egypt: Organization, Courts, and Judges on the Ancient Nile" (2001) 9 Cardozo J of Int'l & Comp Law 105; J G Manning, "The Representation of

presaging those we would recognize today (a high standard of proof, due process, right to be heard, right to reasons for decision, and public trials).[95]

Similarly, Islamic law has also long featured criminal law, including the principle of legality (non-retroactivity)[96] and the principle of personal culpability.[97] Taymor Kamel exposes the assumption that the legality principle is a Western invention, as a factually incorrect and Eurocentric assumption. Kamel shows the principle's long prior roots in Islamic criminal law.[98] Similarly, in Islamic law, the requirement of personal culpability is considered "as old as the law itself," and includes familiar facets such as intent, fault, exculpating conditions, and an age of discretion (capacity).[99] Under Islamic law, one cannot be held vicariously responsible for acts of family members, but only for one's own conduct; "criminal responsibility is individual, nontransferable, and based on the conscious intentional conduct of a person in full possession of his/her mental faculties and who is not acting under ... exonerating conditions."[100]

China also developed criminal law between the eleventh and eighth centuries BC, with royal instructions requiring local rulers to make accessible the laws on offences and punishments, and "to ensure that officials apply the existing law and not on their own initiative introduce innovations."[101] There followed in China a considerable legacy of codification and publication,[102] including placing descriptions of penal laws outside of the palace for the information of the public.[103] Ancient laws reflected not only the principle of legality, but also the principle of culpability, including distinguishing intentional from accidental acts and mitigating punishment for the young.[104]

Justice in Ancient Egypt" (2012) 24 Yale J L & HR 111, esp at 112; D Lorton, "The Treatment of Criminals in Ancient Egypt: Through the New Kingdom" (1977) 20 Journal of the Economic and Social History of the Orient, esp at 5 and 13–14. The *content* of the principles was certainly not identical to those that are familiar today. For example, the ancient Egyptian system at times allowed for punishment of the convicted person's family. See, e.g., *ibid* at 14. At this point, I am simply demonstrating that constraining principles were a concern in more than one region; in Chapter 4, I will deal with the more granular topic of different approaches to the precise content of the principles.

95   VerSteeg, *supra* note 92, at 109–24; Manning, *supra* note 92, at 113; Aristide Théodoridès, "The Concept of Law in Ancient Egypt," in J R Harris, *The Legacy of Egypt*, 2nd ed (Clarendon Press, 1971).

96   S Tellenbach, "Aspects of the Iranian Code of Islamic Punishment: The Principle of Legality" (2009) 9 Int'l Crim L Rev 691; F Malekian "The Homogeneity of the International Criminal Court with Islamic Jurisprudence" (2009) 9 Int'l Crim L Rev 607; M Cherif Bassiouni, *The Shari'a and Islamic Criminal Justice in Time of War and Peace* (Oxford University Press, 2013), esp at 123–30.

97   Malekian, *supra* note 94, at 608–11; Bassiouni, *supra* note 94, at 130–32.

98   T Kamel, "The Principle of Legality and Its Application in Islamic Criminal Justice," in M C Bassiouni, ed, *The Islamic Criminal Justice System* (Oceana, 1982) esp at 150.

99   Malekian, *supra* note 94, at 608–11.

100 Bassiouni, *supra* note 94, at 131.

101 G MacCormack, *Traditional Chinese Penal Law* (Edinburgh University Press, 1990) at 1–2.

102 *Ibid* at 2–22.

103 *Ibid* at 4.

104 *Ibid* at 3, 10, 120, 128. Historical documents also show concern with due process (*ibid* at 2), equality before the law (*ibid* at 5), and that only those properly found guilty should be punished (*ibid* at 8). Of

Such developments, millennia before Europe saw its "Enlightenment," cast critical doubt on claims that principles such as the legality or culpability principles can be credited to and ascribed to a single culture or region. On the contrary, the principles seem to have much deeper roots and broader appeal. The popular view that criminal law and these restraining principles are creations of the West seems to be not only uninformed, but also (ironically) an example of Eurocentrism. Indeed, the direction of influence may have been the opposite: European interest in written criminal law and personal culpability may have been inspired by the Egyptian legal system.[105]

Contemporary empirical evidence also casts serious doubt on claims that concern with personal culpability is a peculiarly Western preoccupation. Studies indicate that widely shared intuitions of justice across cultures reflect the principle of culpability. Popular intuitions of justice include quite subtle distinctions that track criminal law and (deontological) moral theory.[106] Cross-cultural studies show a remarkable confluence of intuitions in subjects from the United States, China, Puerto Rico, India, Indonesia, Iran, Italy, and Yugoslavia.[107] Similarly, anthropological work suggests that very basic concepts of responsibility are quite widely shared.[108] Such findings provide further reason to at least hesitate about the claim that fundamental principles are merely "Western" artifacts. They might instead be rooted in common sense and widely shared moral reasoning.

The more salient historic fault line in approaches to penal sanctions is arguably not between "the West and the rest," but rather between small and large social groups. Smaller social units appear more likely to adopt "traditional" or restorative justice (focusing on problem-solving and restoring communal harmony, with vary-

---

course, as in any system, actual practice often diverged from these aspirations (*ibid* at 8), but the point here is that the *principles* were articulated and valued. The most striking departure from personal culpability concerns the punishment of *relatives* of persons convicted for certain crimes (see, e.g., *ibid* at 9–10, 120–25). Interestingly, jurists of past centuries were concerned with this departure from personal fault; some sought to justify the practice with utilitarian arguments, and others used fault-based arguments (e.g. that the relatives knew of the planning of the crime). Commentators in the Ch'ing dynasty grounded punishment of family members in personal fault by requiring proof of knowledge of the plotting (*ibid* at 124–25).

[105] Lorton, *supra* note 92, at 2; Manning, *supra* note 92, at 111.
[106] P H Robinson & R Kurzban, "Concordance and Conflict in Intuitions of Justice" (2006–07) 91 Minnesota L Rev 1829; P H Robinson, "Natural Law and Lawlessness: Modern Lessons from Pirates, Lepers, Eskimos, and Survivors" (2013) U Illinois L Rev 433.
[107] Robinson & Kurzban, *supra* note 104, at 1863–64. Studies tracked, for example, assessment of relative seriousness of wrongdoing and deserved punishment. There was also cross-cultural convergence with respect to exculpatory principles: *ibid* at 1864–65.
[108] D E Brown, *Human Universals* (McGraw-Hill, 1991), an anthropological work, finds that humans in general seem to punish and sanction infractions (at 138), to recognize personal responsibility and intentionality (at 135 and 139), and to distinguish actions under control from those that are not (at 135).

ing degrees of procedure and formality),[109] whereas larger social units (towns, cities, kingdoms) tend to adopt more formalized criminal justice. Importantly, this pattern of developing criminal law once a society reaches a certain size and heterogeneity emerges in different regions and cultures.[110]

Thus the historical, anthropological, and sociological evidence gives considerable reason to doubt the empirical premise of the cultural *ad hominem* argument. At minimum, in light of the evidence, some burden must fall on those who claim that the legality and culpability principles are merely Western constructs, to offer at least some substantiation of the claim.

The second line of response is normative. Rather than investigating the empirical *origins* of fundamental principles, one would shift to their *merits* and ask whether there is any attractive alternative. Scholars have rightly raised the possibility that support for fundamental principles may be culturally conditioned, but such scholars seem to be generally flagging a hypothetical *possibility* of disagreement with the principles, as opposed to *actually disagreeing* with them. In other words, does anyone actually advocate a criminal law system that punishes human beings without regard for culpability?[111] If so, we should get the arguments on the table, so that they can be discussed. Is that a normatively feasible proposition? Would such doctrines be coherent with the enterprise of ICL? Hopefully, as the conversation continues and broadens over time, we will see whether the disagreement is purely hypothetical or there are actually substantive arguments for punishment without culpability. I suspect that the much stronger case will be for respecting the culpability principle, even if there are some disputes about its boundaries.

I do not know how these empirical and normative debates will end. My point here is that unsubstantiated cultural *ad hominem* arguments are not sufficient reason to close down the debate. There are strong reasons to doubt the arguments, and further empirical and normative considerations would have to be addressed. Unless better

---

[109]   As Val Napolean and Hadley Friedland argue, writing on indigenous legal traditions is "fraught with stereotypes, generalizations, oversimplifications and reductionism"; indigenous laws are often "reduced to over-simplified, idealized foils to critique state criminal justice systems within academic literature": V Napoleon & H Friedland, "Indigenous Legal Traditions: Roots to Renaissance," in M D Dubber & T Hörnle, eds, *The Oxford Handbook of Criminal Law* (Oxford University Press, 2014). The supposed dichotomy between "Western" and "non-Western" justice is at least sometimes overstated: Fisher, *supra* note 75, at 144–64.

[110]   See, e.g., S Larcom, "Accounting for Legal Pluralism: The Impact of Pre-colonial Institutions on Crime" (2013) 6 LDR 25; Y Liu, *Origins of Chinese Law: Penal and Administrative Law in its Early Development* (Oxford University Press, 1998) at 19. Other social conditions may also influence the adoption of formal criminal law, e.g. written language is, of course, a precondition of codified criminal law. See, e.g., E Caldwell, "Social Change and Written Law in Early Chinese Legal Thought" (2014) 32 LHR 1.

[111]   One could also note, rightly, that there are traditions that do not employ "criminal law" as it is now commonly understood. My topic in this book, however, is on the *constraints* of criminal law, i.e. once a decision is made to use criminal law, what are the constraining principles? So the question here is whether people advocate criminal law that does not respect culpability or legality, and if so, what are the arguments for disregarding those principles (or replacing them with others)?

arguments emerge, they do not yet provide enough of a reason that we should stop *trying* to figure out what the constraints of ICL should be.

The three most plausible objections to the proposed conversation are as follows. First, one could object that the shared recognition of these principles sounds plausible only because it is at a high level of generality, whereas legal traditions diverge when they articulate the principles in more detail. However, my point is precisely to distinguish between these levels of generality. Here, I am addressing objections to the constraint of culpability as even an appropriate *general* concern. Once we agree that culpability matters, we *then* turn to the more precise task of formulating the content of the constraint. At this more granular level, we consider the divergent formulations, as they show us solutions worked out through experience and awaken us to different traditions of thought. This more granular analysis is discussed in Chapter 4. What I am establishing here is that culpability matters and is worth exploring.

Second, one could rightly warn that the language of cosmopolitanism has often been used, both advertently and inadvertently, as a mask for hegemony.[112] The point is sobering, but it is an objection to *failed* cosmopolitanism; it not a reason to decline to even *attempt* a genuine cross-cultural cosmopolitan conversation.

The third and weightiest difficulty is that much of the available academic and legal writing about fundamental principles does indeed come from a Western perspective. Given the structural inequality of the world today, this is unfortunately the case for most topics. As a result, it will be difficult to disentangle any biases rooted in a particularly Western philosophical outlook, particularly for those of us raised in a Western culture. That difficulty is daunting indeed: how do we contend with potential biases that may permeate our source materials and shape our own outlook and assumptions?[113] Unfortunately, this problem of undetected biases arises in almost all of our intellectual endeavours. The only alternative to *trying* is to give up. If we say that a possibility of undetected bias should make us stop, then that policy would end almost all inquiries into almost all topics. Abandoning the effort to identify the constraining principles seems more ethically untenable than at least *trying*.

In almost all major undertakings, we have the unenviable problem that we have to be wary of our presuppositions and the almost impossible task of sorting our sound

---

[112]   See, e.g., M Koskenniemi, *"Humanity's Law*, Ruti G. Teitel" (2012) 26 Ethics & International Affairs 395 (book review); R Mani, *Beyond Retribution: Seeking Justice in the Shadows of War* (Wiley, 2002) at 47–48.

[113]   The problem is also touched upon in H Christie, "The Poisoned Chalice: Imperial Justice, Moral Relativism, and the Origins of International Criminal Law" (2010) 72 U Pittsburgh L Rev 361, esp at 366 and 382–85, and in Mani, *supra* note 110, at 47–48. On the problem and opportunity of inevitably coming from some cultural context, see P Bourdieu, "Participant Objectivation" (2003) 9 Journal of the Royal Anthropology Institute 281. For an inspiring agenda rightly calling for critical criminal law theory, see A G Kiyani, "International Crime and the Politics of Criminal Theory: Voices and Conduct of Exclusion" (2015) 48 NYU J Int'l L & Pol 187.

ideas from our cultural conditioning. In Chapter 4, I will discuss these problems. All we can do is work with the best evidence and best arguments that we have, with caution about our assumptions, and with our minds open to other perspectives. I will discuss this revisable, fallible, and human conversation as the best and only available way forward, given uncertain starting points.

3.4 IMPLICATIONS

In this chapter, I have argued that fundamental principles do matter in ICL, even though ICL deals with some extraordinary contexts. I have also argued that we do not necessarily need to replicate the formulations of principles found in national law; we can examine what the deontic commitment to individuals entails in the new contexts of ICL.

One can therefore agree with the best insights of both the liberal critique and the critique of the liberal critique, provided that some caveats are made to each. A synthesis is possible that acknowledges the often-distinct contexts of ICL and yet still requires fidelity to an underlying deontic commitment. Thus ICL should not uncritically replicate principles from national systems, nor should it uncritically abandon them.

Engaging with common critiques of liberal accounts helps to light the way toward a nuanced and humanistic liberal account. I have emphasized the "humanity" of criminal justice in multiple senses. First, principles are not simply stipulations of positive law; we uphold the deontic commitment because of recognition and respect for the humanity of subjects of the system. Second, an account can engage with the subtleties of human experience, including collective action and social context. And, third, an account can engage in genuine inquiry into widely shared human concerns.

In Chapter 4, I will explain the "coherentist" methodology for discussing principles. I argue that we need a conversation that draws on the broadest range of clues for inspiration, including patterns of legal practice and normative arguments.

In Chapter 5, I outline some of the questions raised by ICL that may be explored by this approach. ICL presents some new and interesting problems, the investigation of which might generate new and interesting answers. I argue that this approach might also have exciting implications for general criminal law theory. The study of abnormal situations can help us to discern conditions and parameters embedded in what we had believed, based on our everyday experience, to be elementary principles. Doing so helps us to develop a theory that is truly more "general." Problems in ICL may help us to discover that formulations of principles that seemed basic are actually contextually contingent manifestations of a deeper deontic commitment.

4

Fundamentals without Foundations

OVERVIEW

In Chapter 3, I discussed why we may need to reconsider familiar formulations of fundamental principles when we apply them in new contexts. For example, what does the legality principle require in a system without a legislature? What does the culpability principle require in contexts of collective violence? In this chapter, I ask how we might embark on such evaluations: how do we go about formulating and evaluating the principles themselves?

A traditional and commendable scholarly reflex is that we must "ground" our analysis in a secure foundation. In other words, we should be able to show that each proposition is justified by deeper premises, and those premises, if challenged, should in turn be demonstrably justified, until we reach a bedrock that is certain and self-evident or agreed by all. In this way, we would know we have reached the "correct" deductions.

In this chapter, I show the infeasibility of the classic scholarly reflex of trying to demonstrate grounding in secure moral foundations. We do not have an uncontroversially "correct" foundational moral theory, and furthermore the comprehensive moral theories tend to lack the precision to dictate answers to most granular problems. Happily, this absence of bedrock does not mean that we must abandon thoughtful, rigorous discussion of fundamental principles.

I suggest a non-foundational approach, using a coherentist method: we do the best we can with the available clues and arguments. The clues include patterns of practice, normative arguments, and casuistically-tested considered judgements. We can work with "mid-level principles" (principles intermediate between practice and foundational theories) to carry out fruitful analytical and normative work.

The coherentist approach accepts that our principles are human constructs, that our starting points are contingent, and that we have no guarantees of "correctness." Nonetheless, it is important to *try* to determine whether institutions are just, using the best available methods that we have. Discussion of fundamental principles is not a matter of ethical computations; it is a *conversation*. It is a *human* conversation, a *fallible* conversation, and nonetheless an *important* conversation. I also argue that this method – starting in the middle and reconciling all available clues – offers the best explanatory and justificatory account of the method used in most criminal law theory. In other words, it is the best theory of criminal law theory.

4.1 TERMS: FUNDAMENTALS AND FOUNDATIONS

I should explain some terms. I use the term *fundamental principles* in the same way it is used in criminal law scholarship and jurisprudence: principles such as legality or culpability that are found to be fundamental within the legal system. The principles are "fundamental" in comparison with other rules and doctrines in the system. By *foundations*, I mean ultimate bedrock justifications for beliefs; in ethical discourse, the term is also used to refer to general comprehensive moral theories. My point is that we can make meaningful progress in discussing and refining fundamental principles of a criminal justice system without resolving ultimate moral questions, without necessarily subscribing to one of the main comprehensive theories, and without having to decide which comprehensive theory is the "right" one.

I also use the term *mid-level principle*, but in doing so I am not drawing a hierarchy between "fundamental" and "mid-level"; I am simply adopting terms used in two bodies of literature. In ethics literature, the term "mid-level principles" refers to principles that are arguably immanent within a body of practice. Mid-level principles are analytically useful, because they help to explain and systematize the practice, and they are also normatively convincing. They are "mid-level" because they mediate between legal practice and the foundational moral theories; they are more general than the former and more concrete than the latter. My argument is that fundamental principles of criminal justice, and our specific formulations of those principles, can be fruitfully analyzed as "mid-level principles" in this broader sense.

4.2 WHERE CAN WE FIND FUNDAMENTAL PRINCIPLES?

As I discussed in Chapter 1, there are two distinct reasons why it is valuable to formulate the constraining principles as best we can. First, if we neglect or *under-state* a fundamental principle of justice, we breach a commitment of fair treatment owed to the individual: we are treating the person unjustly. Second, and conversely, if we *overstate* a fundamental principle, we are being unnecessarily conservative; we are sacrificing social desiderata when no deontic constraint requires us to do so. It is "bad policy," because we are failing to fulfill the societal aims of the system for no reason. Thus we have both deontological and consequentialist reasons to develop plausible accounts of fundamental principles: It can help us to avoid unjust treatment, and it also helps us to develop better policy.

But where do we look to find those principles? The literature commonly refers to two principles – culpability and legality – but how do we know to accept those two principles? How would we determine if there might be others? Where do we turn to see how to formulate their specific requirements? By "formulations," I mean the articulations of specific implications. For example, does the legality principle require written legislation or can other notice suffice?[1] Does the culpability principle require some causal contribution to a crime, and if so, how much contribution is enough?[2]

At present, when ICL scholarship and jurisprudence invokes or articulates a principle, it routinely draws on any of three sources of reference: (i) formulations in *ICL authorities*, (ii) induction from *national legal systems*, and (iii) deduction from *philosophical argument*. The way in which all three are freely invoked may at first seem haphazard, but I will suggest that the recourse to these reference sources is justified and appropriate, and that coherentism is actually the best explanation for how these reference sources are employed.[3]

First, however, to show that there are no simple and certain sources or methodologies available to us, I will inspect each source in isolation to demonstrate that each has strengths and weaknesses. We are going to see two recurring problems. One problem is the trade-off between positivity and normativity.[4] By "positivity," I mean recognized legal applicability and ascertainability, and by "normativity," I mean the degree of convincingness that we "ought" to recognize the principle. The second problem is the lack of a reliable foundation even for a purely normative conversation.

For greater certainty, let me specify that the methodology I propose does not purport to *escape* all of these problems; rather, I am simply demonstrating the need for a methodology that openly acknowledges and responds to these problems. I will advocate a method that acknowledges the lack of certainty, that strives to identify and test the weaknesses inherent in each source of reference, and that gives us tools for helpful deliberation despite these challenges.

4.2.1 First Source of Reference: Internal Formulations

The first source of reference is the articulation of principles in ICL jurisprudence itself (i.e. in its legal instruments and judicial pronouncements). This is an internal and doctrinal approach. For example, if we were debating the culpability principle, we might turn to articulation of the principle in Tribunal jurisprudence (i.e. "a person can only be held responsible for a crime if he contributed to it or had an effect on it"[5]). If we were debating the requirements of non-retroactivity and the legality

---

[1]　See Chapter 5.

[2]　See Chapter 6.

[3]　See §4.4.

[4]　M Koskenniemi, *From Apology to Utopia: The Structure of International Legal Argument* (Reissue with new epilogue) (Cambridge University Press, 2005).

[5]　*Prosecutor v Tadić*, Judgment, ICTY A.Ch, IT-94-1-A, 15 July 1999, at para 186; *Prosecutor v Kayishema*, Judgment, ICTR T.Ch, ICTR-95-1, 21 May 1999, at para 199.

principle in a case before the ICC, we might invoke the terms enshrined in the ICC Statute.[6]

The strength of this approach is its "positivity." The principles are clearly legally applicable in ICL, because ICL itself says so. They are also relatively concrete, because we use the articulations provided in the authoritative pronouncements of ICL sources.

The weakness of this source is its limited normativity. The approach does not help at all with the questions of whether ICL has adopted flawed or problematic understandings, or whether it ought to recognize other principles. In other words, we cannot use ICL understandings as a yardstick against which to *critically evaluate* ICL understandings. A purely internal approach also does not help us in liminal cases, in which we need to further specify how a particular principle should be formulated. We need some external framework for these kinds of evaluation.[7]

Furthermore, a purely internal account cannot tell us how to resolve a conflict between a doctrine and a principle. From the standpoint of formal non-contradiction, a conflict between an ICL doctrine and an ICL principle can be resolved by reforming the doctrine, or by reformulating or even rejecting the principle.[8] Internal non-contradiction does not tell us whether to reform the doctrine or to reconsider the current understanding of the principle.

[6]   A person can be held responsible only for a crime that was, at the time of its commission, a crime within the jurisdiction of the ICC: ICC Statute, Arts 21–23.
[7]   To be more precise, the framework must be at least *partly* external if it is to question critically the internally adopted formulations. The account I propose in this chapter draws on both internal and external inputs. Furthermore, while simple *consistency* does not tell us which way to redress a conflict, I argue that broader *coherence* gives significantly more guidance.
[8]   As an illustration, consider e.g. the culpability principle and the command responsibility doctrine. Early Tribunal jurisprudence proceeded from the following premises to the following conclusion:

  (1) ICL respects the culpability principle, which requires that the accused must contribute to or have an effect on a crime to share in liability for it.
  (2) However, under the command responsibility doctrine, the accused need not contribute to or have an effect on a crime to share in liability for it.
  (3) Therefore, the culpability principle's requirement of causal contribution apparently does not apply to command responsibility.

In contrast, I would have reached a different conclusion, as follows:

  (3) Therefore, we should re-examine the command responsibility doctrine to bring it into conformity with the culpability principle.

There are, of course, many subtle details to the command responsibility debate, and you might disagree with how I characterize the ICTY analysis. I will unravel all of that with great care in Chapter 6 (including the "separate offence" characterization that later emerged). The point I am making here is simply that, on a pure *internal consistency* account, the first solution is not "wrong." Cases such as Čelebići assumed rather insouciantly that there must be an exception within the fundamental principle, but in doing so they removed the apparent conflict, at least from the formal logical perspective of internal consistency.

The internal approach is nonetheless analytically valuable, because it can reveal *internal contradictions* between ICL doctrines and principles. Internal non-contradiction is an important value in its own right, and thus internal contradictions should be detected and corrected.[9] Nonetheless, we need some external benchmark with which to *specify* the recognized formulations, to *adapt* them, or to critically *evaluate* them.

4.2.2 Second Source of Reference: Induction from National Systems

The second source of reference is induction from the national legal systems of the world. ICL jurisprudence often canvasses national systems for guidance about principles and their formulations. For example, in the *Erdemović* case at the ICTY, the judges surveyed national systems to see if there was a common approach to when duress is an excusing condition.[10] In the *Lubanga* case at the ICC, chambers adopted the "control theory" as a basis to distinguish principals and accessories, noting that the approach is applied in numerous legal systems.[11] Scholars and jurists frequently employ induction from national sources when articulating fundamental principles.[12]

This approach has *intermediate* levels of positivity and normativity. In terms of *positivity*, the "general principles of law derived … from … legal systems of the world" have recognized legal applicability: they are a well-accepted subsidiary interpretive source of ICL.[13] This technique, adapted from general international

---

You may object that, even on an internal consistency account, there is still a formal problem with the Tribunal's chain of reasoning – namely, it misunderstood the proper "hierarchy" between fundamental principles and doctrines when it took the doctrine as the fixed point and assumed an exception in the principle. That could be a correct critique of the *reasoning* in this instance. But the *outcome* of reinterpreting the principle is not necessarily always wrong, if it is done after careful deontic analysis.

[9] Of course, any dynamic living legal system is a field of contestation, absorbing new values over time, and hence contradictions will arise incidentally as components change. Nonetheless, contradiction cannot be a desideratum of any legal system, and coherence must be a systemic goal.

[10] *Prosecutor v Erdemović*, Judgment, ICTY A.Ch, IT-96-22-A, 7 October 1997 ("*Erdemović* Appeals Judgment") and see more detailed discussion in §5.2.2. In that case, there was too much discrepancy between national approaches to extract a general principle on the issue in dispute (whether duress was available for murder).

[11] See, e.g., *Prosecutor v Thomas Lubanga Dyilo*, Decision on the Confirmation of Charges, ICC PTC, ICC-01/04-01/06, 29 January 2007, at para 330.

[12] Examples of drawing on national systems for guidance are innumerable. As illustrations, see S Dana, "Beyond Retroactivity to Realizing Justice: A Theory on the Principle of Legality in International Criminal Law Sentencing" (2009) 99 JCLC 857, esp at 879–81, canvassing national approaches to *nulla poena sine lege*; K Gallant, *The Principle of Legality in International and Comparative Criminal Law* (Cambridge University Press, 2009); K Ambos, *Treatise on International Criminal Law, Vol I: Foundations and General Part* (Oxford University Press, 2012) at 88 (legality) and 94 (culpability).

[13] See, e.g., ICC Statute, Art 21(1)(c); *Erdemović* Appeals Judgment, *supra* note 10, Opinion of Judges McDonald and Vohra, at paras 56–72. The ICC Appeals Chamber has held affirmed the value of drawing inspiration from national legal systems: "[T]he Appeals Chamber considers it appropriate to

law,[14] involves surveying national systems to identify commonalities that can then guide the international system. General principles also offer some level of concreteness, since there is a broadly agreed methodology drawing on objectively ascertainable data.

However, the positivity is only "intermediate," because there are also significant limits. The immense difficulty of collecting the necessary data reduces the accessibility of this source. More problematically, the process requires one to *generalize* from many differing approaches of national systems, which reduces the specificity of the general principles and thus their concreteness in resolving specific issues. This is particularly a problem if national systems diverge on the precise question one is trying to resolve.[15]

Induction from national systems also has an intermediate level of *normativity*. On the one hand, there are good reasons to accord some normative weight to principles derived from national systems. After all, principles recognized across regions, cultures, and traditions, and worked out based on decades or centuries of experience, offer an excellent guide to widely shared intuitions of justice. They are a valuable reference point in informing our understandings of the proper constraints of the criminal sanction.[16]

On the other hand, there are also limits to that normative weight. One problem is that some national traditions will get "double-counted" if they exported their legal systems through colonization.[17] Thus we must be ready to examine biases and impositions of power that may have led to the predominant formulations.[18]

---

seek guidance from approaches developed in other jurisdictions in order to reach a coherent and persuasive interpretation of the Court's legal texts. This Court is not administrating justice in a vacuum, but, in applying the law, needs to be aware of and can relate to concepts and ideas found in domestic jurisdictions." *Prosecutor v Thomas Lubanga Dyilo*, Judgment on the Appeal of Mr Thomas Lubanga Dyilo against His Conviction, ICC A.Ch, ICC-01/04-01/06-3121-Red, 1 December 2014, at para 470. In that particular case, the method was not a general survey of systems, but rather a reference to German legal thinking, on the grounds that it offered a convincing normative theory that fit well with the ICC Statute and with the nature of the crimes before the Court, as a way of distinguishing principals and accessories. This approach matches the coherentist method discussed later in this chapter.

[14]   ICJ Statute, Art 38(1)(c).

[15]   In addition to the limits on positivity noted here, general principles are only a subsidiarity interpretive source, ranking below an institution's basic instrument, as well as any relevant treaty and custom. See, e.g., ICC Statute, Art 21(1)(c); *Erdemović* Appeals Judgment, *supra* note 10.

[16]   G Fletcher, *The Grammar of Criminal Law: American, Comparative and International*, Vol 1 (Oxford University Press, 2007) at 66–67 and 94(comparative study can inform our philosophical inquiry, attempt to formulate principles that cut across legal systems, avoid parochialism); K Ambos, "Toward a Universal System of Crime: Comments on George Fletcher's *Grammar of Criminal Law*" (2006–07) 28 Cardozo L Rev 2647 at 2647, 2649 and 2672; P H Robinson & R Kurzban, "Concordance and Conflict in Intuitions of Justice" (2006–07) 91 Minnesota L Rev 1829.

[17]   J Stewart & A Kiyani, "The Ahistoricism of Legal Pluralism in International Criminal Law" (2017) 65 Am J Comp L 393.

[18]   *Ibid*. See also A G Kiyani, "International Crime and the Politics of Criminal Theory: Voices and Conduct of Exclusion" (2015) 48 NYU J Int'l L & Pol 187 on the need for searing critical inspection of proposed principles and rationales.

Another problem is that, as discussed in Chapter 3, ICL operates in contexts that are often profoundly different from the "normal" societal context in which the familiar formulations of principles evolved. So, even if every system in the world were to concur in a particular formulation of a principle, that would not necessarily be a conclusive case for its absorption into ICL, because there could be normatively salient differences. For example, even if every legal system in the world were to say that all criminal law must be written law,[19] that would not necessarily support a maxim that all criminal law systems in all circumstances must be based on written law. We might conclude instead that *lex scripta* is merely a manifestation of a deeper underlying principle (perhaps concerning notice or ascertainability) and that the specific requirement of written legislation applies only under certain societal conditions.[20]

Thus the second source, induction from national systems, offers intermediate positivity and normativity. National formulations provide some guidance to widely shared understandings of justice, worked out over time in diverse settings. However, we must be alert to possible biases in existing practice and formulations of principles, as well as possible inaptness outside the societal contexts in which those formulations were developed.[21]

4.2.3 Third Source of Reference: Deduction from Moral Philosophy

The third source of reference is to deduce conclusions from normative argumentation, for example by appealing to basic moral commitments as to how persons should be treated. This is also a frequently employed method, for example when one invokes philosophical thinkers or a school of thought,[22] or when scholars or jurists engage directly with moral questions of justice for the individual.[23]

---

[19] They do not. Consider, e.g., the UK, which still allows common law offences, as well as the many local regimes of customary law in the world. See, e.g., D D Ntanda Nsereko, *Criminal Law in Botswana* (Kluwer, 2011) at 46; D Isser, ed, *Customary Justice and the Rule of Law in War-Torn Societies* (USIP Press, 2011).

[20] Accordingly, ICL, at least in its early phases, provides an interesting context to explore the possible unstated preconditions of the *lex scripta* requirement. See Chapter 5.

[21] For discussion, see Chapter 3.

[22] Examples abound, but one illustration among many would be George Fletcher drawing on ideas from Kant, Hegel, Fuller, Rawls, and so on, to flesh out normative arguments: Fletcher, *supra* note 16.

[23] Again, examples abound, but illustrations would include the direct engagement with what can fairly be expected of a person under duress in the *Erdemović* case or reflection on fair notice to the individual in the *Nuremberg* Judgment, or debates about the limits of personal culpability in command responsibility in the *Bemba* case. See, e.g., *Erdemović* Appeals Judgment, *supra* note 10, Dissenting Opinion of Judge Cassese, paras 47–48; *Judgment of the International Military Tribunal (Nuremberg)*, reproduced in (1947) 41 AJIL (supplement) 172 (arguing that the injustice of prosecution would be outweighed by the injustice of non-prosecution and that the accused did have a form of notice of the illegality of their acts); *Prosecutor v Jean-Pierre Bemba Gombo*, Judgment Pursuant to Article 74 of the Statute, ICC T.Ch, ICC-01/05-01/08, 21 March 2016, in which each judge gave subtle analyses of the requirements of culpability (see further discussion in Chapter 7).

This approach has the highest level of normativity, because it is purely a discussion about what we *ought* to do. The obvious problem with the third approach is, of course, the lack of positivity.[24] It can be difficult to show that any particular moral theory or philosophical argument is legally germane. And, of course, the enormous problem with many discussions of moral principles is the lack of concreteness. Further reducing the concreteness, there are many different theories and sets of values, as well as a lack of guidance as to which is "correct," or at least authoritative.

Here, we encounter a problem that is greater than the positivity-normativity tension. Suppose that we decide not to worry about legal "positivity" at all – that we wish to have a *purely normative* discussion. In other words, we will discuss only what the principles *ought* to be. We might decide, for the reasons discussed in Chapter 3, that we want to avoid assumptions based on formulations of principles in national systems, because they might be inapposite.[25] In this hypothesized conversation, we presumably want to be "rigorous," and we might understand rigour in the traditional Cartesian way: that we must ground our conclusions in solid foundations. There are two major problems with that conception of rigour: the problem of insufficient specification, and the problem of pluralism.

The problem of insufficient specification

When ICL scholars speak of the moral underpinnings of fundamental principles, the most frequently invoked underlying moral theory is that of Immanuel Kant.[26] Thus our first thought might be to adopt that as our foundation: we will apply a Kantian analysis to assess whether new articulations of principles are justifiable in abnormal contexts. An attraction of Kant's deontological theory is that it purports to offer an objective, formal, rational, framework that is not dependent on empirical social, anthropological, or cultural inputs.[27] This would be wonderful for ICL theory, because it would sidestep concerns and objections about social contingency

---

[24] I use the term "source of reference" to avoid any misunderstanding that I am suggesting that philosophical works are a formal source of law. I am saying, rather, that jurists and scholars routinely (and rightly) engage directly in moral reasoning when making arguments about what is entailed by fundamental principles.

[25] See Chapter 3.

[26] I Kant, *Groundwork of the Metaphysics of Morals*, trans M Gregor (Cambridge University Press, 1998) ("*Groundwork*"); I Kant, *The Metaphysics of Morals*, trans M Gregor (Cambridge University Press, 1996) ("*Metaphysics*"). Some features of Kantian thought are that: we must act in accordance with maxims that can be willed as universal law (Kant, *Groundwork*, at 15, 31 4:402, 4:421); we must treat individuals as ends and not solely as means (Kant, *Groundwork*, at 37–38, 41 4:428–429, 4:433); therefore we can punish only where there is desert (Kant, *Metaphysics*, 105 6:331); lawful external coercion is right where it is a response to hindrances of freedom (Kant, *Metaphysics*. at 25 6:232); and the system is reciprocal coercion in accordance with the universal freedom of everyone (Kant, *Metaphysics*, at 26 6:232).

[27] Kant, *Groundwork, supra* note 26, at 1–3 (4:388–89) ("a pure moral philosophy, completely cleansed of anything that may be only empirical," "does not borrow the least thing from acquaintance with [human beings] (from anthropology)"; see also *ibid* at 20–23 (4:408–4:411) (not dependent on

or cultural imposition[28]: principles would be derived by logic from *a priori* premises applicable to all rational beings.

Alas, however, as we look at the conclusions reached by Kant using his methodology of pure reason, we notice that he happens to deduce many of the social institutions familiar in Germany in the 1700s, some of which we would today consider unjust.[29] It seems improbable that those arrangements were dictated by pure reason alone. I am not engaging here in the easy sport of criticizing historical figures for holding views typical of their era; rather, I am highlighting the problem with Kant's claim that his theory was not based on empirical inputs (anthropological, sociological, cultural), and hence with its promise of neutral rational objectivity. The fact that Kant happened to deduce familiar features of his own society strongly suggests that the process is *not* one of pure deductions from *a priori* axioms. Instead, there seems to be considerable gap-filling in deciding what is or is not a "contradiction," and that gap-filling repeatedly draws on empirical presuppositions and contemporary normative opinions.[30]

Of course, there is nothing wrong with the fact that moral reasoning depends on empirical presuppositions and will be influenced by contemporary values. I am simply pointing out the implausibility of the promise of apolitical, objective, logical deductions from *a priori* premises. A neutral, objective system based on rational deductions from universally applicable premises would be wonderful for ICL, because it would avoid criticisms about culture and politics; unfortunately, such a system is not available. Even the most ostensibly formal methodology appears to leave vast latitude as to how one colours in the details.

The general formulas in comprehensive ethical theories usually will not be granular enough to answer the comparatively narrow questions we will be asking about criminal law doctrines. For example, even if we agree that the personal culpability principle requires some "causal contribution" to a crime, we might see multiple plausible formulations for that requirement (e.g. discernible minor impact versus risk aggravation).[31] Most comprehensive moral theories will not

---

"contingent conditions of humanity," "rest only on pure reason independently of all experience," "principles are to be found altogether a priori, free from anything empirical, solely in pure rational concepts and nowhere else even to the slightest extent," "not based on what is peculiar to human nature but must be fixed a priori by themselves," "all moral concepts have their seat and origin completely a priori in reason," "they cannot be abstracted from any empirical and therefore merely contingent cognitions").

[28] See §3.3.

[29] For example, approval of second-class citizens (Kant, *Metaphysics*, *supra* note 26, at 92 6:314–15), no suffrage for women (*ibid* at 92 6:314–15), no right to resist even "unbearable" abuses by ruler (*ibid* at 96–97 6:320), no punishment for a head of state (*ibid* at 104–5 6:331), and a mandatory death penalty for murder (*ibid* at 106 6:333).

[30] See also C Sunstein, "Is Deontology a Heuristic? On Psychology, Neuroscience, Ethics and Law" (2014) 63 Jerusalem Phil Q 83.

[31] See Chapter 7.

generate "answers" to questions at that level of granularity.[32] At best, such theories provide us with helpful ways of thinking about and debating issues. But our problem is even bigger than the lack of granularity in the moral theories; we also have different moral theories.

The problem of pluralism

An even bigger problem is that there are actually multiple plausible moral theories that could conceivably underpin the fundamental principles. Earlier, I referred to "deontic" commitments. I am using the term "deontic" (i.e. relating to a duty) as a helpful contrast to the relatively simplistic consequentialist arguments often seen in ICL (and national criminal law) argumentation.[33] I use the term "deontic" to refer to principled constraints rooted in duties to the individual, which we would respect even if doing so did not optimize social welfare.

Given this framing, it is entirely understandable that our first thought commonly goes to the most famous deontological theory – that of Kant. But there are many other moral theories that might underlie and explain the fundamental principles. Within the deontological school of thought, we could turn instead to Hegel. According to Hegel, the criminal law repudiates a person's claim to be entitled to coerce others. On his account, a person has a "right" to be punished, because it recognizes the person as a moral and rational actor.[34] Alternatively, we could turn away from traditional deontological theories, looking instead to *contractualist* theories to generate the basic principles of culpability and legality. A contractualist might look for principles that persons would adopt if they were laying down general rules when negotiating in the "original position," behind a veil of ignorance as to their actual identity and circumstances.[35] Or, we might look for principles that could not be reasonably rejected by persons moved to find principles for regulating human conduct that others, similarly motivated, could

---

[32]   Of course, consequentialist theories in the abstract may purport to offer determinate answers. In theory, for any given question (e.g. how to formulate a principle in ICL), there is an answer that in fact maximizes the desiderata of that theory (e.g. utility). But, in practice, the desiderata will never be perfectly measurable, and hence the problem of insufficient specificity and granularity remains.

[33]   Utilitarian arguments in criminal law jurisprudence are often fairly simplistic and incomplete, because they focus on only one variable – namely, crime prevention. For example, it is often argued in ICL that we need a broader inculpatory rule for general deterrence, to send a strong message, or to close "loopholes" that would let accused persons "escape conviction" (see Chapter 2). Of course, a more sophisticated utilitarian account would grapple with other long-term consequences. These would include the negative consequences of over-criminalization, "chilling effects" on desirable behaviour, other legitimate social ends (e.g. security or military efficacy), or the optimally efficient limits for the reach of ICL. A more sophisticated consequentialist approach would *reduce* many of the divergences from deontological approaches. However, it would not *eliminate* them, because a true utilitarian would still, e.g., punish the innocent if it served the greatest good over the long term.

[34]   By coercing others, the person has recognized a law permitting violation of the freedom of another and thus has authorized application of that law to him- or herself. G W F Hegel, *Elements of the Philosophy of Right*, A Wood, ed (Cambridge University Press, 1991) at 126–27 (§100).

[35]   J Rawls, *Justice as Fairness: A Restatement*, E Kelly, ed (Harvard University Press, 2001) at 14–18.

not reasonably reject.[36] Or, one might adopt a *communitarian* theory, and yet still share a commitment to these fundamental principles, if one's theory values autonomy and responsibility.[37] It is even possible that one could construct duty-like limits working within a *consequentialist* model. For example, one could conclude that a criminal justice system can optimize its benefits in the long run only if it posits, as a stipulation of the system, that its officials must strictly respect deontic constraints.[38]

Any of these moral foundational theories might underlie the principles of culpability and legality as we know them. In a liminal case, in which we need to further clarify a fundamental principle, each theory might generate a different method of analysis and possibly a different answer. Accordingly, our aspiration to be "rigorous," as classically conceived (i.e. grounded in secure foundations), is challenged by two problems: the malleability and imprecision within each moral theory, and the plurality of plausible moral theories.

4.2.4 We Have No Reliable Foundation

As these arguments show, each of the three commonly invoked sources of reference for fundamental principles is inadequate. First, each source lacks in either positivity or normativity, or both. Second, even if we decide to set aside positivity and have a purely normative discussion about how we *ought* to understand the principles, we are still stuck without a reliable, uncontroverted normative foundation.

A common – even classic – scholarly expectation is that normative analyses and prescriptions should be grounded in a convincing general ethical theory.[39] This chapter is, in part, a reaction to the common attitude that there is something suspect or incomplete about a normative argument that is not rooted in a comprehensive theory. In academia, it is common for scholars to select and adhere to one or the other of the main traditions (e.g. Kantian, Hegelian, contractarian, rule utilitarian) and then offer analyses from that tradition. Such approaches can, of course, offer valuable contributions. However, the problem is that any analyses offered from one particular tradition can then be rejected as unconvincing by any interlocutor who rejects that tradition. As a result, the quest for certain grounding (and of having to declare allegiance to a foundational theory) immediately drags us down into an insoluble preliminary quest to establish which is the "correct" foundational moral theory.

---

[36] T M Scanlon, *What We Owe to Each Other* (Harvard University Press, 1998).

[37] See, e.g., N Lacey, *State Punishment*: Political Principles and Community Values (Routledge, 2002) at 188.

[38] J Rawls, "Two Concepts of Rules" (1955) 64 Philosophical Review 3. Alternatively, one could argue –
given the difficulty of calculating utility in all cases, as well as problems of dangerous precedents and
slippery slopes – that second-order "rules," including "maxims of justice," should be followed because
they generally advance utility, even if they do not do so in a particular case. J S Mill, "Utilitarianism,"
in M Lerner, ed, *Essential Works of John Stuart Mill* (Bantam Books, 1961) at 226–48.

[39] As just one example lamenting this commonplace expectation, see M Engel Jr, "Coherentism and the
Epistemic Justification of Moral Beliefs: A Case Study in How to Do Practical Ethics without Appeal
to a Moral Theory" (2012) 50 Southern J Phil 50.

If I may state explicitly what is implicit in the classic expectation of secure grounding, the resulting methodology would be as follows.

(1) Figure out which moral theory is the correct one.
(2) Extrapolate from that theory to the best principles of justice.
(3) Evaluate ICL using those principles.

Once the implicit expectation is stated explicitly, it can readily be seen that this is not a feasible approach. After some millennia of trying, we have not determined the "correct" moral theory, and there is good reason to be skeptical that the answer is coming any time soon (or ever).

Yet there must be a way for us at least to *talk* about more practical ethical questions of the middle range, such as the justifiability of ICL doctrines. Surely, we do not have to postpone conversation about fundamental principles in ICL until we first identify the ultimately correct moral theory. There are many issues and controversies to discuss here and now, concerning command responsibility, superior orders, aiding and abetting, co-perpetration, and so on. If we want to make our best efforts to ensure that people are being treated fairly, what are we to do?

4.3 FUNDAMENTALS WITHOUT FOUNDATIONS: MID-LEVEL PRINCIPLES AND COHERENTISM

There is a defensible, thoughtful alternative to starting with foundations. A better approach is to "start in the middle."[40] I will outline an account here that works provisionally with "mid-level principles." This approach is best understood[41] as falling within a broader "coherentist" tradition, which sets aside the quest for certain or epistemically privileged basic premises and instead builds models that promote "coherence" between the available clues. This account can enable valuable normative and analytical inquiry. I will argue that this is the best means of advancing the conversation in fruitful ways.

4.3.1 Mid-level Principles

The conceptual tool of "mid-level principles" came to prominence in discussions of ethics,[42] and it has been fruitfully applied in legal contexts such as tort law and

[40] J Coleman, *The Practice of Principle: In Defence of a Pragmatist Approach to Legal Theory* (Oxford University Press, 2003). esp at 5–6.

[41] In §4.3.2, I will discuss a caveat: that some of the "modest" versions of foundationalism could also embrace these methods (mid-level principles, reflective equilibrium). Nonetheless, I will follow the usage in the literature describing the method as coherentist, given that it focuses on reconciling all clues (rather than necessarily building up from a privileged set of premises).

[42] T Beauchamp & J Childress, *Principles of Biomedical Ethics*, 7th ed (Oxford University Press, 2012) (the first edition, working with mid-level principles, was published in 1979); M Bayles, "Mid-level

intellectual property.[43] Mid-level principles *mediate* between foundational moral theories and a specific body of practice (e.g. legal doctrines).[44] They are "mid-level" because they are more abstract and general than specific rules and doctrines, and more specific and concrete than comprehensive moral theories. They are relatively discrete and accessible propositions, applying within a field of practice.[45] Mid-level principles are propositions that are arguably embodied in a body of practice (i.e. they *analytically* fit) and are *normatively* attractive.[46] Mid-level principles can be supported by multiple foundational theories: people may agree on the mid-level principles even if they have different underlying reasons for doing so. I suggest that the culpability principle and the legality principle can fruitfully be analyzed as "mid-level principles" in this broader sense.[47]

One virtue of mid-level principles is *convergence*.[48] Participants in a field may agree on certain mid-level principles even if they differ in their deeper underlying

Principles and Justification," in J R Pennock & J W Chapman, eds, *Justification* (New York University Press, 1986); M Bayles, "Moral Theory and Application," in J Howie, ed, *Ethical Principles and Practice* (SIU Press, 1987) ("Moral Theory"); B Brody, "Quality of Scholarship in Bioethics" (1990) 15 Journal of Medicine and Philosophy 161; Coleman, *supra* note 40; S Diekmann, "Moral Mid-level Principles in Modeling" (2013) 226 Eur J Oper Res 132.

Indeed, the idea of mid-level principles has even earlier forerunners; it was foreshadowed, e.g., by J S Mill, who noted "much greater unanimity among thinking persons than might be supposed from their diametric divergence on the great questions of moral metaphysics ... [T]hey are more likely to agree in their intermediate principles ... than in their first principles": J S Mill, "Bentham," in A Reid, ed, *Utilitarianism and Other Essays* (Penguin Random House, 1987) at 170. Interestingly, Kant also noted the value of "intermediate principles" in helping to enable judgements about what deeper principles require: Kant, "On a Supposed Right to Lie from Philanthropy," in Practical Philosophy, trans M J Gregor (Cambridge University Press, 1999) at 8:430.

43   K Henley, "Abstract Principles, Mid-level Principles and the Rule of Law" (1993)12 L & Phil 121; Coleman, *supra* note 40; R Merges, *Justifying Intellectual Property* (Harvard University Press, 2011) (*Justifying*); R Merges, "Foundations and Principles Redux: A Reply to Professor Blankfein-Tabachnik" (2013) 101 Calif L Rev 1361 ("Foundations"). In tort law, Jules Coleman proposes that the immanent mid-level principle is corrective justice (wrongful loss, responsibility, repair). In intellectual property, Merges proposes that the mid-level principles include proportionality, efficiency, public domain, and dignity.

44   Merges, *Justifying, supra* note 43, provides a typical structure, with "mid-level principles" mediating between "specific practices" and "normative foundations."

45   P Tremblay, "The New Casuistry" (1999) 12 Geo J Legal Ethics 489 at 503.

46   Coleman, *supra* note 40, esp at 29. This is the same process as Dworkin's search for analytical "fit" and normative "value," at least in his earlier works: see, e.g., R Dworkin, *Law's Empire* (Harvard University Press, 1986). Dworkin's approach is also coherentist (see §4.3.3), and see discussion of coherentism and Dworkin in A Amaya, *The Tapestry of Reason: An Inquiry into the Nature of Coherence and Its Role in Legal Argument* (Hart, 2015) at 38 and 46.

47   As noted in the introduction to this chapter, I am not drawing a hierarchy between "fundamental" and "mid-level"; rather, I am simply adopting the terminology used in two bodies of literature. I use the term "fundamental principles" because that is the common terminology within criminal law and criminal law theory: the principles are fundamental within the system of criminal law. I use the term "mid-level principles" because that is the terminology in the relevant ethics literature; they are at a "mid level" between comprehensive moral theories and the legal practice. My argument is that fundamental principles can be fruitfully analyzed as an example of mid-level principles.

48   Henley, *supra* note 43, at 123 uses the terms "convergence virtues" and "practical virtues" (the latter referring to the relative concreteness of mid-level principles).

philosophical outlooks.[49] Different moral theories may support the mid-level principles for different reasons, but nonetheless overlap in supporting the principles. This convergence is like Rawlsian "overlapping consensus"[50] or Sunstein's "incompletely theorized agreements."[51] Where such convergence exists, one can fruitfully work with mid-level principles without having to isolate the soundest ultimate basis for them. Of course, there may be some difficult liminal cases, in which a principle must be further clarified to resolve the case and in which different underlying moral theories may generate different answers, so that a choice must be made when specifying the principle. Nonetheless, the mid-level principles provide a valuable *starting point*. Moreover, for many problems of the middle range, mid-level principles are sufficient tools for valuable work, without need for recourse to deeper theories.[52]

A second virtue of mid-level principles is that they are more *specific* and concrete than general moral theories, and thus offer more *practical guidance* in a particular context.[53] General moral theories may be too abstract to generate ready answers to many specific problems.[54] For example, if we are wondering precisely what degree of causal contribution is required by the culpability principle, we will likely find that foundational reference points, such as the categorical imperative or imagining an ideal conversation, do not generate sufficiently specific answers. Mid-level principles enable us to identify morally or legally relevant characteristics and to note specific normative questions both "more dependably and more quickly" than we could if we were directly applying a foundational theory.[55]

A third virtue is that mid-level principles enable an inclusive, pluralistic conversation.[56] Mid-level principles can enable us to debate and often resolve certain concrete problems without first having to agree on the ultimate answers about morality. A central theme of this book is that discussion of principles is a type of *conversation*. Working with mid-level principles can help to facilitate that conversation. As Paul Tremblay observes, mid-level principles "permit conversation through common language and agreement about normative terms."[57] Similarly, Robert Merges describes mid-level principles as providing "a shared language

---

[49]   Merges, "Foundations," *supra* note 43, at 1364–66.
[50]   Rawls, *supra* note 35, at 32–38.
[51]   C Sunstein, "Incompletely Theorized Agreements" (1995) 108 Harvard L Rev 1733.
[52]   Bayles, "Moral Theory," *supra* note 42, at 112; Merges, *Justifying*, *supra* note 43, at 9. See, e.g., Chapters 7 and 8, querying the requisite level of foresight and the requisite level of involvement for the culpability principle.
[53]   Henley, *supra* note 43, at 123.
[54]   Coleman, *supra* note 40, at 5 and 54.
[55]   Henley, *supra* note 43, at 23.
[56]   Sunstein, *supra* note 51, at 1746. Sunstein does not use the term "mid-level principles"; he refers to "incompletely theorized agreements" and "low-level principles," but the idea is very much the same as the mid-level principles discussed here: see *ibid* at 1740.
[57]   Tremblay, *supra* note 45, at 504.

consistent with diverse foundational commitments";[58] they allow us to "play together even if we disagree about the deep wellspring."[59]

The relationship between moral theories, mid-level principles, and practice is not merely a one-directional deductive chain. In other words, it is not simply that the moral theories support the principles, and then the principles dictate the correct rules and outcomes; the interplay is more complex. For example, new cases or seemingly anomalous bodies of practice might lead us to reconsider, specify, or alter our principles: "[C]onsideration of particular cases and policies can lead one to see effects on moral values and principles not adequately taken into account in the [prior] formulations of mid-level principles."[60] Or, as Jules Coleman notes, we can use the principles to assess and guide the practice, but conversely the practice also *specifies, concretizes,* and *clarifies* the principles by applying them to new problems.[61]

Earlier in the chapter, I drew a contrast between "positivity" and "normativity." Often, we might find that "normativity" can be revealed in the "positive" (i.e. the practice). In other words, patterns of practice worked out by actors seeking to do justice may reveal plausible implicit underlying conceptions of justice.[62] Thus practice is not purely subordinate; practice is not merely the object to be *evaluated* by normative tools. The practice may also provide a *clue* helping us to reflect upon and revise the principles as we have formulated them. Accordingly, where a doctrine departs from our current best theory of the principles, there are two possibilities. In most cases, the analytically elegant and normatively sound conclusion will be that the outlying doctrine is problematic and should be harmonized with the principle. But it is also possible that the outlying practice could provide a normative insight that leads us to revise our understanding of the principles.[63] We would strive to identify which solution provides "coherence" in the deepest sense, which can be a subtle and difficult question, as I will explain further in §4.3.2 and §4.3.3.

As I will develop further in the rest of this chapter, if we take mid-level principles as a starting point, then we can do various tasks, working "upwards" or "downwards,"[64] and working analytically or normatively. Analytically, we can strive

58 Merges, "Foundations," *supra* note 43, at 1364–65.
59 Merges, *Justifying, supra* note 43, at 11. In this connection, it is interesting that both Kant and Mill recognize the value of "intermediate" principles.
60 Bayles, "Moral Theory," *supra* note 35, at 111.
61 Coleman, *supra* note 41, at 54–58.
62 Of particular interest would be patterns of practice by actors with different foundational moral beliefs; where those patterns are consistent with a unifying principle, then that principle may reflect an overlapping consensus.
63 In Chapter 8, I will argue that command responsibility is an example of a seemingly anomalous doctrine, which, on more careful inspection, reveals a useful insight about justice.
64 I should offer a terminological clarification on the metaphor of "up" and "down." In much of the mid-level principle literature, ethical theories are described as "up," and particular practices and cases are "down," with mid-level principles in between. However, in literature on foundationalism, the imagery is that "foundations" are below us: we "dig down" to the "deeper" "underlying" theories so that our arguments are "grounded." For consistency, I am adopting the latter metaphor; thus the

to articulate principles that provide the best descriptive "fit" and which may be seen as unifying the practice, or at least helping to systematize or guide the practice. This analytical approach can also be used to identify aberrant doctrines (i.e. doctrines that contradict the principles that appear to be immanent within the system). Normatively, we can ask whether a particular understanding of a mid-level principle is justified, or which of two candidate formulations is normatively "better." In liminal cases, the normative task may require descending into competing underlying moral theories to flesh out the principles or to choose between formulations.

My argument is that fundamental principles of justice in ICL (and indeed in criminal law) are most fruitfully approached as "mid-level principles" as the term is used in the ethics literature. Notice that I am not saying that the *only* mid-level principles in criminal law are fundamental principles of justice (such as the culpability or legality principles); on the contrary, there are many other organizing ideas in criminal law that are also best understood as mid-level principles.[65] I focus here on fundamental principles of justice because the aim of this book is to explore those principles; however, I believe that coherentism and mid-level principles offer an appropriate method for criminal law theory much more broadly.

4.3.2 A Coherentist Account

The proposed approach, of working with fundamental principles as "mid-level principles," is generally situated within a "coherentist" tradition.[66] In this section, I will explain the broader method[67] of coherentism. To prevent misreading, I should make something clear: Working with "mid-level principles" falls within the broader tradition of coherentism, but that does not mean that all of coherentism works with mid-level principles. Thus, when I say that science uses a coherentist method, that

---

"deeper," "foundational," and "underlying" moral theories are linguistically and metaphorically "downwards," and conversely the doctrine is "above," on the surface.

[65] For example, the "control theory," or any other theory for delineating between principals and accessories, is not a "fundamental principle of justice," but it is an important postulated organizing concept in ICL. Mid-level principles can be postulated at different levels of granularity and scope. In my view, works exploring the organizing concepts of ICL (or criminal law) are best understood as working with mid-level principles and a coherentist approach. For an example of such a methodology, see J D Ohlin, "Second-Order Linking Principles: Combining Vertical and Horizontal Modes of Liability" (2012) 25 LJIL 771.

[66] Beauchamp and Childress, early advocates of the mid-level principles approach, describe their approach as "coherentist": Beauchamp & Childress, *supra* note 42, at 13–25 and 383–85). Coleman, adopting the mid-level principles approach in law, adopts a pragmatist method, which falls within the coherentist tradition. See, e.g., Coleman, *supra* note 40, at 6–8. However, as I will discuss in a moment, there are some moderate versions of foundationalism that could also avail of these types of method.

[67] Coherentism is a theory about how to justify beliefs; as such, it generates a method for how to justify beliefs. See M DePaul, "Two Conceptions of Coherence Methods in Ethics" (1987) 96 Mind 463; M DePaul, "The Problem of the Criterion and Coherence Methods in Ethics" (1988) 18 Canadian J Phil 67; R Stern, "Coherence as a Test for Truth" (2004) 69 PPR 296 (on coherentism as a method of inquiry).

does not mean that science works with "mid-level principles"; coherentism is the broader category.

Coherentism seeks to advance understanding by reconciling all of the available clues as far as possible, without demanding demonstration of ultimate bedrock justification, epistemically privileged basic beliefs, or a comprehensive first-order theory. Indeed, the expectation that every proposition should be "grounded" in an even deeper theory is ultimately unattainable and hence unsound.[68]

Coherentism is the main rival to foundationalism. Foundationalism is the more traditional understanding of justification in which each of our beliefs should be supported by a more basic belief below (in the classical conception, one should reach down to a bedrock of self-evident premises).[69] A common metaphor for foundationalism is that the structure of justification is like a building: each floor relies on the floor below for support, until one reaches the foundation.[70] Some contemporary foundationalist accounts are more "moderate" in that they do not require self-evidence or certainty, but they still require "basic" beliefs that are identified as epistemically privileged (e.g. *prima facie* justified), with other beliefs necessarily supported by those basic beliefs. Some versions of moderate ethical foundationalism use premises about persons to derive a single value or the ground for all values.[71] Coherentism differs from these because it does not require that single underlying theory, but rather draws on all clues. Other versions of moderate foundationalism do not adopt a comprehensive theory, but rather take certain intuitions to be the *prima facie*, but defeasibly, correct starting points. There are subtle differences between coherentism and this latter version,[72] but generally the methods I outline here are largely compatible with that version of foundationalism.

[68] "If anyone really believes that the worth of a theory is dependent on the worth of its philosophical grounding then they would be dubious about physics and many other things": R Rorty, *Consequences of Pragmatism: Essays: 1972–1980* (University of Minnesota Press, 1982) at 168.

[69] The classical foundational method would include Descartes' effort in his *Meditations* to derive a set of beliefs from self-evident axioms.

[70] See, e.g., R Fanselow, "Self-Evidence and Disagreement in Ethics" (2011) 5 J Ethics Soc Philos 1; Amaya, *supra* note 46, at 138.

[71] M Timmons, "Foundationalism and the Structure of Ethical Justification" (1987) 97 Ethics 595 at 600–02.

An ethical foundationalist account could, of course, assert that its foundations are simply *stipulated* as axioms (with the theory exploring the ramifications of those axioms). A coherentist can happily work with such a theory, but would see it as a *model* – an exploration of what might flow from a certain way of looking at things. For example, what flows if we start from a premise of securing equal freedom to all? What flows if we start from a premise of maximizing human flourishing? Those are perfectly interesting questions that a coherentist method can draw upon as valuable *tools*, without accepting any such approach as the ultimately correct and conclusive framework. Furthermore, if anyone were to plausibly challenge the axiom, then I think the resulting conversation has to be a coherentist one.

[72] The coherentist response is to ask how these starting points obtained their supposedly privileged status; if the ultimate reason turns out to be that they are the most strongly supported by one's belief structure, then this is coherentism: G Sayre-McCord, "Coherentism and the Justification of Moral Beliefs," in M Timmons & WS Armstrong, eds, *Moral Knowledge* (Oxford University Press, 1996).

Coherentism accepts that "foundations" are not available. Our beliefs cannot be, and do not have to be, rooted in secure or comprehensive foundations. We do not need the false comfort of trying to select foundational beliefs that are considered privileged; instead, we can do only our best with the entire web of clues available to us. We develop and revise *models* that best reconcile our beliefs and observations; we are given no guarantees of correctness. As William James has written, our beliefs "lean on each other, but the whole of them, if such whole there be, leans on nothing."[73] Where a new, inconsistent experience or observation arises, we modify our beliefs to try to reconcile them in coherent schema. We work with all of the available clues, to make them fit as best we can in a coherent understanding.

The foundationalist objection is that such a process sounds problematically circular: Belief A supports belief B, and belief B supports belief A. However, that objection itself assumes a linear chain of justification.[74] Instead of the metaphor of a building, the coherentist metaphor is of a web.[75] The coherentist approach is not linear, but *holistic*: it aims to refine a *system* of beliefs, rooted in observations and experiences. Our confidence increases the more our beliefs reconcile experiences and inputs. For many, this approach of reconciling available clues and simply accepting foundational uncertainty may sound disturbingly insecure or even flimsy. I address three main objections (conservatism, uncertainty, and untidiness) in §4.3.3.

Perhaps it will be comforting to recall that the coherentist method matches the scientific method: We form models, we make new observations, and we revise models to better reconcile all of the available clues. For example, we can collect diverse clues from fossils, carbon dating, DNA of descendants, and geology to improve our theories about the histories of species and their migration. Each clue in isolation should be approached with caution and skepticism, but we formulate models that best bring the available evidence into coherence, and our confidence in each clue and supposition is bolstered by its coherence with other clues.

One might object that morality is different from science: in science, there can be observations that clearly contradict a model, whereas morality involves more subjective appreciations. However, the methodological similarity is that we still draw on all of the *clues* we can. We draw on our analytical application of theories, our

Furthermore, if supposedly privileged starting points can be dethroned based on their incompatibility with other evidence and considered beliefs, then the underlying method is coherentism: Stern, *supra* note 67. Such accounts match the coherentist method of adopting a model based on premises that appear plausible, given the available evidence, until such time as the model must be modified or rejected based on further evidence. Within a model, certain beliefs are sometimes extremely strongly supported and thus would not be lightly abandoned (e.g. "gravity" in physics, or the importance of the culpability principle in the model presented here). Nonetheless, all beliefs, including extremely strong supported beliefs, could be dethroned by a new conception that offers even stronger coherence.

73   W James, *Pragmatism* (originally published by Longman Green & Co, 1907) at 113.
74   L BonJour, "The Coherence Theory of Empirical Knowledge" (1976) 30 Philosophical Studies 281 at 282–86; Fanselow, *supra* note 70; Amaya, *supra* note 46, at 145 and 535.
75   Fanselow, *supra* note 70.

intuitive reactions to concrete applications, and even the views and arguments of others to test our ideas and to formulate the best understanding that we can with the available inputs.

Coherentism underlies not only the scientific method, but also some normative theories. Examples include the philosophical tradition of pragmatism,[76] the Rawlsian method of reflective equilibrium,[77] and Dworkin's "law as integrity."[78] I will therefore cite scholars in each of these traditions for their insights concerning coherentism in general.

The proposed approach is *anti-Cartesian* and *fallibilist*, meaning that it does not promise "certainty"; rather, it openly acknowledges that its conclusions are fallible.[79] Propositions (such as mid-level principles) are continually revisable based on new experiences and new arguments. At each juncture, we formulate the best hypotheses we can to reconcile the available clues. Coherentism is a form of *practical reasoning*. It does not strive to unearth the ultimate moral truths; it aims to address concrete human problems and questions as best we can.

My proposed account readily acknowledges that the fundamental principles of criminal justice are *human constructs*. As William James noted, "you cannot weed out the human contribution";[80] "the trail of the human serpent is thus over everything."[81] My account is *post-postmodern*: We acknowledge that each of these principles can be endlessly deconstructed, but, rather than falling into nihilism, we are willing to provisionally work with the constructs. We are prepared to question the

---

[76] See, e.g., James, *supra* note 73; J Dewey, *The Quest for Certainty: A Study of the Relation of Knowledge and Action* (Putnam, 1929); Rorty, *supra* note 68; M Dickstein, ed, *The Revival of Pragmatism: New Essays on Social Thought, Law, and Culture* (Duke University Press, 1998); C Misak, *The American Pragmatists* (Oxford University Press, 2013).

[77] Rawls, *supra* note 35, at 29–32. Rawls' approach is coherentist, e.g. he writes: "A conception of justice cannot be deduced from self-evident premises or conditions on principles: instead, its justification is a matter of the mutual support of many considerations, of everything fitting together into one coherent view." See J Rawls, *A Theory of Justice* (Oxford University Press, 1999) at 19. Similarly, *ibid* at 507, he writes that he does not grant a special place to any first principle; justification rests upon the entire conception and how it fits together.

Reflective equilibrium is generally described as coherentist. See, e.g., N Daniels, "Wide Reflective Equilibrium and Theory Acceptance in Ethics" (1979) 76 J Phil 256; Timmons, *supra* note 71, as some illustrations. Some argue that reflective equilibrium is compatible with modest foundationalism (or even best understood as modest foundationalist). See, e.g., R Ebertz, "Is Reflective Equilibrium a Coherentist Model?" (1993) 23 Canadian J Phil 193. Others have rejected this argument. See, e.g., S de Magt, "Reflective Equilibrium and Moral Objective" (2017) 60 Inquiry 443, arguing that the method requires either coherentism or classical intuitionism. In any case, I will follow the common tendency to describe reflective equilibrium as coherentist (given its focus on reconciling inputs rather than identifying reliable foundations), with the caveat that some forms of modest foundationalism employ the method as well.

[78] Dworkin, *supra* note 46, esp at 225–75.

[79] Dewey, *supra* note 76.

[80] James, *supra* note 73, at 110. He continues: "Our nouns and adjectives are all humanized heirlooms, and in the theories we build them into, the inner order and arrangement is wholly dictated by human considerations, intellectual consistency being chief among them."

[81] James, *supra* note 73, at 30.

concepts, but we do not simply discard them all at the outset. After all, if we want to engage in ethical deliberation, then we need to start *somewhere*. We might as well start with the products of the human conversation to date. As Ronald Dworkin acknowledges, "justice ... has a history," and each reinterpretation of it is "built on the rearrangements of practice and attitudes achieved by the last."[82] Thus we can take available formulations of principles[83] as starting hypotheses. We remain ready to examine our biases and the historic contingency of current formulations. We are prepared to argue for alterations to existing principles and ideas based on the best available arguments.

A core theme of this chapter is that analysis of principles of justice is not a set of moral deductions, applying some "ultimate ethical algorithm."[84] The coherentist accepts that we will not develop a mechanical procedure that can generate correct ethical answers to complex questions; there will always be an element of judgement, and hence we need deliberation and conversation.[85] We work with human-created, fallible ideas, and we do so with human-created, fallible processes. But that is the best and only process through which to try to discuss the normative justifiability of practices, laws, and institutions. Thus we should embrace the contingency, fallibility, and humanity of the conversation. As Richard Rorty has argued, "to accept the contingency of starting points is to accept our inheritance from, and our conversation with, our fellow humans as our only source of guidance."[86] Reflecting these themes of humanity and fallibility, he argues:

> Since Kant, philosophers hope to find the a priori structure of any possible inquiry or language or form of social life. If we give up this hope, we shall lose what Nietzsche called "metaphysical comfort," but we may gain a renewed sense of community. ... Our glory is in our participation in fallible and transitory human projects, not in our obedience to permanent nonhuman constraints.[87]

My account is "non-foundational," by which I simply mean I am not *relying* on any particular foundation. The account could perhaps even be described as foundationally "pluralist"[88]: participants in the conversation can draw plausible arguments from different moral theories where they appear to be illuminating, even if we do not yet have a meta-theory that explains how those theories are ultimately tied together. Science does precisely the same, employing *models* in contexts in which

---

[82] Dworkin, *supra* note 46, at 73–74.
[83] For example, that the culpability principle requires that the accused must have participated in or facilitated a crime to be a party to it.
[84] Tremblay, *supra* note 45, at 504 (the quest for the "ultimate ethical algorithm").
[85] Rorty, *supra* note 68, at 164.
[86] Rorty, *supra* note 68, at 166.
[87] Ibid.
[88] Merges, *Justifying*, *supra* note 43.

they are helpful, even if there are unresolved inconsistencies with other models that work in other contexts, until such time as better models emerge.[89]

My account is *melioristic,* meaning that I believe we can improve our institutions, practices, doctrines, and even our formulations of principles through thought and effort. While the principles may be human constructs, we can still strive to develop *better* human constructs. "Better" formulations are ones that better reconcile all of the available clues and inputs.

In the proposed method, we can take existing mid-level principles (e.g. culpability, legality) as provisional starting points. We can then further specify, adjust, or even add or remove principles based on the best available arguments and inputs. Those inputs include moral theories, patterns of practice, and considered judgements (casuistically testing our sense of justice of the outcomes in particular cases, including hypotheticals[90]). We seek "reflective equilibrium": we move back and forth among formulations of principles and our considered judgements of their outcomes in particular cases, adjusting our constructs or re-evaluating our judgements, to reconcile them as far as possible.[91] We look for *deductive* coherence (whether formulated principles match with our considered judgements in particular cases) and *analogical* coherence (whether those judgements fit with judgements in analogous cases). More profoundly, we look for *deliberative* coherence, i.e. whether formulated principles cohere with the plausible accounts of the underlying values and goals of the system.[92] Indeed, the enterprise of law itself may entail recognizing persons as agents, and thus we would seek coherence with "the inner morality of law."[93] The coherentist method also seeks *elegance* and *consilience.* For example,

---

[89] For example, utilitarian and deontological theories both seem to offer valuable insights into particular problems. It is sometimes argued that, because they are seemingly contrasting theories, it is untenable to invoke them both without at least providing a unifying meta-theory. However, I do not think this is necessarily a problem. For example, suppose science offers two seemingly rival theories: that electrons are waves, and that electrons are particles. Each theory is good for handling some problems, but poor for handling others. No one would chide a scientist for invoking each model to handle the problems to which they are suited, even if she did not yet have a unifying meta-theory. On a coherentist model, she can justifiably proceed on the tentative supposition, based on all of the available clues, that both models seem to be valuable and that there probably is a good unifying meta-theory even if it has not yet been articulated.

[90] See Tremblay, *supra* note 46. Markus Dubber explores the "sense of justice," arguing that it involves empathic role-taking with others as fellow moral persons: M D Dubber, *The Sense of Justice: Empathy in Law and Punishment* (Universal Law, 2006). Marjolein Cupido explains casuistic reasoning in M Cupido, *Facts Matter: A Study into the Casuistry of Substantive International Criminal Law* (Eleven International. 2015).

[91] Rawls, *supra* note 35, at 29–32.

[92] Proposals that improve the coherence between the constraints of a system and its aims have an increased plausibility: see, e.g., J Gardner, "Introduction," to G L A Hart, *Punishment and Responsibility,* 2nd ed (Oxford University Press, 2008) at xii–xxxi (constraints and aims of punishment).

[93] L Fuller, *The Morality of Law* (Yale University Press, 1964); K Rundle, *Forms Liberate: Reclaiming the Jurisprudence of Lon L Fuller* (Oxford University Press, 2012).

a simple principle that convincingly explains multiple features of legal practice offers more explanatory coherence than a disjointed series of ad hoc stipulations.[94]

4.3.3 Objections and Clarifications

In this section, I discuss the most important objections to coherentism – namely, conservativism, fallibility, and untidiness.[95]

Conservativism

The most common initial objection is that this method sounds like it cannot be radical. After all, if we work with practice, then we are just going to replicate the practice. However, this reaction underestimates the ambitiousness of coherentism. Coherence is not mere superficial consistency. As I have mentioned, in a coherentist method of identifying the deontic principles, we draw on *all available clues*. We look at patterns of practice for clues about underlying insights of justice, which can include comparative analysis (looking at other jurisdictions, other areas of law, or possibly even other social practices). We look at normative arguments and practical reason, as well as intuition and considered judgements in casuistic testing. We seek coherence in the deepest sense with what appear to be the best understandings of the underlying values.[96] Thus the coherentist method does not simply replicate existing practice.

As Rorty argues, the holistic process of reconciling clues "often does require us to change radically our views on particular subjects."[97] Similarly, Dworkin responds to the conservativism objection by arguing that once "we grasp the difference between [coherence] and narrow consistency," we may come to see that coherence "is a More dynamic and radical standard than it first seemed," because it encourages us to be wide-ranging and imaginative in the search for deep coherence.[98]

I submit that the coherentist process of testing incompatible beliefs and practices has engendered numerous radical changes in human history.[99] Consider, for

---

[94] Amaya, *supra* note 46, at 394–96.
[95] There are many other possible objections. In the interests of space, I am canvassing the strongest and most salient ones. For much more detailed analysis, see Amaya, *supra* note 46, at 57–73, 143–44, 178–87, 308–10, 370–72, 410–12 and 532 (including as to the truth-conduciveness of coherence).
[96] As noted earlier, there may be values and constraints implicit in the enterprise of law itself, e.g. if law is predicated on treating individuals as responsible agents, then its doctrines and principles should reflect that: Fuller, *supra* note 93; Rundle, *supra* note 93.
[97] Rorty, *supra* note 68, at 168. See also M Sullivan & D J Solove, "Radical Pragmatism," in A Malachowski, ed, *The Cambridge Companion to Pragmatism* (Cambridge University Press, 2013) arguing that although the pragmatist method is often perceived as "banal," it can be radical in critically assessing both means and ends.
[98] Dworkin, *supra* note 46, at 220. (Dworkin uses the term "integrity," rather than "coherence," but the term "integrity" refers to legal and moral coherence: *ibid* at 176.)
[99] In this argument, I am making a descriptive claim about how I believe most people in fact engage in moral reasoning. I do not believe that most people start with a particular foundational theory and then deduce correct actions from it. I think people work with a mass of principles, articulated at different

example, the abolition of slavery. Slavery was not abolished because someone proved its unsoundness through analytical deduction from an abstract construct, such as the Aristotelian conception of equality. (Indeed, in his formal model, Aristotle carved out an exception for slaves, alleging their "slave nature."[100]) Instead, arguments drew on diverse important ideas such as freedom, dignity, equality, and happiness. Attempts to justify slavery were repeatedly exposed as jarringly inconsistent with other widely and firmly held moral beliefs, and hinged on fallacies and unconvincing rationalizations.[101] Empathy and intuition, which are sometimes regarded as suspect or inferior to analytical reason in moral philosophy, played an important role.[102] Importantly, many people raised in slave-owning societies, who had been conditioned to accept the practice as "normal," came to change their minds through this process of reflection and argumentation. (I am not attempting to touch on all facets of abolition, such as the racism or paternalism among abolitionists, or the vital contribution of slave uprisings and activists who had escaped slavery; I am simply pointing out that the moral arguments were not a matter of demonstrated deduction from an agreed comprehensive theory. The debate was based on a wide range of considerations, showing the incompatibility of this abhorrent institution with the available web of moral clues.)

Notice the difference here between (i) broad coherence and (ii) superficial consistency among a limited set of propositions. Many slave-owning societies (such as the United States) also espoused principles of equality. At the time, slave-owners argued that slavery was consistent with principles of equality by alleging that they applied only between free people and not enslaved people, who were positioned as something "other." At a superficial level, *consistency* between the practice (slavery) and the principle (equality) might theoretically be achieved either by abolishing

---

levels of generality or specificity, taking the readily available inputs (e.g. considered judgements) and working in a manner akin to reflective equilibrium.

[100] Aristotle, *Politics* (Clarendon Press, 1910) at 1254b 16–21. This is precisely the problem with analytical deductions from abstract constructs: while they purport to be logically pure, they may actually be as distorted and unreliable as any other construct. The best we can do is to constantly test our deductions from any one theory using other theories and judgements (and, iteratively, constantly testing those theories and judgements with other theories and judgements).

[101] An example of this mélange of arguments – consistent with a coherentist method rather than a linear deduction from a single value – is the 1841 presentation by John Quincy Adams in the *Amistad* case, which used each of these points of reference. The statement is available online at https://avalon .law.yale.edu/19th_century/amistad_002.asp.

[102] The slavery example also shows how "intuition" can play different roles and how no source of clues is entirely reliable. Some people in slave-owning societies had been socialized to see the institution as "natural" – particularly those who benefited from the institution. Thus intuition is not necessarily a well spring of wisdom; it is merely one of the clues we take into account in the search for coherence. Reflective equilibrium calls on us to critically assess even our own intuitive reactions. In the slavery example, we might notice that persons whose intuitions were not disturbed by slavery had all undergone particular social conditioning to produce that indifference. We might also discover, through analogical testing, that their indifference is severely inconsistent with their reactions to analogous cases. Testing for these types of bias and anomaly would give us reason to doubt those intuitions.

the practice or by declaring a limitation to the principle. But which is the more normatively convincing answer, all things considered? Coherence is a more ambitious and deeper concept than mere consistency among a limited set of propositions: coherence requires us to draw widely on all available clues, including normative arguments, casuistic testing of our judgements based on empathic role-taking, and noticing biases or argumentative fallacies that have previously led us astray. There is little question that the coherent reconciliation of the full spectrum of available clues is that slavery is wrong.

The example illustrates another merit of coherentism. A proponent of a comprehensive theory rooted in a single value (e.g. freedom, dignity, happiness) might argue that the real problem with slavery was its contradiction of the single value cherished by that theory. But there are many possible values that would entail a rejection of slavery and many possible theories that could draw on those values with different emphases. Often, we will have vastly more confidence in a mid-level determination (e.g. slavery is wrong) than we have about which supportive theory is the correct one. Coherentism allows us to act on that mid-level determination even if we do not know which underlying theory is the ultimately correct one.

The process of continually revising our body of beliefs to better reconcile ideas and experiences is even more ambitious than the foregoing discussion suggests, because it is *iterative*. Each revision of practices and beliefs in turn enables people to notice, analogically, other practices that conflict with better conceptions of equality. Over time, numerous practices that once seemed natural have gradually come to be recognized to be discriminatory in various ways. For example, the institution of marriage, which was until recent decades seen as "inherently" between a man and a woman, has been revised in many societies to include same-sex partners and thus to better reflect equality principles. This continual, iterative revision of beliefs and practices is coherentism at work.

My point is that coherentist methods can require radical changes in our beliefs and practices. The continual effort to reconcile our principles, theories, judgements, and practices can lead to the discovery of previously unnoticed latent conflicts. Coherence can therefore require dramatic revision of our beliefs or practices in particular areas.

There is another, narrower, version of the "conservatism" objection: since coherentist theories start with pre-existing beliefs (or, in this context, widely recognized principles), they may have a tendency to perpetuate received beliefs.[103] There is merit to this objection. For example, the account I suggest here provisionally accepts established formulations of principles as its working hypotheses. By accepting these historically contingent starting points, there is a risk that one may perpetuate past thinking and preclude radical thinking.

---

[103] See, e.g., Amaya, *supra* note 46, at 58, 371 and 474.

My response to this narrower objection is that any account has to start *somewhere*. The coherentist account accepts, as a starting point, the conversation that is already under way. It does so because no other more compelling starting point has been identified. If a more compelling starting point were identified, then coherence would require us to start with the new more compelling starting point, and the conversation would shift accordingly.

Consulting formulations developed in national and international practice is valuable as a "humility check" on our abstract theory-building. One could advance an entirely new normative theory and deduce from it a new set of principles for criminal law systems. However, if we were to look around the world and notice that no legal system on earth satisfies our proposed new requirements, we could rightly take that observation as a clue that there *might* be a problem in our new theory. Patterns of practice, which reflect the understandings of justice of thousands of practitioners over a great many years, are at least a worthwhile checkpoint.[104] Nonetheless, if there are powerful arguments for the new theory that outweigh the old conception, then the totality of available clues would lead us to adopt it.[105]

In §4.3, I spoke about "starting in the middle" – meaning starting with mid-level principles rather than with doctrines or with foundations. But there is another way in which we must always "start in the middle": temporally. We start *in media res* – "in the middle of the action." The story of criminal law, the story of ICL, and the story of criminal law theory are all already under way. Many doctrines and formulations of principles have already been developed, and certain conversations and debates are in progress. So we start from what has already gone before, we draw lessons and form theories, and we suggest modifications to what is there. Some starting assumptions may later turn out to be "wrong," but we nonetheless must start somewhere. As in the famous metaphor of Neurath's boat:

> We are like sailors who on the open sea must reconstruct their ship but are never able to start afresh from the bottom. Where a beam is taken away a new one must at once be put there, and for this the rest of the ship is used as support. In this way, by using the old beams and driftwood the ship can be shaped entirely anew, but only by gradual reconstruction.[106]

---

[104] Parenthetically, another possible objection is that reference to practice seems like a form of the naturalist fallacy – the leap from "is" to "ought." However, as just noted, we consider patterns of practice not to mindlessly replicate them, but out of humility, because they offer clues to understandings of justice worked out by others through extensive practice. Patterns of practice are a helpful common reference point, a valuable check on the imagination of any given individual, and a body of propositions that have at least been tested in practice.

[105] Thus this is not a Burkean conservative position warning against the unknown dangers of making any changes at all to established social institutions. It simply uses practice as a reference point, or possible "humility check," in assessing one's own judgements and constructs. Where it is nonetheless clear that practice should be reformed, then it should be reformed.

[106] O Neurath, "Anti-Spengler," in M Neurath & R Cohen, eds, *Empiricism and Sociology* (D Reidel, 1973) at 201.

Fallibility

The second common objection to the coherentist method is that it does not provide *certainty*. It relies on a series of inputs, each of which *might be wrong*. The objection is correct.

The coherentist method freely acknowledges that any of the inputs might be flawed. For example, familiar formulations of principles might replicate the biases or blind spots of past legal practitioners. Patterns of practice may be similarly problematic. The major ethical theories are contested human creations and may be gravely flawed. Our sense of justice, or intuition, about particular outcomes might sometimes mislead us: it may reflect our prejudices and social conditioning. (There are many possible objections to considering intuition,[107] but, in my view the best argument in favour of consulting our intuition is the absurdity of ignoring it.[108]) A coherentist account attempts to reduce error in each of the available imperfect inputs in the only way available to humans: by testing them against all of the other inputs.

An even greater danger still lurks: it is entirely possible that *every one* of those inputs (principles, practice, theories, and judgements) is erroneous. For example, they might very well all be distorted by the same bias, arising perhaps in the human mind or in the human meta-culture. Thus there is a possibility not merely of error, but of *massive* error.

The coherentist method acknowledges this as well. It acknowledges the fallibility of its inputs and its process, and hence the possibility of error, including potentially massive error. For many scholars and jurists, this acceptance of fallibility is a cause of considerable discomfort. But the response is: *there is no methodology* that furnishes moral certainty. There is no methodology that can guarantee freedom from error, or even from massive error.

The insistence upon or expectation of certainty in relation to ethical questions is itself deeply unsound; it is the Cartesian anxiety. The options actually available are either (i) a false pretense of certainty or (ii) a theory that openly acknowledges uncertainty, but which is committed to taking every possible measure for error-

---

[107]   The strongest objection is that appeals to intuition might reflect our conditioning and cannot be mistaken for infallible innate wisdom. The objection is, of course, correct. However, reflective equilibrium does not take intuition as infallible. Both our reasoning (analytical deductions from our constructed theories) and our intuition (reactions to concrete cases) can be wrong. That is why we use each to test the other as best we can. We search for deductive or analogical incoherence and try to inspect both our reasoning and our judgements. This process is obviously fallible, but no infallible process has been identified. The best we can do is test all available inputs against the other inputs.

[108]   It seems unthinkable that we would apply cerebrally constructed moral theories even when our instincts cry out that the results are monstrous. I think such reactions would be a clue that the moral theory might need re-examination. The coherentist approach sensibly uses all available clues. Markus Dubber convincingly argues that the sense of justice requires empathetic identification, and he rejects the dichotomy between emotion and rationality: Dubber, *supra* note 90, at 7–8, 52, 71–72, 83, 146.

correction (maximum corrigibility). The coherentist argues that the latter is the more mature and honest route. The coherentist abandons "the neurotic Cartesian quest for certainty."[109] Instead of seeking certainty, we simply seek to establish *better-justified* principles, drawing on all available arguments. We have uncertain information and uncertain starting points, and we have to make the best decisions we can with the best evidence and best tools we can produce. Science proceeds in the same way, often provisionally accepting uncertain hypotheses as starting points to see where they lead and generating helpful insights as a result.[110]

Untidiness and imprecision

A third set of objections is that the coherentist method is too untidy, imprecise, vague, or complex.[111] In other words, coherentism does not provide a clear enough "operator's manual" on precisely how to reconcile inconsistent clues to maximize coherence.

For example, where an outlying body of practice conflicts with a formulated principle, should we amend the practice, or is the practice a clue (reflecting sound insights about justice) that should lead to a reformulation or exception in the principle? When there is a conflict between national formulations, moral theories, or considered judgements, which should prevail? The coherentist method does not offer a mechanical protocol for such decisions; there may be plausible arguments for different solutions. Some coherentist thinkers have tried to articulate more precisely what people do when they seek to maximize coherence in their models.[112]

---

[109] Rorty, *supra* note 68, at 161. See also J T Kloppenberg, "Pragmatism: An Old Name for Some New Ways of Thinking?," in M Dickstein, ed, *The Revival of Pragmatism: New Essays on Social Thought, Law, and Culture* (Duke University Press, 1998) (discussing the debilitating "Cartesian anxiety" that demands "the grail of objective knowledge" and "timeless principles").

[110] For example, sciences started with a provisional assumption that the reports of our senses map in some way onto an external reality. Using the observations of those senses, humans developed theories, made deductions, and built tools that allowed them to learn ever more about the apparent world. We eventually learned that, e.g., the world is not composed of "solid objects" in the way that our senses report; instead, "matter" is overwhelmingly composed of empty space, with fields of energy generating what we perceive as "solidity." Similarly, our experience of "colour" turns out to be a subjective translation of certain forms of radiation. Thus science shows us some ways in which our senses are indeed unreliable. But we got there by starting with a provisional working hypothesis that senses are at least somewhat reliable clues.

If, instead, we had said that our senses are not reliable and thus declined to make any further investigations based on them, we would not have worked out that useful information, including about the limits of our senses. In the same manner, a provisional acceptance of familiar formulations, moral theories, and our intuitive responses provides at least a starting point for deliberations, even if the deliberations may lead us to change our minds about some of those inputs.

[111] Amaya, *supra* note 46, at 57, 143, 181–82.

[112] An illustrative and incomplete list includes: N MacCormack, "Coherence in Legal Justification," in A Peczenik, L Lindahl & B van Roermund, eds, *Theory of Legal Science* (Reidel, 1984); L BonJour, *The Structure of Empirical Knowledge* (Cambridge University Press, 1985); S Hurley, *Natural Reasons: Personality and Polity* (Oxford University Press, 1989); R Alexy & A Peczenik, "The Concept of Coherence and Its Significance for Discursive Rationality" (1990) 3 Ratio Iuris 130;

Nonetheless, as in science, there is still room to differ about how best to reconcile contradictory clues. For many people, the consideration of so many elements without a more explicit instruction manual is too untidy and vague, and thus leaves too much room for individual judgement.

The coherentist response is that it is simply an unrealistic expectation that a successful theory must provide a clear formula that mechanically generates morally correct answers. The world is complex. To return to the science analogy, when observations arise that are inconsistent with currently favoured models, scientists often differ on how to reconcile the conflicting clues. Some may adhere to the existing models, with the provisional expectation that the anomalies will be explained away; others may provisionally revise their models to better fit the data. Yet science is not beleaguered with complaints that there should be clear, mechanical rules dictating precisely when a model must be revised and how. Science is not infected with the idea that figuring out really complicated things should be simple.

In a coherentist method, we abandon the "quest for the ultimate ethical algorithm" that can deductively answer all of our moral queries.[113] Accordingly, reasonable people will at times disagree about how to prioritize and reconcile the clues, just as happens in science and every other field. We can only keep striving to collect better inputs, to detect unsound arguments and conclusions, and to develop better understandings. We cannot eliminate judgement and deliberation from moral reasoning.[114]

Conclusion

In conclusion, all three objections are *correct*: The coherentist approach does not guarantee certainty, it does not provide a precise operator's manual, and it draws on past thought and therefore might perpetuate old assumptions. However, these objections can be made against *any* method. There is no method that is certain, straightforward, and divorced from past thought.

These three objections (fallibility, untidiness, and contingency) are actually objections to the human condition. We have imperfect information and no definitive guidance, and the best we can do is do the best we can. Since we must build our structures on sand (i.e. lack of Cartesian certainty), we might as well acknowledge that we are doing so, and attempt to build structures that are as useful and reliable as possible, while also continuing to try to learn more about the sand.[115]

M DePaul, *Balance and Refinement: Beyond Coherence Methods of Moral Inquiry* (Routledge, 1993); H Richardson, *Practical Reasoning about Final Ends* (Cambridge University Press, 1994); P Thagard & K Verbeugt, "Coherence as Constraint Satisfaction" (1998) 22 Cognitive Science 1; K Lehrer, "Justification, Coherence and Knowledge" (1999) 50 Erkenntnis 243; Amaya, *supra* note 46.

[113] Tremblay, *supra* note 45, at 504 (the quest for the "ultimate ethical algorithm").

[114] Rorty, *supra* note 68, at 164 argues against the Platonic idea that we can substitute "method" for "deliberation."

[115] For those who remain uncomfortable with the coherentist method, regarding it as suspect, incomplete or unreliable, I can offer the following additional responses.

4.4 JUSTICE: A COHERENTIST CONVERSATION

In this final section, I outline some features of the envisaged coherentist conversation about the principles of justice.[116]

4.4.1 Resulting Framework for ICL Theory

(1) **Analytical and normative** First, we can use mid-level principles to work both *analytically* and *normatively*, and to work at different levels of abstraction or concreteness. Analytically, we can try to discern principles immanent within the practice, and we can identify doctrines that contradict the best understandings of the principles. Normatively, we can evaluate the competing formulations of principles, we can criticize problematic practices or even criticize principles, and we can try to clarify the best justificatory bases for doctrines. We can work more at the concrete end of the spectrum (assessing doctrines in light of accepted principles) or more at the abstract end of the spectrum (re-examining the principles). The particular emphasis of any given work will depend on the type of contribution it seeks to make, for example explanatory, justificatory, critical, or reconstructive.

(1) For those who prize "certainty," I agree that moral certainty would be *better*, but it is not available. If anyone demonstrates the "correct" moral theory, then I for one would happily root my arguments in the proven-correct moral theory. Until that time, however, we need some other approach.

(2) For those who prize "reliability," it is arguable that a foundationally pluralist account provides *more* reliability. Where multiple foundational theories could converge in supporting a mid-level principle, we should have *more* confidence in the principle than we would in any one theory. Because mid-level principles are formulated in particular contexts and with comparative precision, some people may support the principle even without knowing precisely which theory they favour in support. As Sunstein argues, for fallible human beings, caution and humility about theoretical claims are appropriate, at least when multiple theories can lead in the same direction. Sunstein, *supra* note 51, at 1769.

[116] When I say "conversation," I am emphasizing that refining our understandings is not a matter of mechanically applying an ethical proof; instead, it is a process we engage in as fallible humans, using fallible human processes, testing fallible human ideas, and building on the fallible human conversation that has gone before. Different participants with different experiences might draw on different inputs with different emphases; that interaction and debate can provide more clues and more inspiration about the best way forward. Conversations of this nature commonly feature disagreements, but they also feature points that become largely accepted – until such time as those accepted points are disrupted by new insights and better arguments.

I am attracted to the view that the "best" understanding is that which would be arrived at in an ideal conversation with all attainable information on hand and with all arguments properly considered. This is, of course, only an in-principle aspiration, because we will never achieve an ideal conversation, but I think it correctly states what coherentism strives for (best possible understandings, not ultimate truths). See, e.g., J Habermas, *Moral Consciousness and Communicative Action*, C Lenhart & S Weber Nicholson, trans (MIT Press, 1990) esp at 43–115; T Scanlon, *supra* note 36; Rawls, *supra* note 35, esp at xi; Rorty, *supra* note 68, esp at 160–66.

(2) **External and internal** A conversation about fundamental principles of justice can adopt a perspective that is both *external* and *internal* to the field of ICL. What I mean is that fundamental principles are both an external normative yardstick by which to judge the system, but they are also internally recognized by the system as interpretive guides or even imperatives. Thus, if we identify a doctrine that conflicts with the best understanding of a fundamental principle, we can make external or internal kinds of claim, and indeed we can make both at the same time. From an external perspective, we could say that the system has failed to meet an important normative standard and criticize it for this failing. From an internal perspective, we could say that the apparent doctrine conflicts with fundamental principles, and thus it is *"incorrect"* and needs to be reinterpreted to conform. Fundamental principles are both external tools for criticism and evaluation and internal tools for clarification and reform.

(3) **No fixed priority** There is no single fixed priority among the three commonly used sources of reference I have discussed. These sources are articulations of principles in ICL itself, general principles derived from national systems, and normative argumentation. Each can properly be used in developing our views, but no one of them is paramount.[117] Indeed, we use each source to better evaluate, specify, and understand the others.[118] Each source has different strengths, and each is important for different purposes (analytical, comparative, normative). The emphasis appropriately accorded to each depends on the project. For example, a doctrinal project might accord internal formulations the highest priority, but even that project will be informed by induction from national systems and by normative reflection. For a normative project, the hierarchy might seem to be the reverse, with moral theories being the most important. But simple hierarchies still elude us. For example, scrutiny of national and international practice might reveal insights requiring us to revise our normative theories. Even in a normative account, it is valuable to start with mid-level principles and to consult practice. Doing so helps us to stay tethered, with humble awareness that even the foundational moral theories are also human constructs.[119] Thus the process is necessarily

---

[117] Similarly, Coleman, *supra* note 40, at 56 declines to assign fixed "priority" among the practice, the principles, and the theories.

[118] For example, a review of national and international practice might reveal plausible underlying intuitions of justice that lead us to revise our philosophical suppositions. Our philosophical reflections may lead us to discern patterns in the commonalities of national systems not previously noticed.

[119] Sunstein, *supra* note 51, at 1762:

> But we might think instead that there is no special magic in theories or abstractions, and that theories are simply the (humanly constructed) means by which people make sense of the judgements that constitute their ethical, legal, and political worlds. The abstract deserves no priority over the particular; neither should be treated as foundational. A (poor or crude) abstract theory may simply be a confused way of trying to make sense of our considered judgements about particular constitutional cases, which may be better than the theory.

recursive and untidy. I think that the back-and-forth process, oscillating between practices, principles, theories, and judgements, looking at analytical "fit" and advancing normative justification or criticism, is an essential part of a grounded normative theory *about* international criminal law.

(4) **A framework for frameworks** I am outlining the general framework for a conversation that can incorporate multiple plausible frameworks. I have tried to frame my remarks generally enough to leave space for different outlooks.[120] The justice conversation is inclusive and pluralist, and descends as needed into ethical theories. The method is non-foundational, but it is still receptive to foundational theories as ways of framing a question and potentially generating helpful insights. A coherentist conversation can still draw on the main moral theories not as ultimate truths, but as *models* (i.e. they can show what the implications are if one focuses on a given set of values or adopts a given set of premises).[121] Contributors to the conversation may bring insights drawing on very different foundational theories; a foundationally pluralist conversation is receptive to such arguments. Fortunately, a lot of work can be done with mid-level principles without having to descend into their underpinnings or decide between theories. However, there may be liminal cases in which it is necessary to do so. For example, what is it about human beings that requires us to afford them respectful treatment? Scholars refer variously to attributes such as agency, autonomy, dignity, the capacity for reason-directed behavior, personhood, worth, and so on. For most criminal law problems, we simply would not need to isolate precisely which attributes generate which obligations. However, it is at least conceivable that some criminal law problem may arise that requires us to specify the relevant attribute with more precision or to decide between different foundational theories. The conversation descends as needed into ethical theories.

(5) **Conversation versus contribution** When I map out the numerous possible inputs for a coherentist analysis, that does not mean that any given contribution

---

[120] For example, when I speak of "deontic" commitments, I speak in classic terms: a duty to the individual that will be honoured even when it does not maximize the social desiderata of typical consequentialist accounts. But it is also possible to advance arguments from "moderate" or "threshold" deontology, which permits overrides in the most extreme circumstances. It is possible that moderate deontology has something fruitful to add to the conversation. At the moment, however, we do not seem to have arrived at any conundrum that requires ICL to make a choice on that question. See, e.g., discussion in M S Moore, *Placing Blame: A General Theory of Criminal Law* (Oxford University Press, 1997) at 719–24; T Nagel, *Mortal Questions* (Cambridge University Press, 1979) at 62–63; S Kagan, *Normative Ethics* (Avalon, 1998) at 78–94.

[121] Again, this is the same method as is used in science. The overall method is coherentist, which can entail use of one or more "models." Where a model has been successful, we can even use it to generate (provisional) deductions, and a highly successful model will be widely adopted. Nonetheless, even the most successful model is still a provisional tool and can be discarded on coherentist grounds, such as when a model offering even better coherence emerges.

will have all of those features. For example, it is not feasible that any single contribution will canvass all national systems and all moral theories. I am simply aiming to outline some of the tools and moves that can be usefully employed. Different contributors will bring their different perspectives and expertise to bear on different topics of interest. For example, my own contributions will often draw on English-speaking theorists and common law ideas, because that is my experience and expertise, and it is the best way for me to add value to the conversation at this stage. But, in doing so, I will strive to engage with the ideas of others, who draw on different literatures and legal traditions, in the hopes of building something together that is non-parochial. It will be important for the broader conversation to continue with diverse inputs from diverse contributors, to build more thoughtful, durable, and inclusive understandings of the principles.

(6) **Hypotheses, not answers** Finally, the justice conversation will not produce definitive *answers*. At best, it provides *working hypotheses* about fundamental principles. The conversation is nonetheless valuable because it requires us to grapple with questions of justice. The discourse around mass atrocity is often dominated by revulsion and the wish that someone be punished; the justice conversation recalls that we must consider the constraints of justice. Of course, there are very different plausible views once we try to specify the principles. (Is causal contribution required for culpability, and if so, what does it mean?[122] Is criminal negligence sufficient for culpability?[123]) We will never arrive at conclusive "answers" to these questions. In any human enterprise, the best we can do is make our best efforts to work out the normative underpinnings and to comply with them.

4.4.2 A Theory of Criminal Law Theory

I also think that "mid-level principles" (along with coherentist reconciliation of clues) offers the best explanation of much of the scholarship and juridical practice that works with deontic principles and criminal law theory. I mentioned at the outset that scholarship and juridical argument tend to draw on the three different sources even though each is flawed. They often do so without explaining why we can draw on those three sources in what might seem to be a hodge-podge. One might expect that I would go on to declare a more correct methodology, or unveil a fourth source of reference. Instead, however, I have concluded that most criminal law theory of ICL to date is best explained and best supported as an application of coherentist methods. Scholars are generally drawing on the web of available clues to construct the best understanding that they can of the principles, as opposed to rooting

[122] See Chapter 7.
[123] See Chapter 8.

principles in axiomatic or epistemically privileged foundational propositions. If so, my contribution here is largely to make explicit some of the implicit underpinnings of these efforts.

I close with two clarifications in response to reader queries. First, some readers have understood the proposed approach as seeking to avoid taking any normative positions at all. To be clear, the coherentist approach avoids subscribing to any particular *foundational theory* as the established source of moral truth, but it does not avoid normative debate. On the contrary, as I have explained, the approach engages extensively with normative ideas and normative arguments in an effort to arrive at the most defensible normative positions (and subject to revision based on new arguments). My argument is that we do so by drawing on the web of available clues rather than deducing them from privileged first principles.

A second question is whether coherentism is suitable only for ICL or criminal law theory, or does it have broader applications. As I hope I have explained, coherentism is a general approach to forming beliefs. I have highlighted it here because I believe it to be an underappreciated alternative to a typical scholarly reflex: the Cartesian, "classical foundationalist" expectation that premises should ideally be grounded securely in underlying theories, reaching down to a reliable foundation. My impression is that many scholars assume that the classical foundationalist model is the "proper" standard, but they intuitively apply coherentist methods to work on particular problems. Such scholars have at times operated semi-apologetically, as if they are bad or incomplete foundationalists, when actually they might be good coherentists. For example, I think these thoughts of John Gardner are best explained and justified by a coherentist method:

> My attempts to write an introduction that would paint the bigger picture were unsuccessful, because there is no bigger picture. I don't have a theory of law, let alone what Ernest Weinrib calls a "comprehensive theoretical position ... [with] broad philosophical vistas." I have quite a lot of thoughts about law in general and I can only hope that they turn out to be consistent with one other.[124]

Highlighting the coherentist alternative, and making the implicit methodology more explicit, can help us to build better arguments with a coherentist conception of rigour, and it can help us to better recognize the limitations of our conclusions.

In my view, coherentism is not only defensible, but also preferable as the methodological basis for mid-level theory work. Consciousness of the strengths and limitations of the coherentist method can help us to advance arguments that are more rigorous – rigorous not in a classic Cartesian structure, but in a coherentist structure, relying on the web of available clues.

---

[124] J Gardner, *Law as Leap of Faith* (Oxford University Press, 2012) at v.

4.4.3 Conclusion

The justice conversation is a fallible, human conversation working with fallible, human constructs – but that does not make it superficial or meaningless. Many readers will be tempted to reject an approach that does not guarantee that the constructs map onto "true" justice. But we are faced with three alternatives.

The first is for someone to discover and demonstrate the guaranteed correct theory of justice. That has not happened yet, despite centuries of deliberation.[125]

The second alternative is to give up. Giving up seems far more bankrupt than *trying* to work with the best available evidence. If we care about morality and justice, then we have to try to discuss our practices and institutions – their aims and constraints, and the overall justifications and possible improvement.

The third, and only remaining, alternative is to accept that working with the best available clues is the only practicable moral option we have.

The best and only assurance that our constructs map onto something meaningful is that our analytical reasoning and intuitive responses tell us so. Thus the justice conversation may be fallible, human, contingent, and provisional, but it is nonetheless vital.

---

[125] If someone does discover it, then the coherentist approach would immediately merge with the foundationalist approach in that area, because working with the best clues and models would obviously entail embracing a "guaranteed correct" model.

5

Criminal Law Theory *in Extremis*

OVERVIEW

In this chapter, I outline how the proposed approach can raise new questions, both for ICL and for general criminal law theory.

The study of extreme cases can unsettle and refine our understandings of the principles developed in everyday experience. I will show how studying ICL problems may require us to unpack the roles traditionally played by the state in criminal law thinking, and to re-examine many familiar tools of criminal law thought (such as "community," "citizenship," and "authority"). The criminal law theory of ICL might draw on "cosmopolitan" scholarship, which contemplates forms of governance other than the state, and which is therefore particularly challenging for mainstream criminal law thinking.

I will also highlight "promising problems" in ICL. Exploring such problems can help us to refine ICL doctrines and also make contributions to mainstream criminal law theory. These problems include: legality without a legislature; a humanistic account of duress and social roles; and superior orders and state authority. I will then delve even more deeply into a select set of controversies in Chapters 6–8 to demonstrate the method at work and thereby clarify the method, the work it can do, and the themes it raises.

5.1 NEW CHALLENGES FOR CRIMINAL LAW THEORY

A central aim of this book is to bring criminal law theory to bear on ICL problems. More specifically, I am laying the groundwork for tackling questions of justice and criminal law theory in the unusual contexts of ICL. It turns out, however, that doing so is not simply a matter of applying the accumulated wisdom of general criminal law theory to ICL problems. Instead, the process provides insights in two directions. ICL raises new problems and new questions that have not necessarily been considered in mainstream criminal law theory. The study of ICL problems leads us into some largely unexplored territory, in which we lose the familiar backdrop for most criminal law thinking. ICL invites us to imagine a much more general account of criminal justice, which encompasses new, unusual, or extreme conditions. Thus the endeavour may also generate new insights for mainstream criminal law theory.

5.1.1 The Normal Case and the Special Case

Criminal law scholars and practitioners have, with the benefit of long experience and debate, been developing a fairly elaborate set of propositions about the requirements of criminal justice. The contemporary conversations feature many points of broad agreement and many points of dispute. These debates have generally taken place in one particular context: the "normal" context – that is, the practice of criminal law as known in the modern state. In the normal context, criminal law is applied by authorities of a single modern state to human individuals within that state's jurisdiction. The state has the familiar Westphalian features, which include, for example, a claim to paramount authority within a territory and branches of government playing different roles (legislature, judiciary, and executive). Generally, the model assumes a functioning state and relative stability, so that criminal activity is usually deviant from social norms.

These assumptions are entirely understandable and appropriate given experience with criminal law in recent centuries. Jurists and scholars were correct to focus on the normal case, to try to systematize and make fair the apparatuses of criminal law actually affecting the lives of human persons.

However, the study of "special" cases can lead us to reconsider our theories built on the "normal" cases, by requiring us to notice subtleties and underpinnings. In doing so, we can build a more "general" theory. To draw an analogy with physics, we may have a workable understanding of "mass" or "time" in our common everyday life on Earth, and yet observations near a black hole, or at relativistic speeds, may lead us to realize that these concepts contain subtleties that we had not detected in our everyday experience. It is not that the deeper concepts of "mass" or "time" are *different* on Earth or near a black hole; it is that inherent conditions, limitations, or parameters that are not prominent in "normal" conditions become more noticeable in a different context.

In a similar manner, the study of special cases from ICL may enrich general criminal law theory. We might notice and explore assumptions underpinning articulations of fundamental principles, or indeed other assumptions of criminal law theory. We might even reconsider the role of the state itself, as well as common tools of thought in criminal law theory, as I will explain in a moment.

Issues that are marginal or peripheral in the "normal" case, and hence which can be set aside or ignored in mainstream theory, can become central in ICL and demand more attentive reflection. To return to the physics analogy, it was the study of seemingly "peripheral" issues that ultimately led to paradigm shifts in basic concepts.[1]

---

[1]   T Kuhn, *The Structure of Scientific Revolutions* (University of Chicago Press, 1962).

I have already touched on examples of ICL's special challenges in Chapter 3. Crimes of mass coordination require us to consider the outer limits of inculpating doctrines, which may refine our understanding of culpability. ICL more frequently encounters crimes that are arguably causally overdetermined, which can help us more precisely confront causation and culpability in such circumstances.[2] Crimes of obedience raise questions about deviance and wrongdoing. Criminal governments overturn the normal role of the state as lawprovider. The alternative means of law creation under ICL call for reflection on the parameters of fair warning and the requirements of the legality principle. These and other special problems can lead us to learn more about the principles used in everyday experience.

Let me be clear: I am not suggesting that ICL requires a different concept of justice merely because it is international. I have not suggested that ICL is entirely different from criminal law, or that ICL theory is entirely different from national criminal law theory, or that national criminal law never encounters difficult or extreme cases.[3] What I have said is that ICL can present new contexts and problems, and that *salient differences* in context can help us to reconsider underlying suppositions and clarify ideas in ways that we would not have if we thought only about the normal case (i.e. the normal contexts of domestic criminal law). This might lead us to recognize some caveat or limit or problem with a proposition that previously seemed sound. Familiar propositions might contain an assumption about citizenship, community, a unitary state, or the legislative role that require rethinking when the assumption proves incorrect. My suggestion here is akin to Scanlon's conception of "parametric universalism": sometimes, the same underlying principle might generate different rules where there are salient differences in context.[4]

5.1.2 The Cosmopolitan Challenge to the State-Centric Account

In Chapter 3, I suggested a "humanistic" account; in Chapter 4, I added that the approach should also be "coherentist." I now add the proposal that an account should also be "cosmopolitan," which is a partial challenge to state-centric thinking and thus is potentially perplexing for criminal law theory.

---

[2]   J Stewart, "Overdetermined Atrocities" (2012) 10 JICL 1189.
[3]   For example, I emphasized that national criminal law and theory also deals with collective crimes (§3.3.1) and with problems of constrained agency (§3.3.1).
[4]   TM Scanlon, *What We Owe to Each Other* (Harvard University Press, 1998) at 329. For example, a society in a cold climate might have a rule about always helping a driver whose car has broken down, while a society in a warm climate might not have such a rule, and yet the two different rules may both be consistent with an underlying principle about helping others who are in great danger when it is safe to do so.

The term "cosmopolitanism" has been used in international relations and international legal theory literature,[5] as well as in ICL literature,[6] with differing connotations, but there are three main recurring features. First, cosmopolitanism does not assume the centrality of states to the extent that many other theories do; cosmopolitanism focuses on *human agents* rather than on states per se. Cosmopolitanism regards states as one historically contingent coordination device created by humans to advance human ends. Cosmopolitans are prepared to see states supplemented by other governance structures as needed.[7] This outlook is particularly salient for the study of ICL, because ICL embraces alternative governance structures to supplement state structures and enables them to apply law directly.[8]

Second, cosmopolitan regard for others does not stop at the boundaries of one's own state.[9] This is not to say that borders do not matter at all or that cosmopolitanism is a utopic fantasy. Cosmopolitanism acknowledges the contemporary sociopolitical constructs of states; hence borders do matter, and we may be more involved with members of our own polity. But we also have concern and regard for all human beings. This feature of cosmopolitanism also seems necessary to understand and explain ICL, because ICL delineates violations that are not only of domestic concern, but also of international concern, and hence may be transnationally prosecuted.

Third, cosmopolitanism searches for commonalities between cultures, but it also recognizes and respects differences, and hence it embraces pluralism and the building of a *modus vivendi*.[10] Cosmopolitanism is sometimes incorrectly conflated with universalism, but such conflation misses the key nuances of cosmopolitanism. Cosmopolitanism is a deliberate contrast with universalism: it does not assume that

5   K Appiah, *Cosmopolitanism: Ethics in a World of Strangers* (WW Norton & Co, 2006); D Archibugi, D Held & M Köhler, *Re-imagining Political Community: Studies in Cosmopolitan Democracy* (Stanford University Press, 1998); D Archibugi, "Immanuel Kant, Cosmopolitan Law and Peace" (1995) 1 Eur J Int'l Rel 429; S Benhabib, *Another Cosmopolitanism* (Oxford University Press, 2006); C R Beitz, *Political Theory and International Relations* (Princeton University Press, 1999); J Bohman & M Lutz-Bachmann, eds, *Perpetual Peace: Essays on Kant's Cosmopolitan Ideal* (MIT Press, 1997); D Held, *Democracy and the Global Order: From the Modern State to Cosmopolitan Governance* (Polity, 1995); S van Hooft, *Cosmopolitanism: A Philosophy for Global Ethics* (Cambridge University Press, 2009); T W Pogge, "Cosmopolitanism and Sovereignty" (1992) 103 Ethics 48; R Vernon, *Cosmopolitan Regard: Political Membership and Global Justice* (Cambridge University Press, 2010).

6   G Simpson, *Law, War and Crime: War Crimes Trials and the Reinvention of International Law* (Polity, 2007) at 12, 24, 30–36 and 44–46; M Drumbl, *Atrocity, Punishment, and International Law* (Cambridge University Press, 2007) at 19–20, 185–86; D Hirsh, *Law against Genocide: Cosmopolitan Trials* (Routledge, 2003); P Hayden, "Cosmopolitanism and the Need for Transnational Criminal Justice: The Case of the International Criminal Court" (2004) 104 Theoria 69.

7   See e.g., Beitz, *supra* note 5, at 6, 53, 182; Held, *supra* note 5, at 233–35; J Habermas, "Kant's Idea of Perpetual Peace, with the Benefit of Two Hundred Years' Hindsight," in Bohman & Lutz-Bachmann, *supra* note 5, at 128–29.

8   On ICL and cosmopolitan de-emphasis of the state, see D Koller, "The Faith of the International Criminal Lawyer" (2008) 40 NYU J Int'l L & Pol 1019 at 1052; Simpson, *supra* note 6, at 46; D Luban, "State Criminality and the Ambition of International Criminal Law," in T Isaacs & R Vernon, eds, *Accountability for Collective Wrongdoing* (Cambridge University Press, 2011).

9   Pogge, *supra* note 5, at 49.

10 See, e.g. Appiah, *supra* note 5, at xv, 96–99, 144, 151; van Hooft, *supra* note 5, at 164–69.

we share all the same values. Instead, it assumes that those with different outlooks have enough common ground at least to carry out a *conversation*.[11] Similarly, some warn that cosmopolitanism might be invoked as a mask for hegemony, but this is an objection to failed or false cosmopolitanism; it is not an objection to the prescription of genuine conversation.[12] Interestingly, the cosmopolitan prescription of a genuine conversation is in very much the same spirit as the coherentist method I outlined in Chapter 4.[13]

Cosmopolitanism's departure from a state-centric approach is both very challenging and very promising for criminal law theory. Cosmopolitanism recognizes states as important and prominent centres of authority in the contemporary arrangement of social and political life. However, states are not the *only* possible centre of authority. Cosmopolitanism understands individuals not only as citizens of a given state, but also as members of overlapping networks. A cosmopolitan imagination can easily envisage a "neo-medieval" landscape, featuring overlapping and diverse governance structures.[14]

By contrast, criminal law theory traditionally – and entirely understandably, given the normal historic experience – assumes the modern state as its centrepiece. Most thinking about criminal law regards each country as a separate and more-or-less closed microcosm, with a few peripheral cases of overlapping jurisdiction. Thus criminal law problems are discussed as if the relevant players are that one state and the individual inhabitants. In this picture, one can readily rely on concepts such as citizenship or community to help to explain aspects of criminal law.

ICL, which contemplates the unmediated application of law to individuals by international governance mechanisms,[15] provides many examples that do not readily

---

[11] On a universalist account, I would be trying to discover the deep, "true," universal answers for the "correct" formulation of fundamental principles. I am talking instead about a conversation, in which the participants may have different viewpoints and in which there may be multiple plausible formulations. See Chapter 4.

[12] See, e.g. M Koskenniemi, *"Humanity's Law*, Ruti G. Teitel"* (2012) 26 Ethics & International Affairs 395 (book review); R Mani, *Beyond Retribution: Seeking Justice in the Shadows of War* (Wiley, 2002) at 47–48. Such objections are not a reason to decline to *attempt* a genuine cosmopolitan conversation; they are reminders that we must act with humility, caution about our assumptions, and open-mindedness to other views. See Chapters 4 and 5.

[13] For example, as K Appiah writes, cosmopolitans suppose that persons from different cultures have enough overlap in their vocabulary to begin a conversation. They do not suppose, like some universalists, that we could all come to an agreement if only we had the same vocabulary. See Appiah, *supra* note 5, at 57. Appiah also notes that we might agree on a practice even if we do not agree on the underlying justification. *Ibid* at 67. There are clear parallels with coherentist ideas discussed in Chapter 4 (sufficient vocabulary for conversation, incompletely theorized agreements).
  Similarly, Monica Hakimi, while not explicitly adopting the label "cosmopolitan," advances cosmopolitan ideas when she argues that a community (including the international community) does not require consensus on all values and is not necessarily diminished by discord; instead, a community is partially constituted by its conflicts and disagreements and its efforts to manage disagreements. M Hakimi, "Constructing an International Community" (2017) 111 AJIL 317.

[14] Held, *supra* note 5, at 224–34; Habermas, *supra* note 7, at 128–29.

[15] See generally J K Cogan, "The Regulatory Turn in International Law" (2011) 52 Harvard Int'l LJ 322.

fit this familiar picture. ICL can help us to see that the familiar picture (normal criminal law in a functioning state) is only an *example* of the more general possibilities of criminal law. Although many regard the state as a strictly essential requirement for criminal law, we might find on inspection that what is really required is not the entire package of the modern Westphalian state, but rather certain *features* of the state. We might also see how those features could be allocated differently or vested in other institutions. The emergence of new institutions, such as international courts, can help us to separate out different threads that might be bundled together in the context of a state, giving us a more thorough understanding of what is needed.

A more general theory of the practice of criminal law requires a bigger imagination about the potential configurations of criminal law. We may find that criminal law does not necessarily require a "state" per se; perhaps what is needed can be stated in even more general terms (e.g. public authority). We would then have to explore the ramifications of criminal law under different types of authority structure.

5.1.3 Unpacking "the State," and Common Tools of Thought

I am suggesting, contrary to typical thinking about criminal law, that "the State" is not necessarily always the central and indispensable character. Of course, as a matter of positive law, ICL institutions exercise authority delegated by states. Furthermore, states are obviously ubiquitous in ICL: they may bestow jurisdiction or compete for jurisdiction, they carry out arrests, they shape ICL doctrines and policies, and they may order crimes or try to halt crimes.

What I am saying is that ICL presents criminal law without the familiar *conceptual framework* of "the State": a single Westphalian state sitting in judgement of the humans within its jurisdiction. This central character in criminal law thinking is a single entity, claiming a monopoly of force in a territory and uniquely empowered to sit in judgement of all of the other actors.[16] It is the law-maker, law-interpreter, and law-enforcer; it is the keeper of the peace, custodian of public right, embodiment of the community, and beneficiary of duties of allegiance.

In the normal case, criminal law theory can assume that all of these roles and attributes are merged in one posited entity, which is also the entity creating and enforcing criminal law in the case in question. However, this bundling of roles and attributes in one entity may not be present in ICL contexts. These functions may be disaggregated over different entities, or they may be duplicated in more than one entity, which may even be asserting authority in conflicting ways.

When we lose the single (comparatively) tidy package, we also bring into question many of the tools of thought that have been used in analyzing criminal law. I will give three examples: citizenship, community, and authority. First, criminal law

---

[16]   L Green, *The Authority of the State* (Clarendon Press, 1988).

theorists often invoke the relations between "citizens" in a polity.[17] However, the idea of *citizenship* may not be an appropriate explanatory tool if bonds of citizenship are not present between accused, victims, or other states asserting authority, or international tribunals.[18] Perhaps "citizenship" will prove to be a placeholder for a deeper concept: perhaps what really matters is the relations and duties between persons simply as fellow persons, and shared citizenship might play only a small role.[19]

Second, criminal law theorists sometimes invoke the idea of *community*, which seems plausible enough in normal criminal law, because we have some sense of what the community is.[20] However, in ICL, what was formerly a peripheral issue becomes a central problem. If we want to use "community" as a tool of thought in ICL, we have to think more carefully about how a "community" is constituted and why that idea is relevant.[21]

Third, criminal law theorists sometimes invoke the idea of *state authority*, which is comparatively straightforward in a normal context, in which the state authorizing the act is also the state applying criminal law. In ICL, however, the entity applying the law (possibly an international tribunal) will often not be the entity that authorized the act. Thus new questions would arise about why criminal law accommodates state authority and whether ICL should accommodate the authority of other states, and to what extent and why. In short, when these various roles and attributes, normally bundled in a single entity, are disaggregated, we find ourselves with both the burden and the opportunity of isolating the significance of those different roles and attributes for criminal law.

Another upshot is that we should not assume that tribunals must be "like" states insofar as they apply criminal law, and then find fault if they differ in some respects.[22]

---

[17] See, e.g., R A Duff, *Answering for Crime: Responsibility and Liability in the Criminal Law* (Hart, 2007) at 49–54.

[18] Of course, as a matter of positive law, nationality remains a clear ground of jurisdiction. I am speaking here of citizenship as a theoretical tool for analysis of doctrines.

[19] For example, perhaps shared citizenship is relevant to our thinking only about specific crimes such as treason, foreign enlistment, or tax evasion.

[20] See, e.g., Duff, *supra* note 17, at 44–46 and 52–56.

[21] See preliminary discussions *ibid* at 55–56. Some scholars insist that there is no "international community" because of divergences in values and interests. Such claims appear to overestimate the level of agreement needed to constitute a "community" (e.g. the people of Toronto have diverse social and political views, with many born in different cultures, and yet they constitute a "community"). Alternatively, such claims may underestimate how much we human beings, with nearly identical DNA and stuck to the surface of a single planet, have in common. For thoughts on community, see also Appiah, *supra* note 5, at 57 (on the minimal convergence needed); Hakimi, *supra* note 13 (community is partially constituted by conflict and disagreement). In any case, these questions would have to be unpacked if a criminal law theory drawing on "community" were to be extended to ICL.

[22] One could insist that an international tribunal acts "like a state" insofar as it applies criminal law. But this may be too simplistic (a cow is "like" a horse, in that both are four-legged mammals, but it is not a horse). Perhaps what matters is not similitude to a state, but rather some broader underlying characteristics, such as public authority.

Some features of a state may be needed for criminal law, others may not, and yet others may require modification of our thinking. For example, ICL does not feature a legislature per se, which differentiates it from a typical national criminal legal system. However, that particular feature of a state may not be essential for a system to do *justice*. We must distinguish (i) the rules that have grown around particular contingent features of the modern state from (ii) the requirements actually essential for criminal law practices to be justified.

An even more challenging question is whether it is really ultimately true that only "states" can apply criminal law. Jurists commonly assert that only states have authority to do criminal law. This proposition is largely true, as a statement of currently accepted social and legal conventions within the "normal" case of an orderly modern state. But it is not an absolute truth: it is not something essential, eternal, or intrinsically inherent to the concept of criminal law or the state. Criminal law is, in reality, carried out by human beings; it is only relatively recently in human history that human beings have carried out criminal law primarily through the social institution of the Westphalian state. There have been other configurations of human governance in history, with criminal sanctions applied, for example, by religious institutions, communities, and other organizations.[23] More recently, armed groups carrying out criminal law have raised new questions about legitimacy, legality, and the appropriate standards by which to assess such practices, given the different capacities of armed groups.[24] Thus, on a deeper normative level, it is at least

---

[23] For articles discussing the relatively recent predominance of law through modern states and prior alternatives, such as religious institutions and local communities, see, e.g., F Schechter, "Popular Law and Common Law in Medieval England" (1928) 28 Colum L Rev 269; R T Ford, "Law's Territory (A History of Jurisdiction)" (1998–99) 97 Michigan L Rev 843; A Orford, "Jurisdiction without Territory: From the Holy Roman Empire to the Responsibility to Protect" (2008–09) 30 Michigan J Int'l L 981; J Greenberg & M J Sechler, "Constitutionalism Ancient and Early Modern: The Contributions of Roman Law, Cannon Law, and English Common Law" (2013) 34 Cardozo L Rev 1021; S Dorsett & S McVeigh, "Jurisprudences of Jurisdiction: Matters of Public Authority" (2014) 23 Griffith L Rev 569. Early corporations acted as polities and political communities, including applying criminal law to employees and others. See, e.g., R Smandych & R Linden, "Administering Justice without the State: A Study of the Private Justice System of the Hudson's Bay Company to 1800" (1996) 11 Can J L & Soc 21; P J Stern, " 'A Politie of Civill & Military Power': Political Thought and the Late Seventeenth-Century Foundations of the East India Company-State" (2008) 47 JBS 253; E Cavanagh, "A Company with Sovereignty and Subjects of Its Own? The Case of the Hudson's Bay Company, 1670–1763" (2011) 26 Can J L & Soc 25; N Yahaya, "Legal Pluralism and the English East India Company in the Straits of Malacca during the Early Nineteenth Century" (2015) 33 Law & Hist Rev 945. See also D J Bederman, "The Pirate Code" (2008) 22 Emory Int'l L Rev 707.

[24] See, e.g., S Sivakumaran, "Courts of Armed Opposition Groups: Fair Trials or Summary Justice?" (2009) 7 JICJ 489; J Somer, "Jungle Justice: Passing Sentence on the Equality of Belligerents in Non-international Armed Conflict" (2007) 89 International Review of the Red Cross 655. See also S Sivakumaran, "Ownership of International Humanitarian Law: Non-state Armed Groups and the Formation and Enforcement of IHL Rules," in B Perrin, ed, *Modern Warfare: Armed Groups, Private Militaries, Humanitarian Organizations, and the Law* (UBC Press, 2012) esp at 95–96; H Krieger, "International Law and Governance by Armed Groups: Caught in the Legitimacy Trap?" (2018) 12 Journal of Intervention and Statebuilding 563, esp at 571; René Provost, *Rebel Courts: The Administration of Justice by Armed Insurgents* (Oxford University Press, forthcoming).

conceivable that authorities other than states could legitimately apply criminal law. Perhaps the state is only one possible configuration of governance. Perhaps what is really needed for criminal law is something broader, such as "governance" or "public authority," and the institution of the Westphalian state is simply the most familiar species of that broader genus. ICL may provide a doorway into such questions, because it is routinely carried out not by states, but by international tribunals, directly applying criminal law to persons.[25] ICL provides an opportunity to explore criminal law under alternative forms of governance and, in so doing, to learn more about the more truly general case of criminal law.[26]

Of course, we can still certainly turn to the rich and well-developed thinking in the context of states as a "reservoir" of ideas about governance under international institutions.[27] But my point of caution is that we should draw from that reservoir of ideas with care, so that our net does not include the accumulated detritus that is particular to states, but not necessarily essential to criminal law under other mechanisms of governance.

5.2 PROMISING PROBLEMS

In this section, I outline how a humanistic, coherentist, cosmopolitan account engaging with deontic principles might assist with concrete problems in ICL. I am not attempting to stake out a conclusion on any of these issues; I am simply outlining some of the potential questions and insights for ICL, and possibly for criminal law theory.

5.2.1 Legality without a Legislature

Custom and lex scripta

In a normal criminal law context (i.e. within a modern state), it is comparatively easy to say how the principle of legality is satisfied: through the adoption of legislation prior to the crime.[28] However, ICL raises two challenges. First, ICL has no legislature and ascertains law through a variety of means, including treaties and customary

---

[25] Obviously, as a matter of positive law, tribunals exercise legal authority delegated from states. But I am speaking here not of the black-letter doctrinal basis for jurisdiction, but rather a deeper normative question about the possibilities of criminal law.

[26] See also C Ryngaert, "Territory in the Law of Jurisdiction: Imagining Alternatives" (2017) 47 NYIL 49; P Capps & H P Olsen, eds, *Legal Authority beyond the State* (Cambridge University Press, 2018).

[27] K Knop, "Statehood: Territory, People, Government," in J Crawford & M Koskenniemi, eds, *The Cambridge Companion to International Law* (Cambridge University Press, 2012) at 96–97 and 112–14 (discussing abstracting from the state rather than mapping it directly onto international institutions).

[28] The principle of legality requires that persons be punished only for transgressing existing law, so that persons have fair notice of prohibitions and can order their affairs accordingly. For a careful discussion, see K Gallant, *The Principle of Legality in International and Comparative Criminal Law* (Cambridge University Press, 2009).

international law. Second, ICL periodically confronts horrific and massive crimes for which domestic positive law is lacking and where the parameters of international criminalization are unclear. These features of ICL require us – and enable us – to explore more precisely what the underpinnings and contours of the legality principle really are.

Consider, for example, the principle *nullum crimen sine lege scripta* ("no crime without written law"). In the context of the modern state, which features a separation of powers (and thus a legislature) and diverse societies subject to voluminous regulation, it is very plausible to regard the *lex scripta* requirement as a fundamental principle. Accordingly, scholars have understandably argued that ICL also must comply with *lex scripta* to satisfy fundamental precepts of justice. For example, George Fletcher argues that the reliance on customary international law as a source of prohibitions is an error introduced by international lawyers and reflects a failure to understand the full implications of legality in criminal cases.[29] I certainly agree that some problems in ICL flow from habits and thought patterns of international lawyers (see Chapter 2). This may, however, be an instance in which the seeming departure is one that, on further inspection, proves to be deontically justifiable.

In almost all of contemporary human experience with the criminal sanction, it seems quite plausible to regard *lex scripta* as a precondition for just punishment. However, it is studying the exception that may teach us the most about the rule. *Lex scripta* may simply be a *technique* to satisfy a more elementary requirement. If so, perhaps it manifests as a requirement of justice only under certain conditions.

Through a few thought experiments, we can readily imagine examples in which justice would not require written law. For example, we could imagine a small society trapped on an island developing a system to enforce a few basic prohibitions. Our concept of fair warning would likely not require written prohibitions in that situation, if prohibitions were otherwise known or ascertainable.[30] I am not suggesting that ICL is analogous to the island situation; rather, I am using the island situation to demonstrate that the *lex scripta* requirement is not universally applicable and therefore must be contextually contingent. Such examples can show that written law is not a truly basic requirement, but rather a manifestation of a deeper requirement that generates principles such as *lex scripta* when certain conditions are satisfied.

ICL – a legal system without a legislature, which has largely relied on customary law for its basic rules, and which has recently and rapidly transited from embryonic to relatively mature system – provides a wonderful setting in which to try to explore

---

[29] G Fletcher, *The Grammar of Criminal Law: American, Comparative and International*, Vol 1 (Oxford University Press, 2007) at 164 n 41 and 222.

[30] To investigate the circumstances in which sanction without codification may be justifiable, we could also consider the practice of a great many societies that have not required written penal law and have relied on custom.

the parameters of the *lex scripta* requirement.[31] Under what circumstances does our concept of justice require written law and why? Can it justifiably be connected to the maturity of the system, and if so, how?[32] If writing is required, does it have to be in one place (e.g. a code), or can the writings be scattered in multiple places, as it is in common law jurisprudence or customary international law? What might we learn from studying customary law traditions?

Pluralistic sources and non-retroactivity

ICL also provides an opportunity to explore legality in another way. As already mentioned, ICL frequently confronts massive evils in situations in which positive law is lacking. The stakes in such cases are often higher than in ordinary criminal law, because (i) the atrocities are usually far more horrific, and (ii) it is considerably more difficult to posit new law to remedy any gaps (e.g. by multilateral treaty). ICL jurists have developed various strategies of argument to justify punishment in such cases. I expect that some such punishment can indeed be justified, but each of the major argumentative strategies employed to date has shortcomings.[33]

For example, it is often argued that the prohibition on retroactive law was not applicable in ICL, at least in its early stages.[34] That argument may indeed be correct as a matter of *positive law*, but it does not help us with our question of whether retroactivity is *normatively* acceptable – that is, whether it is "just." One of the arguments raised in the *Nuremberg* judgment in response to the principle of legality was that it was merely a principle of justice and not a rule of international law. But in a system that seeks to do justice, surely we would not want to bat away principles on the grounds that they are "merely" about justice.

A more promising argument is that the "formal justice" enshrined in the principle of legality must give way to the "substantive justice" of not letting persons escape punishment for heinous deeds.[35] That argument is appealing, but incomplete, because it is formally empty: it does not specify any *content* for its exception. How do we know that the prohibition we wish to impose falls within this concept of

[31] These issues do not arise before the ICC specifically, because its crimes are defined in the Rome Statute, and hence it accords with the *lex scripta* requirement. The issue is, however, pertinent (i) before tribunals authorized to apply customary law, (ii) before national systems authorized to apply customary international law, and (iii) as a principled normative inquiry.

[32] See, e.g., the argument advanced in *United States v Alstötter et al (the Justice Case)* 3 *Trials of War Criminals before the Nuremberg Military Tribunal under Control Council Law No 10* at 975 that applying the prohibition in a nascent legal system would strangle the law at birth. The argument is intriguing, but a deontic justification will require a bit more development.

[33] Some such argumentative strategies are discussed in B van Schaack, "*Crimen Sine Lege*: Judicial Lawmaking at the Intersection of Law and Morals" (2008) 97 Georgetown L Rev 119; B Roth, "Coming to Terms with Ruthlessness: Sovereign Equality, Global Pluralism, and the Limits of International Criminal Justice" (2010) 8 Santa Clara J Int'l L 231.

[34] See, e.g., H Kelsen, "Will the Judgment in the Nuremberg Trial Constitute a Precedent in International Law?" (1947) 1 Int'l LQ 153 at 164. The non-retroactivity principle is now formally recognized in Art 22 of the ICC Statute.

[35] *Ibid* at 165; A Cassese, *International Criminal Law*, 2nd ed (Oxford University Press, 2008) at 38–41.

"substantive justice"? There must be some ascertainable limits to the set of norms that could displace the requirement of "formal justice." It is tempting to fall back on natural law or to assert that a certain act is *malum in se* ("wrong in itself"), but presumably we would want rule-appliers to be constrained in some ascertainable way, so that we do not end up with arbitrary retroactive criminalization based purely on revulsion or intuition. Thus we are thrown back into the search for some method or source to delineate the punishable prohibitions.

If we look at patterns of practice in ICL, we see that jurists have used multiple points of reference, such as criminalization in most legal systems of the world, prohibition in general international law, and appeal to a subset of values perceived as warranting a penal response. Article 15 of the International Covenant on Civil and Political Rights suggests that the non-retroactivity principle is not violated where the conduct was criminal according to general principles of law recognized by the community of nations, and this widely adopted provision might be a clue about a justifiable limit. The Sierra Leone Special Court's *Norman* decision on child soldiers provides an excellent attempt, by the majority and the dissent, to delineate when a new crime may crystallize and what sources and methods may be invoked.[36] A coherentist method could examine these and other points of reference to try to identify a convincing account of when an offence can be recognized as giving rise to ICL liability.[37] Such an account will almost inevitably embrace pluralistic sources.[38] More importantly, such an account will require a convincing deontic theory about the underpinnings and outer limits of the legality principle.

Strict construction

At a less radical, but still important and revealing, level: what is the best account of interpretation where there *is* an enacted text? This question may be even more vital than the previous one, given that ICL today is largely codified and given that every text has ambiguities. In Chapter 2, I explored a contrast between (i) ICL's declared commitment to strict construction and (ii) the common practice[39] of maximal

---

[36] *Prosecutor v Norman*, Decision on Preliminary Motion Based on Lack of Jurisdiction, SCSL A.Ch, SCSL-2004-14-AR72(E), 31 May 2004.

[37] This possibility is also noted in E van Sliedregt, "International Criminal Law," in M Dubber & T Hörnle, *The Oxford Handbook of Criminal Law* (Oxford University Press, 2014) esp at 1147–50 and 1162.

[38] By definition, recognition of new ICL crimes must draw from outside ICL. A pluralistic account may provide some anchoring in social facts, which is likely necessary to satisfy the underpinnings of the legality principle, while allowing recognition of offences for which there is sufficient notice. On pluralism in ICL, see, e.g., E van Sliedregt, "Pluralism in International Criminal Law" (2012) 25 LJIL 847; E van Sliedregt & S Vasiliev, eds, *Pluralism in International Criminal Law* (Oxford University Press, 2014); A K A Greenawalt, "The Pluralism of International Criminal Law" (2011) 86 Indiana LJ 1063. More generally, see P S Berman, *Global Legal Pluralism: A Jurisprudence of Law beyond Borders* (Cambridge University Press, 2012); C H Koch Jr, "Judicial Dialogue for Legal Multiculturalism" (2004) 25 Michigan J Int'l L 879, esp at 897–902.

[39] The practice was common in the early stages of the renaissance of ICL; it is now less prevalent, but still appears in some decisions.

construction. From this, one might assume that I have a passion for strict construction.[40] But recall again that, in Chapter 2, I was simply working with principles *as articulated by the system itself*. I was looking at the reasoning that led to those internal contradictions and which led the contradictions to go largely unnoticed because jurists thought they were applying an established rule of interpretation.[41] I noted, however, that the substantive evaluation of those principles themselves would await another day and that more sophisticated formulations might be possible.

What might we conclude from a more careful substantive inquiry? I think that a coherentist deontic inquiry would require some version of strict construction,[42] given the values underlying the principle, but precisely how should that principle be understood? My intuition is that the principle as commonly understood is actually a rather crude proxy for more subtle underlying principles.

As commonly understood, the principle seems to me either too toothless or too dispositive. If one emphasizes the principle's precondition – that all other canons of interpretation must be exhausted first – then the principle is trivially easy to circumvent. One could even apply maximal construction at an earlier stage and thus nullify the principle while claiming formally to respect it.[43] Relevant jurisprudence allows, for example, "foreseeable" judicial innovations, but this leaves almost no limitation on judicial creativity.[44] Conversely, if one does not emphasize the precondition and gives the principle free play earlier in the analysis, then the principle become perversely dominant and simplistic, always dictating the narrower outcome at every interpretive juncture. Such an understanding seems hard to defend in consequentialist, deontic, doctrinal, or institutional terms.[45]

---

[40] As Caroline Davidson notes, "Robinson started the conversation by noting the illiberal tendencies of ICL to construe crimes expansively, at the expense of the legality principle, in order to fight impunity, but in more recent scholarship seems not to embrace a strict version of lenity." C Davidson, "How to Read International Criminal Law: Strict Construction and the Rome Statute of the International Criminal Court" (2017) 91 St John's L Rev 37at 74.

[41] And they were, but it was an established rule of international human rights law interpretation. When transplanted into ICL without sufficient reflection, such an approach nullifies and even reverses the supposed approach of strict construction, because all ambiguities are resolved against the accused. See §2.2.

[42] I am confident that careful analysis would reject maximal construction, which is antithetical to criminal law in multiple ways (its deontic constraints, its scope, its nature and consequences). There are nonetheless many gradations between maximal construction and strict construction. I think, however, that coherentist deontic analysis would require an approach that at least captures some key values underlying strict construction.

[43] Judge Shahabuddeen's aim was, of course, not to nullify the principle, but his analysis does show some of the numerous possible limits to or loopholes in the principle: M Shahabuddeen, "Does the Principle of Legality Stand in the Way of Progressive Development of the Law?" (2004) 2 JICJ 1007.

[44] D Robinson, "Legality and Our Contradictory Commitments: Some Thoughts About the Way We Think" (2009) 103 ASIL Proc 104 at 104.

[45] National systems are rightly consistent in holding that strict construction does not mean that, in any dispute, the narrower interpretation must prevail, because this would have absurd consequences. Such an approach would frustrate legislative objectives and would require legislators to draft overbroad definitions to forestall austere interpretations.

My initial assessment (prior to detailed research) is that the principle, as commonly articulated, has a valuable role in the rare cases in which there is actually equipoise among the different interpretive clues.[46] But I suspect what is also needed is something else: not a crude tie-breaker rule, but a cluster of more complex considerations that I am not able to fully develop here. This cluster of considerations calls for the interpreter to be mindful of the limits of criminal law – that is, of: legality considerations (whether conduct was "innocent when done," the judicial versus legislative role, and predictability); other deontic principles, such as culpability and fair labelling; the proper scope of criminal law; and the even narrower scope appropriate for ICL (which authorizes transnational interventions).

In this connection, a remarkable article by Caroline Davidson engages in precisely the type of analysis I have advocated in this book – what I would describe as a coherentist, deontic, and reconstructivist approach. Rather than simply transplanting the common articulation of the strict construction principle, she examines the values underlying the principle, inspects them in light of the morally salient distinctive features of ICL, and reconstructs a deontically justified understanding that reflects these features.[47] Her proposal is consistent with what I have outlined here, but more advanced and better substantiated. She argues that courts should bear in mind the *values* underlying strict construction: they should avoid unfair surprises to accused persons, avoid extending criminal law to conduct that states parties intended not to cover, avoid usurping legislative authority, and examine whether the proposed resolution makes the law more or less certain.[48]

Conclusion

As may be seen, the account I propose would not simply transplant the familiar articulations of the legality principle from national to international law. Nor would it indulge arguments that simply circumvent legality and fair warning altogether. Instead, we use hard cases to try to isolate what form of prohibition or warning is truly needed before we can prosecute a person. We examine what our deontic commitments entail in light of the distinctive conditions of ICL; morally salient differences may generate different, but deontically justified, approaches. The inquiry into unusual circumstances helps us to better understand the more general underlying rule.

---

[46]   And indeed is established in ICL: see ICC Statute, Art 22(2).

[47]   Davidson, *supra* note 40. Her work does not use terms such as "coherentist," "deontic," or "reconstructivist," but her methodology has those features, as discussed in Chapters 3–5. By "morally salient distinctive features," I mean not simply gesturing toward the gravity of the crimes, but rather looking at the distinct law-making methods of ICL, difficulties of amendment, legitimacy issues, decentralized power, and the fact that states parties may at times deliberately delegate the burden of clarification to a judicial institution and at other times deliberately delineate a prohibition.

[48]   Davidson, *supra* note 40.

5.2.2 Duress and Social Roles

The extreme contexts encountered in ICL can also generate new questions about the defence of duress. For example, in the *Erdemović* case, the accused had enlisted in a non-combat unit of the army.[49] One day, his unit was sent to a farm, where they were informed that they were to shoot Muslim civilians. He protested the order and was presented with a choice of either participating or joining the prisoners and being shot alongside them. Faced with the unappealing alternative of sacrificing his life while saving no lives, Erdemović complied. The majority of the ICTY Appeals Chamber adopted a rule that duress is not a defence to the killing of civilians, following the lead of many common law jurisdictions.[50]

ICL scholars within the liberal tradition have widely, and understandably, criticized the majority decision for its insensitivity to deontic principles and the importance of moral choice for culpability, given that the only way for Erdemović to be innocent was to be dead.[51] In Chapter 2, I criticized the *reasoning* employed by the majority; however, as I emphasized, this did not necessarily exhaust my analysis of the *outcome*.[52] While I agree with the liberal critiques, there is at least room for further analysis if we take into account the social dimension of human experience (§3.3.2).

In classical liberal theories that conceive of individuals as atomistic entities entering into a notional social contract to better advance their personal aims, the freedom to preserve one's own life is the ultimate *domain reservé*.[53] To many, a law that requires one to die to avoid censure is futile.[54] As Paul Kahn has argued, traditional contractarian liberal theories have trouble grappling with sacrifice (both the willingness of individuals to sacrifice themselves and the state's or community's claim to expect sacrifice).[55] However, if we acknowledge the richly social world of human beings, as suggested in §3.3.2, our analysis might change. Social roles can change the expectations placed upon us. A person assuming the role of "soldier" is expected to carry out dangerous acts at risk of death, including for

---

[49] *Prosecutor v Erdemović*, Judgment, ICTY A.Ch, IT-96-22-A, 7 October 1997 ("*Erdemović* Appeal Judgment").

[50] *Ibid* at para 19.

[51] See, e.g., R E Brooks, "Law in the Heart of Darkness: Atrocity and Duress" (2003) 43 Virginia J Int'l L 861; I Wall, "Duress, International Criminal Law and Literature" (2006) 4 JICJ 724; A Fichtelberg, "Liberal Values in International Criminal Law: A Critique of *Erdemović*" (2007) 6 JICJ 3; V Epps, "The Soldier's Obligation to Die When Ordered to Shoot Civilians or Face Death Himself" (2003) 37 New England L Rev 987.

[52] See §2.2.4.

[53] T Hobbes, *Leviathan*, C B MacPherson, ed (Penguin Books, 1985) at 192, 199 and 268–70.

[54] I Kant, The Metaphysics of Morals, trans M Gregor (Cambridge University Press, 1996) at 28 (6:235–236) argues that a drowning person pushing another from a plank in order to survive would be culpable, but not punishable, because the punishment threatened by law could not be greater than the immediate loss of his own life.

[55] P W Kahn, *Putting Liberalism in Its Place* (Princeton University Press, 2005) at 10, 12, 25, 63, 164 and 228–40.

example charging a machine gun nest if ordered to do so. Experience shows that many humans can conceive of outcomes worse than losing one's life (and hence the familiar phrases "death before dishonour" or "a fate worse than death"). Thus punishment for a refusal to fulfill an almost certainly lethal duty is not necessarily an absurdity. Criminal laws may punish soldiers for desertion, or insubordination, or cowardice in the face of the enemy.

Perhaps duress is based on the expectations of firmness that we can fairly expect from members of society.[56] Normally, criminal law would not and could not demand heroism, but it is at least possible that we can justly impose higher expectations on persons assuming the role of soldier. Just as we hold soldiers liable for desertion in the face of the enemy, perhaps we could hold them to a similar standard concerning their duty not to fire on civilians. Although the *reasoning* of the majority decision in *Erdemović* may be faulted for inadequate deontic engagement,[57] it is at least conceivable that the *conclusion* reached might be justified, insofar as it was restricted to soldiers,[58] if we use an account that considers these social dimensions of human experience.

There are still many issues that would have to be worked out. For example, the category of "soldier" is not homogenous, and we should not build an exception for soldiers based on an archetypal impression of a soldier. We would have to at least consider the differences in training and experiences of combatants in different armed groups around the world. We would also have to consider the situation of conscripts. A reflex in many liberal theories would be that roles that are not voluntarily assumed cannot create duties, but that might not always be true and might hinge on relative vulnerabilities (for example accidental parents may incur obligations to babies).[59] I am not taking a position on these issues; I am outlining the type of *question* that a humanistic liberal account can raise.

5.2.3 Superior Orders and State Authority

As mentioned in Chapter 2, the Nuremberg and Tokyo Charters, positing rules for defeated enemies, declared that there would be no defence of superior orders.[60] In the ICC Statute, which was negotiated multilaterally, states reinstated a limited version of the defence.[61] The defence is intensely controversial, but much of the discussion involves source-based and teleological

---

[56]   Fletcher, *supra* note 29, at 117, 322 (discussing the German concept of *Zumutbarkeit*).

[57]   See Chapter 2.

[58]   *Erdemović* Appeal Judgment, *supra* note 49, at para 19.

[59]   See discussion of voluntarily assumed roles in Green, *supra* note 16, at 211 and 238. Also, if soldiers have a duty to die in such circumstances, is it only to protect members of their polity (an allegiance-based duty), or does it entail a more cosmopolitan regard for all non-combatants? I would lean toward the latter.

[60]   Nuremberg Charter, Art 8; Tokyo Charter, Art 6.

[61]   ICC Statute, Art 33.

arguments rather than deontic analysis. Furthermore, many of the criticisms reflect reasoning reflexes discussed in Chapter 2: single-issue reductive teleo-logical analysis and the assumption that departures from Nuremberg must be politicized capitulations to self-interest.[62]

Developing a normative theory of the defence of superior orders could be illuminating both for ICL and for general criminal law theory. The defence of superior orders is controversial both doctrinally and normatively.[63] The defence precludes the international criminal responsibility of persons who are obliged to obey orders, when they carry out orders that they did not know to be unlawful and which were not "manifestly" unlawful, but which turn out to have been unlawful.[64] If we wish to assess whether the doctrine is normatively justified, we would have to start by trying to identify the best explanation of its underpinnings. An initial question is how to conceive of it: is it a justification or an excuse? In normal criminal law, authorization by the state is typically a "justification." However, for reasons I touch on shortly, it may be that, in ICL, such a defence is better conceived of as an "excuse."

What are the possible theoretical underpinnings of the doctrine? Given that the doctrine partially accommodates orders legally binding under national law, a possible starting point is the concept of "state authority." Malcolm Thorburn has helpfully highlighted state authority as an explanation in the context of justifications, with a model that looks into the role of the agent, the agent's reasons for acting, and the relevant scope of discretion.[65] The concept of "state authority" seems likely to be part of the apparatus needed to explain the superior orders doctrine.[66]

Again, however, ICL confronts us with a more complex relationship between state authority and criminal law. In a "normal" context, a single state is both the applier of criminal law and the authorizer of the act. Given that unity, it seems obvious why that state would build deference to its own authorized acts into its criminal law. By

---

[62] As examples, see P Gaeta, "Defence of Superior Orders: The Statute of the International Criminal Court versus Customary International Law" (1999) 10 EJIL 172; M Frulli, "Are Crimes against Humanity More Serious than War Crimes?" (2001) 12 EJIL 329; C Fournet, "When the Child Surpasses the Father: Admissible Defences in International Criminal Law" (2008) 8 Int'l Crim L Rev 509.

[63] For some leading examples of the discussion, see Gaeta, *supra* note 62; Osiel M, Obeying Orders: Atrocity, Military Discipline and the Law of War (Routledge, 2002); R Cryer, "Superior Orders and the International Criminal Court," in R Burchill, N White & J Morris, eds, *International Conflict and Security Law: Essays in Memory of Hilaire McCoubrey* (Cambridge University Press, 2005).

[64] ICC Statute, Art 33.

[65] M Thorburn, "Justifications, Power and Authority" (2008) 117 Yale LJ 1070. See also J Gardner, "Justifications under Authority" (2010) 23 Can JL & Jur 71.

[66] The solution will likely not be a direct application of the approach laid out by Thorburn, because it may be that superior orders is not a justification per se. For example, justifications tend to relate to a particular valued end; the superior orders defence protects obedience to certain orders of the state without regard to the aim or purpose of the order. Thus a theory of superior orders may be more elaborate (excusing the individual for one form of mistake of law, but providing the excuse out of qualified deference to the authority of states).

contrast, in ICL contexts, there may not be a unity of identity between the applier of criminal law and the authorizer of the act. Indeed, there may be multiple authority structures asserting authority in conflicting ways. For example, an official's state of nationality may authorize and order the conduct, the law of the territorial state may forbid it, and the law of an international tribunal with jurisdiction might also proscribe the conduct, but with a defence that accommodates assertions of state authority that are not "manifestly unlawful." In these messier contexts, we are compelled to ask additional questions: why exactly should criminal law accommodate state authority? What is the proper scope for that accommodation?

There are other tools of thought that might be helpful. For example, Meir Dan-Cohen offers the idea of "role distance" in relation to official roles, which may also be of assistance.[67] The defence of superior orders may be rooted in an acknowledgement of the plight of the individual, who will be punished in domestic law for disobeying a lawful order and punished in ICL for obeying an unlawful order. It is often argued in response that there is no dilemma: the soldier needs simply to obey lawful orders and disobey unlawful orders. However, that response is too sanguine and does not empathetically engage with the dilemma: it glibly requires soldiers to immediately and unerringly carry out correct legal assessments of all orders, even in rushed and chaotic circumstances, and even though the laws of war often involve subtle and even perplexing distinctions for which normal peacetime experience is not a reliable guide.

For normal citizens, the "thin ice principle" argues that they should stay clear of possibly criminal conduct, and hence it is not unjust to punish them if they choose to walk the line and the conduct is found to be criminal.[68] However, soldiers (or others obliged to obey) do not have the simple option of steering clear of the thin ice. Their refusal to obey is a crime if the conduct turns out not to have been criminal. There may be a good deontic basis to allow a soldier some margin for good faith error in truly ambiguous situations.

Perhaps the defence is rooted in a combination of considerations: It respects the plight of the individual caught in this conflict, but the conflict is salient only because ICL recognizes some general value in compliance with law or with orders. If we develop a convincing normative account of the defence, it may inform the interpretation of the defence,[69] it may answer some criticisms of the defence, and it may raise new criticisms of the defence (e.g. perhaps it is not too broad, but too narrow).[70]

[67]   M Dan-Cohen, "Responsibility and the Boundaries of the Self" (1992) 105 Harvard L Rev 959 at 999–1001.

[68]   A Ashworth & J Horder, *Principles of Criminal Law*, 7th ed (Oxford University Press, 2013) at 62.

[69]   Under Art 33 of the Rome Statute, the defence of superior orders is available only to state forces and not necessarily to non-state armed forces. Whether judges should extend the defence (or a similar defence) to non-state groups depends on the underlying rationale: is it based in respect for state authority or respect for the operation of armed groups?

[70]   The most common criticism of the defence of superior orders comes from a pro-prosecution, victim-protection angle, arguing that the defence should not exist, because it allows officials to "escape

5.3 CONCLUSION

The framework I have advanced over the last few chapters is liberal, humanistic, coherentist, and cosmopolitan. The term "liberal" is used to mean different things and is often used pejoratively, but in this book I simply mean that the framework accepts deontic constraints on criminal law out of respect for individuals as moral agents. By "humanistic," I emphasize that the framework is not based on rarefied stipulations; it is based on respect for the humanity of persons, it reflects human concerns, and it engages with the nuances of human experience.[71] By "coherentist," I mean that the framework does not purport to deduce propositions from abstract timeless premises, but rather accepts that we are in a human conversation about human constructs.[72] By "cosmopolitan," I mean that we seek conversation between traditions, and our concern extends to all human beings. More ambitiously, cosmopolitanism regards the state as merely one useful human-created device to facilitate human governance. Thus the approach re-examines thinking about criminal law under the Westphalian state, and it considers criminal law under other authority structures and in contexts other than the normal case.

Just as criminal law theory might generate new insights about ICL, ICL might generate new insights about general criminal law theory. Extreme contexts might create an opportunity to isolate, with more specificity, the significance of ideas such as community, citizenship, authority, and legislation, and even to unpack our thoughts on the role of the state itself.

I have tried to show how a thoughtful account can lead to new legal prescriptions and perhaps even lead us to rethink our understanding of fundamental principles. It may be that familiar formulations of principles (e.g. that legality requires written law) might not in fact be elementary. They might be contextually contingent manifestations of deeper underlying commitments.

The coherentist method I advance is consistent with, and provides a methodological underpinning for, those who have called for an international *Dogmatik* – that is, the ideas and building blocks for a just system of criminal law.[73] It will take a long time and a long conversation to clarify those ideas, which will draw inspiration from multiple

---

conviction" for acts that prove to be unlawful. However, if we develop a normative justification, we might wind up criticizing the current defence from a different direction. Article 33 of the Rome Statute precludes the defence in relation to crimes against humanity; however, there can also be borderline, ambiguous orders (e.g. to deport or detain) that are not "manifestly" unlawful, but which, on closer examination, constitute crimes against humanity. It may prove to be unjust to preclude the defence in such circumstances.

[71] For more specification of this term, see Chapter 3.

[72] For more specification of this term, see Chapter 4.

[73] The idea of a *Dogmatik* is drawn from German legal theory. It refers to organizing ideas of a just system of criminal law. See, e.g., G Fletcher, "New Court, Old *Dogmatik*" (2011) 9 JICJ 179; G Vanocore, "Legality, Culpability and *Dogmatik*: A Dialogue between the ECtHR, Comparative and International Criminal Law" (2015) 15 Int'l Crim L Rev 823; K Ambos, "Toward a Universal System of Crime: Comments on George Fletcher's *Grammar of Criminal Law*" (2010) 28 Cardozo L Rev 2647.

systems, require critical inspection of common assumptions, and may demand tailoring and adapting to ICL contexts.[74] The goal could be described as an undogmatic *Dogmatik*.

In Part III, I will provide a more detailed illustration of the method at work by analyzing specific controversies about command responsibility. In doing so, I will showcase the method, the questions it poses, the themes that emerge, and the usefulness of such inquiry.

---

[74] See, e.g., C Steer, *Translating Guilt: Identifying Leadership Liability for Mass Atrocity Crimes* (TMC Asser Press, 2017), proposing a combination of comparative survey of national approaches plus selection of best fit for ICL on functional grounds. A G Kiyani, "International Crime and the Politics of Criminal Theory: Voices and Conduct of Exclusion" (2015) 48 NYU J Int'l L & Pol 187 calls for ambitious, critical interrogation of practices and normative arrangements. As discussed in §4.3.3, coherentism embraces serious reconsideration of patterns of practice where there is incompatibility with more important commitments.

Illustration through Application

OBJECTIVES

In Part III, I demonstrate and clarify the proposed method of inquiry by applying it to specific problems in ICL. In doing so, I will:

(1) show that early legal reasoning in ICL was often inadequately mindful of deontic constraints and concepts of criminal law theory, generating contradictions and problems;

(2) showcase deontic analysis and, in particular, my recommended "mid-level principles" or coherentist approach to such analysis;

(3) show that deontic analysis can help to avoid unjust doctrines and also avoid pointlessly conservative doctrines that overstate the relevant constraints;

(4) generate new doctrinal prescriptions (see especially §8.4); and

(5) show how ICL can raise new questions for general criminal law theory.

WHY FOCUS ON COMMAND RESPONSIBILITY?

I will illustrate these themes with three chapters, each focusing on one particular controversy in the law of command responsibility. Why do I devote three chapters to this one doctrine, when we have all of the myriad puzzles of ICL still awaiting our scrutiny? I could instead offer a broader, but thinner, survey of numerous current controversies in ICL. But if we attend carefully to command responsibility, there is a lot to unravel and a lot to learn. We can "see a world in a grain of sand."[1]

Command responsibility raises fascinating issues for criminal law theory. Whereas other modes of liability in ICL were transplanted from established domestic analogues, command responsibility developed in international law. Accordingly, command responsibility has not yet been scrutinized to the same extent as domestic modes of liability, which have been refined and debated by jurists and scholars in many countries over centuries of experience. Command

---

[1] W Blake, "Auguries of Innocence," in D H S Nicholson & A H E Lee, eds, *The Oxford Book of English Mystical Verse* (Clarendon Press, 1917).

responsibility is a valuable and intriguing doctrine: it responds to a particular pathology of human organization – namely, dangerously inadequate supervision in contexts of power and vulnerability.

OUTLINE OF ARGUMENTS

In Chapter 6, I look at the controversy as to whether command responsibility requires (or should require) some causal contribution to the subordinates' crimes. The culpability principle, as recognized by ICL, requires a person to contribute to a crime in some way to be a party to it. I will show that early reasoning in Tribunal jurisprudence engaged inadequately with the deontic dimension, producing an internal contradiction with the culpability principle. I will also show how this early mis-step led command responsibility jurisprudence to become tangled and how each subsequent manoeuvre to deny or avoid this root contradiction produced increasingly convoluted knots. As a result, this discourse is now so fragmented that even the very *nature* of command responsibility is the subject of multiple conflicting and complex theories. My analysis generates a comparatively simple solution: to go back and untie the first knot.

Chapter 7 moves from analytical[2] to *normative* assessment, modelling a coherentist deontic inquiry. I examine the deontic questions of how much causal contribution is required and whether there are justifiable alternatives. I show that the causal contribution requirement is not unduly onerous; it is satisfied by "risk aggravation." I also consider more radical proposals for culpability without causal contribution, but I conclude that arguments to dispense with causal contribution are as yet too embryonic and undeveloped to provide a convincing basis for punishing human beings.

Chapter 8 tackles another intense controversy: the mental fault requirement of command responsibility. Early Tribunal jurisprudence disavowed criminal negligence, which was a well-intentioned and commendable caution. I argue, however, after a careful deontic analysis, that a criminal negligence standard actually maps *better* onto personal culpability than the tests devised by the Tribunals. I argue that the "should have known" standard in the ICC Statute is deontically justified and that a criminal negligence standard should be openly embraced. This chapter illustrates several of the themes of Part II. First, the tools of criminal law theory can clarify and improve ICL doctrine. Second, careful deontic analysis can sometimes help us to avoid needlessly conservative doctrines that are based on unfounded overestimates of the relevant constraints. Third, ICL can provide new problems and contexts that may lead us to reconsider criminal law theory assumptions. Command responsibility reveals a special set of

---

[2] Exposing a contradiction and the related reasoning.

circumstances that overturns the standard assumption that criminal negligence is categorically less serious that subjective foresight.

SCOPE, TERMS, AND CAVEATS

In these chapters, I will use the term *"command responsibility,"* and I will focus on the situation of military commanders. Of course, the doctrine – more accurately and inclusively known as *"superior responsibility"* – covers a broader set of relationships. In order not to further complicate an already intricate subject, I will focus specifically on command responsibility and military relationships. The arguments for requiring causal contribution apply with equal, or indeed greater, force in non-military relationships. I use terms such as *"doctrine," "doctrinal,"* and *"deontic"* in the manner explained earlier in this book. In particular, I use *"doctrinal"* in the common law sense (which is very different from, for example, the German usage) to refer to source-based and teleological legal arguments, as opposed to arguments engaging with deontic principles or deeper theoretical coherence. As a counterbalance to the widespread use of the masculine pronoun, these chapters will use the feminine pronoun, especially in relation to commanders.

These chapters bring together ICL scholarship and criminal law theory scholarship. For reasons of space, it is impossible to provide a complete treatment of both bodies of work. While this volume is one of the most detailed examinations of the doctrine to date from a deontic and criminal law theory perspective, there are countless issues that could and should be explored in more detail. As for the positive law on command responsibility, I delve into the vast jurisprudence and literature only to the extent needed to illustrate the culpability issues discussed here; numerous other issues are untouched. This work is simply an initial foray, and it is my hope that a longer and broader conversation will continue.

6

An Unresolved Contradiction

OVERVIEW

In this case study, I focus on a particular contradiction emerging from Tribunal jurisprudence and the surrounding discourse. The contradiction is that Tribunal jurisprudence (i) recognizes the principle of personal culpability, pursuant to which a person must contribute to a crime to be party to it, and yet (ii) uses command responsibility to declare persons party to international crimes without a causal contribution. Some readers will protest at this claim, but I will examine each of the major counter-arguments to show that the contradiction does exist.

The contradiction first emerged as a result of surface-level doctrinal reasoning that did not adequately consider the deontic dimension. I will show how the subsequent twists and turns to deny, obscure, evade, or resolve this contradiction have led to increasingly complex and obscure claims about command responsibility. Jurists now disagree about basic requirements of the doctrine and even its very nature: Is it a mode of liability, a separate offence, or a mysterious new category, or does it perhaps even vacillate between both?

The analysis will show the problems of inadequate attention to deontic limits. It will also help us to better understand the trajectory by which the command responsibility debate became so convoluted. Sensitivity to deontic constraints will shed new light on earlier, overly simplistic debates. It can also generate prescriptions: I will argue that a relatively simple solution is available, which relies on established concepts of criminal law. Regardless of whether you agree with my specific solution, however, my examination here should help to clear out the most fallacious arguments, to map out the defensible options, and to pave the way for a simpler, clearer debate that engages seriously with personal culpability.

6.1 ARGUMENT AND RESULTING INSIGHTS

6.1.1 The Structure of the Argument

The syllogism that is at the core of my argument is essentially as follows:

(1) The Tribunals claim to comply with the fundamental principles of justice, including the principle of personal culpability.

(2) The principle of personal culpability requires that persons can be held liable as party only to crimes to which they *contributed*.

(3) Under the doctrine of command responsibility, the Tribunals explicitly hold the commander liable as a party to the crimes of subordinates.[3]

(4) Therefore, to comply with the system's principles, command responsibility as a mode of liability must require that the commander's dereliction contributed to the crimes of subordinates.

This syllogism is quite straightforward and demonstrates a contradiction. However, that contradiction has been thoroughly obscured by several arguments and ambiguities in the jurisprudence. I will explore in turn each of the counter-arguments that have been advanced to resist this syllogism. As a helpful by-product, in discussing each of the counter-arguments, I will also trace the trajectory of the command responsibility debate, thereby showing how each step (or strategy) in the debate led command responsibility to become increasingly mystified and disputed.

(1) **Doctrinal sidestep** The first strategy was to employ technical doctrinal arguments to sidestep fundamental principles. I will show in §6.5 that doctrinal arguments are the wrong *type* of response, because they do not even *attempt* to answer the deontic concern about culpability and the limits of principled punishment.

(2) **Separate offence** The second strategy was to characterize command responsibility as a separate offence. However, the practice of the Tribunals *explicitly* charges, convicts, and sentences the commanders as parties to the underlying offences (see §6.6). The Tribunals cannot answer culpability challenges by claiming that they do not hold the commander liable as party to the underlying crime when they in fact do precisely that.

(3) **Invoke *sui generis* nature** A third strategy has been to simply assert that command responsibility is a "*sui generis*" mode of liability exempt from the contribution requirement. However, simply invoking the adjective *sui generis* does not even attempt to provide a deontic justification for liability without contribution (see §6.7).

(4) **Retreat to obscurity** A fourth move in Tribunal jurisprudence has been to offer muddled and contradictory claims about whether the commander is or is not liable in relation to the acts of the subordinates. I will show that such vagueness is not a suitable solution (see §6.7).

(5) **Reconceptualize culpability** The fifth, and most ambitious and sophisticated, strategy is to build a new account of culpability that does not require

---

[3]   This premise may be particularly controversial for many readers, but, as I will elaborate in §6.6, the Tribunals do in fact charge, convict, and sentence the commander as party to the underlying crimes.

causal contribution. I explore this possibility in Chapter 7. Even in an open-minded, coherentist account that is receptive to reconstructive ideas, such arguments are at this time too undeveloped and problematic to be relied on in punishing human beings.

(6) **Proposed solution: respect the contribution requirement** I will argue that the best solution is the simplest: to go back and untie the first knot that led to all of the subsequent knots. If we undo the first mis-step, in which causal contribution was rejected for hasty and inadequate reasons, we immediately discover an elegant solution. Command responsibility in ICL institutions remains a mode of accessory liability, just as it has long been recognized. As such, it requires causal contribution. This requirement is not burdensome, because it can be satisfied by showing that the commander's dereliction aggravated the risk of the subsequent crimes. The solution instantly reconciles Tribunal jurisprudence with the ICC Statute, the transnational case law (from Nuremberg up to the Tribunals), and fundamental principles of criminal justice.

There are admittedly shortcomings in my proposed solution; no available interpretive solution perfectly reconciles all of the puzzle pieces. The proposed approach somewhat restricts the usefulness of the "failure to punish" branch. My solution also means that a successor commander cannot be held liable for past crimes to which she could not possibly have contributed. However, I will argue that this is a non-problem that has occupied too much attention in ICL already. Non-contributory derelictions can be addressed, if necessary, through legislative addressed through national prosecutions or even treaty amendments; amendments; in my view, this quite narrow problem does not warrant making implausible claims about applicable law or breaching the culpability principle. Presently, ICL institutions, with their limited resources, are struggling to address persons who bear much greater responsibility for core crimes. It is therefore strange that the current debate focuses so keenly on those whose oversights did not facilitate even a single such crime. However, even if you disagree with the particular proposed solution, I hope you will agree with my main point: the need to clear the terrain of overly simplistic arguments that simply disregard deontic principles.

6.1.2 Resulting Insights

Insights about reasoning

My main concern in this chapter is with reasoning and internal contradictions. I will demonstrate problematic tendencies in past reasoning, as well as the need for better engagement with deontic constraints and helpful concepts of criminal law theory. Attentiveness to reasoning also helps us to better understand the trajectory by which command responsibility discourse became so complicated, along with the stakes and the options.

I argue that Tribunal jurisprudence took an early wrong turn when it rejected the fundamental requirement of causal contribution, following hasty reasoning about the "failure to punish" branch of command responsibility. Subsequent twists and turns to escape the contradiction led to increasingly evasive claims about the nature of command responsibility. Literature and jurisprudence has now fractured into claims that command responsibility is a separate offence, a new *sui generis* form of liability (whose nature is never explained), neither-mode-nor-offence, or sometimes-mode-sometimes-offence. It has led to descriptions of command responsibility that are unnecessarily complex, vague, and even contradictory.[4] In the mainstream Tribunal approach, descriptions *have to be* elusive, because any clarity would immediately reveal the contradiction. Tools of criminal law theory can help us to notice such problems and to resolve them with more surgical care.

Insights about law

This analysis sheds new light on ongoing debates. First, the mainstream Tribunal still contains a contradiction that has not been resolved. Second, whereas the ICTY majority decision in *Hadžihasanović* on successor commanders has been vehemently criticized, I place it in a more favourable light: it is best supported by a deontic analysis.[5] Third, many criticisms of a contribution requirement as an "arbitrary" barrier to prosecution are too simplistic: the debate must recognize that if command responsibility is indeed a mode of liability, then the contribution requirement is a principled limitation to *prevent* arbitrariness. Fourth, several of the complexities from Tribunal jurisprudence need not and should not be imported to other jurisdictions: clearer and more principled paths are available. Whatever solution one prefers, a better debate will integrate the culpability principle.

Disclaimers

My inquiry here is not about possible legislative reforms, but rather the legal reasoning applied by the Tribunals (and in surrounding discourse), with the aim of improving on such reasoning in future. Furthermore, my aim here is not to criticize the Tribunals. The Tribunals operated in a pioneering phase of ICL. They were engaged in a fast-paced and complex task of constructing doctrine from diverse authorities. They had to resolve countless legal questions, and they could not give detailed consideration to every fine point, especially in the earliest cases. It is largely thanks to the Tribunals that we now have a corpus of law. My aim here is to take a step back and critically assess that corpus of law, as well as the reasoning employed, to improve upon the law and legal reasoning for the future.

---

[4] For example, Tribunal judgments describe it as responsibility for the act and also as *not* responsibility for the act: see §6.7.2.

[5] In that case, a majority of the ICTY Appeals Chamber declined to create "successor commander liability." That decision has been condemned as "arbitrary," but it should instead be commended as reducing the culpability gap. See §6.4.2.

My discussion of command responsibility and causal contribution is unavoidably lengthy, for two reasons. First, the collective understanding of command responsibility is now a Tower of Babel, remarkably fractured, with many conflicting conceptions of it. Each reader will have different understandings and thus different priorities that they would wish to see addressed first. Second, I am offering observations at quite different levels: about reasoning, about doctrine, and about criminal theory. When all is untangled, I hope to have persuaded you that there is a contradiction, that it has been obscured by the discourse, and that more elegant solutions are available.

6.2 THE NOVEL REACH OF COMMAND RESPONSIBILITY

To appraise command responsibility, we must ask: what is distinctive about it? In what way does command responsibility reach *beyond* other modes of liability, doing something that other modes do not, thereby warranting its separate existence? The command responsibility doctrine, as articulated in the statutes and jurisprudence of the Tribunals, imposes liability where:

(1) there is a superior–subordinate relationship;
(2) the superior knew or had reason to know that a subordinate was about to commit crimes or had done so; and
(3) the superior failed to take the necessary and reasonable measures to prevent such acts or to punish the perpetrators.[6]

The ICC Statute takes a very similar approach,[7] with two notable differences. First, and most importantly for present purposes, the ICC Statute expressly requires that the commander's dereliction causally contributed to the crimes.[8] Second, the ICC Statute also handles the mental element differently; I will discuss this in Chapter 8.

---

[6] ICTY Statute, Art 7(3); ICTR Statute, Art 6(3); *Prosecutor v Kordić and Čerkez*, Judgment, ICTY A.Ch, IT-95–14/2-A, 17 December 2004, at para 839.
[7] ICC Statute, Art 28(a), provides (emphasis added):
   A *military commander* or person effectively acting as a military commander shall be *criminally responsible for crimes* within the jurisdiction of the Court *committed by forces under his or her effective command* and control, or effective authority and control as the case may be, *as a result of his or her failure* to exercise control properly over such forces, where:
   (i) That military commander or person either *knew* or, owing to the circumstances at the time, *should have known* that the forces were committing or about to commit such crimes; and
   (ii) That military commander or person *failed to take all necessary and reasonable measures* within his or her power to prevent or repress their commission or to submit the matter to the competent authorities for investigation and prosecution.
[8] The ICC Statute requires that the crimes were "a result of his or her failure to exercise control properly over such forces." As I will discuss, the culpability principle does not require that this be interpreted as a "but for" causation; the principle is satisfied by contributions that aggravated the risk of the resulting crimes.

I refer here to command responsibility as a mode of accessory liability because that is how it has been understood and applied over the history of ICL, with controversy arising only relatively recently. Prior to the creation of the Tribunals, jurisprudence, legislation, and discourse were consistent that command responsibility is a mode of liability.[9] I will address in §6.6 the more recent contention that command responsibility might constitute an entirely separate offence.

How does command responsibility reach beyond other liability doctrines? First, if a commander actually *orders* or instigates a crime, then she is already liable by virtue of other modes of liability (such as ordering, instigating, or joint commission). Second, where a commander does not initiate the crimes, but *knows* of the crimes and *contributes* to them, then she may still be liable through "aiding and abetting" or other complicity doctrines.[10] Third, where the commander *knows* of the pending or ongoing crimes, but nonetheless *omits to prevent* them, she can still be found complicit: aiding and abetting by omission has, for example, been recognized where the person is under a duty to prevent crimes and is in a position to act, yet fails to do so.[11]

Accordingly, the distinctive reach of command responsibility is that it captures the commander who "had reason to know" or "should have known" of the crimes and failed to prevent or punish them.[12] Other modes of liability in ICL, such as aiding and abetting by omission, require *knowledge* of the crimes. It is the modified mental element that gives command responsibility its additional substantive reach. As I will argue in Chapter 8, command responsibility signals that, given the seriousness of the commander's duties and the danger inherent in supervising troops, a deliberate or criminally negligent failure to fulfill the duty to control troops can be a basis for accessory liability in any crimes resulting from that failure.

---

[9]   See references in §6.6.

[10] Other complicity doctrines include "joint criminal enterprise" before the Tribunals and contribution to a "common purpose" before the ICC. See, e.g., ICC Statute, Art 25.

[11] *Prosecutor v Orić*, Judgment, ICTY T.Ch, IT-03-68-T, 30 June 2006 ("*Orić* Trial Judgment") at para 283; *Prosecutor v Orić*, Judgment, ICTY A.Ch, IT-03-68-A, 3 July 2008 ("*Orić* Appeals Judgment") at para 43; *Prosecutor v Halilović*, Judgment, ICTY T.Ch, IT-01-48-T, 16 November 2005, at para 303–04 ("*Halilović* Trial Judgment"); *Prosecutor v Kvočka*, Judgment, ICTY A.Ch, IT-98-30/1-A, 28 February 2005, at para 187; with particularly detailed discussion at *Prosecutor v Mrkšić et al*, Appeal Judgment, ICTY A.Ch, IT-IT-95-13/1-A, 27 September 2007, at paras 49, 134–35, 146, and see survey of aiding and abetting by omission in M Jackson, *Complicity in International Law* (Oxford University Press, 2015) at 98–110. For comparable approaches in national (common law) systems, see A P Simester & G R Sullivan, *Criminal Law: Theory and Doctrine*, 3d ed (Hart, 2007) at 204–07; A Ashworth, *Principles of Criminal Law*, 5th ed (Oxford University Press, 2006) at 410.

[12] Of course, beyond this additional *substantive* reach, command responsibility also has an *expressive* or pedagogic value. It helps to reinforce the message that superiors must take steps to prevent and repress crimes by subordinates. Thus cases in which commanders had actual knowledge – which technically could be prosecuted as aiding and abetting by omission – can be prosecuted under command responsibility. Doing so advances the didactic function of the command responsibility doctrine, which is to reinforce that superiors must take steps to prevent and repress crimes by subordinates. My point in this section is simply that, in terms of substantive reach, command responsibility is distinct from other modes by virtue of its modified mental element.

Tribunal jurisprudence claims that there is an additional difference: that command responsibility is a special mode of liability that does not require any contribution to the subordinate's crimes. It is this claim (and the lack of any attempt at deontic justification) that I examine in this chapter.

6.3 THE CULPABILITY CONTRADICTION

In this section, I demonstrate the internal contradiction between Tribunal jurisprudence and the fundamental principle of personal culpability as recognized by the Tribunal itself.

6.3.1 Tribunal Jurisprudence Recognizes the Culpability Principle, Including the Contribution Requirement

Tribunal jurisprudence declares its exemplary compliance with fundamental principles, including the culpability principle.[13] For example, in *Tadić* it was recognized that "the foundation of criminal responsibility is the principle of personal culpability: nobody may be held criminally responsible for acts or transactions in which he has not personally engaged or in some other way participated."[14] The principle means that we punish people only for deeds for which they are personally culpable. The principle of personal culpability has an objective aspect (a connection to the crime) and a subjective aspect (a blameworthy mental state). My focus in this chapter is on the objective aspect – that is, that we hold persons responsible only for their own conduct and the consequences thereof. Culpability is personal, and hence we cannot punish a person for crimes in which she was not involved.

An individual may, of course, share liability relating to acts physically perpetrated by others, provided that the individual *contributed* to the acts and did so with a mental state sufficient for accessory liability. Criminality often involves multiple actors, each contributing to a crime in different ways and to differing degrees. The commitment to punish persons only for their own wrongdoing means that the accused must contribute in some way to a crime to be liable for it. ICL scholars Guénaël Mettraux and Ilias Bantekas have, respectively, observed that the requirement that the accused be "causally linked to the crime itself is a general and

---

[13] UN Secretary General, *Report of the Secretary-General Pursuant to Paragraph 2 of Security Council Resolution 808 (1993)*, UN Doc S/25704 (1993) at paras 34 and 106; *Prosecutor v Tadić*, Decision on the Defence Motion for Interlocutory Appeal on Jurisdiction, ICTY A.Ch, IT-94-1-A, 2 October 1995, at paras 42, 45 and 62; J Pejic, "The International Criminal Court Statute: An Appraisal of the Rome Package" (2000) 34 International Lawyer 65 at 69.

[14] *Prosecutor v Tadić*, Judgment, ICTY A.Ch, IT-94-1-A, 15 July 1999 (*"Tadić* Appeal Judgment") at para 186; see also *Judgment of the International Military Tribunal (Nuremberg)*, reproduced in (1947) 41 AJIL (supplement) 172 at 251 ("criminal guilt is personal").

fundamental requirement of criminal law"[15] and that, "in all criminal justice systems, some form of causality is required."[16]

ICL jurisprudence recognizes that, for personal culpability, accessory liability requires some contribution to the underlying crime. For example, in *Kayishema* the ICTR affirmed that it is "firmly established that for the accused to be criminally culpable his conduct must … have contributed to, or have had an effect on, the commission of the crime."[17] Tribunal jurisprudence has also recognized that conduct *after* the completion of crime cannot be regarded as contributing to the commission of the crime.[18]

Those parties to a crime who are most directly responsible are liable as *principals*, and more indirect contributors are liable as *accessories*. I will discuss the principal–accessory distinction at greater length in Chapter 8, where I will discuss some controversies and different approaches to the distinction.[19] For the present purpose of simply demonstrating an internal contradiction, it suffices to work with the distinction as recognized in ICL.[20]

Whereas principals "cause" the crime (or make an "essential" contribution, often expressed as *sine qua non*, or "but for," causation of some aspect of the crime), accessories need only "contribute" in a more peripheral way.[21] A principal brings

---

[15] G Mettraux, *The Law of Command Responsibility* (Oxford University Press, 2009) at 82. Mettraux suggests, however, that causal contribution can be satisfied by contributing to impunity for the crime (*ibid* at 43 and 80). This position differs from the generally recognized conception of culpability, which requires a contribution to the crime itself, and is reminiscent of earlier doctrines such as "accessory after the fact."

[16] I Bantekas, "On Stretching the Boundaries of Responsible Command" (2009) 7 JICJ 1197 at 1199.

[17] *Prosecutor v Kayishema*, Judgment, ICTR T.Ch, ICTR-95-1T, 21 May 1999, at para 199. Similarly, ICTY jurisprudence has held that "rendering a substantial contribution to the commission of a crime is indeed expressing a feature which is common to all forms of participation": *Orić* Trial Judgment, *supra* note 9, at para 280.

[18] Tribunal jurisprudence indicates that the only "exception," in which conduct after the crime can be regarded as contributing to the commission of the crime, is where there is a prior agreement to subsequently aid or abet: *Prosecutor v Blagojević and Jokić*, Judgment, ICTY T.Ch, IT-02-60-T, 17 January 2005, at para 731. However, this is not really an exception, given that there is a *prior* agreement, and it is the agreement that can facilitate, encourage, or have an effect on the crime.

[19] This accords with the "mid-level principles" and coherentist approach outlined in Chapter 4. Because the distinction is so well established in ICL and in most national systems, we can at least adopt it as a starting hypothesis or point of departure. As I will discuss in Chapter 8, some scholars and some systems do not support the distinction. See, e.g., J Stewart, "The End of 'Modes of Liability' for International Crimes" (2011) 25 LJIL 165. In my view, the arguments against do not displace the weight of extensive practice and normative argument in favour of the distinction.

[20] See, e.g., H Olásolo, "Developments in the Distinction between Principal and Accessory Liability in Light of the First Case Law of the International Criminal Court," in C Stahn & G Sluiter, eds, *The Emerging Practice of the International Criminal Court* (Brill, 2009).

[21] There are different possible ways of distinguishing between accessories and principals. In this chapter, I focus on the essential contribution, which has support in ICL jurisprudence and ICL literature. See, e.g., *Prosecutor v Katanga and Chui*, Decision on Confirmation of Charges, ICC PTC, ICC-01/04-01/07, 30 September 2008, at paras 480–86; *Prosecutor v Lubanga*, Decision on the Confirmation of Charges, ICC PTC, ICC-01/04-01/06, 29 January 2007, at paras 322–40. See also H Olásolo, *supra* note 18; M Dubber, "Criminalizing Complicity: A Comparative Analysis" (2007) 5 JICJ 977. It also

about the *actus reus* through her own acts (direct perpetration) or otherwise makes an essential contribution, including by acting through others while still having "control" over the crimes. By contrast, the contribution of an accessory may be more indirect: the accessory's actions either *influence* or *facilitate* the voluntary acts and choices of the principal(s).[22]

Importantly, to "contribute" to a crime is a less demanding standard than to "cause" the crime.[23] Merely contributing requires only that one's conduct was of a nature that would facilitate or encourage the crime. After all, accessories are liable for assisting and encouraging others, and "causation" can rarely be traced through the voluntary and informed acts of other human beings. Accordingly, it is not required that an accessory "cause" the crime in the sense of a *sine qua non* causal relation; all that is required is some "contribution."[24]

A typical and plausible elaboration on the contribution requirement in Tribunal jurisprudence is that it is "enough to make the performance of the crime *possible or at least easier*"[25] and that the contribution can be any assistance or support, whether present or removed in place and time, *furthering or facilitating* the performance of the crime, provided that it is "prior to the full completion of the crime."[26] As I will discuss in Chapter 7, the contribution requirement is not onerous: it can be satisfied by conduct of a nature that would encourage or facilitate the crime (elevating the risk).

Furthermore, the contribution may be in the form of an omission if the accused was under an obligation to prevent the crime.[27] (It is sometimes argued that omissions cannot make contributions; I discuss this in Chapter 7. ICL jurisprudence follows the mainstream and common-sense position that our failures can indeed

---

has support in scholarship on normative underpinnings of criminal law. To take some prominent examples from the English-language literature, S H Kadish, "Complicity, Cause and Blame: A Study in the Interpretation of Doctrine" (1985) 73 Calif L Rev 323, explains in a seminal article how principals make a *sine qua non* ("but for") contribution, whereas the accomplice aids or influences the principal; the consequence of her act is the influence on the choices and actions of others. See also M S Moore, "Causing, Aiding, and the Superfluity of Accomplice Liability" (2007) 156 U Pa L Rev 395 at 401; J Dressler, "Reassessing the Theoretical Underpinnings of Accomplice Liability: New Solutions to an Old Problem" (1985) 37 Hastings LJ 91 at 99–102.

Another difference between accessories and principals, discussed in Chapter 8, is that a principal must have the paradigmatic *mens rea* for the offence, whereas an accessory has a different *mens rea* requirement stipulated by the mode of liability.

[22]   Kadish, *supra* note 19, at 328 and 343–46; Dressler, *supra* note 19, at 139.
[23]   See, e.g., J Gardner, "Complicity and Causality" (2007) 1 Crim Law & Philos 127 at 128; I Bantekas, "The Contemporary Law of Superior Responsibility" (1999) 93 AJIL 573 at 577; Kadish, *supra* note 19, at 337–42; Simester & Sullivan, *supra* note 9, at 193–96.
[24]   In Chapter 7, I explore the outer limits of causal contribution, i.e. the minimum level of involvement entailed by the culpability principle for any form of accessory liability.
[25]   *Orić* Trial Judgment, *supra* note 9, at para 282 (emphasis added).
[26]   *Ibid* (emphasis added). The *Orić* case also confirms that the contribution standard is not "but for" causation; it simply requires a significant effect that furthers or facilitates the crime: *ibid* at para 338.
[27]   *Ibid* at para 283.

have consequences. For example, failing to lock a door facilitates escape or entry through that door.[28])

I should address two possible points of confusion. First, a surprisingly common misperception in ICL jurisprudence and literature is that the accessory liability model entails "pretending" or "deeming" the accessory to have "committed" the crime.[29] Accessory liability is not deemed commission; accessories are held responsible for their own role in contributing to the crime with the requisite level of fault. Second, you might be thinking of attempts, incitement, or "accessory after the fact" as possible examples of noncontributory modes of liability. Those, however, are separate offences. The common law concept of "accessory after the fact" was rejected in modern times as a form of accessory liability, specifically because it is considered unsound to hold someone as accessory to a crime to which they made no contribution.[30]

6.3.2 Yet Tribunal Jurisprudence Rejects Contribution in Command Responsibility

Despite affirming the culpability principle and the contribution requirement entailed therein, Tribunal jurisprudence nonetheless goes on to assert that the requirement does not apply to command responsibility. For example, the Tribunal's decision in *Orić* acknowledges that modes of liability require a causal contribution and thus that superior responsibility "would require a causal contribution to the principal crime," yet asserts that causal contribution is not required, "for good reasons."[31] I will scrutinize the quality of those "good reasons" in a moment (see §6.5). First, however, I will outline how the anticontribution position emerged and show the implications of that position.

The doctrine of command responsibility provides two distinct ways of proving dereliction by the commander: (i) failure to *prevent* crimes, and (ii) failure to *punish* crimes.[32] The first branch is satisfied where that the commander "failed to take the necessary and reasonable measures" to try to *prevent* the crimes.[33] The "failure to *prevent*" branch does not pose culpability problems. Given that the commander has

---

[28]   Tribunal jurisprudence has followed the mainstream position that the "substantial effect" requirement, when applied to omissions, requires that "had the accused acted the commission of the crime would have been substantially less likely": *Prosecutor v Popović*, Judgment, ICTY A.Ch, IT-05–88-A, 30 January 2015, at para 1741.

[29]   For examples of this misunderstanding, see discussion in §8.3.2.

[30]   See §7.2.1.

[31]   *Orić* Trial Judgment, *supra* note 9, at para 338.

[32]   The ICTY and ICTR Statutes refer to failures to prevent and failures to punish. The ICC Statute actually splits the possible derelictions into three categories: failure to prevent, failure to repress, and failure to submit the matter to other authorities for punishment. While the three-prong ICC approach may be useful for highlighting different obligations of commanders, I will, for simplicity, continue to refer to the two conceptually different stages: failures to prevent (referring to actions required prior to a particular crime) and failures to punish (referring to actions required after a particular crime). The three options in the ICC Statute ultimately collapse into these two conceptual categories.

[33]   ICTY Statute, Art 7(3); ICTR Statute, Art 6(3). A similar requirement appears in ICC Statute, Art 28 (a)(ii) and 28(b)(iii). The obligation is one of means and not results; the mere fact that crimes

a duty to provide training and to establish preventive systems, the failure to do so facilitates crimes in comparison with the situation that would exist had she met her duty.[34]

It is the second branch, the "failure to *punish*" crimes, that has caused confusion and difficulty. This branch refers to the failure of the commander to take the reasonable and necessary measures to investigate and punish or to refer the matter to competent authorities for investigation and prosecution.[35] Obviously, a commander's failure to punish in relation to a particular crime can occur only *after* that crime; hence it cannot causally contribute to that particular crime. For this reason, Tribunal jurisprudence has declared that it is "illogical"[36] and "would make no sense"[37] to require that the failure to punish the crime contribute to that same crime. From this observation, the ICTY reasoned that "the very existence" of the failure to punish branch in Article 7(3) of its Statute "demonstrates the absence of a requirement of causality."[38] Accordingly, the Tribunal rejected the contribution requirement.[39]

It is true that a failure to punish a crime cannot retroactively causally contribute to that same crime. However, this does not demonstrate that the "failure to punish" branch is incompatible with the contribution requirement. It seems incompatible only if we fail to consider the possibility of a *series* of crimes.

FIG 1 If we conceive only of the one-crime scenario, there would seem to be a contradiction between the "failure to *punish*" branch and requiring causal contribution

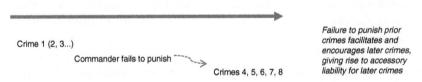

FIG 2 However, if we conceive of multiple crimes, the seeming paradox is solved

nonetheless occurred does not mean that the commander failed to meet her duty to take reasonable preventive steps.

[34] Some may argue that a failure to prevent, being an omission, cannot be regarded as "contributing" to any events. This argument is discussed in §7.1.2.

[35] ICTY Statute, Art 7(3); ICTR Statute, Art 6(3); ICC Statute, Art 28(a)(ii) and 28(b)(iii).

[36] *Prosecutor v Blaškić*, Judgment, ICTY A.Ch, IT-95–14-A, 29 July 2004 ("*Blaškić* Appeal Judgment").

[37] *Orić* Trial Judgment, *supra* note 9, at para 338.

[38] *Prosecutor v Delalić et al (Čelebići)*, Judgment, ICTY T.Ch, IT-96–21-T, 16 November 1998 ("*Čelebići* Trial Judgment") at para 400. The prosecution similarly rejected the possibility of causal nexus "as a matter of logic" (*ibid* at para 397).

[39] *Ibid* at paras 396–40; endorsed in *Blaškić* Appeal Judgment, *supra* note 34 at para 76.

Consider the scenario in which subordinates commit not one crime, but a *series* of crimes, which is indeed the typical situation in ICL. The first crime(s) are committed. At some point, the commander either learns of the crimes or has enough information that she "should have known" or "had reason to know" of the crimes. The commander fails to take reasonable steps to have the crimes investigated and prosecuted, and crimes continue to occur. Although this failure of the commander cannot retroactively contribute to the *initial* crimes, it can and does contribute to each *subsequent* crime. Her failure to punish the prior crimes facilitates the subsequent crimes, in comparison with the legally required baseline of a diligent response to her subordinates' crimes. Her dereliction facilitates and elevates the risk of crimes in multiple ways. If the subordinates know of the lack of punishment, they may perceive a reduced risk of punishment or may perceive a permissive signal. But we do not even need a showing of such knowledge, because the commander has failed to deliver the deterrent and repudiative message that she was obligated to give, and thus she has, by omission, elevated the risk in comparison to the situation that would pertain had she met her obligation.[40] The commander properly shares in accessory liability for the subsequent crimes, because her failure to punish prior crimes is a culpable omission that facilitated those crimes.

Once we consider the scenario of multiple crimes, which is actually the most common scenario in ICL, we see that the "failure to punish" branch can indeed be reconciled with a requirement of causal contribution. Thus there was no incompatibility or contradiction that would require, or even permit, the Tribunal to reject a requirement of the fundamental principle of personal culpability.

I believe that the Tribunal's reasoning in those cases is an example of hurried doctrinal reasoning that does not engage adequately with deontic constraints. The Tribunal abandoned the culpability principle all too insouciantly because of a surface-level doctrinal argument (textual construction). Indeed, the seeds of confusion can be traced even further back, to the drafters of the ICTY Statute, who blithely merged criminal and non-criminal provisions of Additional Protocol I to the Geneva Conventions (AP I), without considering the culpability principle.[41] Had the chambers approached the text with the culpability principle more carefully in mind, the provision could readily have been interpreted compatibly with the requirement.

---

[40] See §7.1.2 on omissions.

[41] See discussion at §2.3.2. The criminal law provision of AP I (Art 86(2)) referred only to ongoing or imminent crimes, which complies with the culpability principle. It was a different provision, Art 87, which set out a more general civil duty of commanders and rightly included the duty to punish past crimes (but which did not purport to render the commander retroactively personally liable for the past crimes). The merger is an example of what I call "conflation," i.e. assuming that the rule in criminal law must be co-extensive with the rule in international humanitarian law, without pausing to reflect on the different context of criminal law.

6.4 THE STAKES

To illuminate the implications of allowing convictions without contributions, I will outline two scenarios of "non-contributory" failures to punish. By "non-contributory," I mean that the failure was not followed by any subsequent crimes, and thus it did not facilitate or encourage any crimes by subordinates. One scenario is the problem of the isolated crime; the other is the problem of the successor commander. I will also address the main objections to respecting the culpability requirement.

6.4.1 The Problem of the Isolated (or Initial) Crime

The first problem is where a crime occurs, the commander fails to punish, and yet no other crimes occur. The problematic scenario arises only where the commander has adequately met her "preventive" duties; otherwise, the failure to prevent could facilitate or encourage crimes, and there is no problem with causal contribution. On my account – an account that respects the contribution requirement – the commander cannot be retroactively liable as party to the isolated crime, because she did not contribute to it. She could be held liable for subsequent crimes following that failure to punish, but not for the isolated crime to which she did not contribute.

A variation on this scenario is what we may call the "problem of the initial crime." In this variation, following the commander's failure to punish, further crimes do indeed occur. The commander may be properly liable for the *subsequent* crimes because her failure to punish prior crimes facilitated or encouraged those crimes.[42] However, she should not be liable for the *initial* crime or crimes (the crimes prior to the time at which she knew or had reason to know that crimes were occurring), because she made no culpable contribution, by act or omission, to those crimes.

In the isolated crime scenario, the commander has clearly failed in her responsibilities, and she may face various consequences for her dereliction, including criminal liability for dereliction of duty offences. But, I argue, we cannot convict her as a party to the core crime. She has done something wrong, but "party to genocide" is not an accurate or fair description of her wrong.[43] By contrast, Tribunal jurisprudence would allow her conviction as a party to that initial crime by virtue of command responsibility, in the absence of any contribution, in violation of the culpability principle as currently understood.

6.4.2 The Problem of the Successor Commander

An even more glaring problem of non-contributory dereliction arises in the scenario of the "successor commander." This scenario arose in *Hadžihasanović*, in which a

---

[42] It facilitates or encourages in comparison to the legally required baseline behaviour of diligent action. See §7.1.2 explaining the causal contribution of omissions to fulfill a duty.

[43] Unless a new conception of retroactive culpability is developed (see Chapter 8).

commander, Kubura, had taken up his command position *after* certain crimes were committed.[44] Kubura was nonetheless charged with crimes committed *prior to his assignment* by virtue of command responsibility and his failure to punish those crimes once he took up the post.

The prosecution, the Trial Chamber, and the two dissenting judges in the Appeals Chamber pressed the proposition that causal contribution is not required to its furthest extension. If no causal contribution is required, then it follows that the accused need not even have been in command or involved in the outfit at the time of the crimes. Indeed, it would equally follow that the accused need not even have been *born* at the time of the crimes. All that would matter is that, at some point, the accused assumed command, became aware of past crimes or had reason to know of them, and failed to punish the persons responsible. If we apply the doctrine mechanistically and without any concern for fundamental principles, this approach would meet all of the formal requirements of Article 7(3) of the ICTY Statute.

On appeal, a bare 3–2 majority of the Appeals Chamber recoiled from successor commander liability, over some strong dissents and with some heated judicial language on all sides.[45] The majority held that the commander must at least have been in command at the time of the crimes. The reasoning of the majority was not explicitly based on concern for the culpability principle, but rather on the doctrinal grounds that prior sources and authorities did not seem to support successor commander liability for past crimes.[46] Judges Shahabuddeen and Hunt, in dissent, would have allowed successor commander liability.

The *Hadžihasanović* decision generated major controversy and has spawned an extensive literature on successor commander liability. Rather than receiving applause for its principled restraint, the majority position has come under extensive criticism. Much of the discourse illustrates the reasoning habits discussed in Chapter 2, focusing on international humanitarian law sources and the goal of maximizing deterrence, but neglecting the deontic constraint on personal criminal culpability. Many scholars argue that the majority position creates a "loophole," an "arbitrary limitation," and a "gaping hole" through which perpetrators will "escape liability."[47] Within the ICTY, trial chambers have openly expressed their discontent

---

[44] *Prosecutor v Hadžihasanović*, Decision on Interlocutory Appeal Challenging Jurisdiction in Relation to Command Responsibility, ICTY A.Ch, IT-01-47-AR72, 16 July 2003 ("*Hadžihasanović* Interlocutory Appeal"). Appended to the decision are the dissenting opinions of Judge Shahabuddeen and Judge Hunt.

[45] *Ibid.*

[46] *Ibid* at paras 37–56. See also T Meron, "Revival of Customary Humanitarian Law" (2005) 99 AJIL 817 at 824–26. While the approach does not directly reference the culpability principle, it does reflect concern for the legality principle.

[47] See, e.g., C Fox, "Closing a Loophole in Accountability for War Crimes: Successor Commanders' Duty to Punish Known Past Offences" (2004) 55 Case W Res L Rev 443; D Akerson & N Knowlton, "President Obama and the International Criminal Law of Successor Liability" (2009) 37 Denver J Int L & Pol'y 615; Mettraux, *supra* note 13, and the declarations of Judges Shahabuddeen, Liu, and Schomburg in the *Orić* Appeals Judgment, *supra* note 9, as well as further examples in Chapter 6.

and disapproval of the majority decision.[48] A trial chamber of the Sierra Leone Special Court declined to follow the majority approach and instead adopted the dissent approach.[49] The ICTY Appeals Chamber itself almost overturned the majority position in a later decision (*Orić*). Separate opinions in the *Orić* decision described the *Hadžihasanović* majority decision as "an erroneous decision," "highly questionable," and an "arbitrary limitation,"[50] and noted that there "is a new majority of appellate thought."[51] The Appeals Chamber narrowly declined to overturn *Hadžihasanović* on the grounds that the facts in *Orić* did not squarely require a determination on that issue.[52]

The judicial debate was framed in terms of precedents and teleological arguments. What was largely missing from the conversation is the deontic dimension – that is, that convicting a person for crimes completed before she even joined the unit would be a startling departure from the culpability principle at least as hitherto understood. If such a proposition is to be entertained at all, it would require a new understanding of culpability, backed by convincing deontic justification.[53]

The culpability problem was not entirely overlooked. Judge Shahabuddeen, dissenting in *Hadžiihasanović*, acknowledged that modes of liability require causal contribution.[54] His solution to the impasse was that he "prefers" to characterize command responsibility as a separate offence. This was the origin of the "separate offence" versus "mode of liability" controversy that still burns today. While that characterization would indeed solve the problem, I argue in §6.6 that it is not

---

[48] *Orić* Trial Judgment, *supra* note 9, at para 335 ("it should be immaterial whether he or she had assumed control over the relevant subordinates prior to their committing the crime. Since the Appeals Chamber, however, has taken a different view for reasons which will not be questioned here, the Trial Chamber finds itself bound"); *Halilović* Trial Judgment, *supra* note 9, at para 53.

[49] *Prosecutor v Sesay, Kallon and Gbao*, Judgment, SCSL T.Ch, SCSL-04-15-T, 2 March 2009 ("*RUF Case*") at para 306 ("this Chamber is satisfied that the principle of superior responsibility as it exists in customary international law does include the situation in which a Commander can be held liable for a failure to punish subordinates for a crime that occurred before he assumed effective control"). But see *contra Prosecutor v Brima, Kamara and Kanu*, Judgment, SCSL T.Ch, SCLC-04-16-T, 20 June 2007 ("*AFRC Case*") at para 799 ("there is no support in customary international law for the proposition that a commander can be held responsible for crimes committed by a subordinate prior to the commander's assumption of command over that subordinate"); *Prosecutor v Fofana and Kondewa*, Judgment, SCSL T.Ch, SCSL-04-14-T, 2 August 2007 ("*CDF Case*") at para 240 ("The Chamber further endorses the finding of the ICTY Appeals Chamber that an Accused could not be held liable under Article 6(3) of the Statute for crimes committed by a subordinate before the said Accused assumed command over that subordinate").

[50] *Orić* Appeals Judgment, *supra* note 9, Liu Declaration, paras 5 and 8; *ibid*, Schomberg Declaration at para 2.

[51] *Ibid*, Shahabuddeen Declaration at para 3; see also *ibid* at para 12.

[52] *Ibid* at para 167 ("The Appeals Chamber, Judge Liu and Judge Schomburg dissenting, declines to address the *ratio decidendi* of the *Hadžihasanović* Appeal Decision on Jurisdiction, which, in light of the conclusion in the previous paragraph, could not have an impact on the outcome of the present case").

[53] Possible alternative understandings of culpability, including an intriguing argument advanced by Amy Sepinwall, are touched upon in §7.2.

[54] *Orić* Appeals Judgment, *supra* note 9, Shahabuddeen Declaration at para 17.

available to the judges of the Tribunals and the ICC. In any case, Tribunal jurisprudence is explicit that it is a mode of liability, and hence the unresolved contradiction persists.

The position taken by the prosecution[55] and by most of the jurisprudence[56] is the greater puzzle, because it involves a stark contradiction. That position (i) regards command responsibility as a mode of accessory liability, (ii) rejects the contribution requirement, and yet (iii) proclaims compliance with the culpability principle. Such a position could be defended only with a new deontic account of personal culpability, which the Tribunals have not offered or even attempted.

This culpability contradiction is not immediately evident, because several arguments have obscured it. The remaining sections in this chapter (§6.5–§6.7) examine the evolution of the legal argumentation, showing how the culpability contradiction was long obscured from view.

6.4.3 Common Objections to the Contribution Requirement

The main recurring objection is that the constraint of requiring contribution would create a "gap" that will allow commanders to "escape justice" for the isolated or initial crimes.[57] Such arguments are an illustration of one of the problematic structures of argument that I discussed in Chapter 2. They adopt a purely utilitarian approach focusing on the single variable of maximizing deterrence, and they fail to engage with the deontic question of whether conviction in such circumstances would constitute "*justice*." If the commander is not culpable for the core crime, then our inability to convict her does not mean she is "escaping justice." On the contrary: our inability to convict constitutes "justice."

The second common objection is that that the scope of criminal liability would be narrower than the full scope of the humanitarian law duty.[58] This objection illustrates another of the problematic structures of argument that I discussed in Chapter 2. The objection assumes that ICL norms must be coextensive with human rights or humanitarian law norms. The humanitarian law duty certainly does require the commander to punish all past crimes, regardless of whether she contributed to them.[59] Thus any failure to punish would indeed breach *humanitarian* law. It is, however, an entirely different question whether we can hold her retroactively *personally criminally liable* as an accessory to those crimes. Before transplanting the humanitarian law rules into ICL prohibitions, we must pause and reflect on the

---

[55] As discussed, e.g., *ibid* at para 18.
[56] The ambiguities of the jurisprudence are discussed in §6.7.
[57] See examples cited at §6.4.2 (loophole, gaping hole, escape justice, etc.).
[58] See, e.g., *Hadžihasanović* Interlocutory Appeal, *supra* note 42, esp Judge Hunt at paras 21–22 and Judge Shahabuddeen at paras 23, 25 and 38. See also *Orić* Appeals Judgment, *supra* note 9, esp Judge Liu at paras 19–21 and 30–31 and Judge Schomberg at parass 8 and 18–19.
[59] See, e.g., AP I, Art 87(3).

limits of personal criminal culpability. The personal criminal liability of the individual may rightly be narrower than the civil obligation of her state or armed group; that is not necessarily a "lacuna."

Respecting the culpability principle does not mean that commanders are free to ignore past crimes. First, a failure to punish would mean that the state or armed group has breached *humanitarian* law, triggering any relevant remedies under that law. Second, the commander may also personally face *criminal* law repercussions if a lawmaker with jurisdiction has criminalized non-contributory derelictions of duty. But what it does preclude[60] is holding the commander liable as an accessory, via command responsibility, for past crimes on which her derelictions had no possible influence.

6.5 FIRST STRATEGY: DOCTRINAL ARGUMENTS TO SIDESTEP THE CONTRIBUTION REQUIREMENT

The initial responses to complaints about the culpability contradiction were technical doctrinal[61] arguments. I will argue that not only are these doctrinal arguments wrong *qua* doctrinal arguments, but also they are the wrong *type* of answer. They do not even attempt to address the objection that the system is contradicting its recognized fundamental principles.

6.5.1 The Perceived Incompatibility with "Failure to Punish"

As explained in §6.3, the contribution requirement was initially rejected on the grounds that it cannot be reconciled with the "failure to punish" branch of command responsibility. In *Čelebići*, the defence argued that a "failure to punish" should give rise to accessory liability only if that failure is "the cause of *future offences*."[62] The Chamber appears to have missed the subtlety of the defence argument and instead considered whether a failure to punish a crime can cause that *same crime*. The Chamber held that "no such causal link can possibly exist" between a failure to punish an offence and "that same offence."[63] The Chamber opined that "the very existence" of the failure to punish branch in Article 7(3) of the ICTY Statute "demonstrates the absence of a requirement of causality."[64] The prosecution similarly rejected the possibility of causal nexus "as a matter of logic."[65] In *Blaškić*, the defence again argued that a contribution to crimes must

---

[60] Unless a new conception of retroactive culpability is developed (see Chapter 8).
[61] I use the term "doctrinal" in the sense used among common law scholars. It refers to technical legal arguments, often employed in a piecemeal way, which do not necessarily engage with broader systemic coherence and deeper underlying principles.
[62] *Čelebići* Trial Judgment, *supra* note 36, at para 396.
[63] *Ibid* at para 400.
[64] *Ibid*.
[65] *Ibid* at para 397.

be shown even under the "failure to punish" branch, and the Appeals Chamber found the defence argument to be "illogical," because "disciplinary and penal action can only be initiated after a violation is discovered."[66]

The Chambers' reasoning is sound as far as it goes, but it is too simplistic. The defence was not arguing that a failure to punish a crime can retroactively cause that same crime. The defence argument – consistent with the culpability principle – was that a failure to punish can create accessory liability only with respect to *subsequent* crimes encouraged or facilitated by that failure.[67] There is nothing "illogical" about recognizing the "failure to prevent" branch while also respecting the contribution requirement.

It is often argued that recognizing the contribution requirement would render the "failure to punish" branch redundant.[68] However, the two branches ("failure to prevent" and "failure to punish") offer two distinct ways of proving the failure of the commander. A prosecutor may prove *either* a failure to take adequate preventative measures *or* inadequate efforts to investigate and prosecute crimes. Either provides the dereliction that, if accompanied by a blameworthy state of mind and a contribution to crimes, can ground accomplice liability for resulting crimes.

Respecting the contribution requirement does, admittedly, partly restrict the use of the "failure to punish" branch in this mode of criminal liability, because such failures are significant only if subsequent crimes occur. I consider this more subtle concern in §6.8, where I discuss how every possible solution has at least a minor incongruity, and I show how other solutions create even greater incongruities. For now, I note that the solution slightly restricts the "failure to punish" branch, but is not "irreconcileable" with it, nor does it render it redundant or outright ineffective.

6.5.2 The Claim that Precedents Did not Require Contribution

The second doctrinal response is the claim that past precedent did not require causal contribution for command responsibility. For example, in *Čelebići*, the defence argued that the commander's failure to punish must contribute to the commission of criminal acts.[69] The Trial Chamber acknowledged "the central place assumed by the principle of causation in criminal law,"[70] but nonetheless asserted that a causal contribution "has not traditionally been postulated" as a condition for liability under command responsibility.[71] In a one-sentence analysis, the Chamber asserted that it "found no support" for a requirement of causal contribution for command

---

[66] *Blaškić* Appeal Judgment, *supra* note 34, at para 83.

[67] *Čelebići* Trial Judgment, *supra* note 36, at 396.

[68] For this form of argument, see, e.g., *Orić* Trial Judgment, *supra* note 9, at para 335; *Orić* Appeals Judgment, *supra* note 9, Judge Liu at para 7; *ibid*, Judge Schomberg at para 8, all in the context of successor commander liability.

[69] *Čelebići* Trial Judgment, *supra* note 36, at paras 345 and 396.

[70] *Ibid* at para 398.

[71] *Ibid* (emphasis added).

responsibility in the case law, treaty law, or (with one exception) the literature.[72] Similar defence arguments were advanced again in a later case,[73] but the Appeals Chamber cited with approval the analysis in *Čelebići* and rejected causal contribution as an element of command responsibility.[74]

The problem with responses pointing to past authority is that they are the wrong *type* of answer. These responses give a technical, mechanical, "source-based" analysis.[75] But a culpability challenge requires a deontic analysis: one must actually assess compatibility with the fundamental principles that limit our licence to punish individuals. This deontic task requires an assessment of whether the rules are *just*.[76]

Interestingly, in addition to being the wrong *type* of response, the precedent argument was inaccurate even as a doctrinal argument. Numerous scholars have shown that past cases and authorities actually do provide ample authority for a contribution requirement.[77] I will not repeat those efforts by embarking here on a doctrinal review of the past authorities; my concern here is not with source-based doctrinal analysis, but rather with the culpability principle and with reasoning. We can, however, glean from this example a fantastic lesson about reasoning: curiously, the *Čelebići* Chamber somehow managed to detect "no support" for a contribution requirement even though the *Čelebići* decision itself *directly* quoted passages from authorities that *explicitly* support the requirement. To give two examples, *Čelebići* cites the post-World War II *Toyoda* decision, which described the principle as covering the commander who, "by his failure to take any action to punish the perpetrators, permitted the atrocities to continue."[78] *Čelebići* also cites legislation of the former Yugoslavia providing that "a military commander is responsible as a participant or an instigator if, by not taking measures against subordinates who

---

[72] *Ibid* (emphases added). The exception that the Chamber noted was the work of Cherif Bassiouni, arguing that causal contribution was an essential element.

[73] *Blaškić* Appeal Judgment, *supra* note 34, paras 73–77, with similar issues also arising in paras 78–85.

[74] *Ibid* at paras 76 and 77. Subsequent cases have, in turn, cited *Čelebići* and *Blaškić* as authoritatively settling this question See, e.g., *Halilović* Trial Judgment, *supra* note 9; *Prosecutor v Brdjanin*, Judgment, ICTY T.Ch, IT-99-36-T, 1 September 2004, at para 280.

[75] See §1.2.1.

[76] Of course, precedent would matter where there is a formally binding or discursively persuasive precedent that specifically considers and rules on compatibility with the culpability principle.
In fairness to the precedent-based reasoning in the *Čelebići* and *Blaškić* decisions, the defence lawyers in those cases primarily characterized their challenge as one based on the principle of legality (*nullum crimen sine lege*). Thus reference to doctrine was an appropriate response to that challenge. The problem is that subsequent chambers have regarded *Čelebići* and *Blaškić* as conclusively settling all debate on the issue, and hence they have not engaged seriously with the distinct problem of culpability.

[77] O Triffterer, "Causality, a Separate Element of the Doctrine of Superior Responsibility as Expressed in Article 28 Rome Statute?" (2002) 15 LJIL 179; Mettraux, *supra* note 13, at 82–86 and 236; A Cassese, *International Criminal Law*, 2nd ed (Oxford University Press, 2008) at 236–42; C Greenwood, "Command Responsibility and the *Hadžihasanović* Decision" (2004) 2 JICJ 598; Bantekas, *supra* note 14; V Nerlich, "Superior Responsibility under Article 28 ICC Statute: For What Exactly Is the Superior Held Responsible?" (2007) 5 JICJ 665 at 672–73.

[78] *Čelebići* Trial Judgment, *supra* note 36, at para 339.

violate the law of war, he allows his subordinate units to continue to commit the acts."[79] These and other authorities highlight other courts' and lawmakers' under-standing that, *even for failures to punish*, liability arises when the commander's failure *permitted other crimes* to continue. The clues were there for those attuned to see them. The lesson I draw from this is that, even in source-based analysis, what we see – and what we overlook – is influenced by our sensitivities. If we are mindful of fundamental principles, we are more likely to see the patterns in authorities that are consistent with those principles; if we are not mindful, we may miss those patterns.

6.5.3 The Argument that Respecting the Contribution Requirement Would Render Command Responsibility Superfluous

The third major doctrinal argument against a contribution requirement is that it would render command responsibility "redundant" with other modes of liability. The *Halilović* and *Orić* decisions argued that, if causal contribution were required, then the "borderline between article 7(3) [command responsibility] and ... 7(1) [the other modes] ... would be transgressed and, thus, superior criminal responsibility would become superfluous."[80]

This argument overlooks that command responsibility is already distinct from other modes of liability by virtue of the modified mental element. Command responsibility allows conviction based on a "had reason to know" or "should have known" standard.[81] Thus it is not true that recognizing the contribution requirement – and hence respecting the culpability principle – would render command responsibility superfluous.

A related argument is that "[i]f a causal link were required this would change the basis of command responsibility" because "it would practically require involvement on the part of the commander ... thus altering the very nature of the liability imposed under Article 7(3)."[82] This argument is also incorrect: the essence of command responsibility remains the *failure to become involved* where there was a duty to do so. The failure to intervene facilitates the crime in comparison with the situation that would have existed had the commander met her duty.[83]

In conclusion, each of the doctrinal responses is problematic on two levels. First, they are unsound even as doctrinal arguments because their premises (the alleged incompatibility with text, absence of precedent, or redundancy with other modes) are false. Second, and more fundamentally, these arguments engage at entirely the wrong *level*. They do not even *attempt* to engage with the deontic argument: the

---

[79]　*Ibid* at para 341.
[80]　*Orić* Trial Judgment, *supra* note 9, at para 338. See also *Halilović* Trial Judgment, *supra* note 9, at para 78.
[81]　This fault standard is examined in Chapter 8.
[82]　*Halilović* Trial Judgment, *supra* note 9, at para 79.
[83]　This crime-facilitating effect of the commander's failure satisfies the contribution requirement. On omissions and causation, see §7.1.2.

violation of the fundamental principle of culpability. ICL claims to respect the culpability principle as "the foundation of criminal responsibility" and thus to hold persons responsible only for transactions in which they "personally engaged or in some other way participated."[84] Technical doctrinal arguments, such as reconciling one provision with another, are no answer to the challenge that one is contradicting one's own stated fundamental principles. To answer such a challenge, one must consider the normative question of compliance with deontic constraints.[85]

6.6 SECOND STRATEGY: CHARACTERIZATION AS A SEPARATE OFFENCE

6.6.1 Emergence of the "Separate Offence" Characterization

We now arrive at the next twist in the discourse on command responsibility. In *Hadžihasanović*, the Appeals Chamber confronted the scenario of the "successor commander," which places the problems of not requiring causation in particularly stark relief. Faced with defence objections to liability in the absence of "any involvement whatsoever in the *actus reus*,"[86] Judge Shahabuddeen, dissenting, advanced an innovative solution: "I prefer to interpret the provision as making the commander guilty for failing in his supervisory capacity to take the necessary corrective action … Reading the provision reasonably, it could not have been designed to make the commander a party to the particular crime committed by his subordinate."[87] Several subsequent trial-level decisions seized on this approach,[88] giving birth to a new and vigorous controversy over the very nature of command responsibility.[89]

---

[84] *Tadić* Appeal Judgment, *supra* note 12, at para 186.

[85] One might be able to uphold the no-contribution approach by reconceptualizing the principle of culpability, but this would require careful deontological justification (see §7.2), not technical doctrinal arguments.

[86] *Hadžihasanović* Interlocutory Appeal, *supra* note 42, Judge Shahabuddeen at para 32.

[87] *Ibid.*

[88] *Orić* Trial Judgment, *supra* note 9, at para 335 ("it should be immaterial whether he or she had assumed control over the relevant subordinates prior to their committing the crime. Since the Appeals Chamber, however, has taken a different view for reasons which will not be questioned here, the Trial Chamber finds itself bound"); *Halilović* Trial Judgment, *supra* note 9, at para 53; *RUF Case, supra* note 47, at para 306 ("this Chamber is satisfied that the principle of superior responsibility as it exists in customary international law does include the situation in which a Commander can be held liable for a failure to punish subordinates for a crime that occurred before he assumed effective control"); *Prosecutor v Ndindiliyiman*, Judgment, ICTR T.Ch, ICTR-00-56-T, 17 May 2011, at paras 1960–61.

But see *contra* AFRC Case, *supra* note 47, at para 799 ("there is no support in customary international law for the proposition that a commander can be held responsible for crimes committed by a subordinate prior to the commander's assumption of command over that subordinate"); *CDF Case, supra* note 47, at para 240 ("The Chamber further endorses the finding of the ICTY Appeals Chamber that an Accused could not be held liable under Article 6(3) of the Statute for crimes committed by a subordinate before the said Accused assumed command over that subordinate").

[89] See, e.g., Fox, *supra* note 45; Greenwood, *supra* note 75; B B Jia, "The Doctrine of Command Responsibility Revisited" (2004) 3 Chinese J Int'l L 1; Mettraux, *supra* note 13, 190–92; Nerlich, *supra*

6.6.2 The "Separate Offence" Approach Would Avoid the Culpability Problem

The "separate offence" approach is preferable to the doctrinal arguments canvassed in the previous section, because it does not simply ignore the culpability principle. If breach of command responsibility were legally established as a separate offence, the concerns about culpability would be resolved. The commander would not be held indirectly liable as a party to crimes to which she in no way contributed; instead, she would be held directly liable for her own dereliction. However, I believe that the option of declaring a new offence of breach of command responsibility is not legally available to the Tribunals, for reasons I will explain in a moment.

To be clear, in this case study, I am looking at the plausible interpretive options for the Tribunals (and, by extension, the ICC); I am not engaged in the legislative policy debate of which approach would be preferable for a national legislator or treaty drafter. I have no objection to "separate offence" legislation. Indeed, I helped to draft the Canadian legislation, which, for domestic legal reasons, was one of the first to establish "breach of command responsibility" as a separate offence.[90] Both approaches have merits. The "mode" approach has the advantage of reflecting the grave harm flowing from the commander's failure to act. The "dereliction"

---

note 75; C Meloni, "Command Responsibility: Mode of Liability for the Crimes of Subordinates or Separate Offence of the Superior?" (2007) 5 JICJ 619; R Arnold & O Triffterer, "Article 28: Responsibility of Commanders and Other Superiors," in O Triffterer, ed, *Commentary on the Rome Statute of the International Criminal Court: Observers' Notes, Article by Article*, 2nd ed (Beck, 2008); Akerson & Knowlton, *supra* note 45, at 627; A J Sepinwall, "Failures to Punish: Command Responsibility in Domestic and International Law" (2009) 30 Michigan J Int'l L 251; E van Sliedregt, "Article 28 of the ICC Statute: Mode of Liability and/or Separate Offence?" (2009) 12 New Crim L Rev 420; B J Moloto, "Command Responsibility in International Criminal Tribunals" (2009) 3 Publicist 12; S Trechsel, "Command Responsibility as a Separate Offence" (2009) 3 Publicist 26; B Sander, "Unravelling the Confusion Concerning Successor Superior Responsibility in the ICTY Jurisprudence" (2010) 23 LJIL 105; R Cryer, "The Ad Hoc Tribunals and the Law of Command Responsibility: A Quiet Earthquake," in S Darcy & J Powderly, eds, *Judicial Creativity at the International Criminal Tribunals* (Oxford University Press, 2010); J Dungel & S Ghadiri, "The Temporal Scope of Command Responsibility Revisited: Why Commanders Have a Duty to Prevent Crimes Committed after the Cessation of Effective Control" (2010) 17 U C Davis J Intl L & Pol'y 1; T Weigend, "Superior Responsibility: Complicity, Omission or Over-Extension of the Criminal Law?," in C Burchard, O Triffterer & J Vogel, eds, *The Review Conference and the Future of International Criminal Law* (Kluwer, 2010); N Tsagourias, "Command Responsibility and the Principle of Individual Criminal Responsibility: A Critical Analysis of International Jurisprudence," in C Eboe-Osuji, ed, *Essays in International Law and Policy in Honour of Navanethem Pillay* (Martinus Nijhoff, 2010); C Meloni, *Command Responsibility in International Criminal Law* (TMC Asser, 2010); E van Sliedregt, "Command Responsibility at the ICTY: Three Generations of Case Law and Still Ambiguity," in A H Swart, A Zahar & G Sluiter, eds, *The Legacy of the ICTY* (Oxford University Press, 2011); E van Sliedregt, *Individual Criminal Responsibility in International Law* (Oxford University Press, 2012); K Ambos, *Treatise on International Criminal Law, Vol I: Foundations and General Part* (Oxford University Press, 2012) at 219–26; J Root, "Some Other Mens Rea? The Nature of Command Responsibility in the Rome Statute" (2013) 23 Transnat'l L & Pol'y 119; Jackson, *supra* note 9.

90 K Prost & D Robinson, "Canada," in C Kress et al, eds, *The Rome Statute and Domestic Legal Orders, Vol 2* (Nomos, 2000–05) at 54–55.

approach has the advantage of capturing non-contributory derelictions. Indeed, national legislation or a treaty amendment could even posit *both* concepts, recognizing command responsibility as a mode of participation *and* establishing a separate offence for non-contributory derelictions. The German and Korean legislation are commendable models.[91] My case study here, however, focuses on problems in the reasoning applied in the interpretation of the existing ICL statutes.

6.6.3 The Legality Problem: Departure from Applicable Law

In my view, the difficulty with the "separate offence" approach is that it is an implausible departure from the applicable law of the Tribunals (and the ICC), and hence it is a change that should not be made by judicial fiat, but rather by lawmakers (legislators or treaty drafters), if it must be made.

The Tribunal Statutes (and the ICC Statute) appear to recognize command responsibility as a mode of liability, not as a crime. For example, Article 28 of the ICC Statute is *explicit* that the commander is held "criminally responsible *for crimes … committed by forces* under his or her effective command and control."[92] It is hard to see how drafters could make it clearer that the commander is held criminally responsible for the crimes of the subordinates, other than saying so explicitly, as they did. The ICTY Statute is not as explicit. However, as Robert Cryer notes, we should not lightly conclude that command responsibility has an entirely different nature in different statutes, lest we create unnecessary fragmentation between instruments that purport to reflect customary law.[93] Furthermore, command responsibility appears in the general principles of liability,[94] and in the ICTY Statute, inchoate offences are not listed among the principles of liability; they are all listed in the

---

91   Tae Hyun Choi & Sangkul Kim, "Nationalized International Criminal Law: Genocidal Intent, Command Responsibility, and an Overview of the South Korean Implementing Legislation of the ICC Statute" (2011) 19 Michigan State J Int'l L 589 at 616–21; Gesetz zur Einführung des Völkerstrafgesetzbuches [Act to Introduce the Code of Crimes against International Law], 26 June 2002, Bundesgesetzblatt Jahrgang 2002 Teil II, Nr. 42, 2254), online: www.mpicc.de/shared/data/pdf/vstgbleng2.pdf. See art 1, §4(1) (intentional omission to prevent the commission of a crime is a mode of liability) and art 1, §§13, 14 (failure to properly supervise and/or report crimes are separate offences). The German legislation recognizes a mode of liability only where there is both a contribution and subjective *mens rea*; the latter requirement is plausibly cautious to ensure constitutionality. In Chapter 8, I argue that the departure from subjective *mens rea* in ICL may be justifiable in a liberal system; however, the argument remains to be judicially tested.

92   ICC Statute, Art 28(1)(a); see similarly ICC Statute, Art 28(1)(b).

93   Cryer, *supra* note 87, at 182 (also warning against judicial adoption of a separate offence approach, which would be a "legislative move, fundamentally altering the basis of command responsibility").

94   For example, in the ICTY Statute, the crimes are listed in Arts 2–5, whereas command responsibility appears in Art 7, which contains principles of "individual criminal responsibility," including the other modes of liability, such as planning, instigating, ordering, and aiding and abetting. Similarly, in the ICC Statute, definitions of crimes appear in Pt II, whereas command responsibility appears in Pt III, "General Principles of Criminal Law."

definitions of crimes (attempt, conspiracy, and incitement appear only in the definition of crimes attached to the crime of genocide).[95]

More importantly, the ICTY Statute purports to reflect customary law, and customary law precedent was overwhelmingly consistent that command responsibility is a mode of liability. The consistent understanding is seen in jurisprudence from Nuremberg up to the Tribunals, in national legislation, and in state practice. For example, in the negotiation of the Rome Statute, it was uncontroversial that command responsibility is a mode of liability.[96] I will not embark here on a lengthy review of the doctrinal precedents; to do so would require an additional chapter of this book, and my aim here is to explore the Tribunal's handling of the culpability principle, not to recount earlier precedents. Other scholars have admirably canvassed the precedents showing that it was a mode of liability.[97] If any doubts remain on this score, consultation of these works canvassing the precedents will likely allay them.

Indeed, Tribunal jurisprudence itself acknowledges that previous customary law authorities regarded command responsibility as accessory liability.[98] Significantly, even the *Halilović* decision, in which an ICTY Trial Chamber creatively advocated for the separate offence interpretation, actually demonstrates the long consistency of the "mode" approach. Although the *Halilović* decision attempted to characterize post-World War II jurisprudence as "divergent," in fact every authority it cited adopted the "mode" approach, with the exception of only one passage from one case that only arguably supported a separate dereliction offence. The *Halilović* decision also acknowledged that national legislation treated command responsibility as a mode of accomplice liability and that the jurisprudence of the Tribunal itself had consistently done so.[99] Thus even the *Halilović* decision could not find contrary precedents. Prior to the *Hadžihasanović* controversy, academic literature had long recognized command responsibility as a mode of liability.[100] The mode-versus-

---

95 ICTY Statute, Art 4(3); ICTR Statute, Art 2(3).

96 See, e.g., UN Diplomatic Conference of Plenipotentiaries on the Establishment of an International Criminal Court, Rome, 15 June–17 July 1998, Official Records, A/CONF.183/13 (Vol 2) at 136–38 (responsibility for acts of subordinates).

97 Sepinwall, *supra* note 87, at 265–69; Sander, *supra* note 87; Meloni, *supra* note 87; Cryer, *supra* note 87; van Sliedregt, *supra* note 87, at 192–96.

98 For examples cited in Tribunal jurisprudence, see the *Čelebići* Trial Judgment, *supra* note 34, at para 336, citing French law ("accomplices"); *ibid* at 337, citing Chinese law ("accomplices"); *ibid* at 341, citing Yugoslav law ("participant"); *ibid* at 338, citing the *Hostages (List)* case ("held responsible for the acts of his subordinates").

99 *Halilović* Trial Judgment, *supra* note 9, para 42–53.

100 See, e.g., Greenwood, *supra* note 75, at 603–04 (punished for the subordinate's act); Sepinwall, *supra* note 87, at 267 (doctrinal history gives "overwhelming support for the mode of liability view"); Cryer, *supra* note 87, at 171–82 (form of liability for the underlying offence); Bantekas, *supra* note 14, at 577 (imputed liability); Cassese, *supra* note 75, at 206; Triffterer, *supra* note 75, at 229 (mode of participation); Arnold & Triffterer, *supra* note 87, at 843; D L Nersessian, "Whoops, I Committed Genocide! The Anomaly of Constructive Liability for Serious International Crimes" (2006) 30 Fletcher F World Aff 81at 89; Meloni, *supra* note 87, at 621–25; Darcy & Powderly, *supra* note 87,

offence controversy arose only out of an effort to square the Tribunals' refusal to recognize a contribution requirement with the culpability principle.

My position about the applicable law is not rooted in a rigidly formalistic approach. I would allow judges latitude to interpret and reinterpret provisions of their respective statutes, especially given that ICL is a nascent discipline that is being developed each day. It is always possible that the earliest authorities did not consider all of the implications or did not express themselves perfectly, so that judges may later need to interpret them in new and better ways. However, a precedent-based argument that command responsibility was a separate offence all along collides with the facts. Moreover, as Barrie Sander notes, we must be wary where the proposal is to judicially recognize a new crime, because that may contravene the legality principle.[101] In any event, Appeal Chamber jurisprudence has expressly rejected the "separate offence" characterization and affirmed that command responsibility is a mode of liability.[102]

6.6.4 Explicit Contradiction with Actual Practice

There is another problem with the oft-repeated claim that the Tribunals do not charge the commander with the underlying crimes – namely, that it is demonstrably, empirically untrue. When we look at the actual charges, convictions, and sentences entered by the Tribunal, we see that the commanders are *expressly* charged, convicted, and sentenced for the underlying offences of genocide, crimes against humanity, and war crimes.

Judges and scholars claiming that the commander is not charged with the underlying crime often cite an "entirely unreasoned" and "throwaway"[103] line in

at 391; W J Fenrick, "Some International Law Problems Related to Prosecutions before the International Criminal Tribunal for the former Yugoslavia" (1995) 6 Duke J Comp & Int'l L 103 at 111–12 (party to offence, not a separate offence); W H Parks, "Command Responsibility for War Crimes" (1973) 62 Military L Rev 1 at 113–14; Y Shany & K R Michaeli, "The Case against Ariel Sharon: Revisiting the Doctrine of Command Responsibility" (2001–02) 34 NYU J Int'l L & Pol 797 at 803 and 829–31; A Zahar, "Command Responsibility of Civilian Superiors for Genocide" (2001) 14 LJIL 591 at 596 (mode of participation, not a crime); M Smidt, "*Yamashita, Medina*, and beyond: Command Responsibility in Contemporary Military Operations" (2000) 164 Military L Rev 155, 168–69; K J Heller, *The Nuremberg Military Tribunals and the Origins of International Criminal Law* (Oxford University Press, 2011) at 271. But see Jia, *supra* note 87, at 34; Trechsel, *supra* note 87; K Ambos, "Superior Responsibility," in A Cassese, P Gaeta & J R W D Jones, eds, *The Rome Statute of the International Criminal Court: A Commentary, Vol 2* (Oxford University Press, 2002) at 823 (separate offence). Ambos suggests a separate offence approach not because of precedents, but on principled grounds that it is the only way in which to comply with deontic principles given the "should have known" standard. This argument is more convincing than other arguments, but in Chapter 9 I map out the argument that this route is not necessary, and thus precedent and principles can be reconciled.

[101] Sander, *supra* note 87, at 122.
[102] *Prosecutor v Ntabakuze*, Judgment, ICTR A.Ch, ICTR-98-4-A, 8 May 2012.
[103] Cryer, *supra* note 87, at 177–79.

the *Krnojelac* case: "It cannot be overemphasized that, where superior responsibility is concerned, an accused is not charged with the crimes of his subordinates but with his failure to carry out his duty as a superior to exercise control."[104] This passage is sound insofar as it emphasizes that the commander's liability is not vicarious, but rather rooted in fault, or that she is not charged with *perpetrating* the crimes. However, if the passage is to be construed as meaning that the commander is literally not charged as a party to the underlying core crime, but rather is charged for a distinct crime of "failure to exercise her duty to exercise control," then the passage is plainly factually untrue. For example, in that very case, Krnojelac was in fact charged with "crimes against humanity and violations of the laws and customs of war," including torture, murder, persecution, unlawful confinement, and enslavement – that is, the core crimes carried out by his subordinates.[105] He was also *convicted* of those crimes.[106] For example, he was found "guilty of … murder as a crime against humanity and murder as a violation of the laws or customs of war)," pursuant to Article 7(3) (command responsibility), and "guilty of … torture as a crime against humanity and a violation of the laws or customs of war," pursuant to Article 7(3). He was found guilty of those crimes by virtue of command responsibility. Other cases follow the same pattern: By virtue of command responsibility, commanders are charged not with a separate dereliction offence, but with the underlying crimes of subordinates, and the commanders are sentenced as parties to those crimes.[107]

Notice that I am not here advancing a doctrinal argument that there is "precedent" for treating command responsibility as a mode; rather, my point is about *veracity*. One cannot deflect a culpability challenge by claiming that the commander is not held responsible as a party to the core crime when, in reality, the charges and convictions do precisely that. In the actual command responsibility practice of the Tribunals, commanders are explicitly charged with the underlying crimes and sentenced as parties to the underlying crimes.

6.6.5 Principled Arguments for Separate Offence Interpretation

There are alternative and more sophisticated argument for a separate offence approach. Some scholars have argued for a separate offence interpretation, based

---

[104]   *Prosecutor v Krnojelac*, Judgment, ICTY A.Ch, IT-97-25-A, 17 September 2003 ("*Krnojelac* Appeal Judgment") at para 171.
[105]   *Prosecutor v Krnojelac*, Third Amended Indictment, ICTY T.Ch, IT-27-95-I, 25 June 2001.
[106]   *Krnojelac* Appeal Judgment, *supra* note 102, at Pt VI, Disposition.
[107]   Sander, *supra* note 87, at 116 provides additional examples. In one trial decision, *Orić* Trial Judgment, *supra* note 9, the Trial Chamber purported to convict the accused for a separate offence of "failing to discharge his duty to prevent." The prosecution appealed on the grounds that this was a mischaracterization of command responsibility, which is a mode of liability, and that the sentence failed to reflect its gravity as a mode of liability. The Appeals Chamber found that the factual findings for a command responsibility conviction had not been made and thus that the issue was moot: *Orić* Appeals Judgment, *supra* note 9, at para 79.

not on disingenuous claims about applicable law, nor as an expedient device to enable convictions of successor commanders, but for the principled reason that it is the only way of complying with fundamental principles.[108] I would endorse such an approach if it were the only way of complying with fundamental principles: in that case, canons of construction could allow a strained textual reading and a departure from precedents to avoid violating fundamental principles.[109] A coherentist legal interpretation would endorse a creative re-reading, if it were the best way of making sense of all considerations. However, in my view, that route is not necessary, because the precedents and principles can be reconciled, and hence a creative judicial recharacterization (creating a new crime) is not warranted.[110]

(There is still one more possibility for a separate offence approach: those who are adamant about prosecuting successor commanders before international courts could embrace an admittedly imaginative and reconstructive "separate offence" interpretation. After completing my discussion of the trajectory of the main arguments, I will discuss disadvantages of this alternative approach in §6.8, under "Implications.")

6.7 OTHER RESPONSES (AND THE INCREASING MYSTIFICATION OF COMMAND RESPONSIBILITY)

For the reasons just given in §6.5 and §6.6, neither of the first two strategies solved the culpability problem in Tribunal jurisprudence. Command responsibility discourse then became even more fractured and convoluted. Positions on the nature of command responsibility proliferated: mode of liability separate offence, neither-mode-nor-offence, sort-of-mode-sort-of-offence, and sometimes-mode-sometimes-offence. In the resulting climate of uncertainty, Tribunal judgments began to include muddled and self-contradictory statements about the nature of command responsibility.

6.7.1 Invoking *Sui Generis* Nature

One of the later lines of response in Tribunal jurisprudence was to assert that command responsibility is a *"sui generis"* mode of liability, to which the contribution requirement simply does not apply. For example, the *Halilović* decision

---

[108]   Ambos, *supra* note 98, at 825, 851–52; Meloni, *supra* note 87, at 637.
[109]   One could argue that the "context" includes fundamental principles of justice, or that the object and purpose includes compliance with fundamental principles of justice.
[110]   The precedents (which overwhelmingly support the "mode" approach) can be reconciled with principles by respecting the contribution requirement. The requirement is not onerous (see Chapter 7). It is well established that omissions can make contributions (see Chapter 7). The trickiest aspect is the "should have known" standard, but I argue that the special insight of command responsibility is that this too is deontically justified (see Chapter 8).

declares that "the nature of command responsibility itself, as a *sui generis* form of liability, which is distinct from the modes of individual responsibility set out in Article 7(1), does not require a causal link."[111] However, simply invoking the label *sui generis* and declaring *per definitionem* that this new mode does not require causal contribution does not even attempt to address the culpability problem. It is a hand-waving gesture, or a naked assertion; it is not a deontic justification.[112]

6.7.2 The Retreat to Obscurity (Neither Mode Nor Offence)

Some scholars and some decisions appear to argue that command responsibility is *neither* a mode of liability *nor* a separate offence and is instead some hitherto unknown *category* altogether.[113] Such arguments are intriguing. One of the themes of this book is that ICL can raise new problems that lead to new thinking for general criminal law theory. The discovery of an entirely new category of liability, falling outside any known category (i.e. separate offence, principal liability, accessory liability), would be an excellent illustration of this point.

My concern, however, is that this particular characterization simply creates a shroud of ambiguity to obscure the culpability problem. This vagueness about the nature of command responsibility enables a kind of "shell game": Jurists can downplay the "mode" nature of command responsibility whenever the culpability problem is raised, and they can then shift back to treating it as a mode of liability just in time for conviction and sentencing. James Stewart has aptly described such arguments as "more of a smokescreen to ward off conceptual criticisms than a marked normative change."[114]

Subsequent contortions in Tribunal jurisprudence are a fascinating case study of how problems from a contradiction can compound. Tribunal jurisprudence has tied itself into increasingly tortuous knots trying to deny the contradiction between (i) a mode that does not require contribution and (ii) the accepted principle that modes require contribution. An illustration of this convolution is the equivocation

---

[111] *Halilović* Trial Judgment, *supra* note 9, at para 78.

[112] There is nothing wrong per se in describing command responsibility as *sui generis*, in the sense that it has differences from other modes. Indeed, any mode must be distinct from other modes in some way; otherwise, it would not need to exist. However, each mode must still be justified in accordance with fundamental principles.

[113] See, e.g., A M M Orie, "*Stare Decisis* in the ICTY Appeal System: Successor Responsibility in the *Hadžihasanović* Case" (2012) 10 JICJ 635 at 636 ("Superior responsibility is increasingly considered to be of a *sui generis* character rather than a mode of liability"). See also Mettraux, *supra* note 13, at 37–47 and 80–88, who also appears to suggest this. Mettraux rejects accessory liability as the appropriate category, on the grounds that accessory liability requires knowledge. However, as I argue in Chapter 8, a subjective knowledge requirement does not appear to be an immutable defining feature of accessory liability. It is possible to construct a deontic justification for a "should have known" standard in the context of command responsibility. Accordingly, command responsibility can be a mode of accessory liability.

[114] Stewart, *supra* note 17, at 25.

and self-contradiction over whether responsibility "for" the crimes means responsibility "for" the crimes.[115] Some judgments seek to downplay the culpability
problem by insisting that the commander is not held responsible "for" the crimes
committed by subordinates, but ironically those very same judgments slip and
contradict themselves, acknowledging it as responsibility for the acts.[116]
Frequently, the judges struggle to describe an indirect liability that is neither
personal commission nor a separate offence.[117] But the indirect liability that
these passages struggle to describe is already beautifully and elegantly captured
by an existing concept: *accessory liability*. I think that this conceptual and terminological haziness is a sign that ICL is still a relatively young field. Careful, systematic criminal law theory has helpful tools to offer ICL.

If there is indeed a new category that is neither a mode nor an offence, its
proponents must clarify what this new twilight category *is*. Once we are told what
relationship this purported new category signifies between the accused and the
subordinate crime, we can try to discern the appropriate deontic requirements.
Conceptually, however, the existing categories – direct or indirect liability in the
subordinate crimes, or a separate offence – appear to exhaust the logically conceivable universe of alternatives. If the claim is to be made that another category is

---

[115] Early jurisprudence forthrightly acknowledged that the commander is held responsible for the crimes
of the subordinates. See, e.g., *Čelebići* Trial Judgement, *supra* note 36, at para 333 (commanders are
"held criminally responsible for the unlawful conduct of their subordinates"). Later cases, seeking to
downplay the culpability problem, struggle to clarify that responsibility "for" the crimes does not
actually mean responsibility "for" the crimes, but rather "because of" the crimes.

[116] See, e.g., *Prosecutor v Aleksovski*, Judgment, ICTY T.Ch, IT-95-14/1-T, 25 June 1999, at para 72
("superior responsibility … must *not be seen as responsibility for the act of another person*"). Yet see
also *ibid* at para 67: "A superior is *held responsible for the acts of his subordinates* if he did not prevent
the perpetration of the crimes of his subordinates or punish them for the crimes" (emphasis added).
Similarly, *Halilović* Trial Judgment, *supra* note 9, at para 54 emphasizes that the commander is not
held liable *"for"* the crimes, but "because of" the crimes. Then, *ibid* at para 95, the same judgment
asserts that failure to punish is so "grave that international law imposes upon [the commander]
responsibility for those crimes" (emphasis added).

[117] Consider the following attempt to square the circle in the *Halilović* Trial Judgment, *supra* note 9, at
para 54:

> "For the acts of his subordinates" as generally referred to the in the jurisprudence of the
> Tribunal does not mean that the commander shares the same responsibility as the
> subordinates which committed the crimes, but rather that because of the crimes commit-
> ted by his subordinates, the commander should bear responsibility for his failure to act …
> [A] commander is responsible not as though he committed the crime himself, but his
> responsibility is considered in proportion to the gravity of the offences committed.

> The passage is sound in insisting that the commander is deemed to be neither a perpetrator nor even
> principal of the crimes ("not a direct responsibility"; not the "same responsibility"). Often, such passages
> emphasize the commander's dereliction and fault, rightly distinguishing command responsibility from
> vicarious liability (i.e. she is not liable by virtue of the relationship alone). These features – that the
> commander is not deemed a perpetrator and that she is held responsible for her fault in relation to the
> crime – are already elegantly reflected in an existing concept: accessory liability. We do not need to
> fabricate an entire new category to capture these features of command responsibility.

possible, the gap should be explained.[118] Applying Occam's razor, it is for now more parsimonious and elegant to work with the known categories, given that they appear to be mutually exclusive and jointly exhaustive.

6.7.3 The Variegated Approach (Sometimes Mode, Sometimes Offence)

The final alternative solution that I will review in this chapter is what I will call the "variegated" approach. Some scholars suggest a variegated account in which command responsibility operates sometimes as a mode and sometimes as a separate offence. Its nature in each case depends on variables such as failure to prevent versus failure to punish, knowledge versus "should have known," or contributory versus non-contributory dereliction.[119]

The variegated approach is vastly preferable to the previous approaches. It is fully compliant with the culpability principle, and it does not rely on obscurity. It rightly recognizes the indirect liability of the commander where she contributed to crimes, it avoids the overreach of a noncausal mode of liability, and it still responds to failure-to-punish derelictions. Lawmakers are certainly welcome to adopt the variegated approach, for example, by recognizing contributory derelictions as a mode of liability and non-contributory derelictions as a separate offence.

Nonetheless, I have two concerns with reading the existing texts (the Tribunal Statutes or the ICC Statute) in line with the variegated approach. First, reading such approaches into the existing ICL texts injects a level of complexity that is textually implausible and unnecessarily complicated. The relevant texts do not suggest, on their face, that command responsibility operates differently in different instances, switching from mode to separate offence. For example, Article 28 of the ICC Statute gives no indication that an offence provision is hidden inside it.[120] Thus my objections are similar to those in relation to the "separate offence" characterization: I see difficulties with the legality principle, given the implausibility of the portrayal of applicable law. Second, I believe it is not *necessary* to read in a variegated approach: I will argue in the next section why the limited nature of this problem does not

---

[118] I do not reject the possibility that there might be some hitherto undetected gap in the categories known to criminal theory. Indeed, ICL may present new problems that help us to discover such gaps (see Chapters 3 and 5). I simply ask for greater precision as to what the alleged gap is.

[119] Some sophisticated examples of works that draw distinctions between different forms of command responsibility include Meloni, *supra* note 87, and Nerlich, *supra* note 75. Both plausibly distinguish between contributory and non-contributory derelictions and between those with and without subjective knowledge. These approaches are an advance over other approaches, because they grapple with culpability and acknowledge significant distinctions. My suggestion, however, is that simpler solutions can be found. Nerlich's solution does not refer expressly to a separate offence, but would distinguish between holding the commander responsible for the *crime* and holding the commander responsible for the *consequences of the crime* (see *ibid* at 680–82).

[120] I accept that interpreters can read counter-textual terms into a provision where it is necessary or valuable to do so and does not contradict fundamental principles, such as legality. Here, however, there is no need for a counter-textual reading.

warrant such a dramatic, results-driven counter-textual recharacterization of what the Statute and precedents actually say.

6.8 IMPLICATIONS

6.8.1 Toward a Better Debate with Deontic Engagement

My main objective in this chapter was to explore the often problematic reasoning on this topic and to show examples of inadequate deontic engagement, as well as how they triggered a cascade of problems. My secondary objective was to suggest a prescription that resolves the contradiction. Even if you disagree with my prescription, I hope you are at least convinced of the following points about reasoning and the need for a more clear and thoughtful debate.

(1) The Tribunal's initial rejection of causal contribution, in what was then clearly understood to be a mode of liability, was based on hasty and inadequate doctrinal reasoning (a perceived textual inconsistency) that did not adequately consider the culpability principle.

(2) A lot of the argumentation on this topic (in judicial decisions and surrounding literature) has featured overly simplistic arguments, based on types of reasoning discussed in Chapter 2, such as simply maximizing crime control or attempted transplants from international humanitarian law without considering the context shift.[121]

(3) Several of the main responses (the doctrinal responses, or simply invoking the adjective "*sui generis*" without any further attempt at justification) do not even *attempt* to address the violation of a stated fundamental principle.

(4) Many of the objections to the *Hadžihasanović* decision, or the contribution requirement in Article 28, as an "arbitrary" barrier to prosecution[122] failed to consider that the contribution requirement is a principled requirement for accessory culpability in order to prevent arbitrary punishment. Thus arguments against causal contribution must either (i) acknowledge and overcome the extensive applicable law indicating that command responsibility is a mode of liability, or (ii) advance a new conception of retroactive culpability (a possibility discussed in Chapter 8).

(5) The debate over the *Hadžihasanović* decision largely centred on doctrinal and teleological arguments, but I argue that the *better* basis to support the majority decision is the deontic argument: the need to respect the culpability principle.

---

[121] See, e.g., at §6.4.3.

[122] See, e.g., Akerson & Knowlton, *supra* note 45, at 360 ("obvious flaw"); Fox, *supra* note 45, at 480 ("weaknesses and limitations"); E Langston, "The Superior Responsibility Doctrine in International Law: Historical Continuities, Innovation and Criminality – Can East Timor's Special Panels Bring Militia Leaders to Justice?" (2004) 4 Int'l Crim L Rev 141 at 161 ("retreat").

(6) The contradiction remains unresolved in Tribunal jurisprudence, which recognizes command responsibility as a mode of liability and yet rejects the contribution requirement. The *Hadžihasanović* decision removes the problem of retroactively punishing successor commanders for crimes in which they were not involved, but it still allows retroactive culpability for "isolated" or "initial" crimes to which a commander in no way contributed.[123]

(7) Any legal systems that draw from Tribunal jurisprudence should carefully examine these particular aspects of the jurisprudence before importing them. Many of the convoluted claims (e.g. "neither mode nor offence") were generated by a particular problem that may not arise at other institutions. For example, the ICC Statute expressly requires causal contribution; if judges respect that explicit requirement, then the contradiction that necessitated those complex claims is entirely avoided.

(8) A better debate on these issues can at least set aside the most fallacious arguments (e.g. those that fail to consider culpability at all) and focus on the deontically tenable options.

6.8.2 The Way(s) Forward

In this chapter, I also suggested a prescription to resolve these problems. The prescription has implications for other institutions with similar statutes or who consult Tribunal jurisprudence. My thoughts in this section will turn particularly to implications for interpreting the ICC Statute.

My prescription is to undo the first mis-step that triggered the entire cascade of complexities. By repairing the initial contradiction, we can restore command responsibility to relative simplicity. Command responsibility can remain, simply and elegantly, a mode of accessory liability. The proposed approach instantly reconciles the pre-Tribunal authorities and cases, the ICC Statute, and the culpability principle. The solution has the advantage of clarity, because it relies on an established concept of criminal law (accessory liability). Accessory liability beautifully captures the idea of indirect liability that some Tribunal cases have struggled so hard to describe.[124]

There are several possible legitimate concerns about this proposed solution. First, one might fear that proving the "contribution" to a subsequent crime might be unacceptably difficult, posing a barrier to meritorious cases. I argue, however, that the contribution requirement, properly understood (see §6.3.1 and §7.1.3), is satisfied by conduct of a nature that elevated the risk of the ensuing crimes – a standard that in general is obviously met by failures to prevent or punish. Early ICC decisions are consistent with this understanding (see Annex 3).

[123] See §6.4.1.
[124] See §6.7.2.

Another legitimate concern is that the solution partly restricts the utility of the "failure to punish" branch, because such a failure must be followed by subsequent crimes. Erasmus Mayr rightly voices the concern that, "on Robinson's reading, responsibility from failure to punish begins to appear redundant, because it is reduced to one case of failure to prevent."[125] I concede that the interpretation I advocate does restrict the role of the "failure to punish" branch, because we cannot convict the commander for past crimes to which she did not contribute. However, this does not quite render the "failure to punish" branch a dead letter; it still provides the prosecutor with an alternative route to prove a dereliction. The prosecutor can show a failure to establish preventive systems or a failure to punish, or both. Furthermore, there is no interpretation that perfectly reconciles the various puzzle pieces. In the ICC Statute, this partial limitation on the usefulness of one branch of one element is necessary not only to comply with the culpability principle, but also to comply with the *explicit* contribution requirement in Article 28. The alternatives are either (i) to partly restrict the scenarios in which one branch of one element can be applied, or (ii) to ignore an explicit statutory requirement (and, along with it, the culpability principle). I believe the former is by far the more plausible.

The remaining concern arises if one is adamant that successor commanders must be punished before international courts and tribunals, even without any statute amendments. In that case, one could embrace a "separate offence" interpretation, or even the variegated approach, and to do so in a way that forthrightly acknowledges that it is a departure from precedent and a creative reinterpretation of the text.[126] However, if adopted at the ICC, such an approach would mean ignoring the explicit statement in Article 28 that the commander is held "criminally responsible for crimes committed by" subordinates. Furthermore, one would also have to commit to ignoring the explicit statutory causal contribution requirement in Article 28 for all command responsibility charges. There are legality problems with ignoring explicit statutory conditions for liability. In addition, while I am open to some creative readings to solve inadvertent problems in texts, to adopt an interpretation so contrary to the text and precedent would incur credibility and legitimacy costs that are not warranted by the limited problem.[127]

In my view, the inability to punish non-contributory derelictions before international courts is an acceptable price for (and the only apparent way of) reconciling

---

[125] E Mayr, "International Criminal Law, Causation and Responsibility" (2014) 14 Int'l Crim L Rev 855. Similarly, Miles Jackson has objected that "Robinson's interpretation would render criminal responsibility based on the well-established customary law obligation of commanders to punish the crimes of their subordinates a dead letter": Jackson, *supra* note 9, at 119. I agree that the obligation is well established *in humanitarian law*; the question here, however, is the proper role of that obligation in a criminal law mode of liability.

[126] Alternatively, one could try to offer a convincing deontic account allowing retroactive culpability: see Chapter 7.

[127] If adopted at another international tribunal, a less serious drawback of the separate offence approach is that it introduces fragmentation between instruments that all purport to reflect customary law.

the applicable law (mode of liability) with fundamental principles (culpability). The reason I do not consider this "lacuna" to be fatal is as follows. International courts and tribunals have to devote their limited resources to those persons most responsible for the most serious core crimes. In the debate over non-contributory derelictions, we are fixating on commanders who did not contribute to even a single core crime. I could conceive of prosecuting persons who contributed to no crime if they committed an inchoate offence such as attempts or incitement, because those crimes require the highest level of mental culpability: *purpose*. In attempt or incitement cases, the person is acting purposively with the *aim* of producing core crimes, so their wrongdoing entails high moral culpability and deliberate risk-creation. But with mere non-contributory failures to punish, we have *neither* that highest standard of culpability (purpose) *nor* any material contribution. I am not sure a case of non-contributory failure to punish would even make it through case selection under foreseeable conditions, for surely a prosecutor would rather charge persons with actual responsibility for the core crime itself. This is why, in my view, this lacuna does not warrant twisting the applicable law. If we want to add separate dereliction crimes to the ICC Statute (perhaps for expressive purposes), then it can be done through law-making avenues. In the meanwhile, national systems can continue to prosecute such derelictions just as they prosecute almost all serious crimes in the world.

However, even if you disagree with that particular prescription, I hope we at least agree on the main point, which is that the debate should better engage with deontic principles. I would not object strenuously to a "separate offence" approach if it were adopted transparently and at least applied consistently. My real objections are to:

(1) treating command responsibility as a mode of liability and simply ignoring the culpability contradiction;

(2) claiming that it is not a mode of liability while, in fact, charging and convicting persons as party to the subordinates' core crimes; or

(3) creating a "smokescreen" category by which the "mode" nature is downplayed whenever the culpability principle is raised, but then emphasized at the time of conviction and sentencing.

In Chapter 7, I will turn from the analytical question of "internal contradictions" to the more nuanced normative question of what precisely the contribution requirement entails and whether a non-causal alternative is available.

7

The Outer Limits of Culpability

OVERVIEW

In Chapter 6, I worked *analytically*. I compared Tribunal doctrine with the culpability principle as commonly understood, even within ICL. That inquiry was fruitful: we discerned an internal contradiction, we examined the reasoning that produced it, and we saw the tangled consequences of it. In this chapter, I move on to resulting *normative* questions: I engage in deontic analysis of what the culpability principle actually requires and whether it might be reconceived.

First, I will examine why criminal law requires causal contribution and the degree of contribution required. I will argue that the requirement in relation to accessories is not onerous; "risk aggravation" satisfies the culpability principle.

Second, I consider ambitious proposals to reimagine culpability – that is, to develop a new deontic account that does not require any causal contribution. A theme of this book is that ICL may present us with new questions that can lead us to adjust the basic assumptions common in criminal law theory.[1] Although the arguments for culpability without contribution are intriguing, my conclusion is that, on a coherentist "all things considered" judgement, they are as yet far too tentative and undeveloped to provide a convincing basis for criminal sanctions. Accordingly, the current best theory is that accessories must at least elevate the risk of the crimes occurring.

7.1 WHAT ARE THE PARAMETERS OF "CONTRIBUTION"?

7.1.1 General Recognition of a Contribution Requirement

As with any organizing concept in criminal law, it is difficult to reach unassailable "bedrock" when digging down into *why* we require a contribution to a deed to consider a person culpable for that deed.[2] Fortunately, as discussed in Chapter 4, we do not have to find "bedrock" for all of our beliefs. On a coherentist approach (which

---

[1] See, e.g. Chapters 1, 3 and esp 5.
[2] DH Husak, "Omissions, Causation and Liability" (1980) 30 The Philosophical Quarterly 323 observes that there is no objective "fact" that requires causation for culpability. H L A Hart & A M Honoré, *Causation in the Law*, 2d ed (Clarendon Press, 1985) at 132 and 64 observe that there is nothing to

I argue in Chapter 4 is the most appropriate approach), it is sufficient to follow the best evidence available, taking into account all available clues, such as patterns of practice and normative argumentation.

Turning to those clues, there is extremely strong support for a requirement that one must contribute to a crime in order to be culpable for it. First, the legal systems of the world converge in this understanding of responsibility.[3] Second, normative arguments about principles of criminal justice generally reach the same conclusion.[4] The requirement of causal contribution matches the principled commitment that we hold persons culpable for their acts and the blameworthy consequences thereof, and not for events in which they did not participate or to which they made no contribution. Causal connection is "the instrument we employ to ensure that responsibility is personal."[5] As John Gardner argues, there is no way of participating in the wrongs of another other than by making a contribution to them.[6] Similarly, Michael Moore argues that, in a justice-oriented system of criminal law, criminal responsibility must track moral responsibility, which in turn tracks natural relations such as causation.[7] Causation has been described as "deeply characteristic of human thought," appearing among diverse societies.[8]

As mentioned in Chapter 6, a different degree of causal connection is required for principals and accessories. Principal liability appears to require a *sine qua non*, "but for," type of causation. Accessory liability merely requires "contribution," which is more indirect: it suffices to encourage or facilitate the crime.[9] In the remainder of this chapter, I will try to distinguish "causation" in this narrower sense from mere "contribution."

---

compel a legal system to accept a causal connection as either necessary or sufficient for liability, yet most systems generally do so.

[3] See, e.g., Hart & Honoré, *supra* note 2, at 62–68. They mention the seeming exception of vicarious liability, which is discussed at §7.2.1.

[4] For an exception to the main trend, see C Kutz, "Causeless Complicity" (2007) 1 Crim L & Phil 289. Scholars sometimes argue that "causation" should not be required for accomplice liability, but, on closer inspection, it emerges that they are simply arguing that "but for" causation is not required for accessory liability. Such positions are consistent with the view expressed here. For example, J Dressler, "Reassessing the Theoretical Underpinnings of Accomplice Liability: New Solutions to an Old Problem" (1985) 37 Hastings LJ 91 at 102 argues that "causation" is not required for accessory liability, but by "causation," he means "but for" causation. He acknowledges the need for assistance or influence (*ibid* at 139). See also discussion by M S Moore, *Causation and Responsibility: An Essay in Law, Morals and Metaphysics* (Oxford University Press, 2009) at 402–07.

[5] Dressler, *supra* note 4, at 103.

[6] J Gardner, "Complicity and Causality" (2007) 1 Crim L & Phil 127 at 127.

[7] Moore, *supra* note 4, at 3–5 and 110.

[8] J Hall, *General Principles of Criminal Law*, 2nd ed (Bobbs Merrill, 1960) at 248.

[9] S H Kadish, "Complicity, Cause and Blame: A Study in the Interpretation of Doctrine" (1985) 73 Calif L Rev 323 at 346; Gardner, *supra* note 6; Dressler, *supra* note 4; A Ashworth, *Principles of Criminal Law*, 5th ed (Oxford University Press, 2006) at 415. As Michael Moore writes, "[t]o be an accomplice, my act must have something to do with why, how or with what ease the legally prohibited result was brought about by someone else": Moore, *supra* note 4, at 401.

7.1.2 Do Failures Have Consequences?

Some scholars argue that an omission merely *fails to avert* an outcome and cannot "cause" or "contribute" to an outcome.[10] Such arguments rely on a "naturalistic" conception of causation, which looks only at sufficient physical causes. In contrast, legal practice and normative argumentation overwhelmingly support the "normative" conception, which considers that humans have duties and that failures to meet those duties can have consequences. On the normative conception, we compare what happened to the situation that would have existed had the person met her duty.[11] If I am obliged to guard prisoners and I do not do so, the normative conception has no difficulty recognizing that my failure to guard may facilitate their escape.

My aim in this chapter is not to delve into or add to the already extensive discussion on that philosophical debate; my aim is to explore other specific issues in command responsibility and culpability. The position that I adopt (the "normative" conception of causation) already accords with ICL doctrine, with the jurisprudence of national systems, and with the preponderance of arguments on normative theory. Thus my arguments rely on the excellent responses already provided in the ample discourse on the issue.[12] In this chapter, I accept and build on the well-established normative conception of causation to unpack the implications for command responsibility.

I will nonetheless provide the following quick summation, simply to make sure that my discussion of omissions and causal contributions is clear. The counterfactual analysis of an omission mirrors the counterfactual analysis of an act. Where there was a positive act by the accused, we imagine the world in which she did not do the prohibited act to assess the difference that her act likely made. In the case of an omission, we imagine a counterfactual world in which the accused did what was legally required, and we assess the likely difference.[13]

---

[10]   *Ibid* at 446, Moore argues that that an omission is a nothingness, or an absence, and that an absence cannot produce effects; "nothing comes from nothing." While Moore concludes that counterfactual dependency does not warrant the label "causation," he holds that counterfactual dependency can give rise to liability. In this respect, he reaches a similar endpoint to other scholars, albeit with different labels. See *ibid* at 139–42 and 351–54.

[11]   See, e.g., K Ambos, *Treatise on International Criminal Law, Vol I: Foundations and General Part* (Oxford University Press, 2012) at 215–17.

[12]   See, e.g., G Fletcher, *Basic Concepts of Criminal Law* (Oxford University Press, 1998) at 67–69; G Fletcher, *Rethinking Criminal Law*, 3rd ed (Oxford University Press, 2000) at 585–625; Ashworth, *supra* note 9, at 418–20; Husak, *supra* note 2, at 160–65; Hart & Honoré, *supra* note 2, at 30–31, 40 and 447–49; C Sartoria, "Causation and Responsibility by Michael Moore" (2010) 119 Mind 475; J Schaffer, "Contrastive Causation in the Law" (2010) 16 Legal Theory 259; R W Wright, "Causation: Metaphysics or Intuition?," in K Ferzan & S Morse, eds, *Legal, Moral and Metaphysical Truths: The Philosophy of Michael Moore* (Oxford University Press, 2016).

[13]   See similarly K Ambos, "Superior Responsibility," in A Cassese, P Gaeta & J R W D Jones, eds, *The Rome Statute of the International Criminal Court: A Commentary, Vol 2* (Oxford University Press, 2002) at 860.

For example, if a pilot aboard an aircraft has a duty to operate and land the aircraft, yet chooses instead to do nothing and allow the plane to crash, most jurists (and laypersons) would conclude that the pilot's omission contributed to the crash. A purely "naturalistic" conception of causation, looking only at active physical forces, would insist that the plane crashed on its own because of gravity and inertia, and that the pilot merely "did nothing." Legal practice and ordinary language reject this as a contrived and myopic way of describing events.[14] On a "normative" conception of causation, we compare the result against what would have resulted if the pilot had met the baseline expectation of carrying out her legal duty. Under common notions of causation and responsibility, we would not hesitate to find that the pilot's omission to fulfill her duty was indeed a contributing factor and that the crash was a result of her culpable inaction.

To give other examples, most people have no difficulty recognizing that a failure to feed prisoners, despite a duty to do so, contributes to their starvation. Or, as Miles Jackson notes, a cleaner who deliberately omits to lock a door in order to assist robbers thereby facilitates the robbery.[15] The naturalistic conception neglects morally salient features of causation because it focuses incorrectly on only one aspect of causation ("causal energy") and neglects other aspects ("counterfactual dependence").[16] As Victor Tadros argues, any theory that ignores the fact that a lack of rain causes crops to fail is not a viable theory of causation.[17] Tribunal jurisprudence reflects the mainstream understanding: the "substantial effect" test, for example, when applied to omissions, means that "had the accused acted, the commission of the crime would have been substantially less likely."[18] Similarly, ICC jurisprudence has generally supported the normative conception (see discussion in Annex 3).

---

[14] See, e.g., Hart & Honoré, *supra* note 2, at 139 and other works cited in the previous two footnotes.

[15] M Jackson, *Complicity in International Law* (Oxford University Press, 2015) at 103.

[16] I believe that the debate arises because there are at least two major conceptions underlying causation. One conception looks at counterfactual dependence (the "but for" test), examining what would have happened in an alternative universe without the variable in question. Another looks at the chain of events as they actually occurred, looking at the "causal energy" or "causal efficacy" of the forces sufficient to bring about the result. But causation is more subtle than either of these conceptions on its own.

For example, it is well recognized that exclusive reliance on the counterfactual ("but for") test can, at times, generate absurd results. In "overdetermined" events, where there are multiple concurring sufficient causes, the "but for" test would absurdly absolve all contributors, because each can accurately say that the event would have happened anyway. Thus the "but for" test cannot be the entirety of the test, and we must resort to other tools. See, e.g. Dressler, *supra* note 4, at 99–102; Hart & Honoré, *supra* note 2, at 122–25.

Similarly, the difficulties with omissions arise only when one relies *exclusively* on concepts such as "causal energy" or "causal efficacy" and sets aside counterfactual analysis. That limited analysis can also generate counter-intuitive results, such as not conceding that failures by humans to fulfill their duties can have consequences. Causation (and contribution) are more subtle than either "counterfactual dependence" or looking for "sufficient" causes. Both types of analysis are needed to capture the nuances of causation.

[17] V Tadros, *Criminal Responsibility* (Oxford University Press, 2010) at 155–81.

[18] *Prosecutor v Popović*, Judgment, ICTY A.Ch, IT-05–88-A, 30 January 2015, at para 1741.

On the normative conception, it is easy to see that a commander's omission to take appropriate steps to inculcate respect for humanitarian law, to establish a system of discipline, and to repudiate and punish crimes thereby encourages or facilitates subsequent crimes, in comparison with the situation that would have existed had she met her duty. Whether one prefers to use labels such as hypothetical causation, counterfactual causation, quasi-causation, or negative causation is not of interest at this point. What matters is that there is ample ground to conclude that omissions can satisfy the causal contribution requirement. To deny this is to deny that failures by humans to fulfill their duties can ever have consequences.

It is sometimes thought that the assessment of the impact of omissions is more difficult or more speculative than the assessment of the impact of acts.[19] This view overestimates the clarity of the impact of acts. Assessing the impact of an act also entails a "hypothetical" assessment. Whether for acts or omissions, the counterfactual analysis equally involves imagining a hypothetical alternative world. Furthermore, the daily practice of criminal law shows that the impact of acts can often be equally difficult to assess. For example, did one blow among many other blows hasten the death? Conversely, the impact of omissions can be quite clear, as in the case of the pilot choosing to slump passively during a routine landing and thus crashing the plane. The real difficulty is not the difference between acts and omissions, but rather the inherent challenges of assessing impacts on the behaviour of other human beings. This is why accessory liability only requires "contribution" (see §7.1.3 and Annex 3).

7.1.3 How Much Contribution Is Required?

National legal systems converge in the conclusion that accessory liability requires a "contribution" to the underlying crime. ICL jurisprudence adheres to this understanding. For example, ICTY cases stipulate that it is "firmly established that for the accused to be criminally culpable his conduct must . . . have contributed to, or have had an effect on, the commission of the crime."[20] The contribution may "make the performance of the crime possible or at least easier."[21] The contribution must have some substantial or significant effect that furthers or facilitates the commission of the crime,[22] as long as it is prior to the full completion of the crime.[23] This approach is consistent with the most common articulation of the requirement in criminal law

---

[19]   See, e.g. *Prosecutor v Jean-Pierre Bemba Gombo*, Decision Pursuant to Article 61(7)(a) and (b) of the Rome Statute on the Charges of the Prosecutor against Jean-Pierre Bemba Gombo, ICC PTC, ICC-01/05–01/08, 15 June 2009 ("*Bemba* Confirmation Decision") at para 425; *Prosecutor v Jean-Pierre Bemba Gombo*, Judgment Pursuant to Article 74 of the Statute, ICC T.Ch, ICC-01/05–01/08, 21 March 2016 ("*Bemba* Trial Judgment") at para 212.

[20]   *Prosecutor v Kayishema*, ICTR T.Ch., ICTR-95–1, 21 May 1999, at para 199.

[21]   *Prosecutor v Orić*, Judgment, ICTY T.Ch., IT-03–68-T, 30 June 2006, at para 282.

[22]   *Ibid* at para 284.

[23]   *Ibid* at para 282.

theory – namely, that the accessory's conduct must encourage, contribute to, or facilitate the crime, render the crime easier, or put the victim at a disadvantage.[24]

There are convincing reasons why the "contribution" standard for accessories is lower than the "causation" standard often used for principals. A principal is typically accused of bringing the crime about in the world. For accessories, however, the accusation is merely that they culpably contributed to voluntary and intentional acts of others, making them indirectly responsible. As many have noted, it is very difficult to assess the influence of one person's conduct on the voluntary and informed acts of other human beings, because we are dealing with other people's volition, freedom of choice, or autonomy.[25] Some believe that influencing human behaviour is of a different *nature* than influencing the physical universe,[26] whereas others would simply say that human behaviour is less *predictable*.[27] Either way, it is not necessary to decide if the accessory "caused" the principal's behaviour, because the accessory is blamed only for having culpably contributed and thus being indirectly responsible.

It is widely accepted that the accessory's contribution need not make the difference between the crime *happening* or *not happening*. Indeed, that would be tantamount to having "control" of the crime; that heightened level of contribution is generally considered to satisfy the requirements for principal liability.

Some scholars, looking at patterns of practice and normative arguments, conclude that an accessory must make some demonstrable concrete difference in *how* the crime came about, even if that difference is small – for example that the perpetrators entered by that particular entrance or used that particular weapon. However, such solutions may not be perfectly satisfactory because they hinge on proof of differences that are arguably not that important (e.g. whether the victim was killed with one gun or another).[28] This difficulty gives us reason to suspect that this approach is not the best explanation.

Experience shows that it often cannot be said with certainty whether the act of a potential accomplice had a specific effect on the crime. For example, if the

---

[24] See, e.g., Kadish, *supra* note 9, at 357; G Mettraux, *The Law of Command Responsibility* (Oxford University Press, 2009) at 14 ("significant contributing factor"); K Ambos, "Article 25," in O Triffterer, ed, *Commentary on the Rome Statute of the International Criminal Court*, 2nd ed (Beck, 2008) at 756–58.

[25] See, e.g., Hart & Honoré, *supra* note 2, at 51–59; Kadish, *supra* note 9, at 329–36; Dressler, *supra* note 4, at 127–28; Ashworth, *supra* note 9, at 415. An extreme form of belief in free will rejects the possibility of *any* causal contribution to the informed and voluntary decision of another human, but this position has fallen out of favour, and it is well accepted that one may speak of humans influencing other humans. S J Morse, "The Moral Metaphysics of Causation and Results" (2000) 88 Calif L Rev 879; Moore, *supra* note 4, at 414. Another justification for the more elastic approaches – which, for reasons of space, I will not explore here – is the problem of "moral luck"; it is often argued, with some plausibility, that persons should be held responsible for prohibited acts of risk-creation, not for the lucky or unlucky fortuities of what consequences actually flow.

[26] Kadish, *supra* note 9, at 334; Hart & Honoré, *supra* note 2, at 51–57.

[27] Dressler, *supra* note 4, at 127–28; Kutz, *supra* note 4, at 294; Morse, *supra* note 25, at 883–86.

[28] See discussion in Kutz, *supra* note 4, at 297; Moore, *supra* note 4, at 406–07.

accomplice had not provided the keys to the door, might the perpetrator have found an equally effective means of entry?[29] Acts of encouragement are even more difficult (or impossible) to weigh: Did the words of encouragement, or suggestions for a plan, actually have an impact on the perpetrator, or might the perpetrator have done the exact same thing in any event? This is why legal practice does not require proof of the actual impact on the perpetrator; it is sufficient that the accused culpably carried out acts of encouragement.

In light of these features of human behaviour, there is both jurisprudential and normative support that a particular concrete impact need not be shown. It is sufficient if the accused's conduct *increased the risk* of the crime occurring or being successfully completed.

For example, Sanford Kadish, reviewing common law jurisprudence, shows that the contribution requirement is satisfied as long as the accused does something that *could* make a difference.[30] This follows the risk aggravation approach. A great illustration arises in the US case of *State v Tally*.[31] In this case, the victim's relatives had sent the victim a warning by telegraph that the principals were coming to kill him. The accused, seeking to facilitate the killing, sent a telegram to the telegraph operator not to deliver the warning telegraph and thus thwarted that warning. We do not know whether the warning telegraph would have actually helped the victim to escape, but we do know that the accused deprived the victim of that chance and hence elevated the risk of the crime being completed. The decision held that:

> The assistance given ... need not contribute to the criminal result in the sense that but for it the result would not have ensued. It is quite sufficient if it facilitated a result that would have transpired without it. It is quite enough if the aid merely rendered it easier for the principal actor to accomplish the end intended by him and the aider and abettor, though in all human probability the end would have been attained without it.[32]

Kadish argues that the contribution requirement is satisfied by elevating the probability of the crime and that it is found to be unsatisfied only where there was *no possibility* that the accomplice's conduct could have contributed, such as where the attempted contribution demonstrably "never reached its target."[33]

Both common law and civil law systems appear to converge in requiring that the conduct was of a type that can facilitate or encourage the crimes, without necessarily requiring proof that it actually made an identifiable difference (e.g. actually

---

[29] This issue is sometimes resolved by defining the crime with increasing granularity, i.e. the accomplice contributed to the crime in which the perpetrators entered by that particular entrance or used that particular weapon. Such solutions are not perfectly satisfactory: see discussion in Kutz, *supra* note 4, at 297; Moore, *supra* note 4, at 406–07.

[30] Kadish, *supra* note 9.

[31] 102 Ala. 25, 15 So. 722 (1894). See also Kadish, *supra* note 9, at 357.

[32] *Tally*, *supra* note 31, at 738.

[33] Kadish, *supra* note 9, at 358.

persuading the principal).[34] The latter would often be impossible to show and, in any case, unnecessary: culpability flows from engaging in conduct of a nature that would tend to encourage and facilitate the crime, and doing so with the requisite mental state (on which, see Chapter 8).

Risk aggravation is a plausible and helpful restatement of what it means to make a crime easier or more likely. Kai Ambos has argued convincingly that risk aggravation is appropriate for culpability in command responsibility,[35] and Roberta Arnold has explored similar lines.[36] Hart and Honoré discuss the significance of risk aggravation in notions of causal contribution as used in common law and continental systems, as well as everyday usage.[37] Hart and Honoré also show that, in law and in common usage, a culpable dereliction in providing an opportunity for others to commit crimes can be considered a contribution to crimes that occur within the ambit of the created risk.[38]

Some readers might still be hesitant as to whether elevating the risk of the crime is sufficient to constitute a "contribution." However, that objection implicitly assumes and reverts to the more rigid conception, which requires proof of some particular concrete impact. The reasons for the rejection of that approach in practice and theory were discussed earlier (it hinges on showing of some trivial differences, and this arbitrariness does not map well onto what the culpability principle is about). Recall that deontic principles are not abstract, other-worldly, metaphysical constructs, which can be satisfied only in a laboratory of the mind. They are human principles, designed for the social practice of criminal law; they are intended to prevent injustice, not to generate fastidious stipulations. Culpable risk-creation is a core concern of a rational and compassionate justice system. If one engages in

---

[34] See, e.g., S Bock & F Stark, "Preparatory Offences," in K Ambos et al, *Core Concepts in Criminal Law and Criminal Justice, Vol I* (Cambridge University Press, 2019) at §IV.3. Some cases are satisfied even when the attempted assistance does not reach its target (e.g. a letter does not arrive), but Bock and Stark plausibly argue that the assistance should at least reach the target so that there is a possibility of facilitation or encouragement.

[35] Ambos, *supra* note 13, at 860. And for risk aggravation theory as appropriate in accessory liability, see Ambos, *supra* note 24, at 758–59. See also N Jain, *Perpetrators and Accessories in International Criminal Law* (Hart, 2014) at 191 (conduct of a nature objectively recognizable as increasing the probability that the crime will occur and succeed).

[36] R Arnold, "Command Responsibility: A Case Study of Alleged Violations of the Laws of War at Khiam Detention Centre" (2002) 7 J Conflict & Sec L 191 at 207–08.

[37] Hart & Honoré, *supra* note 2, at lxii–lxv, 6, 81–82, 286, 478–95. Moore, *supra* note 4, at 432–40, would decline to apply the label of "causation" to risk aggravation, but regards risk aggravation as a sufficient basis for liability, which again brings us to a similar endpoint, albeit with different terminology and conceptualizations. See also *ibid* at 308–10.

[38] Hart & Honoré, *supra* note 2, at 59–61 and 80–82. Some might object that it seems problematic to be contemplating mere possibilities. After all, if the evidentiary standard is "beyond reasonable doubt," it may seem strange that mere increases in risk can suffice. However, this concern confuses the evidentiary standard with the substantive test. The evidentiary standard stipulates the degree of confidence required. The legal test stipulates the proposition to be proven. There is no contradiction in requiring a high degree of confidence (evidentiary standard) that the accessory's conduct was of a nature that would at least facilitate or encourage the crimes (substantive test).

culpable risk-creation, elevating the risk of that very crime, then we are no longer in the domain of – for example – *ex post* gestures of approval; that person has crossed the minimal threshold for material culpability. Of course, liability will depend on satisfying any other material and mental culpability requirements stipulated by the relevant mode of liability.

7.2 CULPABILITY WITHOUT CONTRIBUTION?

We now come to a more ambitious normative question: whether a new deontically justified conception of culpability might support culpability without causal contribution. This is the final possible avenue to justify holding a commander personally criminally liable for a past crime by virtue of her failure to punish that crime.[39] For example, it might be argued that the commander thereby "ratifies," endorses, or acquiesces in the crime and thus voluntarily absorbs liability for it *ex post facto*. Such a theory would be innovative, but, as was mentioned in Chapter 3, we should be ready to re-examine and rearticulate our principles if a convincing deontic account can be developed. The coherentist framework that I suggest starts with widely accepted formulations of principles as a starting points or initial hypotheses, but it is ready to embrace convincing arguments for new conceptions.

7.2.1 The "Accessory after the Fact" Analogy and Other Unlikely Avenues

Before outlining some potentially plausible avenues toward such an account, I will briefly raise and dismiss three avenues that I believe are unlikely to succeed. Each draws on broader legal practices, which are another helpful clue in a coherentist account, but in this instance the practices do not provide convincing bases for criminal liability as an accessory to serious crimes.

Analogy to "accessory after the fact"

One obvious strategy would be to highlight the similarity with the concept of "accessory after the fact." The doctrine of "accessory after the fact" was once familiar in common law systems, and a comparable concept of *assistance après coup*, or "facilitation after the fact," is known in some civil law systems.[40] In early common law, the conception was that a person assisting a perpetrator to avoid arrest, trial, or conviction thereby becomes party to the original felony.[41] The parallel with command responsibility is clear, because failing to meet the "duty to punish" clearly

---

[39] In Chapter 6, I discussed various strategies to avoid or resolve the culpability contradiction; this strategy is the most ambitious of them – it aims to reconceive the culpability principle itself.

[40] M D Dubber, "Criminalizing Complicity: A Comparative Analysis" (2007) 5 JICJ 977 at 979–81 and 997–98; M Damaška, "The Shadow Side of Command Responsibility" (2001) 49 Am J Comp L 455 at 468–69.

[41] A P Simester & G R Sullivan, *Criminal Law: Theory and Doctrine*, 3rd ed (Hart, 2007) at 195.

helps the perpetrators to avoid arrest, trial, or conviction. One could argue that if "accessory after the fact" is justifiable under the culpability principle, then a concept of command responsibility without causation is also justifiable, because the commander similarly contributes to the frustration of justice.

The problem with this analogy, however, is that legal systems have moved away from treating assistance after the fact as creating liability for the crime itself, precisely because of concerns about culpability.[42] The contemporary approach is to punish aiders after the fact for what they actually did – such as obstructing justice or harbouring a fugitive. We do not hold them retroactively responsible for an already-completed crime in which they did not participate and to which they did not contribute; that crime is not in any way their deed.[43] Thus post-offence assistance in frustrating justice is no longer seen as a mode of liability in the crime, but rather as a separate crime. Accordingly, analogy to accessory after the fact does not provide a principled basis on which to treat non-contributory derelictions as a mode of liability.

Analogy to "acknowledgement and adoption"

A second strategy could be to draw on the international law state responsibility doctrine of "acknowledgement and adoption."[44] However, this analogy is also problematic. State responsibility creates civil liability. It is a different question whether an *individual* may endorse the conduct of other persons after the fact and thereby become personally *criminally* complicit in it. When one individual commits a crime, there may be many others who approve of the act. Nonetheless, no matter how hearty their approval and how fervent their desire to make it "their" act, they cannot voluntarily assume criminal liability for the act. It is not their act. The concept of "ratification" exists in private law, but not in criminal law, where "consent" to be criminally liable is irrelevant; in criminal law, responsibility is personal, and thus we need a contribution to the deed.[45]

---

[42] See, e.g., US Model Penal Code §242.3; Damaška, *supra* note 40, at 468–69; Dubber, *supra* note 40, at 998; A Eser, "Individual Criminal Responsibility," in Cassese, Gaeta & Jones, *supra* note 13, at 806–07; Ambos, *supra* note 24, at 769–70; Fletcher, *supra* note 12, at 646.

[43] The aider after the offence "bears no causal responsibility for the offence; his conduct does not even rise to the level of a contributory cause": Dubber, *supra* note 40, at 998. I should reiterate that steps taken *before* completion of the crime, such as agreeing in advance to help to ensure that the perpetrators escape justice, may of course facilitate or encourage the crime and thus can satisfy the causal contribution requirement.

[44] United Nations General Assembly, *Draft Articles on Responsibility of States for Internationally Wrongful Acts*, Annex to GA Res 58/83, UNGAOR, 58th Sess, UN Doc A/56/49(Vol I)/Corr.4 (2001), Art 11; *Case Concerning United States Diplomatic and Consular Staff in Tehran (United States of America v. Iran)* [1980] ICJ Rep 3 at paras 71–74. Under this doctrine, where conduct was carried out by persons who were not agents of a particular state, the state may nonetheless "acknowledge and adopt" that conduct *ex post facto* as its own conduct, thereby acquiring liability for that conduct.

[45] F B Sayre, "Criminal Responsibility for the Acts of Another" (1930) 43 Harvard L Rev 689 at 708; Kadish, *supra* note 9, at 354. Hart & Honoré, *supra* note 2, at 387–88 discuss cases suggesting

Analogy to vicarious regulatory liability

A third strategy would be to draw an analogy with regulatory enterprise liability, such as the vicarious liability of owners of enterprises for regulatory offences. However, such regimes apply to regulatory offences that are not regarded as creating a "stigma" to be borne by the accused. The culpability principle requires a personal contribution for those crimes that bear a stigma, such that the person is being "blamed" for the crime and exposed to significant punishment. Thus this model does not seem viable as a solution in a liberal system of justice.[46]

7.2.2 Possible Arguments for Commander Culpability without Contribution

In a coherentist account, we draw on all available clues to help us to develop the soundest understanding of the principles that we can.[47] Those clues include patterns of juridical practice, which might reveal insightful underlying intuitions of justice.

While most of the early jurisprudence seems to require causal contribution,[48] there are some traces of doctrinal support for a "ratification" theory in command responsibility jurisprudence. For example, in the *High Command* case (*Kuechler*), a commander was held liable for crimes prior to his failure to punish, on the grounds that his failure to take corrective action showed that he tolerated and approved of the crimes.[49] If the judgment simply means that conveying such tolerance and approval aggravates the risk of further crimes, it is consistent with the contribution requirement. But the thinking may instead have been that tolerance and approval of the crime provided a sufficient nexus.

Similarly, in the *Sawada* case, before the Tokyo Tribunal, a commander learned of crimes that occurred while he was away and failed to punish those responsible. The Tokyo Tribunal held that, by his failure to punish, he "ratified" the crimes.[50] Furthermore, an ICTY Trial Chamber has described the "tacit acceptance"

"ratification" of past criminal acts as "doubtful cases" and express doubt that approval constitutes a separate ground of liability.

[46] As Francis Sayre has written:

> Where the offense is in the nature of a true crime, that is, where it involves moral delinquency or is punishable by imprisonment or a serious penalty, it seems clear that the doctrine of *respondeat superior* must be repudiated as a foundation for criminal liability. For it is of the very essence of our deep-rooted notions of criminal liability that guilt be personal and individual; and in the last analysis the … sense of justice … is the only sure foundation of law.

> Sayre, *supra* note 45, at 717. See also T Wu & Y-S Kang, "Criminal Liability for the Actions of Subordinates: The Doctrine of Command Responsibility and Its Analogues in United States Law" (1997) 38 Harvard Int'l LJ 272 at 278–85.

[47] See Chapter 4.
[48] See §9.1.2.
[49] *United States v Wilhelm von Leeb et al (The High Command Trial)*, 9 Trials of War Criminals before the Nuremberg Military Tribunals (1950) 9 TWC 462 at 568.
[50] *Trial of Lieutenant-General Shigeru Sawada and Three Others*, Case No 25, 5 UN War Crimes Comm'n L Rep Trials War Criminals I (US Mil Comm'n in Shanghai, 1948).

argument as "not without merits," because a failure to punish is so "grave that international law imposes upon him responsibility for those crimes."[51]

In Chapter 4, I discussed the possible coherentist responses to "outlier" cases. When should such cases be set aside as questionable because they do not follow the accepted pattern, and when might they be prophetic indications of a viable exception or alternative normative approach? There is no mechanical algorithm to decide such questions; we must consider all of the clues, including whether there are compelling normative arguments to support the seemingly anomalous practice.[52]

Some scholars, including Christopher Kutz, Amy Sepinwall, and Guénaël Mettraux, have advanced normative arguments for culpability without causal contribution. Christopher Kutz has tentatively outlined the most careful exploration of this possibility, noting the inclusiveness of the contribution requirement – for example, that it does not require a showing of successful impact, but rather conduct of a nature that typically would facilitate or encourage the crime.[53]

Noting this elasticity, Kutz asks "whether the boundaries of complicity might stretch further, to encompass acts of ratification and endorsement."[54] He suggests that perhaps the reason we require a causal contribution is simply to distinguish non-culpable gestures, such as declarations of support, from types of conduct likely to enhance the risks of harm or wrongdoing. He notes that, in some organizational situations, such as supervisors or lawyers providing advice, endorsement after the fact may be "more than an expression of approval"; it may be an act "with real institutional consequences."[55] He acknowledges that "ratification has not been a recognized basis of criminal liability," but argues that there are "good reasons to recognize it in a well-defined context."[56]

Working along similar lines, Amy Sepinwall advances a deontic argument that the endorsement or acquiescence of a commander in failing to punish a crime might be a legitimate basis for liability in that crime.[57] She acknowledges that this approach does not fit within the formulation of the culpability principle in ICL, because the commander does not make a contribution to the crime itself.[58] However, she advances an innovative, but potentially plausible, argument about culpability based on the *expressive harm* of endorsing crimes.[59]

---

[51] *Prosecutor v Halilović*, Judgment, ICTY T.Ch, IT-01–48-T, 16 November 2005, at para 95.

[52] See §4.3.1 and §4.3.3.

[53] Kutz, *supra* note 4.

[54] *Ibid* at 300.

[55] *Ibid* at 304.

[56] *Ibid*. The reasons include that ratification expresses an agent's identification with the acts, that it reveals the dangerousness of the ratifying accomplice, and that, in an institutional context, ratification may have future effects and exacerbate the dangerousness of future principals.

[57] A Sepinwall, "Failures to Punish: Command Responsibility in Domestic and International Law" (2008–09) 30 Michigan Int'l LJ 251 at 255.

[58] *Ibid* at 296.

[59] *Ibid* at 286–302.

Guénaël Mettraux advances a similar argument. He argues that causation is required by fundamental principles, but he regards causal contribution as satisfied by the *ex post* enabling of *impunity* – that is, allowing the crime to remain unpunished.[60] While structured differently from Sepinwall's approach, Mettraux's approach produces a comparable outcome. It would constitute a departure from the contribution requirement as articulated in ICL jurisprudence and other sources (see §7.1). Generally, contributing to impunity for a previous and completed crime is considered to affect a different legal interest from the initial crime itself, and thus it is not regarded as part of the initial crime.[61] However, one could try to build an argument for an expanded concept of culpability in which a contribution to impunity for the crime is a sufficient contribution.

Another possible avenue would be to appeal to a concept of crime as "moral pollution." On this view, the unpunished crime is a "stain" that pollutes the moral order and thus requires "cleansing or expatiation," which restores the law.[62] By failing to punish, the commander perpetuates the stain; the "bloodguilt" comes to rest with her.[63] I suspect that this sentiment about moral pollution undergirded early concepts of accessory after the fact or *assistance après coup*. This line of thought is intriguing. However, while the non-contributing dereliction of the commander may give rise to moral or metaphysical guilt for the deed, it may not be an adequate basis to assign *criminal* guilt for the deed.[64] The idea of bloodguilt and of moral pollution tainting other actors is arguably a rather poetic or metaphorical basis for a contemporary system of justice to assign criminal guilt. Indeed, George Fletcher, even as he toyed with the idea of "bloodguilt," concluded that criminal liability based on such ideas would "jar our modern sensitivities."[65] Without more development, it seems unlikely that ideas of bloodguilt and moral pollution can provide a reliable deontic justification to ascribe criminal culpability for the initial crime.

In my view, these arguments are intriguing initial forays into a possible new conception, but at this point they are too skeletal to provide a sufficient basis for criminal sanction. The arguments go against extensive practice and fairly well-established understandings. I refer to practice not because I am taking a doctrinal approach (i.e. that we are bound by precedent), nor because I am committing the naturalist fallacy (i.e. assuming that what was done in the past must be right). I refer

---

[60] Mettraux, *supra* note 24, at 43, 80 and 86.

[61] I am speaking here of entirely after-the-fact conduct. Of course, if one signals prior to completion of the crime that one would help to facilitate impunity (e.g. enabling escape, concealing evidence, or breaching a duty to punish), then that signal in itself facilitates or encourages the crime and hence could give rise to accessory liability.

[62] See, e.g., discussion in a different context in G Fletcher, "Collective Guilt and Collective Punishment" (2004) 5 Theoretical Inq L 163 at 169–72.

[63] Sepinwall, *supra* note 57, at 295, tracing the concept to Kant.

[64] K Jaspers, *The Question of German Guilt*, trans E B Ashton (Fordham University Press, 1947) at 73–74.

[65] Fletcher, *supra* note 62, at 171.

to practice because, where an approach is the product of many minds striving for just solutions, worked out in practice with consequences at stake, it is at least a good "humility check" on theory-building. Furthermore, analytically, to alter this understanding of the culpability principle is a major revision, for which we would at least need a strong normative case. The arguments so far are beset with problems that have not been satisfactorily addressed. For example, the "expressive harm" and "impunity" arguments both appeal to legal interests that are usually understood to be different from those injured by the initial crime. For the time being, there are major difficulties still to be overcome before we embrace culpability without contribution and seek to punish individual human beings in accordance with that theory.

7.3 IMPLICATIONS

The implication of this analysis is that ICL should continue at present to adhere to the mainstream understanding, which requires that an accessory encouraged or facilitated the crime, by at least elevating the risk of the crime occurring or being successfully completed. Such a requirement maintains fidelity to the culpability principle.

In the context of command responsibility, this is not a particularly onerous requirement. In most circumstances in which a command relationship is proven, it should be evident that a serious dereliction worthy of prosecution will be of a type that would at least elevate the risk of crimes occurring or being successfully completed, when compared with the baseline of a commander non-negligently striving to fulfill her duties. The exceptions will be where there was no possibility that her dereliction made any contribution to the charged crimes, such as the "successor commander" scenario, or the "initial crimes" scenario (see §6.4).[66]

Significantly, Tribunal jurisprudence still falls short even on the risk aggravation approach, because it permits convictions even where there is *no possibility* that the commander's failure contributed to core crimes or elevated the risk of the crimes that occurred. The *Hadžihasanović* decision partially solves the problem by precluding the "successor commander" scenario, but it still permits convictions in other

---

[66] In the "successor commander" scenario, the commander fails to punish crimes that occurred when she was not even in command. In the "initial crimes" or "isolated crimes" scenario, a commander adequately fulfills her preventive duties, but crimes occur nonetheless (it is an obligation of effort, not result), and she fails to punish. She would be derelict in her duties (and could be punished for a dereliction offence), but she would not become liable as a party to the war crimes of her subordinates. In the "initial crimes" scenario, she could be liable for subsequent crimes that were encouraged or facilitated by her failure to act. Another possible example could be where a commander was non-negligently out of contact with troops for an extended period (such as where communications lines were disrupted by enemy action) and thus had no possibility of constraining the relevant behavior. The *Yamashita* case may be an example of this, in which case the punishment would be unfair.

scenarios in which there is no *possibility* that the commander's failure elevated the risk of the crimes that occurred.

For the ICC, the prescriptions resulting from the present and previous chapters are that command responsibility should be seen as a mode of accessory liability, that it requires causal contribution, and that causal contribution is satisfied by risk aggravation. This approach reconciles the ICC Statute, the pre-Tribunal transnational jurisprudence, and the culpability principle.

It is too early to say whether the ICC will adopt these prescriptions, but initial jurisprudence has generally conformed to these conclusions. So far, the ICC has considered command responsibility in the *Bemba* case, in a Pre-Trial Chamber confirmation decision, a Trial Chamber judgment, and an Appeals Chamber judgment.[67] The confirmation decision and trial judgment forthrightly recognized command responsibility as a mode of liability.[68] Furthermore, they affirmed the requirement of causal contribution and did so not only for technical doctrinal reasons, but also out of respect for the culpability principle.[69]

Matters were left less clear after the Appeals Chamber decision. Despite a unanimous conviction by the Trial Chamber, the Appeals Chamber substituted an acquittal, by a 3–2 majority. The Appeals Chamber majority decision did not address the specific controversies discussed here; instead, the appeal decision was based on the commander's duty to take measures.[70] Thus questions about causal contribution and the nature of command responsibility remain somewhat open. However, if we count up the separate opinions, three out of five judges expressly recognized command responsibility as a mode of accessory liability, and they expressly recognized the causal contribution requirement, again consistent with the analysis advanced here.[71]

---

[67] The ICC has considered command responsibility in the *Bemba* case, at confirmation of charges, at trial, and at appeal. See *Bemba* Confirmation Decision, *supra* note 19; *Bemba* Trial Judgment, *supra* note 19; *Prosecutor v Jean-Pierre Bemba Gombo*, Judgment on the Appeal of Mr Jean-Pierre Bemba Gombo against Trial Chamber III's Judgment Pursuant to Article 74 of the Statute, ICC A.Ch, ICC-01/05–01/08 A, 8 June 2018 ("*Bemba* Appeal Judgment").

[68] *Bemba* Trial Judgment, *supra* note 19, at para 171, concurring with *Bemba* Confirmation Decision, *supra* note 19, at para 341.

[69] See, e.g., *Bemba* Trial Judgment, *supra* note 19, at para 211 ("It is a core principle of criminal law that a person should not be found individually criminally responsible for a crime in the absence of some form of personal nexus to it"). I discuss the Trial Judgment analysis in more detail in Annex 3.

[70] *Bemba* Appeal Judgment, *supra* note 67.

[71] Although the *Bemba* Appeal Judgment, *ibid*, took no view on the "mode versus offence" debate, the "mode of liability" understanding was actually supported by three of the five Appeal Chamber judges (separate opinion of Judge Eboe-Osuji at paras 194–215 and separate dissenting opinion of Judges Monageng and Hofmanski at para 333). Similarly, although the *Bemba* Appeal Judgment took no view on the contribution requirement, three of the five Appeal Chambers judges upheld the requirement. They did so both for textual reasons and out of respect for the culpability principle (separate opinion of Judge Eboe-Osuji at para 202; separate dissenting opinion of Judges Monageng and Hofmanski at para 333). But see *contra* separate opinion of Judges Van den Wyngaert and Morrison at paras 51–56. See also Annex 3 for more careful discussion.

For those who are interested, I review the deontic arguments of the different chambers, and comment on some nuances, in Annex 3. I relegate this analysis to an annex because some readers may not be interested in an involved discussion of jurisprudence. Other readers, who are interested in the future of command responsibility or in studying judicial engagement with deontic principles, will find the annex of interest. The most important points are that: the lower chambers essentially followed the prescriptions advanced here, as did three of the five Appeals Chamber judges; all levels engaged thoughtfully with deontic principles; and criminal law theory can further assist with some of the points of debate.

The ICC jurisprudence differs from a lot of the reasoning criticized in the previous chapter, because all three chambers engaged with the deontic dimension of criminal law reasoning in addition to the source-based and consequentialist dimensions. Indeed, the Appeals Chamber decision has been plausibly criticized by many scholars for lurching too far and overstating deontic constraints – a theme I touched on in Chapters 1 and 3 – but it did so on grounds outside of those addressed in Chapters 6 and 7.[72] I outline possible examples of such "overcorrection" in Annex 4. But, in any event, at all levels the judges were at least engaging in thoughtful deontic analysis and drew soundly on organizing concepts of criminal law theory, which is commendable.

One theme illustrated by this chapter is that deontic analysis is valuable not only for protecting potential accused persons, but also for shaping better criminal law policy. On a mid-level principles (or coherentist) approach to deontic principles, we can better avoid (on the one hand) neglect of principles and (on the other hand) unsupported, overly rigid misconceptions of principles.[73] For example, my analysis of causal contribution both (i) rejects popular proposals to hold commanders liable for crimes to which they could not have contributed and (ii) shows that the requirement is not onerous and is satisfied by elevating the risk that the crimes would occur or be successfully completed.[74]

Early ICC decisions are consistent not only with my prescriptions, but also, for the most part, with the coherentist and humanistic approach to deontic principles that

---

[72] L N Sadat, "Fiddling While Rome Burns? The Appeals Chamber's Curious Decision in *Prosecutor v Jean-Pierre Bemba Gombo*" (12 June 2018) EJIL Talk (blog); D M Amann, "In *Bemba* and beyond, Crimes Adjudged to Commit Themselves" (13 June 2018) EJIL Talk (blog); M Jackson, "Commanders' Motivations in *Bemba*" (15 June 2018) EJIL Talk (blog); S SáCouto, "The Impact of the Appeals Chamber Decision in *Bemba*: Impunity for Sexual and Gender-Based Crimes?" (22 June 2018) IJ Monitor (blog); J Trahan, "Bemba Acquittal Rests on Erroneous Application of Appellate Review Standard" (25 June 2018) Opinio Juris (blog); J Powderly & N Hayes, "The *Bemba* Appeal: A Fragmented Appeals Chamber Destabilises the Law and Practice of the ICC" (26 June 2018) Human Rights Doctorate (blog); F F Taffo, "Analysis of Jean-Pierre Bemba's Acquittal by the International Criminal Court" (13 December 2018) Conflict Trends (blog); S SaCouto & P Viseur Sellers, "The *Bemba* Appeals Chamber Judgment: Impunity for Sexual and Gender-Based Crimes" (2019) 27 Wm & Mary Bill Rts J 599.

[73] See §1.1.3 and §2.5.

[74] See also Annex 3, showing that ICC jurisprudence largely follows this recommended path.

I recommend here.[75] Most of the judges are seeking faithfully to uphold the constraints, while avoiding unnecessarily rigid conceptions of them. Most of the judges draw on patterns of practice, the best available normative arguments, and considered judgments. I believe that the method outlined in Chapter 4 (mid-level principles, reflective equilibrium, coherentism) is both the best explanation of the underlying method in how we engage in deontic reasoning and the best model for how we should do it. By clarifying the underlying method, we can improve how we examine and construct arguments, test them with appropriate rigour, and continue to build better understandings.

---

[75] See Chapters 3 and 4.

8

The Genius of Command Responsibility

OVERVIEW

In this chapter, I examine a different controversy in command responsibility: the mental element. Scholars and jurists have raised powerful, principled objections to the modified fault standards in command responsibility, such as the "should have known" standard in the ICC Statute. They are absolutely right to raise such questions, because a negligence standard in a mode of accessory liability seems to chafe against our normal analytical and normative constructs. However, I advance, in three steps, a culpability-based justification for command responsibility. I argue that the intuition of justice underlying the doctrine is sound.

I argue that the "should have known" standard in the ICC Statute should be embraced, rather than shunned. I argue that the "should have known" standard actually maps better onto personal culpability than the rival formulations developed by the Tribunals.

This chapter gives an example of the two-way conversation between criminal law theory and ICL. This is an instance in which ICL, by highlighting special contexts and problems, can lead us to reconsider some of our initial reactions and conclusions. Command responsibility delineates a set of circumstances in which our normal reflexes about the lesser culpability of criminal negligence may be unsound.

8.1 PROBLEM, OBJECTIVE, AND THEMES

8.1.1 Principled Concerns about Fault in Command Responsibility

In Chapter 6, I argued that command responsibility can be greatly simplified. I argued that the Tribunals made an early mis-step when, based on hasty reasoning, they rejected the requirement of causal contribution and that this contradiction led to the subsequent convolutions in the doctrine. I argued that if we undo the first knot, the other knots untangle. Command responsibility remains a mode of accessory liability, and it accordingly requires that the commander at least elevated the risk of the crimes through her derelictions.

But there is a problem for my account. Or, at least, it seems to be a problem, but perhaps it is something more exciting: an opportunity for discovery. The apparent problem is the modified mental element. The fault element departs from normal subjective standards of awareness: the Tribunal test is "had reason to know" (HRTK), whereas the ICC test for commanders[1] is "should have known" (SHK). Are such standards justifiable in a mode of liability? Both scholarly literature and Tribunal jurisprudence assert that negligence would be problematic in command responsibility as a mode of liability. If the SHK standard cannot be justified in a mode of liability, this would be a problem not only for my account, but also for the ICC Statute, which expressly creates a mode of liability relying on that standard.

A wealth of thoughtful, principled scholarship advances strong concerns about negligence in command responsibility. These scholars have rightly pressed beyond a discourse that tended to focus on precedential arguments (parsing authorities) and consequentialist arguments (maximizing impact). They helped to usher in more sophisticated scholarship engaging with deeper principles and the *justice* of the doctrines. For example, Mirjan Damaška, in his ground-breaking work on the "shadow side of command responsibility," warned that "a negligent omission has been transformed into intentional criminality of the most serious nature: a superior who may not even have condoned the misdeeds of his subordinates is to be stigmatized in the same way as the intentional perpetrators of those misdeeds."[2] He argued that "it appears inappropriate to associate an official superior with murderers, torturers, or rapists just because he negligently failed to realize that his subordinates are about to kill, torture or rape."[3] Many scholars have carefully developed these principled concerns. Some scholars regard both the HRTK and the SHK tests as suspect; others regard only the SHK test as problematic.[4] The most forceful criticisms arise with respect to the crime of genocide, because it requires a special intent. Command responsibility liability for genocide without that special intent is widely and understandably considered to be contradictory, incoherent, illogical, or unfair.[5]

---

[1] For civilian superiors, ICC Statute, Art 28, offers a more generous subjective test: "consciously disregarded." I discuss this briefly in §8.4.

[2] M Damaška, "The Shadow Side of Command Responsibility" (2001) 49 Am J Comp L 455 at 463.

[3] *Ibid* at 466.

[4] For the most careful development of the latter position, see G Mettraux, *The Law of Command Responsibility* (Oxford University Press, 2009) at 73–79, 101, 210 ("The ICC Statute greatly dilutes the principle of personal culpability"), 211 (the fault element is "emptied of its content"), 212 ("the injuries which the text of the Statute appears to have inflicted upon basic principles of personal guilt").

[5] W A Schabas, "General Principles of Criminal Law in the International Criminal Court (Part III)" (1998) 6 Eur J Crime Cr L Cr J 400 at 417–18 ("doubtful . . . whether negligent behaviour . . . can be reconciled with a crime requiring the highest level of intent. Logically, it is impossible to commit a crime of intent by negligence"); K Ambos, "Superior Responsibility," in A Cassese, P Gaeta & J R W D Jones, eds, *The Rome Statute of the International Criminal Court: A Commentary, Vol 2* (Oxford University Press, 2002) at 852 ("stunning contradiction"); D L Nersessian, "Whoops, I Committed Genocide! The Anomaly of Constructive Liability for Serious International Crimes"

These features of command responsibility do indeed require either justification or revision.

8.1.2 Summary of Argument: A Deontic Justification

My contribution in this chapter is to suggest that a culpability-based justification of the modified fault element is possible. A typical response to culpability concerns would be to argue, in a consequentialist tradition, that they are overridden by the urgent need to reduce mass atrocious crimes. That is not my argument. I am working within the same principled tradition as the scholars cited above. My contribution here is not in opposition to this body of scholarship. On the contrary: I seek to build on it.

Accordingly, my goal is most similar to that of Jenny Martinez, who has lamented that "sensitivity to criticism about the looseness of the mens rea requirement for command responsibility has been unfortunately coupled with reluctance to explore explicitly the theoretical justifications for the doctrine."[6] Like her, I seek to help to develop that theoretical justification.[7] Whereas Martinez considered precedential, consequentialist, and deontic dimensions, I will focus particularly on the deontic justification, developing it in more detail. Other scholars, such as David Luban and Thomas Weigend, have also touched on the deontic justification of command

---

(2006) 30 Fletcher F World Aff 81 at 92–96 ("far below what is required ... for ... genocide"; inconsistent with personal fault and fair labelling); M Osiel, *Making Sense of Mass Atrocity* (Cambridge University Press, 2009) at 27 n 50 and at 113 n 80 (must prove commander's specific intent for genocide); M L Nybondas, *Command Responsibility and Its Applicability to Civilian Superiors* (TMC Asser Press, 2010) at 125–39; T Weigend, "Superior Responsibility: Complicity, Omission or Over-Extension of the Criminal Law?," in C Burchard, O Triffterer & J Vogel, eds, *The Review Conference and the Future of International Criminal Law* (Kluwer, 2010) at 80; E van Sliedregt, "Command Responsibility at the ICTY: Three Generations of Case Law and Still Ambiguity," in A H Swart, A Zahar & G Sluiter, eds, *The Legacy of the ICTY* (Oxford University Press, 2011) at 397 ("incoherence"); E van Sliedregt, *Individual Criminal Responsibility in International Law* (Oxford University Press, 2012) at 205–07 ("conceptually awkward," "gap"); K Ambos, *Treatise on International Criminal Law, Vol I: Foundations and General Part* (Oxford University Press, 2012) at 220–21 and 231 ("logically only possible" if not a "direct liability," but rather liability for the dereliction); M G Karnavas, "Forms of Perpetration," in P Behrens & R Henham, *Elements of Genocide* (Routledge, 2013) at 137 ("obvious tension between specific genocidal intent ... and ... 'knew or should have known' "); J Root, "Some Other Mens Rea? The Nature of Command Responsibility in the Rome Statute" (2013) 23 Transnat'l L & Pol'y 119 at 143 ("Negligence is anathema to specific intent, and it is not an appropriate level of culpability to convict a commander of a specific intent crime"), 125 ("offends basic notions of justice and fairness") and 127 ("objectivize[d]" mental state "divorces it from ... personal accountability"); Mettraux, *supra* note 4, at 226–27 (commander must share in the special intent). C Meloni, *Command Responsibility in International Criminal Law* (TMC Asser, 2010) at 200–02 more cautiously describes it as "theoretically possible although problematic."

6   J S Martinez, "Understanding *Mens Rea* in Command Responsibility: From *Yamashita* to *Blaškić* and beyond" (2007) 5 JICJ 638 at 641.

7   The account here is very briefly foreshadowed in D Robinson, "The Two Liberalisms of International Criminal Law," in C Stahn & L van den Herik, eds, *Future Perspectives on International Criminal Justice* (TMC Asser, 2010) at 115 n 76.

responsibility.[8] In this chapter, I develop what I believe to be the most detailed normative account of command responsibility to date. The account will address the most frequently raised objections.

My argument has three planks. First, I address the unease expressed about negligence in ICL. I show that criminal negligence is a robust concept reflecting personal culpability (it is not concerned with minor slips by a harried commander). Furthermore, criminal negligence is not simply an "absence" of a mental state; rather, it reflects a degree of disregard for the lives and safety of others that is morally reprehensible, socially dangerous, and properly punishable.

Second, I address concerns about liability without the requisite *mens rea* for crimes such as genocide. Many of the criticisms of command responsibility overlook the distinction between principal and accessory liability; they condemn command responsibility for not satisfying the requirements for principal liability, but it is actually a mode of accessory liability.[9] Accessories need not share the *mens rea* for the principal's offence. Accessory and principal liability signify different things and have correspondingly different requirements.

Third, I argue that command responsibility is a justified extension of aiding and abetting by omission. Normally, we would consider "mere" negligence to be much less serious than subjective foresight and perhaps inadequate for accessory liability. But we must look at the context. The activity of overseeing armed forces has repeatedly entailed horrific dangers for vulnerable civilians, giving rise to a duty of vigilance. The commander who criminally neglects such a duty, and such a danger, shows a staggering disregard for the lives and legal interests that she was entrusted to protect. The commander cannot evade responsibility by creating her own ignorance through defiance of this duty. Using a framework outlined by Paul Robinson, I will try to show that culpability-based justifications of "causation" and "equivalence" furnish sufficient fault for accessory liability.

I argue that this is the "genius" of command responsibility: that it recognizes that criminal negligence is sufficiently culpable for accessory liability in this context. I use the term "genius" in its older and less-used sense, such as in Frederick Pollock's lectures on the "genius of the common law."[10] It refers to an underlying, emergent character of

---

[8] Weigend, *supra* note 5, at 73 succinctly outlines the deontic case for the commander's duty. My approach also resonates with more general suggestions of David Luban and others, who have argued that legal rules must be adapted to the special problems of bureaucracy and organized human action. See D Luban, "Contrived Ignorance" (1999) 87 Georgetown LJ 957; D Luban, A Strudler & D Wasserman, "Moral Responsibility in the Age of Bureaucracy" (1992) 90 Michigan L Rev 2348. My prescription is also similar to that of Mark Osiel; he focuses on consequentialist arguments, whereas I am focused on the deontic justification. M Osiel, "The Banality of Good: Aligning Incentives against Mass Atrocity" (2005) 105 Columbia L Rev 1751.

[9] Importantly, I do not argue that the commander's dereliction is equivalent to *committing* war crimes. The idea that command responsibility "deems" a commander to have "committed" the crimes is one of the persistent misunderstandings in the command responsibility discourse: see §8.3.2.

[10] F Pollock, *The Genius of the Common Law* (Columbia University Press, 1912) esp at 4–5. This is similar to the usage that refers, for example, to the genius of an era. Interestingly, Pollock's proposed

a collective endeavour over time, which may be discerned in retrospect even if not consciously intended by its participants. My point is that the many different practitioners who shaped the doctrine were actually reflecting a deontically sound intuition of justice about culpability in a particular set of circumstances, even if the groundwork for that intuition was neither explicitly articulated nor analytically developed.

While our normally reliable understandings tell us that criminal negligence is less culpable than subjective advertence, command responsibility delineates and responds to a special set of circumstances in which that familiar prioritization breaks down. A negligently ignorant commander, who cares so little about the danger to civilians that she does not bother with *even the first step* of monitoring, actually shows *greater* contempt than the commander who monitors and learns of a risk, but hopes it will not materialize. Contrary to our normal assumption that "knowing" is *ipso facto* more culpable than "not knowing," the relative culpability in these circumstances hinges on *why* the commander does not know.

Accordingly, even though a negligence-based mode of accessory liability may seem to challenge our normal analytical constructs, I think that, on closer inspection, the intuition of justice underlying command responsibility is sound. While we should look at post-World War II rules with critical care (because they may reflect overreaching "victors' justice"), command responsibility reveals a valuable insight and contribution to criminal law. It responds to a particular pathology of human organization. It recognizes that, in some circumstances, criminal negligence supplies adequate fault for accessory liability. The criminally indifferent supervisor of dangerous forces does not merely commit her own separate dereliction offence; she is rightly held to account as a culpable facilitator (accessory) of the resulting crimes.

Among the implications of this account is that the SHK standard in the ICC Statute should be defended. The SHK standard has been wrongly equated with strict liability and has fallen under suspicion. The Tribunals shied away from a negligence standard for understandable reasons and fashioned their own test. But I argue that the SHK standard is preferable not only on precedential and consequentialist grounds, but also on deontic grounds. It is less arbitrary than the test developed by the Tribunals and reflects a more consistent, meaningful standard of criminal culpability.

8.1.3 Broader Themes

In this chapter, I demonstrate the application of the coherentist method. The coherentist method draws on all available clues, including patterns of juridical practice, normative argumentation, practical reason, and casuistic testing. These considerations are familiar in both legal and normative argument; I am simply

usage also includes looking for a "clarified" image that brings forth the "best possible" underlying values. This matches well with the coherentist method (see Chapter 4); and with Dworkin's coherentist approach in *Law's Empire*, looking for theory with analytical fit and values that put the practice in the best possible light: R Dworkin, *Law's Empire* (Harvard University Press, 1986).

parsing these techniques to lay bare that coherentism is the best explanation of the underlying methodology.

The inquiry in this chapter will also illustrate some of the main themes of this book. First, ICL can benefit from careful application of the tools of criminal law theory.[11] Second, ICL can in turn illuminate general criminal law theory.[12] Third, the study of deontic principles can be *enabling* as well as restraining, by helping to avoid unnecessarily conservative doctrines.[13] Fourth, a seemingly anomalous area of practice can sometimes reveal a sound insight about justice.[14]

8.1.4 Scope and Terms

In this chapter, I focus on the traditional central case of military command relationships, and thus I speak of "commanders." I will touch on implications for civilian superiors only at the end.[15] In this chapter, I merely *outline* the justificatory account. I am acutely aware that I am skimming the surface of many intricate debates. This chapter offers the most detailed deontic account of command responsibility to date (as far as I know), and yet it remains only a preliminary sketch.

8.2 THE ALLERGY TO NEGLIGENCE

8.2.1 The Tribunals Turn away from Negligence

Under international humanitarian law, commanders have a duty to try to remain apprised of possible crimes by subordinates, by monitoring and requiring reports

---

[11] Some of the reasoning in the field, particularly in its pioneering phase, was a bit superficial. An example is the inadequate distinction between principal and accessory liability, and hence the common argument that command responsibility would entail "pretending" that the commander committed the crimes herself. See §8.3.2.

[12] The novel problems of ICL can invite us to reconsider our normally reliable assumptions. A negligence-based mode of liability seems to depart from our principles, but if we return to the basic building blocks bearing in mind the specific context, we may make some discoveries. As I outlined briefly in §6.1.1, command responsibility responds to a special set of circumstances that challenge our reflexes about subjective advertence and criminal negligence, and about knowing and not knowing.

[13] Sometimes, a doctrine will prove to be unnecessarily conservative because of an incorrect overstatement of the relevant principles. In such a case, the system is forgoing consequentialist benefits for no actual deontic reason. This may have happened in early command responsibility cases, with the understandable but unnecessary decision to steer away from uncertainties around criminal negligence. The study of deontic constraints reveals not only the zone of prohibition, but also the zone of permission to pursue sound policy.

[14] Normally, where there is a conflict between a practice and our understanding of our principles, it is the practice that we will consider "wrong" and in need of alignment. However, the anomaly may sometimes prove to be an appropriate adaptation to a distinct circumstance. In that case, we can articulate a new and better understanding of our principles. The improved understanding takes into account not only the familiar and normal cases, but also more diverse circumstances. In so doing, we learn about our principles and build a more general theory.

[15] See §8.4.

("duty to inquire" or "duty of vigilance").[16] Should command responsibility take into account the commander's proactive duty to inquire?[17]

Post-World War II jurisprudence, which developed the command responsibility doctrine, had "almost universally" held that the commander cannot plead her lack of knowledge where it was created by her criminally negligent breach of her duty to inquire.[18] Tribunal jurisprudence acknowledges this clear pattern in the prior case law.[19]

Nonetheless, the ad hoc Tribunals departed from those precedents and struck a different path. In an early case, *Čelebići*, the prosecution argued, consistently with prior transnational jurisprudence, that the fault requirement is satisfied where the commander did not know of the crimes because of a "serious dereliction" in her duty to obtain information within her reasonable access.[20] The Appeals Chamber demurred. The Chamber held that failure to set up a reporting system "may constitute a neglect of duty which results in liability within the military disciplinary framework," but the Chamber was unwilling to incorporate such failures into command responsibility.[21] The Chamber felt that the prosecution's position "comes close to the imposition of criminal liability on a strict or negligence basis."[22]

To avoid these perceived pitfalls, the Appeals Chamber required that the commander must have in her *"possession"* information sufficient to put her on notice

---

[16]   J-M Hencaerts & L Doswald-Beck, *Customary International Law, Vol II: Practice* (Cambridge University Press, 2005) at 3733–91.

[17]   As discussed in Chapter 6, the bare bones of command responsibility are: (i) a superior–subordinate relationship; (ii) that the superior knew or "had reason to know" (or "should have known") of subordinate crimes; and (iii) that the superior failed to take reasonable measures to prevent such crimes or to punish the subordinates.

[18]   I will not embark here on a doctrinal review of those precedents, because my focus is normative justification, not precedential support, but many other scholars have admirably demonstrated this pattern in the jurisprudence. For example, the massive survey by William Parks concludes, "[a]lmost universally," that post-World War II tribunals adopted the "knew or should have known" standard: W H Parks, "Command Responsibility for War Crimes" (1973) 62 Military L Rev 1 at 95. See also Martinez, *supra* note 6, at 647–54; Meloni, *supra* note 5, at 33–76; K Ambos, *Der Allgemeine Teil des Völkerstrafrechts* (Duncker & Humblot, 2002) at 97–101, 133–36 and 147–50; O Triffterer & R Arnold, "Article 28," in O Triffterer & K Ambos, eds, *The Rome Statute of the International Criminal Court: A Commentary*, 3rd ed (Beck, Hart, Nomos, 2016) at 1070–73 and 1089–91.

[19]   For example, the *Blaškić* Trial Judgment reviews authorities including the Tokyo Judgment, *Toyoda*, *Roechling*, the *Hostage* case, and the *High Command* case, as well as the Commission of Experts (which noted the duty to remain informed and that "such serious personal dereliction on the part of the commander as to constitute wilful and wanton disregard of the possible consequences" would satisfy the *mens rea* requirement). *Prosecutor v Blaškić*, Judgment, ICTY T.Ch, IT-95-14-T, 3 March 2000 ("*Blaškić* Trial Judgment") at paras 309–30. Similarly, *Prosecutor v Delalić et al (Čelebići)*, ICTY T.Ch, IT-96-21-T, 16 November 1998 ("*Čelebići* Trial Judgment") at para 388 held that, "from a study of these decisions, the principle can be obtained that the absence of knowledge should not be considered a defence if, in the words of the Tokyo judgement, the superior was 'at fault in having failed to acquire such knowledge.' "

[20]   *Prosecutor v Delalić et al (Čelebići)*, Judgment, ICTY A.Ch, IT-96-21-A, 20 February 2001 ("*Čelebići* Appeals Judgment") at para 224.

[21]   *Ibid* at para 226.

[22]   *Ibid*.

that crimes were being committed ("alarming information").[23] Thus a commander can generally remain passive; it is only once alarming information makes it into her "possession" that she is required to take steps.

Other trial chambers in early cases – *Bagilishema* (ICTR) and *Blaškić* (ICTY) – attempted to adopt interpretations consistent with earlier jurisprudence (i.e. the SHK test).[24] Again, in both cases, the Appeals Chamber rejected those attempts. In *Bagilishema*, the Appeals Chamber warned that "[r]eferences to 'negligence' in the context of superior responsibility are likely to lead to confusion of thought."[25] In *Blaškić*, the Chamber again "rejected criminal negligence as a basis of liability in the context of command responsibility."[26] The Appeals Chamber reconfirmed that the commander is liable "only if information was available to him which would have put him on notice of offences committed by subordinates."[27]

I have three points about the Chambers' reasoning. First, it was entirely appropriate and commendable that the Chambers showed concern for personal culpability. Their caution was preferable to the oft-seen tendency (especially in early jurisprudence) to use reasoning techniques that maximized liability with inadequate attention to fundamental principles.[28] (As I noted in Chapter 2, these techniques reflect a "tendency," but are not an "iron rule," i.e. I in no way suggest that jurists always fall afoul of them.[29]) Working in the early days of ICL, and confronted with the unexplored implications of incorporating negligence and the duty to inquire, it was a prudent reflex for the judges to steer clear. Now, however, with the luxury of more time and given that the Rome Statute expressly reaffirms the SHK standard, we can and must study with more care whether that standard may in fact be deontically justified.

Second, the Chamber seems to have misunderstood or mis-stated the prosecution's submission. Whereas the prosecution was arguing for the SHK standard, the Chamber instead refuted a "duty to know" about "all" crimes.[30] For brevity, I will refer to this as

---

[23] *Ibid* at para 231–33.

[24] *Prosecutor v Bagilishema*, Judgment, ICTR T.Ch, ICTR-95-1A-T, 7 June 2001, at para 46 held that the fault element is met where "the absence of knowledge is the *result of negligence* in the discharge of the superior's duties, that is where the superior *failed to exercise the means available* to him or her to learn of the offences and, under the circumstances, he or she *should have known*." The *Blaškić* Trial Judgment, *supra* note 19, at para 322, held that the fault element was satisfied if the commander "*failed to exercise the means available* to him to learn of the offence and, under the circumstances, he *should have known* and such failure to know constitutes *criminal dereliction*." Notice that both of these formulations match the test reflected in the Rome Statute and the World War II jurisprudence, and would harmonize the HRTK and SHK standards.

[25] *Prosecutor v Bagilishema*, Judgment, ICTR A.Ch, ICTR-95-1A-A, 3 July 2002, at para 35.

[26] *Prosecutor v Blaškić*, Judgment, ICTY A.Ch, IT-95-14-A, 29 July 2004 ("*Blaškić* Appeal Judgment") at para 63.

[27] *Blaškić* Appeal Judgment, *supra* note 26, at para 62.

[28] See Chapter 2.

[29] See §2.1.3.

[30] *Čelebići* Appeals Judgment, *supra* note 20, at paras 227–30. Similarly, the Chamber also overstated the question as whether failure in this duty will "*always*" (*ibid* at para 220) or "*necessarily*" (*ibid* at para 226) result in criminal liability. Obviously, the answer must be "no." The failure would have to result

the "duty to know everything." The Chamber firmly rejected the "duty to know everything" standard – and rightly so. A "duty to know everything" would indeed pose an unfair "Catch-22": the commander would either (i) *know* and thus be liable or (ii) *not know* and thus be liable. Such a standard would indeed be a strict liability standard, because its logically jointly exhaustive alternatives – knowing or not knowing – would always be met.

Crucially, however, the prosecution was *not* arguing for a "duty to know everything," nor was that the upshot of prior jurisprudence. Notice the following three nuances of the SHK test.

(1) It is a duty of conduct (effort), not a duty of *result*. In other words, it is not a duty to *know*, but simply is a duty to *inquire*.[31] One is exculpated if one exercises due diligence.

(2) The SHK test requires not only that the commander failed to exercise due diligence to inquire, but also that the commander had the "*means* to obtain the knowledge."[32] In other words, the commander *would have found out* had she tried.[33]

(3) The dereliction must be "serious."[34] In other words, it is a standard of criminal negligence, not of simple civil negligence.

Notice too that the commander is not instantly liable if she inherits a force with poor reporting mechanisms; the requirement is simply that she exercise diligence to stay apprised, to the extent that can be expected in the circumstances.

Thus the liability standard in the prior law – and as advanced by the prosecution – was not *strict liability*, but rather *criminal negligence*. These are not synonyms. Unfortunately, following the Appeals Chamber's analysis, jurists and scholars frequently equate the SHK standard with strict liability and a "duty to know everything." The SHK is often regarded as having been decisively discredited in *Čelebići*. But it was not: *Čelebići* actually discredited the "duty to know everything" standard, not the SHK standard. One of my aims here is to untangle these very different ideas so that they can be seen afresh on their own merits.

Third, even though the Tribunals emphatically purported to reject a negligence standard, the HRTK test actually still entails constructive knowledge. The Chambers

from criminal negligence, and all of the other requirements of command responsibility would also have to be met.

[31] See, e.g., the *High Command* case, in which a "duty to know everything" standard was rejected, recognizing that a "commander cannot keep completely informed" of all details and can assume that subordinates are executing orders legally. The commander's disregard must amount to "criminal negligence." *United States v Wilhelm von Leeb et al (The High Command Trial)* (1950) 9 TWC 462 at 543–44.

[32] *Čelebići* Appeals Judgment, *supra* note 20, at para 226. See also the proposed requirement that the information be within her "reasonable access" (*ibid* at para 224).

[33] *Ibid* at para 226.

[34] *Ibid* at para 224.

have held that "possession" does not mean "actual possession"[35] – which sounds contradictory, but presumably means that the commander does not need reports physically in hand. More importantly, the commander need not have *"actually acquainted* himself" with the information; the information needs only to *"have been provided or available"* to the commander.[36] Thus it would suffice, for example, that reports made it to the commander's immediate office. Accordingly, the HRTK test is not actually subjective. The test purports to be subjective, but effectively fixes the commander with knowledge of all information that reached her vicinity.

8.2.2 The "Possession" Test Is a Poor Fit with Actual Culpability

Let me offer a particularly stark example to illustrate the problem with the "possession" requirement. Suppose a commander instructs her team at the outset, "No one is to report to me any information about any crimes by our forces." As a result, her subordinates manage to keep from her any information about the ongoing crimes. On the Tribunals' approach, she would be acquitted, because she does not have such information. Yet the *reason* she does not have the information is the egregiously inadequate reporting system she herself created.[37]

By contrast, the SHK test, in earlier jurisprudence and in the ICC Statute, is slightly broader.[38] The SHK test can be satisfied where the commander does *not*

---

[35] *Ibid* at para 238.

[36] *Ibid* at para 239.

[37] However, one line in the *Blaškić* Appeal Judgment, *supra* note 26, at para 62 seems to suggest otherwise. The line asserts that the commander can be liable if she *"deliberately refrains"* from obtaining information. This is a welcome suggestion, consistent with the normative position I recommend here. However, the assertion cannot be reconciled with the actual rule laid down by the Tribunals, since the central requirement is that alarming information must be in the commander's "possession." Everything I say in this chapter is based on taking the "possession" test at face value.

   Alternatively, however, if future interpreters were to breathe life into the "deliberately refrains from obtaining" line, that would introduce a large and welcome exception to the "possession" requirement. Creating that exception would reduce the gap between the ICC approach and the Tribunal approach. As I argue here, a "deliberately refraining" test would be deontically justified. (Furthermore, while "criminally negligent" failure and "deliberate" failure sound like very different thresholds, they are not so different. Any criminal negligence requires a gross dereliction, which means that there had to be available alternatives, and thus a choice was made not to inquire. In other words, the criminal negligence standard already requires a deliberate failure.) Thus, if the "deliberately refrains" alternative is taken seriously, it leads to a test very much like the test I advocate here. However, it would also contradict the rest of the Tribunals' jurisprudence on the matter, such as their requirement of possession, the rejection of the proactive duty, and the rejection of SHK.

[38] See *Čelebići* Trial Judgment, *supra* note 19, at para 393; *Čelebići* Appeals Judgment, *supra* note 20, at paras 222–42; *Prosecutor v Jean-Pierre Bemba Gombo*, Decision Pursuant to Article 61(7)(a) and (b) of the Rome Statute on the Charges of the Prosecutor against Jean-Pierre Bemba Gombo, ICC PTC, ICC-01/05–01/08, 15 June 2009 ("*Bemba* Confirmation Decision") at paras 433–34. For analysis, see Meloni, *supra* note 5, at 182–86.

possess information about subordinate criminal activity *if* that lack is the result of a gross dereliction of her duty to try to stay apprised, displaying a culpable indifference to the lives and interests she was entrusted to protect.[39]

In consequentialist terms, it is fairly evident that the Tribunals' test creates a perverse incentive: to avoid receiving reports. This achieves the opposite of the purpose of the command responsibility doctrine. The SHK test better advances the aims of the law – that is, to incentivize diligent monitoring and supervision of troops, and thereby to reduce crimes.[40] However, my focus here is not on *consequentialist* arguments, but on *deontic* ones. My aim here is to ask whether the SHK test is justified in terms of the personal culpability of the commander. My conclusion is that the SHK test is not merely *justified* (i.e. permissible); it is actually *preferable* on deontic grounds, because it corresponds better to personal culpability.

The HRTK test, as developed by the Tribunals, is actually both *underinclusive* and *overinclusive*. The test is underinclusive because it acquits the commander who contrives her own ignorance by creating a system that keeps her in the dark about subordinate crimes.[41] But the test is also overinclusive, because it fixes the commander with knowledge of reports that made it to her desk even if exigent demands of her work understandably delayed her from reading the reports.[42] In that case, she is fixed with knowledge even though she was not negligent in the circumstances. The Tribunal test hinges too dramatically on whether other actors or external events bring the alarming information into the nebulously defined "possession" of the passive commander. It lurches from *too low* an expectation – indulging and even encouraging the commander to be passive – to *too high* an expectation – deeming knowledge of all submitted reports, even where the commander was not negligent in not getting to the report.

A metaphor may illustrate the problem. Imagine that an airline pilot has a duty (i) to activate the warning light system and (ii) to follow up on any warning lights. In this metaphor, the Tribunal approach rightly reaches pilots who ignore a warning light, but

---

[39] *Bemba* Confirmation Decision, *supra* note 38, at para 433 ("the 'should have known' standard requires more of an active duty on the part of the superior to take the necessary measures to secure knowledge of the conduct of his troops and to inquire, regardless of the availability of information at the time on the commission of the crime ..."). The *Bemba* decision describes the SHK standard as one of negligence: *ibid* at paras 427–34. On negligence, see §8.3.1.

[40] Osiel, *supra* note 8.

[41] Subject to one untested passage in the *Blaškić* Appeal Judgment, *supra* note 26, which, in any event, is difficult to reconcile with the overarching requirement that information must be in the commander's "possession."

[42] I am referring here to the rule *as stated* by the Tribunals. It might be that, confronted with such a case, the judges would rein in the stated rule to avoid the possible injustice. In that eventuality, however, the test would collapse into simple "knowledge," and thus the HRTK alternative would become nugatory. A more sensible alternative would be to embrace the criminal negligence standard advocated here.

acquits pilots who choose not to turn the system on in the first place.[43] That narrowness is not required by deontic principles.[44] The duty to stay apprised logically entails requiring subordinates to report crimes; it is artificial to try to divide the two.

The SHK standard much more simply and faithfully tracks the proper contours of fault for this mode of liability. It recognizes the commander's basic duty of diligence in requiring reports and monitoring activity. Moreover, the SHK standard does not require heroic efforts; it simply requires efforts that are *not criminally negligent*. The SHK standard does not "deem" the commander to have read reports she had no reasonable opportunity to read. It applies a single, consistent yardstick that reflects both the purpose of command responsibility and a recognized criminal law fault standard. That yardstick is contextually sensitive to the circumstances faced by the commander.[45]

Both the Tribunals and the ICC now understand the SHK test and the HRTK test as differing.[46] Accordingly, I will use the labels as a descriptive shorthand. However, just to be clear, I do not think that the wording of these two extremely similar formulations ever required divergent interpretations.[47] I think that a national or international court applying the words "had reason to know" in future could choose to incorporate post-World War II and ICC jurisprudence. Moreover, while the academic literature often portrays Tribunal jurisprudence as unquestioned customary law, and thus it portrays the ICC test as a departure, I argue that it is actually the Tribunal jurisprudence that departs from prior sources, whereas the ICC Statute returns to the previously established standard of criminal negligence.

---

43 You might object that there is a difference between "choosing" not to turn on the system and negligently "forgetting." In §8.3.3, we will look at the morality of "forgetting" to monitor whether one's troops are killing and raping civilians.

44 The Tribunal approach departed from precedent and went against the consequentialist aims of the provisions, but it would have been right to do both of those things if it were necessary to comply with the culpability principle. However, the restriction is not required by the culpability principle; indeed, the Tribunal creation is actually a *worse* match for culpability.

45 See §8.3.1 and §8.3.3. For example, it is not criminally negligent if a commander takes over a group in harried circumstances and, in the immediate aftermath, does not have a realistic opportunity to set up reporting systems. A commander would also not be considered criminally negligent simply because she operates within a dysfunctional army; we would look at her diligence in its context to assess what measures could be expected of her (and thus which derelictions meet the criminal negligence threshold).

46 See *Čelebići* Trial Judgment, *supra* note 19, at para 393; *Čelebići* Appeals Judgment, *supra* note 20, at paras 222–42 (contrasting with the SHK test); *Bemba* Confirmation Decision, *supra* note 38, at paras 427–34.

47 The Tribunal judges thought that the words "had reason to know" in Additional Protocol I to the Geneva Conventions ("AP I") marked a movement away from criminal negligence and the SHK standard. But, actually, the delegates accepted criminal negligence and were debating its proper parameters. See International Committee of the Red Cross (ICRC), *Commentary on the Additional Protocols of 8 June 1977 to the Geneva Conventions of 12 August 1949* (Martinus Nijhoff, 1987) at 1012; I Bantekas, "The Contemporary Law of Superior Responsibility" (1999) 93 AJIL 573 at 589–90; C Garraway, "Command Responsibility: Victors' Justice or Just Deserts?," in R Burchill, N D White & J Morris, eds, *International Conflict and Security Law: Essays in Memory of Hilaire McCoubrey* (Cambridge University Press, 2005) at 81.

8.3 A PROPOSED JUSTIFICATION OF COMMAND RESPONSIBILITY

I will now offer a normative account of command responsibility as a mode of liability that includes a criminal negligence standard. My argument has three planks. First, I respond to unease about criminal negligence, showing that it can be an appropriate standard for criminal liability, reflecting personal culpability. Second, I address concerns that the commander may not share the *mens rea* for the offence, by highlighting the different standards and implications of accessory and principal liability. Third, I will use Paul Robinson's helpful framework for assessing inculpatory doctrines[48] to show that culpability-based justifications can account for the novel doctrine of command responsibility.

8.3.1 The Personal Culpability of Criminal Negligence

As I have noted, Tribunal jurisprudence (and some ICL literature) expresses discomfort with negligence as a basis for liability.[49] Jenny Martinez rightly questions the tendency in ICL discourse to denigrate the command responsibility standard as "simple negligence" and to conflate it with strict liability.[50] Indeed, to describe the standard as "simple" negligence understates the rigour and nuance of criminal negligence. George Fletcher describes the common "disdainful attitude toward negligence as a basis of liability" as a source of "major distortion of criminal law."[51]

This wariness toward negligence may reflect traces of the "subjectivist bug" – the belief that subjective mental states are the only *proper* grounds for criminal culpability.[52] On the "subjectivist" view, one needs, at a minimum, conscious advertence to a risk in order to ground criminal liability. Thus, where a person did not advert at all to a risk, that person cannot be held responsible. On this view, negligence is seen as non-awareness, a mere "absence" of thought, a "nullity," which does not correspond to any mental state deserving punishment.[53] It is also sometimes argued that negligence cannot be deterred, which seems to equate negligence with

---

[48] P Robinson, "Imputed Criminal Liability" (1984) 93 Yale LJ 609.

[49] See §8.1 for concerns of scholars and §8.2 for Tribunal jurisprudence.

[50] Martinez, *supra* note 6, at 660.

[51] G Fletcher, *The Grammar of Criminal Law: American, Comparative and International*, Vol 1 (Oxford University Press, 2007) at 309.

[52] R Frost, "Centenary Reflections on *Prince's Case*" (1975) 91 LQR 540 at 551; C Wells, "Swatting the Subjectivist Bug" (1982) 1 Crim L Rev 209.

[53] J Hall, *General Principles of Criminal Law* (Bobbs Merrill, 1947) at 366–67; G Williams, *Criminal Law: The General Part*, 2nd ed (Stevens, 1961) at 122–23. More recently, careful arguments for the subjectivist approach have been advanced in A Brudner, *Punishment and Freedom: A Liberal Theory of Penal Justice* (Oxford University Press, 2009) at 59–97 and in L Alexander & K Kessler Ferzan, *Crime and Culpability: A Theory of Criminal Law* (Cambridge University Press, 2011) at 69–85. See also the counter-arguments advanced by Fletcher, *supra* note 51, at 313.

accidents or mindlessness.[54] Such arguments conclude that there is neither a consequentialist nor a deontic justification for punishing negligence.

To respond to such concerns, I offer a very rudimentary sketch[55] of criminal negligence, to distinguish criminal negligence from mere blunders or simple civil negligence. Criminal negligence requires two things. First, the accused must be engaged in an activity that presents an obvious risk to others – such as driving, performing surgery, or supervising factory workers. Second, the accused must not only fail to meet the requisite standard of care, but also fail "by a considerable margin."[56] The requirement has been described as a "marked" departure[57] or a "gross" departure.[58] This standard excludes, among other things, a "momentary lapse of attention" consistent with a good faith effort to fulfill one's responsibilities.[59] Criminal law is concerned only with transgressions that warrant *penal* sanction.

Like many others, I was long convinced by the argument that criminal negligence does not correspond to any personal mental state. After all, a negligence analysis seems simply to compare the accused's (objective) conduct with an objective standard. However, as many scholars have shown, criminal negligence does indeed display a particular blameworthy mental state, for which personal culpability is rightly assigned. A gross departure from the standard of care, in the course of an activity bearing obvious risks for others, demonstrates a *"culpable indifference"*[60] or *"culpable disregard"*[61] for the lives and safety of others. Hart's careful discussion is still illuminating today. He reminds us that failure to advert to a risk can indeed be blameworthy. "I just didn't think" is no excuse when we have a responsibility to *exert*

---

[54] Hall, *supra* note 53; Williams, *supra* note 53. This thinking is echoed in command responsibility literature. For example, Root, *supra* note 5, at 152 argues that "deterrence . . . will not deter individuals from inaction when they were not aware there was a need to act."

[55] For this quick sketch, I draw heavily on my own tradition: the common law. If I were attempting to advance a definitive doctrinal interpretation of "should have known" in ICL, I would need a much more detailed survey of different legal traditions. Here, I am simply providing enough of a sketch to address the preliminary normative objections.

[56] A P Simester & G R Sullivan, *Criminal Law: Theory and Doctrine*, 3rd ed (Hart, 2007) at 146.

[57] See, e.g., *R v Creighton* [1993] 3 SCR 3.

[58] J Horder, *Ashworth's Principles of Criminal Law*, 8th ed (Oxford, 2016) at 196; The American Law Institute, *Model Penal Code: Official Draft and Explanatory Notes: Complete Text of Model Penal Code as Adopted at the 1962 Annual Meeting of the American Law Institute at Washington, D.C., May 24, 1962* (ALI, 1985) at §2.02(2)(d) ("gross deviation"); Ambos, *Treatise, supra* note 5, at 225 ("gross deviation").

[59] K Simons, "Culpability and Retributive Theory: The Problem of Criminal Negligence" (1994) 5 J Contemp Legal Iss 365 at 365. For a helpful illustration, see *R v Beatty* [2008] 1 SCR 49.

[60] A Duff, *Intention, Agency and Criminal Liability* (Blackwell, 1990) at 162–63 ("practical indifference"); Simons, *supra* note 59, at 365 ("culpable indifference"); J Horder, "Gross Negligence and Criminal Culpability" (1997) 47 U Toronto LJ 495 ("indifference").

[61] See, e.g., s 219 of the Canadian Criminal Code. See also *R v Bateman* (1925) 19 Cr App Rep 8 at 11 ("the negligence of the accused went beyond a mere matter of compensation between subjects and showed such disregard for the life and safety of others, as to amount to a crime against the state and conduct deserving of punishment").

our faculties, to be mindful, and to take precautions.[62] Thus where a driver pays absolutely no attention to the road, or a railway switch operator plays cards and completely forgets about the incoming train, we do not take these failures to advert as mere non-culpable "absences" of a mental state. We punish the persons for *failing to exert their faculties* to advert to risks and control their conduct when their activity required them to exert their faculties.[63]

As Antony Duff points out, "what I notice or attend to reflects what I care about; and my very failure to notice something can display my utter indifference to it."[64] Kenneth Simons notes that the culpable indifference standard "asks *why* the actor was unaware. If the reason for the actor's ignorance is itself blameworthy, then the actor might satisfy the culpable indifference criterion."[65] Criminal negligence shows a disregard for others that is morally reprehensible, socially dangerous, and properly punishable.[66]

These arguments also address the claim that negligence cannot be deterred, because they remind us that criminal negligence is confined to serious transgressions and that it can be avoided through effort. Criminal sanctions can remind people that they have to *pay attention* when they engage in certain activities and exert themselves to try to fulfill their duties. Hart gives the example of a man driving his car while gazing into a partner's eyes rather than at the road. It is not unrealistic that punishment could remind him and others in future that, "this time, I must attend to my driving."[67] The claim that criminal negligence cannot be deterred is simply untrue.

A recurring concern in the ICL literature about a "mere" negligence standard is that minor slips, or ineptness, or falling behind in reading, or taking an ill-timed vacation could lead the hapless commander to be held liable as party to serious crimes.[68] Scholars are quite right to consider such scenarios in order to test doctrines. I hope that these clarifications address such concerns. Precedents on

---

[62] H L A Hart, *Punishment and Responsibility: Essays in the Philosophy of Law*, 2nd ed (Oxford University Press, 2008) at 136.

[63] *Ibid* at 150–57.

[64] Duff, *supra* note 60, at 162–63.

[65] Simons, *supra* note 59, at 388 (emphasis added). See also G P Fletcher, "The Fault of Not Knowing" (2002) 3 Theoretical Inq L 265; Horder, *supra* note 58, at 204–06.

[66] Some scholars and some systems (e.g. Germany, Spain) distinguish between "advertent" and "inadvertent" (or "conscious" and "unconscious") negligence, depending on whether the accused was aware of the risk to others. But, as these arguments show, even with "inadvertence," the legal and moral question is *why* the accused did not advert to the risk and whether this itself was rooted in culpable disregard.

[67] Hart, *supra* note 62, at 134.

[68] See, e.g., Nersessian, *supra* note 5, at 93 ("getting drunk at the wrong time, taking an ill-advised holiday, or being woefully incompetent, careless, or distracted"); A B Ching, "Evolution of the Command Responsibility Doctrine in Light of the Čelebići Decision of the International Criminal Tribunal for the Former Yugoslavia" (1999) 25 NC J Int'l L & Comm Reg 167 at 204; Y Shany & K Michaeli, "The Case against Ariel Sharon: Revisiting the Doctrine of Command Responsibility" (2002) 34 NYU J Int'l L & Pol 797 at 841.

command responsibility rightly emphasize that the negligence must be of an extent showing a criminally blameworthy state (e.g. a culpable disregard for the lives and interests that the duty is intended to safeguard).[69]

Of course, the philosophical debate about criminal negligence is not conclusively settled; there are some theorists who argue against it and insist on subjective advertence.[70] For present purposes, rather than digressing further into this debate, we can observe that most legal systems and most of the scholarly literature, backed by convincing normative arguments as outlined here, supports the analysis and intuition that criminal negligence is a suitable basis for criminal liability.[71] On a coherentist account, we accept that we may not arrive at complete consensus or Cartesian certainty. Instead, we make best judgements drawing on all available clues, and the clues overwhelmingly support criminal negligence as a basis for personal culpability.

8.3.2 Accessories Need Not Share the Paradigmatic *Mens Rea* of the Offence

The major concern in ICL literature is not with the appropriateness of criminal negligence liability per se. The major concern is with negligence linking the accused to serious crimes of subjective *mens rea*.[72] That objection is particularly acute for crimes with special intent, such as genocide. As noted earlier, many consider the mismatch between the commander's mental state and the mental state required for genocide to be a contradiction or incoherence.[73]

This seeming mismatch is indeed striking, and scholars are right to raise principled concerns. However, many of the criticisms of command responsibility judge it by the standards expected for *principal* liability. Command responsibility is a mode of *accessory* liability and should be evaluated accordingly. I will point out in this section that it is not problematic, or even unusual, that an accessory does not satisfy the *dolus specialis*, or "special intent," required for the principal's crime.

---

[69] For example, the *High Command* case required "criminal negligence," i.e. "personal neglect amounting to a wanton, immoral disregard." *High Command, supra* note 31, at 543–44. The Commentary to AP I required negligence "so serious that it is tantamount to malicious intent": ICRC, *supra* note 47, at 1012. Many of these precedents use what we would today regard as clumsy terminology. This reflects, I believe, the relative nascence of ICL. Today, we would not equate criminal negligence with "malicious intent" (*dolus specialis*). I think that these and other passages were struggling to convey that the departure is so severe that it shows a culpable attitude worthy of criminal punishment.

[70] See, e.g., Alexander & Ferzan, *supra* note 53, at 69–85.

[71] M E Badar, *The Concept of* Mens Rea *in International Criminal Law: The Case for a Unified Approach* (Hart, 2013) at 66–68, 116–18, 145–46, 166, 186–88; K J Heller & M D Dubber, *The Handbook of Comparative Criminal Law* (Stanford Law Books, 2011) at 25–27, 59, 109, 148–49, 188, 216–19, 263, 294–95, 326–28, 365–66; Ambos, *Treatise, supra* note 5, at 94–95 (esp n 113).

[72] Most ICL scholars accept the appropriateness of criminal negligence, e.g. in a separate dereliction offence. See, e.g., Ambos, *Treatise, supra* note 5, at 231 (see esp n 477); Root, *supra* note 5, at 136; Schabas, *supra* note 5, at 417.

[73] See citations at §8.1.1.

Like most criminal law systems, ICL distinguishes between principals and accessories.[74] Those parties who are most directly responsible are liable as *principals*. Other, more indirect, contributors may be liable as *accessories*. Systems have drawn the dividing line in different ways; each approach has different strengths and shortcomings.[75] ICL has avoided a purely mental or a purely material approach and has instead emphasized "control" over the crime as a distinguishing criterion. This approach was explicitly adopted in some ICC decisions drawing on German legal theory,[76] but it is also implicit in Tribunal jurisprudence,[77] and it has support in other legal systems and traditions of criminal theory.[78]

There are two main differences between accessories and principals. One difference, as discussed in Chapter 6, is the *material* requirement. Principals make an "essential" (*sine qua non*, integral) contribution to some aspect of the crime,[79] whereas accessories merely "contribute" more indirectly, by influencing or assisting the acts and choices of the principals.[80] The more important difference for this chapter is the *mental* requirement. Principals must satisfy all mental elements stipulated for the crime. In other words, they satisfy the "paradigm" of *mens rea* for

---

[74] ICL does not include fixed sentencing discounts; rather, the difference is a factor reflected in sentencing. See, e.g., H Olásolo, "Developments in the Distinction between Principal and Accessory Liability in Light of the First Case Law of the International Criminal Court," in C Stahn & G Sluiter, eds, *The Emerging Practice of the International Criminal Court* (Brill, 2009) at 339; Ambos, *Treatise, supra* note 5, at 144–48 and 176–79; K Ambos, "Article 25," in O Triffterer & K Ambos, eds, *The Rome Statute of the International Criminal Court: A Commentary*, 3rd ed (Beck, Hart, Nomos, 2016); van Sliedregt, *Individual Criminal Responsibility, supra* note 5, at 65–81.

[75] See, e.g., M Dubber, "Criminalizing Complicity: A Comparative Analysis" (2007) 5 JICJ 977; G Werle & B Burghardt, "Introductory Note" (2011) 9 JICJ 191.

[76] See, e.g., *Prosecutor v Katanga and Chui*, Decision on Confirmation of Charges, ICC PTC, ICC-01/04–01/07, 30 September 2008 ("*Katanga* Confirmation Decision") at paras 480–86; *Prosecutor v Lubanga*, Decision on Confirmation of Charges, ICC PTC, ICC-01/04–01/06, 29 January 2007 ("*Lubanga* Confirmation Decision") at paras 322–40. See also Olásolo, *supra* note 74; Dubber, *supra* note 75; T Weigend, "Perpetration through an Organization: The Unexpected Career of a German Legal Concept" (2011) 9 JICJ 91; Ambos, *Treatise, supra* note 5, at 145–60.

[77] For example, *Furundžija* explains that a principal must participate in an "integral part" of the *actus reus*, whereas an accessory need only "encourage or assist" (making a "substantial contribution"). A principal must "partake in the purpose" (i.e. the paradigmatic *mens rea* for torture), whereas the aider and abettor need only "know" that torture is taking place. *Prosecutor v Furundžija*, Judgment, ICTY T.Ch, IT-95–17/1-T, 10 December 1998 ("*Furundžija* Trial Judgment") at para 257.

[78] To take some prominent examples from the English-language literature, see S H Kadish, "Complicity, Cause and Blame: A Study in the Interpretation of Doctrine" (1985) 73 Calif L Rev 323; M S Moore, "Causing, Aiding, and the Superfluity of Accomplice Liability" (2007) 156 U Pa L Rev 395 at 401; J Dressler, "Reassessing the Theoretical Underpinnings of Accomplice Liability: New Solutions to an Old Problem" (1985) 37 Hastings LJ 91 at 99–102.

[79] *Lubanga* Confirmation Decision, *supra* note 76; *Katanga* Confirmation Decision, *supra* note 76; *Furundžija* Trial Judgment, *supra* note 77 ("integral part"); Kadish, *supra* note 78; Moore, *supra* note 78; Dressler, *supra* note 78; Dubber, *supra* note 75.

[80] As John Gardner explains, "Both principals and accomplices make a difference, change the world, have an influence ... [A]ccomplices make their difference through principals, in other words, by making a difference to the difference that principals make." J Gardner, "Complicity and Causality" (2007) 1 Crim L & Phil 127 at 128. See also Kadish, *supra* note 78, at 328 and 343–46; Dressler, *supra* note 78, at 139; Ambos, *Treatise, supra* note 5, at 128–30 and 164–66.

the crime.[81] For accessories, the requisite mental state in relation to the crime is not stipulated by the definition of the crime; it is stipulated by the relevant mode of accessory liability.[82]

As a result, accessories need not share in the paradigmatic *mens rea* for a given offence.[83] As the ICTR noted in *Akayesu*, "an accomplice to genocide need not necessarily possess the *dolus specialis* of genocide."[84] In *Kayishema*, the ICTR held that aiders and abettors "need not necessarily have the same mens rea as the principal offender."[85] Cases from the ICTY, including Appeals Chamber judgments, have repeatedly confirmed that an accessory need not share the *mens rea* for the crime itself. For example, an aider and abettor must know of the crime, but need not personally satisfy the mental elements, such as special intent elements.[86] The ICTY Appeals Chamber has also shown the support of national systems for this approach.[87] National systems seem largely to converge in this respect,[88] with limited exceptions.[89]

---

[81] Robinson, *supra* note 48.

[82] Of course, the mode of liability must itself be deontically justified for liability to be just.

[83] G Werle & F Jessberger, *Principles of International Criminal Law*, 3rd ed (Oxford University Press, 2014) at 219–20.

[84] *Prosecutor v Akayesu*, Judgment, ICTR T.Ch, ICTR-96-4-T, 2 September 1998, at para 540. See discussion in H van der Wilt, "Genocide, Complicity in Genocide and International v Domestic Jurisdiction: Reflections on the *van Anraat Case*" (2006) 4 JICJ 239 at 244–46.

[85] *Prosecutor v Kayishema*, Judgment, ICTR T.Ch, ICTR-95-1T, 21 May 1999, at para 205.

[86] *Prosecutor v Aleksovski*, Judgment, ICTY A.Ch, IT-95-14/1-A, 24 March 2000, at para 162; *Prosecutor v Krnojelać*, Judgment, ICTY A.Ch, IT-97-25-A, 17 September 2003, at para 52 (for aiding and abetting persecution, need not share the discriminatory intent, but must be aware of discriminatory context); *Prosecutor v Simić*, Judgment, ICTY A.Ch, IT-95-9-A, 28 November 2006 ("*Simić* Appeal Judgment") at para 86; *Prosecutor v Blagojević and Jokić*, Judgment, ICTY A.Ch, IT-02-60-A, 9 May 2007; *Prosecutor v Seromba*, Judgment, ICTR A.Ch, ICTR-2001-66-A, 12 March 2008, at para 56.
There is currently a lively debate now as to whether aiding and abetting requires "knowledge," "purpose," or something in between, such as "specific direction." That debate is not pertinent here; my point is that, whatever the ultimately correct details for aiding and abetting may be, the accessory does not have to share the *mens rea* for the crime.

[87] *Prosecutor v Krstić*, Judgment, ICTY A.Ch, IT-98-33-A, 19 April 2004, at para 141.

[88] van der Wilt, *supra* note 84, at 246 notes that, in "both national criminal law systems and international criminal law," "the intentions and purposes of accomplice and principal need not coincide." For example, "Dutch criminal law ... explicitly allows the mens rea of accomplices and principals to differ" (*ibid* at 249). See also Ambos, *Treatise*, *supra* note 5, at 288–89 and 299–300.

[89] Some US states take a "shared intent" approach, in which the aider and abettor must share in the *mens rea* for the crime itself. See A Ramasastry & R C Thompson, *Commerce, Crime and Conflict: Legal Remedies for Private Sector Liability for Grave Breaches of International Law – A Survey of Sixteen Countries* (FAFO, 2006). The Model Penal Code (§2.06(4)) suggests that, for consequence elements, an aider and abettor must have the level of culpability required for a principal. If one is convinced that it is a bedrock principle that an accessory must have the same level of fault as a principal, then my account fails. Not only does my account fail, but also any account of command responsibility as a mode of liability will fail.
Fortunately, there are reasons to doubt that "shared intent" is a necessary requirement. Such a requirement would partially negate the point of distinguishing accessories from principals. It is not followed in most legal systems. Even US jurisdictions that declare a "shared intent" approach do not

You may be familiar with one of the criticisms commonly made against joint criminal enterprise (JCE) – namely, that JCE enables conviction without satisfaction of special mental elements. That criticism cannot simply be transplanted to command responsibility. The criticism is sound in relation to JCE, because JCE is a form of *principal* liability.[90] The extended form (JCE-III) is rightly criticized for imposing principal liability without meeting the culpability requirements for principal liability. But command responsibility is accessory liability and thus does not require paradigmatic *mens rea*. Modes of accessory liability must be evaluated under the respective standards.

Unfortunately, the accessory–principal distinction has been frequently overlooked in command responsibility debates. For example, Joshua Root objects that command responsibility as a mode of liability involves "pretending [that the commander] committed the crime himself."[91] Judge Shahabuddeen disparaged the plausibility of a commander "committing" hundreds of rapes in a day.[92] Guénaël Mettraux argues that "turning a commander into a murderer, a rapist or a *génocidaire* because he failed to keep properly informed seems excessive, inappropriate, and plainly unfair."[93] Mirjan Damaška objects that the negligent commander is "stigmatized in the same way as the intentional perpetrators of those misdeeds."[94]

---

actually adhere to "shared intent" for all accessories. For example, under the Pinkerton doctrine, or "intention in common" liability, one can become an accomplice to foreseeable ancillary crimes, without the fault required for a principal. Thus even those jurisdictions do not uphold a fundamental principle that accessories must have the *mens rea* of a principal.

    I think that the passage in the Model Penal Code commentary was made in the context of a particular debate (where a mode of liability requires subjective advertence, one would not include liability for result offences with more inclusive fault elements not satisfied by the accessory). I do not believe it was intended to contradict the more general proposition that the level of fault for an accessory is stipulated by the mode of liability. If that were the intent, it would contradict extensive juridical practice, and it would be normatively unconvincing, not least because it treats one type of material element differently from others.

[90] The Tribunals assert that JCE is implicit within the term "committed," and thus they maintain it is a form of *commission*, rendering one a principal and "equally guilty" with all JCE members. *Prosecutor v Vasiljević*, Judgment, ICTY A.Ch, IT-98-32-A, 25 February 2004, at para 111 ("*equally guilty* of the crime regardless of the part played by each in its commission"). Notice that I am taking no position on whether JCE would be fine if it were a mode of accessory liability. I am simply pointing out that criticisms and standards appropriate for doctrines of principal liability cannot necessarily be transplanted to doctrines of accessory liability.

[91] Root, *supra* note 5, at 156 ("pretending he committed the crime himself"), 123 ("as if he had committed the crimes himself"), 146 ("Despite Robinson's assertion, there is nothing in this language to suggest that the commander is responsible as if he committed the crimes himself"). The objection overlooks the difference between accessory liability and commission; accessory liability does not entail "pretending" that the accessory "committed" the offence.

[92] *Prosecutor v Hadžihasanović*, Decision on Interlocutory Appeal Challenging Jurisdiction in Relation to Command Responsibility, ICTY A.Ch, IT-01-47-AR72, 16 July 2003, Shahabuddeen Opinion, at para 32.

[93] Mettraux, *supra* note 4, at 211.

[94] Damaška, *supra* note 2, at 463.

As for the first two objections (Root and Shahabuddeen), it is an error to equate all modes of liability with commission, and especially with personal commission.[95] Modes are much more varied and nuanced in what they signify. The latter two objections (Mettraux and Damaška) were valuable correctives in the debate at the time, because the debate sometimes overlooked deontic constraints. However, on reflection those objections are also slightly overstated. Command responsibility does not "turn" a commander into a "murderer" or "rapist." Interestingly, even ordinary language tracks the difference between principal and accessory. Nor does it apply a stigma equal to that which attaches to the perpetrators. Command responsibility is a form of accessory liability, which conveys – accurately – that the commander facilitated crimes in a criminally blameworthy manner.

You might object that I am placing too much emphasis on the distinction between accessories and principals. For example, James Stewart has argued against the distinction, emphasizing that accessory and principal alike are still held criminally liable in relation to "one and the same crime."[96] My answer is that *roles matter*. It is the same crime, but one's *role* in the crime is also very important. The intuition that roles matter is reflected in ICL and in most national systems.[97] When Charles Taylor is convicted of "aiding and abetting" crimes, or Jean-Pierre Bemba Gombo is convicted for command responsibility for sexual violence, those convictions express something more indirect than ordering the crimes. There are many different roles a person might play in relation to a given crime. These different roles entail different censure and different legal consequences, and they have correspondingly different standards. Accessories are condemned not for perpetrating or directing the crime, but for encouraging or facilitating the crime in a culpable manner. The requirements of accessory liability track that diminished level of blame.

8.3.3 Culpable Neglect Is Sufficiently Blameworthy for Accessory Liability in the Command Context

That still leaves the hardest question. So far, I have shown that (i) criminal negligence is an appropriate building block in criminal law, and (ii) accessories need not share the paradigmatic *mens rea* for the principal's offence. But you may still ask: is it

---

[95] Alas, contrary to the Shahabuddeen argument, ICL cases demonstrate all too often that it is in fact entirely possible for a person to be an accessory, or indeed even a joint principal, to hundreds of crimes in a day.

[96] J Stewart, "The End of 'Modes of Liability' for International Crimes" (2012) 25 LJIJ 165 at 212, as well as 168 and 179 n 59. James Stewart argues for an abolition of modes of liability. For a response, see M Jackson, "The Attribution of Responsibility and Modes of Liability in International Criminal Law" (2016) 29 LJIJ 879, drawing a helpful illustrative analogy to being the *author* of a work versus *assisting* the author. See also Ambos, "Article 25," *supra* note 74, at 985 n 11.

[97] Gardner, *supra* note 80, at 136 argues that the distinction between principals and accessories reflects an important moral difference, "embedded in the structure of rational agency."

justified to use that particular building block – negligence – in a mode of liability for serious crimes?

An understandable initial reaction to that question would be to answer in the negative. A standard reflex in criminal law thinking is that negligence is categorically less blameworthy than subjective foresight, and it is probably not blameworthy enough to use in a mode of liability. But our reflexes are likely conditioned and predicated on the "normal" context of typical private citizens interacting in a polity. Before answering, we must give measured consideration to the command context.

In my discussion of the first two planks, I simply recalled familiar understandings from general criminal law thinking. Now we venture into new territory. Perhaps ICL, by focusing on unusual contexts, can lead us to reconsider how building blocks may be put together in new ways that still respect underlying principles.

A framework to assess deontic justification of inculpatory doctrines

How do we even embark on this assessment? Criminal law theorist Paul Robinson has provided a useful framework for the principled analysis of inculpatory doctrines in his writings on "imputed criminal liability."[98] He notes that, for any given offence, the "paradigm of liability" – that is, the satisfaction of every element of the offence – does not always determine criminal liability. Even where all of the elements of the paradigm are proven, there are exceptions that can *exculpate* the accused. These exceptions are commonly grouped together and analyzed as "defences."[99] Paul Robinson's key insight was to look at the *mirror image* of defences.

Paul Robinson pointed out that there is another type of exception to the "paradigm of liability" – namely, *inculpatory* exceptions, whereby a person can be convicted even though the person did not personally satisfy some elements of the offence. Examples include acting through an innocent agent or transferred intent. These inculpatory doctrines are not traditionally grouped together and analyzed as a category. Robinson proposed a search for consistent principles underlying these established inculpatory exceptions, in order to assess the justifiability of the doctrines and to elaborate appropriate doctrinal details.[100]

Paul Robinson identified two deontic (culpability-based) justifications. The first is "causation": the actor is held responsible despite the absence of an element because she is causally responsible or causally contributed to its commission by another.[101] The second is "equivalence," arising, for example, where the accused had a mental state that is equally blameworthy to the requisite mental state.[102] Some doctrines

---

[98]   Robinson, *supra* note 48.
[99]   *Ibid* at 611.
[100] *Ibid* at 676.
[101] *Ibid* at 619, 630 and 676.
[102] An example would be a mistake of fact, where the accused would still be guilty of a comparably serious crime if the facts were as supposed.

may rely on an aggregation of rationales to cumulatively provide an adequate level of culpability.[103] For example, some doctrines inculpate the accused who creates the *absence* of an element in a blameworthy manner (for example willful blindness, or deliberate self-intoxication in preparation for an offence).[104] This rationale will be particularly pertinent to the military commander who creates her own absence of knowledge through culpable disregard for lives and legal interests that she was obligated to protect.

An activity posing extraordinary dangers to others

Because the institution of armed forces is a familiar one to us, we might be tempted to fall back on our usual habits of thought about liability for "mere" negligence. But those habits of thoughts were shaped in the context of normal interactions between civilians. We should try to see with fresh eyes the extraordinary risks of this remarkable activity. The institution of military command is a socially created institution, not a natural "given," and it grants licences for activity that would otherwise be seriously criminal.

Contemporary international law tolerates armed conflict because there are instances in which the use of force may be beneficial to society, such as in self-defence or for collective security.[105] However, armed conflict is rife with horrific social costs and dangers: not only does it unleash deliberate and collateral killing and destruction, but also it routinely entails serious crimes initiated by subordinates. Armed conflict creates a toxic mix of dehumanization, groupthink, vengeance, and habituation to violence. Accordingly, while international law gives a certain licence to military leaders, it accompanies this licence with duties to monitor and restrain the tragically frequent criminal violence of subordinates who exploit their power.[106]

Many factors aggravate the grievous risks for society. First and most obviously, military leaders train people to make them proficient in the use of violence and equip them with weapons that magnify their power. Second, military leaders indoctrinate soldiers to desensitize them to violence to make them more effective fighters. As Martinez notes, military leaders are "given licence to turn ordinary men into lethally destructive, and legally privileged, soldiers; indeed, military training and command structures are expressly designed to dissolve the social inhibitions that normally prevent people from committing acts of extreme violence, and to remove their sense of moral agency when committing such acts."[107] In warfare, many of the normal moral heuristics ("don't kill," "don't destroy") are displaced by more complicated rules that regulate the special contexts in which collective violence may be justified. Thus military leaders break down normal inhibitions against violence and

---

[103] Robinson, *supra* note 48, at 644.
[104] *Ibid* at 619 and 639–42.
[105] *Charter of the United Nations*, 26 June 1945, 1 UNTS XVI, Arts 2(4), 48, 51.
[106] Martinez, *supra* note 6, at 662; Parks, *supra* note 18, at 102 ("massive responsibility").
[107] Martinez, *supra* note 6, at 662. See also Weigend, *supra* note 5, at 73.

even instincts of self-preservation, replacing them with habits of obedience and loyalty to the group. The result is a more effective fighting force, but it also breeds a highly obvious danger of pathological organizational behaviour.

The danger is never far away. Even the most well-trained armies, acting for humanitarian ends, have frequently committed serious international crimes. Even in peacetime, standing armed forces present a danger to the public, because their relative power, desensitization to violence, and cadre loyalty often fuel crimes against civilians. Thus, even if modern law has good reasons to accept the creation of armed forces, the law also recognizes that the activity bristles with danger, and hence engagement in it comes with serious responsibilities.

The culpability of not inquiring

Command responsibility is a justified extension of aiding and abetting by omission to recognize the special duty of commanders. In normal contexts, "I didn't know" would often exculpate. But it does not exculpate where the commander has created her own ignorance through a criminal dereliction of the duty of vigilance entrusted to her to guard against precisely this danger. Culpability-based rationales of causation and equivalence apply to the commander who, contrary to this duty, buries her head in the sand.

You may still object at this point that there is a quantum difference between negligent ignorance and subjective foresight, so that the causation/substitution rationale requires too great a leap. But there are three reasons why, on closer inspection, the gulf is not as stark as it seems on first glance.

First, we must not overestimate what the subjective standard requires. As a matter of practical reason, accessory liability does not and cannot require knowledge of a *certainty* of a crime, because the crimes typically have not started (or finished) at the time of the accessory's contribution. Thus it must always be a matter of risk. Accordingly, juridical practice across legal systems contemplates different *degrees* of subjective awareness or foresight, such as recklessness, willful blindness, or *dolus eventualis*.[108] Not only is there leeway with respect to the degree of certainty, but also the accessory need not anticipate the "precise crime"; it is enough if one is "aware that one of a number of crimes will probably be committed, and one of those crimes is in fact committed."[109] Thus even the subjective standard must deal in uncertainties about both the *likelihood* and the *nature* of crimes.

Second, we must not underestimate the culpability of criminal negligence. Criminal negligence does not encompass modest lapses and imperfect choices. As

---

[108] International Commission of Jurists, *Corporate Complicity and Legal Accountability, Report of the International Commission of Jurists Expert Legal Panel on Corporate Complicity in International Crimes* (ICJ, 2008) at 25; van der Wilt, *supra* note 84, at 247–49.
[109] *Blaškić* Appeal Judgment, *supra* note 26, at para 50; *Simić* Appeal Judgment, *supra* note 86, at para 86.

discussed, the fault standard requires a gross dereliction that shows a culpable disregard for the lives and legal interests of others.[110]

Third, in the aggravating context of command responsibility, that culpable disregard is especially wrongful. In the context of the exceptional dangerousness of the activity, the repeatedly demonstrated risks of egregious crimes, and the imbalance of military power and civilian vulnerability, a culpable disregard for the dangers is simply staggering. In sum, the commander does not get exonerated by creating her own ignorance through defiance of a duty of vigilance that exists precisely because of the glaring danger.

When I first began this project, I accepted the standard prioritization that subjective fault is, in principle, always worse than objective fault. However, command responsibility reveals a set of circumstances in which that prioritization does not hold. Consider two commanders. Commander A requires proper reporting. As a result, she learns of a strong risk that crimes will occur. She decides to run that risk and hopes it will not materialize. Commander B does not care at all about possible crimes. Thus she does not even bother to set up system of reporting, and, as a result, she does not get the reports and she does not learn of the specific risk. Under the classical prioritization, Commander A is more culpable because she has "subjective" foresight. But who is actually more culpable? Unlike Commander A, Commander B did not bother even to take the first steps. Contrary to the standard prioritization, it is Commander B who has shown even greater disdain for protected persons. She created her own lack of knowledge thanks to that disdain. On a subjective approach (and under the HRTK test), she would get exonerated for that lack of knowledge, but that outcome is the reverse of the actual disregard for legal interests shown by the two commanders.

The implication may be surprising. Normally, "knowing" would be categorically worse than "not knowing." But there can be very grave criminal fault in not knowing.[111] To assess the actual degree of fault, we have to go back a step and ask *why* the commander does not know. We would be wrong to consider "knowing" to be *ipso facto* worse than "not knowing." After all, "*not knowing*" includes the commander who is too contemptuous to find out, or even the commander who sets up systems at the outset to frustrate reporting.[112] The "knowing" commander includes the commander who runs a risk with the hope it will not materialize. Any of

---

[110]   See §8.3.1. As noted, I am not attempting to advance a definitive doctrinal interpretation of the fault standard in ICL. In some legal systems, "gross" dereliction may not be required for criminal negligence. If ICL were to follow that route, then deontic justification might be slightly more difficult, because this particular safeguard would be absent. As noted in §8.3.1, ICL precedents tend to emphasize that the negligence must be "serious," conveying that the dereliction must be severe enough to show a criminally culpable disregard.

[111]   Fletcher, *supra* note 65.

[112]   One line in the *Blaškić* Appeal Judgment, *supra* note 26, suggests that a deliberate system to frustrate reporting might qualify, but it is not explained how this is reconciled with the actual legal test, which still requires "possession."

these hypothetical commanders are rightly held accountable for the harms within the risk they culpably created.

In this hypothetical, I stipulated an example in which criminal negligence is worse, for the purpose of illustrating that the categorical prioritization of subjective foresight is not always correct. Of course, whether criminal negligence or knowledge is more blameworthy in any instance will depend on the facts. But my argument is that criminal negligence is *sufficient* for liability: a marked departure showing that culpable disregard, in the context of that level of danger and responsibility, satisfies the Paul Robinson "causation" and "equivalence" theories of culpability.[113]

My two main points are as follows. First, criminal negligence is *adequately* blameworthy, at least in this special context, to meet the culpability requirement for accessory liability. Second, criminal negligence is also *sufficiently equivalent* to subjective foresight to be included in the same doctrine. In other words, they are close enough to address "fair labelling" objections. When I embarked on this work, I initially thought that negligence would still be *generally somewhat less blameworthy* than subjective foresight, and I thought that the differences should be teased out at sentencing. However, I am no longer certain that even this in-principle ranking applies in command responsibility. The actual ranking will depend on the facts of any particular case, including *why* the commander does not know and the degree of disregard that produced her ignorance.

8.4 IMPLICATIONS

8.4.1 The General Conception of Command Responsibility

The foregoing account has several implications for how we understand command responsibility.

Criminal negligence

First, rather than disavowing criminal negligence as an aspect of command responsibility, ICL should openly defend and embrace it. Tribunal jurisprudence has led people to shun criminal negligence as somehow inappropriate in command responsibility. However, the incorporation of criminal negligence is the core innovation of command responsibility, and it is a justified and valuable innovation.

Duty to inquire

Second, it is perfectly appropriate for command responsibility to encompass the commander's proactive duty to inquire. Early Tribunal jurisprudence shied away from this, which was understandable in those early days, given the unexplored normative implications. For example, one might imagine hectic circumstances in which it would be perfectly reasonable that the commander did not have time to set

[113]   Robinson, *supra* note 48.

up reporting systems. In such a case, incorporating the proactive duty might have seemed too harsh. But the response is: any scenario in which the conduct was reasonable is, by definition, not criminal negligence. By recalling the rigour of criminal negligence, we address plausible concerns. Moreover, the point of command responsibility is that it can address egregious breaches of the duty to inquire. It is deontically justified in doing so. Insofar as Tribunal jurisprudence has excised such cases from its ambit, that jurisprudence misses the point of the doctrine. Thus it is not surprising that the HRTK test has not played a significant role in prosecutions.

The "possession" test

Third, command responsibility need not and should not hinge on the requirement that information made it to the commander's "possession." The Tribunals invented the "possession" requirement in their efforts to disavow negligence and to make the HRTK test appear subjective. While the caution was understandable, we can now say on reflection that the requirement of "possession" is required neither by the precedents, nor by deontic considerations (culpability), nor by consequentialist considerations. The "possession" test is muddled, misleading, unfair, and inadequate. It is *muddled* because "possession" does not mean "actual" possession.[114] It is *misleading* because, despite the vocal disavowals of negligence, the test is actually still constructive knowledge, since the commander need not actually be "acquainted" with the information.[115] The test is *unfair (overreaching)* because the commander is deemed to have knowledge of all reports made available to her even if exigent demands at the time meant that she was not negligent in not getting to the reports. The test is *inadequate (underreaching)*, because where a commander arranges inadequate reporting so that no alarming information makes it to her "possession," she gets an acquittal.[116] The test does not reflect individual desert, and it also creates perverse incentives to avoid receiving reports of criminal activity. We must be grateful for the many helpful contributions of Tribunal jurisprudence,[117] but I hope that in coming decades national and international courts will reconsider the ambiguous "possession" test and its unnecessary indulgence of the passive commander.

The "should have known" test

Fourth, the SHK test – which overtly embraces criminal negligence and the duty to inquiry – should be openly defended. The SHK test is a better match with precedents and has better consequences, but was rejected because it was thought to be

---

[114] *Blaškić* Appeal Judgment, *supra* note 26, at para 58.
[115] *Čelebići* Appeal Judgment, *supra* note 20, at para 239.
[116] A line in the *Blaškić* Appeals Judgment, *supra* note 26, at para 62 asserts that the commander can be liable if she "deliberately refrains" from obtaining information, which is a welcome suggestion, consistent with what I advance here, but difficult to square with the actual rule posited in that case.
[117] Including the requisite degree of control and the measures expected of a commander.

unfair. However, on closer reflection, the SHK test is not merely deontically *justifiable*; it actually maps *better* onto personal culpability.[118] Thus ICL should return to the post-World War II jurisprudence: where the commander has created her own ignorance deliberately or through criminal negligence in her duty to inquire, that is adequate to establish the fault element for command responsibility.[119] The ICC seems to have returned to this path in its early jurisprudence.[120] Even for courts and tribunals whose statutes use the phrase "had reason to know," that phrase can be interpreted in better accordance with the World War II jurisprudence and the ICC Statute, as Tribunal prosecutors initially urged.[121]

Accessory liability

Fifth, and finally, command responsibility can indeed be recognized as a mode of liability. Thoughtful scholars, uncertain about whether negligence in a mode of liability can be justified, have suggested that it should be recast as a separate offence. I have attempted here to address the principled concerns, or at least to outline the path to do so. The account I have offered complies with personal culpability. It also maintains fidelity to the long line of precedents indicating that command responsibility is a mode of accessory liability, so that creative reinterpretation is not needed. Command responsibility, as a mode of liability, rightly expresses the commander's indirect responsibility for the crimes facilitated by her culpable dereliction.[122] A "separate offence" approach understates the harm unleashed and the indirect liability for the crimes facilitated by one's dereliction.

8.4.2 Further Refinement of Command Responsibility

If the general account I have outlined is correct, then there are three additional implications for our interpretation and refinement of the doctrine. These pertain to (i) recognizing a capacity exception, (ii) the scope of the doctrine (and which types of organization it covers), and (iii) civilian superiors. For each of these three areas, I am simply outlining an area for *future* study and analysis; in none of them am I attempting to provide an answer.

Capacity exception

First, because this account endorses a criminal negligence standard, it arguably should also recognize a potential exception where the commander lacks the *capacity*

---

[118]   The HRTK test fixes the commander with knowledge of all reports submitted to her – which does not take into account that there may be circumstances in which it was not criminally negligent that she did not have an opportunity to acquaint herself with the report.

[119]   See §8.2.1 for pre-Tribunal jurisprudence.

[120]   *Bemba* Confirmation Decision, *supra* note 38, at paras 433–34.

[121]   See §8.2.1.

[122]   The mode approach, I argue, also entails that the causal contribution requirement must be respected: see Chapter 6.

to meet the requisite standard. I have emphasized that, with criminal negligence, we condemn persons for *failing to exert their faculties* as the activity obviously required, and thereby showing a culpable disregard for the lives and legal interests safeguarded by the duty.[123] However, if the person's gross dereliction resulted not from a culpable disregard, but rather from a lack of capacity (such as severe mental limitations), then blame and punishment would not be appropriate.[124] In such a case, the problem is not that they failed to exert their faculties, but that their faculties were limited.

Appropriate scope (command relation)

Second, the account provides additional guideposts for interpreting the scope of the doctrine, and particularly the types of organization within which it applies. I have argued that a mode of liability incorporating criminal negligence can be justified within the special context of a military command relationship. What are the outer parameters of that justifying context? After all, there are very diverse forms of armed groups, with different degrees of organization (professional armies, paramilitaries, loose armed groups). In determining the outer parameters of the doctrine, we must be sensitive not only to doctrinal and teleological considerations, but also to the *deontic justification*.[125] When considering what types of group or level of organization are needed, we have to consider at what point the rationale for the deontic justification for this mode of liability no longer pertains. Beyond that outer limit, one must fall back on the other remaining complicity doctrines that deal with collective action.

Civilian superiors

Third, the account here may not apply to civilian superiors. Accordingly, this account may cast a more positive light on the bifurcated approach of the ICC Statute. The ICC Statute distinguishes between military and non-military superiors, and gives non-military superiors a more generous test (that the superior "consciously disregarded" information). The bifurcation in the ICC Statute has been strongly criticized.[126] The dominant criticism is that the more generous test for civilian

---

[123] Hart, *supra* note 62, at 150–57.

[124] *Ibid* at 149–54; Horder, *supra* note 58, at 186; *Creighton, supra* note 57. Chinese criminal law reaches the same conclusion – "should have" entails both a duty and capacity: Badar, *supra* note 71, at 186–88. See also Parks, *supra* note 18, at 90–93 suggesting some subjective factors pertinent in the command responsibility context.

[125] Some scholars have already started to helpfully explore these parameters. H van der Wilt, "Command Responsibility in the Jungle: Some Reflections on the Elements of Effective Command and Control," in C C Jalloh, ed, *The Sierra Leone Special Court and Its Legacy; The Impact for Africa and International Criminal Law* (Cambridge University Press, 2014); R Provost, "Authority, Responsibility, and Witchcraft: From Tintin to the SCSL," in Jalloh, *op cit*, at 159; I Bantekas, "Legal Anthropology and the Construction of Complex Liabilities," in Jalloh, *op cit*, at 181; A Zahar, "Command Responsibility of Civilian Superiors for Genocide" (2001)14 LJIJ 591 at 602–12; Nybondas, *supra* note 5, at 191–94.

[126] The *legal* criticism is that the Rome Statute differs from the Tribunal approach and therefore from customary law. Such arguments may underestimate the nuance of the broader body of transnational

superiors represents a tragic watering down of liability for the self-serving reasons of protecting political leaders.[127]

But perhaps the more generous treatment for civilian leaders should not be so quickly condemned. One of the tendencies I discussed in Chapter 2 is that ICL scholars often assume that harsher, unilaterally imposed rules are the "true" law and that negotiated, more permissive, rules are mere political "compromise."[128] Where such an assumption is too hastily applied, it may lead us to favour rules rooted in victors' justice and to overlook fundamental constraining principles. I argued that we should pause to consider that the problematic rule might be the unilaterally imposed one; perhaps potential exposure can have a salutary effect of sharpening drafters' sensitivity to unfairness.[129] Article 28 of the ICC Statute presents an illustration. An alternative explanation of Article 28 is that an issue of principle was raised and delegates were persuaded of its merits.[130] It could be that the deliberative process unearthed a plausible intuition of justice.

Further study may show that there is a principled case for the bifurcated approach. The considerations outlined in this chapter – the extreme danger of the activity, training and equipping people for violence, indoctrination and desensitization, extensive control, military discipline, and the explicit duties of active supervision – do not apply to most civilian superiors. Before purporting to extend the SHK standard to civilians, one would need to do very careful work on the precise parameters of the deontic justification. At this time, it seems to me quite plausible that the SHK test is justifiable for persons effectively acting as military commanders, whereas a subjective test may be appropriate for other superiors.[131]

8.5 CONCLUSION

At first glance, command responsibility seems problematic, because it does not comport with our usual heuristics and constructs developed in typical criminal law settings. However, this an instance in which ICL settings and doctrines can enable us to reconsider our normal reflexes in criminal law theory (a major theme of this book). The command responsibility doctrine was created in international law to deal with a specific set of circumstances that are not the usual context of citizens

---

precedents. Early ICTY and ICTR jurisprudence acknowledged these uncertainties. Thus the custom question may not be as conclusively settled as some suggest.

[127] See, e.g., G Vetter, "Command Responsibility of Non-military Superiors in the International Criminal Court" (2000) 25 Yale J Int'l L 89; E Langston, "The Superior Responsibility Doctrine in International Law: Historical Continuities, Innovation and Criminality – Can East Timor's Special Panels Bring Militia Leaders to Justice?" (2004) 4 Int'l Crim L Rev 141 at 159–61.

[128] See §2.4.

[129] *Ibid.*

[130] See, e.g., P Saland, "International Criminal Law Principles," in R Lee, ed, *The International Criminal Court: The Making of the Rome Statute* (Kluwer, 1999) at 203.

[131] Also noting the different context and responsibilities, see Nybondas, *supra* note 5, at 183–88; Meloni, *supra* note 5, at 250; Martinez, *supra* note 6, at 662; Weigend, *supra* note 5, at 73–74.

interacting. The doctrine takes account of specific responsibilities that are necessary to avert a special pathology of human organizations. This is the "genius" of command responsibility: the practice reveals an underlying insight of justice, shared by the many jurists who helped to create it, even if they did not articulate the deontic justification.

The mental element of command responsibility may differ from familiar national *doctrines*, but it is not a departure from the deeper underlying principles. The concept of complicity by omission, by those under a duty to prevent crimes, is already established. Command responsibility extends this concept with a modified fault element. That modified fault element is rooted in personal culpability, recognizing the responsibilities assumed by the commander and the dangerousness of the activity. Given the extraordinary danger of the activity, the historically demonstrated frequency of abuse, and the imbalance of power of vulnerability, the commander has a duty to try to monitor, prevent, and respond to crimes. The baseline expected of a commander is diligence in monitoring and repressing crimes, and a failure to meet that baseline effectively facilitates and encourages crimes.

Command responsibility rightly conveys that the commander defying this duty is indirectly responsible for the harms unleashed, just as a person criminally derelict in monitoring a dam may be responsible if the dam bursts on civilians below. This message of command responsibility is expressively valuable and deontically justified. Furthermore, the commander choosing not to *try* to require reports makes a choice every bit as dangerous and reprehensible as those who ignore warning signs, because that initial choice already subsumes and enables all the harms within the risk and removes the possibility of responding properly.[132] The driver who dons a blindfold is inculpated, not exculpated, for the harms within the risk generated. Command responsibility may seem at first to chafe against our normal analytical constructs, but I believe that the many jurists who shaped the doctrine over the years were articulating an intuition of justice that is, on careful inspection, justifiable and valuable.

---

[132] One might object that criminal negligence does not entail a "choice," but that line of thought looks at criminal negligence in the abstract rather than considers how concrete cases will unfold in command responsibility. A criminally negligent failure to require reports will always involve a choice; without a choice, there can be no gross departure.

9

Horizons: The Future of the Justice Conversation

OVERVIEW

I conclude with three final overarching sets of observations. First, I make explicit some aspects of the coherentist method, which I modelled in the last three chapters. Second, I highlight some emerging themes for criminal law theory of ICL – particularly the exploration of deontic principles. Third, I survey some additional issues in ICL and criminal law theory, to which the proposed frame of inquiry could be fruitfully applied in the future.

9.1 MID-LEVEL PRINCIPLES AND COHERENTISM AT WORK

9.1.1 Coherentist Moves

In Chapters 6–8, I was not only dissecting current controversies in ICL, but also demonstrating the proposed method. The types of consideration I invoked in my analysis would have seemed quite familiar from most legal and normative analysis – that is, patterns of practice, consistency with analytical constructs, normative argumentation, and casuistic testing. And, indeed, they are the same considerations. I suggest that coherentism is the best underlying theory to explain how we engage in both legal and normative analysis. We form the best understandings that we can by drawing on all available clues.[1]

I think this method (mid-level principles, coherentist reconciliation of clues) implicitly underlies a lot of valuable criminal law theory. For example, in Chapter 8, I employed a framework advanced by Paul Robinson, in which he explored the theories that underpin inculpatory doctrines (causation, equivalence, and so on).[2] His work in formulating that framework was itself an exercise in mid-level principles. He noted that exculpatory doctrines (defences) are often studied as a class, but that inculpatory doctrines had not been studied as a class for unifying principles. He studied patterns of practice, he hypothesized some mid-level

---

[1] See Chapter 4.
[2] See §8.3.3 and see P Robinson, "Imputed Criminal Liability" (1984) 93 Yale LJ 609.

constructs to categorize and explain the practice, he assessed which of those constructs are normatively justifiable, and then he generated prescriptions for a more analytically consistent and normatively sound body of law. In the case of Paul Robinson's framework, the method enabled both analytical systematization and normative evaluation of the underlying justifications for inculpatory doctrines.

I modelled this method in Part III of this book. I worked with propositions that were arguably immanent within ICL practice (e.g. that culpability requires causal contribution, or that principals have paradigmatic *mens rea*). I took those propositions as starting hypotheses, although I was prepared to rethink and reconstruct them if there were convincing reasons to do so. Both propositions proved to be analytically and normatively helpful. The exploration of command responsibility led me to question the assumptions that criminal negligence is always less blameworthy than subjective foresight and that knowing is always worse than not knowing: where a failure to know arises from culpable neglect, it can be equally, or sometimes even more, blameworthy.[3]

I showed how the method can do *analytical* work by unearthing internal contradictions between doctrines and stated principles (Chapter 6). I also showed how it can do *normative* work, by clarifying deontic constraints (Chapter 7) or by examining the justification of doctrines and producing prescriptions (Chapter 8). I drew on patterns of practice, normative arguments, and casuistic testing (e.g. comparing the fault of commanders in different hypothetical scenarios). I showed how such inquiry can help us to put basic building blocks together in a novel way. For example, I argued that command responsibility responds to a specific set of circumstances in which the special fault standard can be deontically justified.

I also showed how the method copes with uncertainty. For example, criminal negligence is not absolutely settled: some scholars argue against criminal negligence as a standard of culpability. Nonetheless, most legal systems, most practice, most scholars, and indeed the weight of the arguments, favour the standard.[4] Similarly, the distinction between principals and accessories has its doubters, but it is a construct that is adopted in ICL, and which is well supported in national practice and by normative argumentation, even if the boundaries between direct and indirect roles can sometimes be contested.[5] There are also philosophers who dispute that omissions can make causal contributions, but again the overwhelming weight of legal practice and normative argumentation concludes that our failures to fulfill duties can have consequences.[6]

If we were insisting on Cartesian certainty, we would be paralyzed by those doubts, because we cannot say for sure that these ideas are "right." We would also be paralyzed by the unreliability of each source (practice, moral theories, our intuitions). The coherentist method draws a wide range of inputs, while being

---

[3] See Chapter 8.
[4] See §8.3.1.
[5] See §8.3.2.
[6] See §7.1.2.

mindful of the limitations of each input, and it seeks to develop the best possible model to reconcile those inputs. The proposed method accepts up front that philosophical certainty is unattainable; we seek a level of confidence sufficient for the decision at hand. For the punishment of individuals, a high level of confidence is appropriate. But the body of available clues provides more than enough support for these practices, unless and until more convincing arguments are developed against the practice.

9.1.2 Why Does Practice Matter in Normative Analysis?

You might wonder whether recourse to practice reflects the "naturalist fallacy": am I impermissibly conflating an "is" (legal practice) with an "ought" (deontic principles)? I refer to practice for two reasons, one analytical and one normative. When we are working *analytically* – trying to formulate mid-level principles that can categorize and explain practice – of course we must consider the practice that we seek to categorize and explain. More profoundly, however, practice can help to inform us even on *normative* questions. Patterns of practice, worked out over time by jurists based on experience – and especially patterns of practice that reoccur in different legal traditions and cultures – may reflect broadly shared intuitions of justice.[7]

The obvious follow-up question is, "But what if all of those people's intuitions of justice were wrong?" That is absolutely a possibility, which the coherentist approach unflinchingly recognizes. There is no guidepost available to human beings that is free from the risk of error.[8] Thus we must approach each clue, including patterns of practice, with appropriate skepticism. We bear in mind that established patterns might reflect arbitrary traditions, or they may reflect biases and assumptions of a culture, or they may even reflect quirks of the human mind. The coherentist method is aware of these risks and seeks to guard against them in the best and only way possible: by testing every clue against all of the other clues (e.g. normative arguments, considered judgements, casuistic testing). This method does not guarantee certainty or freedom from error. No method does. The strength of the coherentist method is precisely that it is constantly testing the components of our beliefs using all other available beliefs and experiences. Widespread juridical practice can assist us as one possible "humility check" to test the moral theories and systems that we spin from our own minds.

9.1.3 Two Levels of Coherentism: Legal and Normative Reasoning

I think that we apply coherentism on two levels: in legal reasoning and normative reasoning. Legal reasoning is a special form of reasoning, distinct from other

---

[7] See §4.3.1 on the "normativity of the positive."
[8] See §4.3.3.

practical or normative reasoning, because it circumscribes the relevant sources and the permissible argumentative moves. I believe that legal reasoning is nonetheless coherentist. We seek the best reconciliation of all of the types of consideration that are recognized in legal analysis: text, context, objects and purposes, coherence with surrounding legal norms, pertinent precedents, and general principles.[9] Often, we cannot achieve perfect "coherence" among all of the clues; some may outright conflict. An example of this is command responsibility. Given the confused state of the authorities, every possible interpretative solution requires rejection of some authorities as inconsistent with the proposed solution. Furthermore, every possible interpretation of Article 28 of the ICC Statute entails downplaying some aspect of the text in favour of others.[10] My proposed solution does not perfectly reconcile all of the considerations, but I believe it offers the highest level of coherence of any solution.[11]

More importantly, and somewhat more unconventionally, I believe that we also use a coherentist method in our normative reasoning, including in our deontic analysis. As discussed in Chapter 4, no single comprehensive ethical theory presents itself to all sober minds as the self-evident, *a priori* starting point. Instead, we find ourselves alive in the world, and we have to draw on all available clues to try to make sense of things, including making moral sense of things. We draw, among other things, on normative arguments, moral theories, and our intuitive reactions to try to form models that reconcile experiences and beliefs to the best extent possible.[12]

9.1.4 Starting in the Middle and Coherentism as Valuable Method

One of my main contributions here is to highlight that there is an attractive alternative to the traditional scholarly Cartesian impulse that all propositions must be rooted in a deeper underlying theory, in turn supported by a deeper underlying theory, until we reach some reliable foundation. Our traditional insecurity is that an

---

[9] See, e.g., ICC Statute, Art 21, which incorporates, along with the Statute, the Rules and the Elements, as well as custom (state practice reflecting a sense of legal obligation) and general principles; see also the Vienna Convention on the Law of Treaties, Art 31, which includes Article 31(3)(c) (systemic integration with other relevant rules).

[10] One must either disregard the express contribution requirement, or narrow the role of the "failure to punish" branch, or strain against the express wording indicating that it is a mode of liability. My own proposed solution admittedly narrows the utility of the "failure to punish" branch, but overall it offers the highest coherence between the text, the culpability principle, the purposes of command responsibility, and the broad body of precedents (beyond only the ICTY) since World War II.

[11] See Chapters 6–8.

[12] One may even choose to adopt a comprehensive theory, such as a Kantian or contractarian theory, but I would suggest that the reasons leading one to do so are still coherentist: one adopts such theories insofar as they seem to be useful models in reconciling the clues. Similarly, in science, models are often provisionally adopted for as long they are helpful in reconciling the clues. But the models may still be set aside if they contradict too much experience, or if experience leads us to replace them with better models.

account that is not grounded in solid foundations is flimsy or insecure. In my view, this Cartesian conception of rigour is not viable, because we could never discuss any of the current ethical questions before us until all foundational moral questions are resolved.

On the coherentist approach, the structure supporting our beliefs is not a linear chain, but rather a web. This is the method used in science and elsewhere in human inquiry to advance our understandings. We can still be "rigorous," but rigour requires a different structure of substantiation from the archetypal model of linear deduction.

It may seem particularly counter-intuitive to engage in debates about deontic principles without committing to a single underlying philosophical theory. But the quest to identify the "correct" theory of morality is endless, and our conclusions may actually be more reliable, not less reliable, if they are supported by multiple theories as well as the wider range of clues.

Of course, scholars attracted to a particular comprehensive ethical theory can still make valuable contributions to debates by drawing on their preferred theory. But I think the field as a whole will absorb those contributions in a coherentist manner – that is, taking the contributions as provisional insights generated by a specific model.

Even on a coherentist approach, it is still desirable to work on grand unifying theories. If a model or theory can address a greater range of problems in an elegant way, then that theory has greater "consilience," which is a desideratum of coherentism. But a grand unifying theory is not a precondition. Working on problems of mid-level theory can also be valuable, if that is where headway can be made.

In my view, mid-level principles and coherentist reconciliation of clues offer the best theory of criminal law theory: it is the best account of how most scholars generally do make contributions in this field. Many scholars I know implicitly assume a classical foundationalist model, and yet they apply coherentist methods, even without formal awareness of coherentism, and hence perceive themselves to be inadequate foundationalists taking shortcuts or being otherwise incomplete. I draw attention to the "web of justification" alternative to the classical linear model, so that it can be applied more consciously and carefully. We can avoid haphazard bricolage and instead seek rigour in a coherentist sense. Coherentism is not a lazy invitation that "anything goes"; it requires a different type of rigour, tested by all-things-considered judgements. It can involve searing scrutiny of the underlying concepts that are employed and the extent to which they are convincing and suitable. Awareness of the coherentist structure of justification helps us to better see its strengths, its demands, and its limitations. We can also be suitably humble about our conclusions, recognizing that they are in all cases provisional and revisable.

9.2 MAJOR AND MINOR THEMES

9.2.1 Major Themes: Criminal Law Theory Meets ICL

(1) **The deontic dimension** Legal analysis in criminal law, including ICL, requires not only the familiar source-based analysis and teleological analysis, but also a third type of reasoning, which I have called deontic analysis. I hope that this term can be added to the ICL lexicon, because it succinctly conveys this distinctive type of reasoning, focused on justice for the individual as opposed to broader social impact. Deontic analysis directly considers the principled limits of institutional punishment in light of the personhood, dignity, and agency of human beings affected by the system.[13]

(2) **Two reasons** The study of deontic principles is important for at least two reasons. First, it clarifies important normative constraints, in order to ensure that the system does not treat persons unjustly. Second, and less obviously, it can also help to shape better policy. Where doctrines are needlessly conservative because of an unmoored, fallaciously restrictive impression of the constraining principles, coherentist deontic analysis can pave the way toward more effective laws.[14]

(3) **Learning from criticisms** I examined the most important criticisms of "liberal" accounts (accounts concerned with deontic constraints). I argued that a sophisticated and humanistic approach to deontic principles can learn from and avoid common criticisms of liberal accounts. A "liberal" account need not entail unsound individualistic methodologies, nor invocation of timeless metaphysical axioms, nor disregard for social context. A sophisticated and humanistic liberal account can draw on human experience and social context.[15] In the minimalist sense in which I use the term "liberal" (and in which it is commonly used in criminal law theory), it simply requires respect for individuals and thus requires justification for the punishment of individuals.

(4) **Open-minded and reconstructive** I examined thoughtful arguments that familiar (deontic) principles of justice from national systems may not be appropriate or applicable in ICL contexts. I concluded that deontic principles do matter in ICL, but that the special contexts of ICL may lead us to refine our understanding of the principles. To ignore deontic principles would not only contravene moral duties owed to the individual, but also probably contradict values inherent to the enterprise of ICL (e.g. the "inner morality of law").[16]

---

[13] See §1.2.1.

[14] See §1.1.3 and §2.5, and Annex 4.

[15] See §3.3. For example, criminal law theory inquires about the responsibility of the individual not because of ideological or methodological blinders that leave theorists able to perceive only individuals, but rather because, once we employ criminal law and choose to punish individuals, we necessarily must inquire what the individuals are accountable for. Similarly, criminal law theory does not require imagining humans as socially unencumbered beings; it can look at actions in their social context and with their social meaning.

[16] See, e.g., L L Fuller, *The Morality of Law*, 2nd ed (Yale University Press, 1969).

However, I advocate an open-minded approach that is prepared to re-evaluate familiar principles: salient differences in contexts may generate deontically justified refinements of principles to recognize special cases.[17]

(5) **A two-way conversation** Accordingly, the encounter between criminal law theory and ICL is not a one-way conversation, in which criminal law theory is deployed to clarify, critique, systematize, and improve ICL. It is a two-way conversation. ICL raises new problems that put formerly peripheral questions at the centre. Mainstream criminal law theory understandably assumes the "normal" case of an interaction between a modern state and the individuals within its jurisdiction, in a society that is relatively stable. ICL routinely confronts situations that fall outside of that paradigm. As a result, ICL problems require us to clarify assumptions about law-making, fair notice, authority, citizenship, community, legitimacy, and many other concepts. The study of extreme or special cases may lead us to realize that there are implicit preconditions and limitations in propositions that we had thought to be elementary. Thus the study of special cases can help to foster a more truly general theory of criminal law.[18]

(6) **Coherentist** As discussed in §9.1, in the absence of an uncontroverted and reliable foundational ethical theory, I argue that coherentism is the best method for identifying and refining deontic principles. More specifically, I advocated working with "mid-level principles." That approach looks for principles that are both arguably immanent within a body of practice and normatively compelling. The approach acknowledges that current understandings of principles are historically contingent human creations, but it works with them as a starting hypothesis while continuing to search for better understandings.[19]

(7) **The humanity of justice** I have emphasized the "humanity" of justice. I do so in response to criticisms that the constraints are doctrinal artifacts, or products of abstract philosophies, or concerns particular to Western culture. Criminal law is carried out for prospective human aims (it is not pointlessly retributive). Its constraints reflect respect for humanity. The constraints are human-created concepts (as opposed to *a priori* Platonic forms), and they are clarified through human processes. We seek to identify widely shared human concerns. There is reason to doubt the common claim that criminal law, or constraints such as the culpability or legality principle, are purely Western preoccupations, given similarities emerging in practices in diverse regions (before colonization and even before the emergence of criminal law in Europe) and empirical studies showing widely shared commonalities in senses of justice. Because the principles are human constructs, shaped and refined through human processes, any discussion of the principles is, of course, fallible, but it is nonetheless

---

[17] See §3.2.
[18] See Chapter 5.
[19] See Chapter 4.

a valuable endeavour. The best we can do is do the best we can to verify that practices and institutions are justified.

9.2.2 Minor Themes: Improving Reasoning

I have also argued that scholarship should be especially attentive to *reasoning*. Problematic reasoning will eventually generate problematic outcomes. I have highlighted some recurring themes about reasoning. Mindfulness of these themes can help us to foster more sophisticated and sound legal reasoning.

(1) **Need for deontic analysis** As mentioned at §9.2.1, early ICL discourse tended to rely heavily on source-based and teleological reasoning, with somewhat weaker deontic reasoning. Early ICL jurisprudence often approached fundamental principles with technical doctrinal arguments rather than deontic analysis.[20] More recently, the system has matured considerably, making it all the more essential to have a framework for deontic analysis.

(2) **Value of criminal law theory** Furthermore, early ICL discourse was not always conversant with helpful tools of criminal law theory. Thus, for example, early arguments equated accessory liability with "commission,"[21] or made inelegant statements about criminal negligence.[22] The tools of criminal law theory can help to clarify ICL. The use of organizing concepts of criminal law theory in ICL has already improved tremendously.[23]

(3) **Alertness to patterns** It is important to be alert to possible systematic distortions in reasoning. I have pointed out numerous illustrations of some problematic habits of reasoning, particularly in the earlier days of ICL, which would tend to distort reasoning away from fundamental principles.[24]

9.3 FURTHER QUESTIONS

The following are some topics that await, ripe for coherentist deontic inquiry. The inquiry can challenge and improve ICL, and it can also challenge and improve criminal law theory.

---

[20] For examples of doctrinal reasoning that failed to engage with the deontic constraints, see §6.3.3 and §6.5.
[21] See, e.g., §8.3.2.
[22] See §8.2.1 and §8.3.1.
[23] See §2.5.
[24] See Chapter 2. Even though I have distinguished between doctrinal and deontic reasoning, sensitivity to deontic considerations can improve our doctrinal analysis, e.g. it can influence what we notice when we survey precedents. I gave examples such as the *Čelebići* decision, in which a chamber found "no support" for a contribution requirement even after citing passages of authorities that expressly supported it. Had the judges examined those precedents with the culpability principle in mind, they might have at least detected that pattern in the precedent. Thus what we are sensitive to may influence what we perceive.

9.3.1 Further Questions in Command Responsibility

I have dissected some specific controversies in command responsibility in consider-able detail. Nonetheless, those chapters were only a toe dipped in the water. As I noted, I skimmed over several debates in the interests of providing succinct illustrations. Many depths remain unplumbed.

Civilian superiors

To contain the scope of my inquiry, I focused on military commanders. I only outlined some thoughts on civilian superiors. Tribunal jurisprudence holds civilian superiors to the same standard as military commanders; the ICC Statute grants them a more generous standard – a "consciously disregarded" standard. There is a vast area here for fruitful study: the deontic case for civilian superior responsibility, its appropriate scope, the appropriate understanding of the fault element, and how it differs from aiding and abetting by omission.[25]

The parameters of "effective control"

Command responsibility requires a relationship of "effective control." What pre-cisely is required for "effective control"? The jurisprudence has approached this question using doctrinal (source-based) and teleological analyses. However, as I outlined in Chapter 8, the "effective control" test can be illuminated by deontic analysis as well.[26] After all, if the "should have known" test is deontically justified in specific circumstances, then the "effective control" test should track the limits of those justifying circumstances. The requirement of being "military" arguably maps well onto both the dangerousness of the enterprise and the extensive control that warrants the doctrine. More specifically still, the test should be confined to the types of control – and to the types of hierarchical organization – that furnish the deontic justification for this special doctrine. In more irregular armed groups, a command responsibility doctrine might be *useful* (from a consequentialist perspective focused on deterrence), but it might not be *fair*. The deontic limits have not been mapped. Other standard modes of liability still apply in contexts in which command respon-sibility is not justified.

Failure to take measures

I have not touched on the third element of command responsibility: the "failure to take all necessary and reasonable measures." The *Bemba* Appeal Judgment hinged on interpretation of that element.[27] That judgment can at least be commended for

---

[25] See §8.4.
[26] See *ibid*.
[27] *Prosecutor v Jean-Pierre Bemba Gombo*, Judgment on the Appeal of Mr Jean-Pierre Bemba Gombo against Trial Chamber III's Judgment Pursuant to Article 74 of the Statute, ICC A.Ch, ICC-01/05-01/08 A, 8 June 2018 ("*Bemba* Appeal Judgment").

being empathetic to the position of a commander[28] and focusing on the deontic question of what criminal law can expected of a commander. It has, however, been extensively criticized by numerous scholars, among other things for its narrow construal of command responsibility and other new requirements announced without legal authority.[29] In Annex 4, I outline how some aspects of the *Bemba* Appeal Judgment are arguably examples of the "overcorrection" I described in §1.1.2 and §2.5: conceptions more rigid than careful deontic analysis would support. The proper scope of the "failure to take all necessary and reasonable measures" test awaits a more careful deontic assessment.

9.3.2 The Next Frontiers

Legality, superior orders, and duress

In Chapter 5, I noted several other questions for which a reconstructive coherentist approach might create new insights not only for ICL, but also for mainstream criminal law theory. First, ICL – a system without a legislature, which has often encountered mass atrocities that are not clearly criminalized in positive law – provides an excellent context in which to explore the parameters of the legality principle.[30] Second, the doctrine of superior orders has been hotly debated in doctrinal terms, but the normative grounding is surprisingly unexplored. Such an inquiry may provide lessons about state authority, role morality, and mistakes of law that could illuminate both this specific doctrine and general criminal law theory.[31] Third, situations of extreme duress, such as in the *Erdemović* case,[32] can help us to better articulate the deontic underpinnings of the duress defences; there has not yet been much discussion about how "social roles" may influence the expectations we rightly place on individuals to resist pressure.[33]

Tools of criminal theory

In Chapter 5, I also highlighted various tools of criminal law theory, such as "community," "citizenship," "authority," and even the basic framework of "the state" itself.[34] Scrutiny of ICL problems would likely reveal problematic cases for each of these tools, leading us to refine (or possibly even reject) some of the tools.

---

[28] Empathy is an important facet of deontic analysis. See §3.2.2 and see M D Dubber, *The Sense of Justice: Empathy in Law and Punishment* (Universal Law, 2006).

[29] See Annex 4.

[30] See §5.2.1.

[31] See §5.2.3.

[32] *Prosecutor v Erdemović*, Judgment, ICTY A.Ch, IT-96-22-A, 7 October 1997.

[33] See §5.2.2.

[34] See §5.1.3.

Aiding and abetting, and neutral contributions

Beyond the issues I have already listed, there are countless others to be examined. For example, the ICL "aiding and abetting" doctrine has engendered fierce controversy – such as the dispute in ICTY jurisprudence over whether the assistance must be "specifically directed" toward the crimes.[35] The battlefield is drawn into two camps, one favouring a "knowledge" test and another favouring a "purpose" test. Most legal systems support one or the other. However, it seems to me that each of the two main contenders is flawed. The "knowledge" test seems too broad, because it encompasses contributions that do not seem culpable, whereas the "purpose" test seems too narrow, because it excludes contributions that do seem culpable. A coherentist account would search for more convincing accounts.[36] The problem is particularly fierce with respect to so-called neutral contributions, and ICL provides new fact patterns with which to explore that problem. For example, if a state is assisting a rebel group that is fighting for a legal and worthy cause, but the group is committing crimes, at what point do officials of the assisting state become personally criminally liable? These are ways in which ICL doctrine can still be refined and in which ICL may help to inform general criminal law theory.[37]

Co-perpetration in crimes of massive scale

ICL also provides a rich context in which to examine individual responsibility in massive collective enterprises. ICL has adopted co-perpetration doctrines from national systems, but those doctrines were generally designed for much smaller groups of perpetrators. Contexts involving hundreds or thousands of contributors, with very different degrees of contribution from different participants, invite and challenge us to identify the proper limits of culpability.

Control theory

The coherentist method is useful for studying not only fundamental principles, but also the other organizing constructs of criminal law. For example, the ICC has adopted the "control theory" to delineate between principals and accessories.[38] The

---

[35] See, e.g., L N Sadat, "Can the ICTY Šainović and Perišić Cases Be Reconciled?" (2014) 108 AJIL 475; K Heller, "Why the ICTY's 'Specifically Directed' Requirement Is Justified" (2 June 2013) Opinio Juris (blog); J Stewart, " 'Specific Direction' is Indefensible: A Response to Heller on Complicity" (12 June 2013) Opinio Juris (blog); J Ohlin, "Specific Direction Again" (17 December 2015), Opinio Juris (blog).

[36] See, e.g., A Sarch, "Condoning the Crime: The Elusive Mens Rea for Complicity" (2015–16) 47 Loy U Chi LJ 131, suggesting an intermediate element of "condoning."

[37] See, already exploring this issue, M Jackson, "Virtuous Accomplices in International Criminal Law" (2019) 68 Int'l & Comp LQ 818. See also, on questions around arms trades that are legal under domestic law, K Ambos, "Complicity in War Crimes through (Legal) Arms Supplies?" (20 January 2020) EJIL Talk (blog).

[38] The control theory regards principals as having "control" over an aspect of the crime, e.g. by making an essential contribution. Prosecutor v Thomas Lubanga Dyilo, Judgment Pursuant to Article 74 of the Statute, T.Ch, ICC-01/04–01/06, 14 March 2012, at paras 918–33 and 976–1006.

control theory is a construct that can be analyzed as a "mid-level principle."[39] It is analytically helpful, because it helps to systematize the practice, and normatively attractive, because it provides a sufficiently convincing basis on which to distinguish principals from accessories. Of course, there are many controversies and disputes about the control theory,[40] but it is sufficiently well established to at least work with it as a starting hypothesis. On a coherentist method, we would then ask: is it useful? What are its implications? Are there better (more normatively convincing and analytically fitting) theories?

Indirect intent

Early ICC case law has adopted a stringent interpretation of indirect intent (holding that it requires foresight of a "virtually certainty"). On the one hand, this stringent interpretation is commendable, as it shows an impulse to respect deontic constraints and the rights of the accused, and it has support in national practice. On the other hand, national jurisdictions can adopt such a narrow construction because they can also rely on broader forms of *mens rea* that typically supplement the "intent" standard (such as recklessness and *dolus eventualis*). As a matter of source-based analysis, it may not be the case that the ICC Statute's intent standard was meant to be quite as narrow as early jurisprudence suggests, and deontic constraints certainly do not necessitate such a narrow conception. It may be that a more careful study, including textual, deontic, and teleological dimensions, would encompass foresight of at least high probabilities (rather than only "virtual certainties").[41]

Other criminal law theory problems

I have advocated a coherentist method for approaching deontic questions. But coherentism is useful for a broader set of criminal law theory problems, including the purpose of the system, its justification, the proper or optimal scope of criminalization, the theory of crimes, and the identification of other appropriate limits on ICL.

At the time of writing, the resurgence of ICL has been under way for some twenty-five years, which seems quite a while in the context of our lifetimes. Nonetheless,

---

[39] See §4.3.1.

[40] N Jain, "The Control Theory of Perpetration in International Criminal Law" (2011) 12 Chicago J Int'l L 159; T Weigend, "Perpetration through an Organization: The Unexpected Career of a German Legal Concept" (2011) 9 JICJ 91; J D Ohlin, E van Sliedregt & T Weigend, "Assessing the Control Theory" (2013) 26 LJIL 725; L N Sadat & J Jolly, "Seven Canons of ICC Treaty Interpretation: Making Sense of Article 25's Rorschach Blot" (2014) 27 LJIL 755; J D Ohlin, "Co-perpetration: German *Dogmatik* or German Invasion?," in C Stahn, ed, *The Law and Practice of the International Criminal Court: A Critical Account of Challenges and Achievements* (Oxford University Press, 2015).

[41] For an initial sketch, see D Piragoff & D Robinson, "Article 30," in K Ambos, ed, *Commentary on the Rome Statute of the International Criminal Court: Observers' Notes, Article by Article*, 4th ed (Beck, 2020). The phrase "will occur in the ordinary course of events" is probabilistic and thus arguably includes high probabilities.

compared to the history of criminal law, it is a nascent development. There remains a great deal to learn for both ICL and criminal law theory.

I end this book with a series of annexes, which address subsidiary issues that may be of interest to particular groups of readers.

- In Annex 1, I respond to some criticisms and questions about the "identity crisis," in order to clarify my claims.[42]
- In Annex 2, I discuss the rise of joint criminal enterprise (JCE) and lessons for reasoning. I truncated that discussion in Chapter 2 to maintain a brisk pace, but the discussion may be of interest for readers relatively new to ICL.[43]
- In Annex 3, I review how the ICC has engaged in the *Bemba* case with the deontic issues canvassed in Chapters 6 and 7 (command responsibility and causal contribution). I find that, for the most part and to their credit, ICC judges have engaged thoughtfully with deontic argumentation, that their analyses make several valuable contributions, and that most judges conform to these prescriptions.[44]
- In Annex 4, I touch on aspects of the intensely controversial *Bemba* Appeal Judgment, which are arguably examples of the "overcorrection": adopting excessively rigid conceptions that are not supported by credible deontic analysis.[45]

ICL is a fast-moving field. When I started working on this book, my main concern was hasty reasoning that overlooked deontic constraints. Now that deontic constraints are a mainstream preoccupation in ICL – following what I have called the "deontic turn in ICL"[46] – the potential problems of ungrounded and idealized conceptions have started to materialize. Accordingly, it is all the more urgent to have a methodology with which to discuss and explore the best understandings of those constraints. It is not the case that the narrowest conception of the constraints is *ipso facto* the best and most principled conception. A coherentist method draws on many points of reference and delivers at least a common basis for debates. I will conclude by recalling that deontic principles are human principles: they are not rarefied, cerebral, abstract, or metaphysical constructions; we inform ourselves by drawing on empathy, experience, and practical wisdom.

---

[42]   See Annex 1.
[43]   See Annex 2.
[44]   See Annex 3.
[45]   See Annex 4.
[46]   See §2.5.

Annex 1 After the Identity Crisis: Responses and Clarifications

I am extremely grateful for the positive and enthusiastic reception of "The Identity Crisis of International Criminal Law," published in 2008.[1] The focus of the article was unusual: rather than weighing in on a particular substantive debate, it was instead a diagnosis about reasoning itself, systematic distortions, unnoticed contradictions, and the need for more careful reasoning.

These observations and these new kinds of questions aroused considerable interest. The article became one of the most cited and most downloaded papers in the field of ICL. It has received strong praise from many scholars whose views I respect greatly.[2] People have built on the ideas in "Identity Crisis" in many different ways. For example, many scholars have worked to replace problematic interpretive approaches with new and sophisticated approaches for a criminal law system that draws appropriately from human rights and humanitarian law precedents.[3]

The purpose of this annex is to address some of the responses to "Identity Crisis," to better clarify five main points of confusion. Scholarly and judicial reactions have revealed to me which of my points were clumsily stated, overly simplistic, or

---

[1] D Robinson, "The Identity Crisis of International Criminal Law" (2008) 21 LJIL 925.

[2] The article has been described by scholars as "iconic," "magisterial," "enlightening," "seminal," "remarkable," "perceptive," a "must read," and "a genuine classic." For an example of its invocation, see, e.g. C Kreß, "On the Outer Limits of Crimes against Humanity: The Concept of Organization within the Policy Requirement: Some Reflections on the March 2010 ICC Kenya Decision" (2010) 23 LJIJ 855 at 861.

[3] B McGonigle Leyh, "Pragmatism over Principles: The International Criminal Court and a Human Rights-Based Approach to Judicial Interpretation" (2018) 41 Fordham Int'l LJ 697; L Grover, "A Call to Arms: Fundamental Dilemmas Confronting the Interpretation of Crimes in the Rome Statute of the International Criminal Court" (2010) 21 EJIL 543; L Grover, *Interpreting Crimes in the Rome Statute of the International Criminal Court* (Cambridge University Press, 2014); A Grabert, *Dynamic Interpretation in International Criminal Law: Striking a Balance between Stability and Change* (Herbert Utz Verlag, 2014); N Jain, "Judicial Lawmaking and General Principles of Law in International Criminal Law" (2016) 57 Harvard Int'l LJ 111; T Rauter, *Judicial Practice, Customary International Criminal Law and* Nullum Crimen Sine Lege (Springer, 2017); C Davidson, "How to Read International Criminal Law: Strict Construction and the Rome Statute of the International Criminal Court" (2017) 91 St John's L Rev 37.

inadequately clear. I have lightly updated my arguments in Chapter 2, but this annex offers additional clarification for readers who have followed the debates or who are otherwise interested in these themes.

A preliminary and crucial caveat, of course, is that the field has already matured considerably since the article was published. The identified reasoning habits can still often be seen in ICL argumentation today, but they are less common. Happily, the article's *descriptive* accuracy has been diminished because its *prescriptive* concern has been widely absorbed. That is the outcome desired by anyone writing about a normative problem. In Chapter 2, I discuss this "deontic turn" in ICL. The themes of "Identity Crisis" about the value of studying the discourse and argumentation nonetheless remain pertinent today.

A1.1 "IDENTITY CRISIS" WAS ABOUT REASONING, NOT EVALUATING OUTCOMES

There are hazards in writing about structures of argument while almost everyone else is fixated on the *outcomes* of the arguments (i.e. staking out and defending their various positions about doctrine). Often, my object of interest is to study the discourse itself – the structures of argument, patterns, and tendencies – because I think there is a lot to be learned from doing so.[4] However, because that focus is atypical, it is particularly susceptible to misunderstanding.

For example, Mark Osiel's thoughtful and engaging work, *Making Sense of Mass Atrocity*, contains several vigorous criticisms of what he believes to be the evaluative thesis of "Identity Crisis." He perceives the article as evaluating the departures and reaching negative conclusions about the doctrines: "Robinson attacks the ad hoc international criminal tribunals for their illiberalism; . . . Robinson decries . . . the doctrinal innovations."[5]

I have spent much of my professional life helping to create, sustain, and improve the Tribunals, so it is a misperception to think that I "attacked" them. As I noted, my observations were "offered in the spirit of improving a relatively new discipline."[6] I was drawing attention to overly simplistic structures of argument that should not continue unchecked. More importantly, the words used to describe my arguments

---

[4] I have described the topic of such inquiries as "discursive," i.e. studying the discourse itself, as opposed to normative, doctrinal, or theoretical inquiries. In my view, such inquiries can be a form of meta-scholarship (scholarship about scholarship). For other examples, see D Robinson, "Inescapable Dyads: Why the ICC Cannot Win" (2015) 28 LJIL 323; D Robinson, "The Controversy over Territorial State Referrals and Reflections on ICL Discourse" (2011) 9 JICJ 355; D Robinson, "The Strangest Debate in Complementarity and the Better Debate Ahead," in C Stahn & M El Zeidy, eds, *The International Criminal Court and Complementarity: From Theory to Practice*, 2nd ed (Cambridge University Press, 2020).

[5] M Osiel, *Making Sense of Mass Atrocity* (Cambridge University Press, 2009) at 123; see also *ibid* at 118.

[6] Robinson, *supra* note 1, at 931.

("attack," "condemn," "decry," "lambaste") assume that I was aiming to substantively *evaluate* the outcomes, and that I had definitively reached a negative assessment. Of course, there certainly is a valuable and important literature that engages in precisely that kind of substantive and critical evaluation. A prominent example would be the critiques of Tribunal jurisprudence by Osiel himself, who described joint criminal enterprise (JCE) as "dangerously illiberal."[7] But in "Identity Crisis" I was discussing the *habits of argument* that were often culminating in the contradictions that others were already noticing.

In an effort to avoid misunderstandings, I specified that my topic was reasoning habits[8] and that I was not yet offering conclusive substantive *evaluations* of particular outcomes.[9] I explained that I was working with internal contradictions (i.e. taking the principles as articulated within ICL itself), specifically to avoid getting into substantive evaluations, so that I could maintain the focus on reasoning.[10] Thus, "where the article exposes an internal contradiction, it should not be assumed that the author believes that the doctrine is wrong and the articulation of the principle is necessarily correct."[11] For example, with the *Erdemović* case, I stated that my interest "for present purposes ... is not whether the decision was correct or incorrect, but, rather, how the majority framed the issue and hence sidestepped the deontological discussion."[12] I emphasized that some doctrines that contravened the system's stated principles might actually be *justified* on a deeper, richer account of fundamental principles.[13] I also explained *why* I was not purporting to evaluate the departures at that time: "An evaluation of how best to resolve those contradictions – which would require inter alia a philosophical analysis of the merits of particular principles and doctrines – will be part of a much larger research project and will remain

---

7 See M Osiel, "The Banality of Good: Aligning Incentives against Mass Atrocity" (2005) 105 Columbia L Rev 1751 at 1772. Interestingly, Osiel energetically responds to various "critics" who have called the JCE doctrine "illiberal," but earlier in the same book he himself describes it as "dangerously illiberal" and advances the same criticisms as liberal scholars, such as overreliance on prosecutorial discretion, vagueness, and other problems: see Osiel, *supra* note 5, at 30; see more generally *ibid* at 48–90. My sense is that Osiel is trying to argue for compliance with liberal principles, while also resisting overly rigid conceptions of those principles – a posture with which I completely agree – but some details were simply not quite settled.

8 See, e.g. Robinson, *supra* note 1, at 961–62: "The focus of this article is on the discourse, the structures of argument and reasoning employed in ICL, that are assumed to be sound, legitimate and even liberal ..."

9 *Ibid* at 932. The fact that the subject of the article is the discourse and arguments is also noted *ibid* at 930, 932–34, 942, 945, and 961. I also explained that I was not embarking upon the substantive normative questions of what principles ICL *ought* to follow, nor the *merits* of compliance with principles: see, e.g., *ibid* at 927 and 962.

10 *Ibid* at 926, 927, 932, 933, 953, 962 and 963.

11 *Ibid* at 932 (emphasis added).

12 *Ibid* at 945 (emphasis added).

13 *Ibid* at 963 (scope to re-examine the principles; contradictions could be resolved by refining the principles). I highlighted that these formal "[c]ontradictions between doctrines and principles may be resolved by correcting the doctrine, refining the principles, or both." *Ibid*.

for future exploration."[14] I foreshadowed that my substantive position would entail a richer account that would be able to re-examine the appropriate principles.[15] I hope that these points clarify both the object of inquiry in "Identity Crisis" and the ambition of the broader project it foreshadowed.

In another example of understandable misunderstanding, Osiel perceived me as having disagreed with his positions, and hence he quite naturally responded with vigour and passion to defend his position from the perceived criticisms.[16] This perception was understandable, because my focus on arguments rather than outcomes was atypical. However, my concern was not with Osiel's conclusions, but rather with the arguments in two cited passages.[17] My topic was recurring forms of argument; academic discipline required that I support my discussion with examples,[18] and two particular passages were prominent illustrations of a recurring type of argument.[19] My point was that it is not enough to argue that a negligence standard in command responsibility is a more effective deterrent; we also need to provide a convincing account of culpability. I indicated, however, that I thought a principled justification of this feature of command responsibility is possible.[20] I developed that deontic justification in later articles and now in this book.[21] Thus

---

[14] *Ibid* at 932.

[15] *Ibid* at 962–63 and 932, also sketching out some of the complexities for such an account.

[16] Osiel, *supra* note 5, at 127 and 129. Osiel asserts that his favoured approaches (broad readings of intent where statute ambiguity permits, or reconceived "effective control" requirements) were accused (by me) of "seeking to overcompensate for material weakness through normative harshness." *Ibid* at 129. However, I made the observation about the temptations of normative harshness in a different context and on a different issue (duress): see Robinson, *supra* note 1, at 944–46. For a preliminary sketch of my position on interpreting intent, see §9.3.2, which seems potentially consistent with Osiel's position. On effective control, see §8.4.

[17] I happen to think that Osiel's books and articles bringing "law and economics" tools to bear on ICL problems are insightful and valuable. As discussed in Chapter 4, good criminal law policy must consider consequentialist and criminological dimensions; we also have to consider deontic constraints.

[18] Providing such examples is understandably a sensitive matter; others have noted the sensitivities in writing about the patterns and practices of academics themselves: see, e.g., P Bourdieu, "Participant Objectivation" (2003) 9 Journal of the Royal Anthropology Institute 281 at 283.

[19] The two arguments were that "the scope of liability is formally over-inclusive, but only to make up for severe practical dangers of under-inclusiveness," and that "the hope is that the threat of serious criminal liability for 'mere' negligence will lead even the most reluctant commander . . . to take all reasonable measures . . .": Robinson, *supra* note 1, at 938. Many scholars have already written on the problems with reliance on prosecutorial discretion to blunt overly inclusive criminal prohibitions: see *ibid* at 941. The consequentialist argument in favour of a negligence standard is sound as far as it goes, but we also need to deal with culpability.

[20] *Ibid* at 950 (noting that principled justification may be possible). The expanded companion piece to "Identity Crisis" outlined the argument in more detail: D Robinson, "The Two Liberalisms of International Criminal Law," in C Stahn & L van den Herik, eds, *Future Perspectives on International Criminal Justice* (TMC Asser, 2010) 115 at 126.

[21] I developed the argument *ibid* at 126. See also D Robinson, "How Command Responsibility Got So Complicated: A Culpability Contradiction, Its Obfuscation, and a Simple Solution" (2012) 13 Melbourne J Int'l L 1; D Robinson, "A Justification of Command Responsibility" (2017) 28 Crim L Forum 633. See Chapters 6–8.

I believe that Mark Osiel and I are actually broadly in agreement both on doctrine and method.[22]

These clarifications should clear up most of the points of supposed disagreement. For example, Osiel responds to the perceived evaluative claims of "Identity Crisis" by arguing that some outcomes of Tribunal decisions could still be defended by more sophisticated reasoning.[23] I agree entirely. However, "Identity Crisis" was *about the reasoning* that the cases actually employed. If scholars and jurists attempt to provide better, more sophisticated reasoning to justify or critique decisions, then that is precisely what "Identity Crisis" was urging. Insofar as Osiel's work strives for a principled and contextualized inquiry into the *justification* of doctrines, our projects have much in common.

Similarly, Osiel also ascribes to me some startlingly rigid views, including an alleged libertarian philosophy,[24] an inflexible textualist approach,[25] and (perhaps most puzzlingly) a hostility to common lawyers.[26] These perceptions of my views seem to flow from the same initial divergence as to the object of inquiry in "Identity Crisis." Accordingly, I hope they are adequately addressed by the

---

[22] As for doctrine, it appears that we have similar views on command responsibility. As for method, thoughtful consequentialist analysis is important and is a vast improvement on the reductive single-issue teleological reasoning that is sometimes employed, because it also includes counter-vailing consequentialist considerations such as over-deterrence and ineffectiveness. My caveat, however, is that we must also attend to the deontic dimension (e.g. culpability). Here, again, it seems that we at least largely agree. In *Making Sense, supra* note 5, Osiel also engages with the constraints of culpability. He expresses subtly different levels of commitment to deontic con-straints, so his approach may be consistent or slightly different from the account I advance: see discussion in §3.2.4.

[23] *Ibid* at 124–44, Osiel advances an intriguing argument that character theory might provide a justification for some of the ambiguities of JCE. I think a lively debate could be had about the use of character theory in this way and about whether it could properly justify the more extensive features of JCE-III that have caused particular concern. Nonetheless, his argument is the right *kind* of discussion, because it at least engages with questions of culpability and fairness, which is exactly what I was encouraging in "Identity Crisis."

[24] Osiel asserts that I adopt an "unduly libertarian understanding of liberalism" (*ibid* at 119). He purports to deduce this outlook from my statement that a liberal criminal law system requires justification of public coercion of human beings. However, that is a commonplace proposition supported under a wide range of outlooks. My account is now outlined in more detail in this book. As you can see in Chapter 4, my account is "liberal" in the minimalist sense that it embraces deontic constraints; this aspiration is compatible with multiple philosophical and political outlooks.

[25] Osiel appears to cite me for the view that "the law must ... clarify ex ante, with consummate linguistic rigor, all details of every legal rule that may later be applied against any defendant" (*ibid* at 120). I have not advanced such a view. For my views on the principle of legality, which, among other things, allow consideration of custom, as well as my nuanced position on strict construction, see §5.2.1.

[26] Most perplexingly, Osiel cites me as an example of "those claiming to defend the systematic integrity of the general part against us from the common law world, in all our slovenly, atheoretical torpor" (*ibid* at 123). I am myself from the common law world (Canada). I at no point claimed to defend ICL from common lawyers (which would include myself), nor did I make any of the ascribed remarks about common lawyers.

above clarifications. Osiel also offers thoughtful objections to rigid deontological approaches, with which I largely agree; these are discussed in Chapter 4.[27]

In "Identity Crisis," I sketched out the anticipated evaluative framework in a manner that I hoped would dispel any perception that the proposed account was a simplistic or rigid one.[28] The proposed account is now developed in this book. I hope that this book will illuminate the brief clarifications and foreshadowing that I sought to provide in previous works.

A1.2 "IDENTITY CRISIS" CRITICIZES *REDUCTIVE* TELEOLOGICAL REASONING

"Identity Crisis" is sometimes thought to suggest that teleological reasoning is per se inappropriate in criminal law. However, as I noted, "[t]his article does not suggest that teleological reasoning is per se inappropriate."[29] Similarly, "[t]he application of the fairly self-evident factors listed in the Vienna Convention (textual, contextual, and purposive) is not necessarily problematic."[30]

My concern was with a recurring form of *reductive* teleological reasoning: a "blinkered," "victim-focused," "exuberant," and "extensive" form.[31] I identified two features of this form of reasoning. First, it assumed a *single purpose* – maximizing the protection of victims – even where an enactment might reflect a richer multiplicity of purposes. Second, it allowed that single presumed purpose to override all other interpretive considerations, including the text.[32]

My concern with this one-dimensional form of reasoning was that it reduces legal reasoning to a simple syllogism, and it resolves all ambiguities in the same way: with further expansion. It puts a heavy thumb on the scale, always on the same side, introducing a systemic distortion. My concern with this reductive approach is that it does not engage with other purposes, it does not give weight to other interpretive considerations, and most importantly it does not engage with fundamental constraining principles such as culpability, legality or fair labelling.[33] Unfortunately, my

---

[27] Osiel objects that the questions are normative, not "metaphysical," and that they cannot be resolved by reference to the "timeless and essential nature of responsibility": *ibid* at 127 and 129. I agree on the first point, but the normative questions still include the deontic dimensions (i.e. what is "right," as distinct from what is "good"). I also agree on the second point; the coherentist account that I develop in Chapter 5 avoids those kinds of objections.

[28] Robinson, *supra* note 1, at 962. Osiel objects that my article "makes no gesture" in that direction: Osiel, *supra* note 5, at 123. However – and I realize I am repeating myself – the topic of "Identity Crisis" was recurring problematic habits of reasoning, which was an elaborate topic on its own. I outlined the future and rather large research project that would build a framework for substantive evaluation. I developed that framework in later works, and the product is this book.

[29] Robinson, *supra* note 1, at 938.

[30] *Ibid* at 935.

[31] *Ibid* at 933, 935, 938, and 961.

[32] *Ibid* at 934.

[33] *Ibid* at 929 and 938.

objection to oversimplified teleological analysis has itself at times been oversimplified into an objection to all teleological analysis.

To give an example from ICC jurisprudence, Judge (later President) Chile Eboe-Osuji cited "Identity Crisis" for this broader proposition in the *Ruto and Sang* case.[34] Judge Eboe-Osuji responds that teleological interpretation can be accompanied by insistence on the procedural rights of the accused. I agree – and I assume he meant to include not only procedural rights, but also fundamental principles. My objection, however, was to the reductive and aggressive form of teleological interpretation, seen in cases and literature discussed in Chapter 2,[35] which reduces analysis to a one-dimensional question.

The *Katanga* judgment, the second conviction by the ICC, also cites "Identity Crisis" as raising concerns about teleological interpretation and the principle of legality.[36] The cite can be read as accurately reflecting my message, insofar as it refers to the use of teleological interpretation (putting an end to impunity) in a *"determinative"* manner. With this caveat, the cite is accurate: it seems to refer to the reductive and aggressive form of teleological reasoning, to which I do object. To be clear, however, I agree with the approach, laid out by the majority in *Katanga*, of looking at text, context, and purpose together, while being constrained by the principle of legality.[37]

Law is a purposive endeavour. Laws, including criminal laws, are created for reasons. It would be unusual and unwise to refrain deliberately from considering those reasons. In each legal system with which I am familiar, purpose is one of the appropriate considerations in interpreting criminal enactments. Moreover, societal protection is certainly one important and weighty purpose of criminal law enactments.

My modest point is that invocation of one single purpose cannot be used to decisively resolve all interpretive disputes in criminal law.[38] There are at least three distinct problems with that approach. First, one-dimensional analysis is not even good *qua* purposive analysis. Most legal enactments delineate a boundary between at least two competing social goods.[39] Thus a good purposive analysis has to consider the multiple purposes in play. Crime control will of course be a central

---

[34] *Prosecutor v Ruto and Sang*, Decision on Defence Applications for Judgments of Acquittal, ICC T. Ch, ICC-01/09-01-11, 5 April 2016, at para 328.

[35] See §2.2.

[36] *Prosecutor v Katanga*, Judgment Pursuant to Article 74 of the Statute, ICC T.Ch-II, ICC-01/04-01-07, 7 March 2014, at para 54.

[37] *Ibid* at paras 43–57.

[38] An analogy offered by George Fletcher is that the purpose of a tax regime may be to raise revenue, but we do not use that purpose to resolve every interpretive dispute: G Fletcher, *Rethinking Criminal Law*, 3rd ed (Oxford University Press, 2000) at 419.

[39] For example, a provision rooted in humanitarian law might reflect a trade-off of different social goods, such as improving protections for non-combatants, military efficacy, and national security. This observation has previously been made by A M Danner, "When Courts Make Law: How the International Criminal Tribunals Recast the Laws of War" (2006) 59 Vanderbilt L Rev 1 at 32.

purpose, but there may often be other competing values underlying a provision (e.g. individual autonomy, military efficacy, national security, jurisdictional allocation). We should also consider more subtle consequentialist implications such as over-deterrence, the appropriate scope of ICL, or whether a problem is better addressed by mechanisms other than criminal law. Second, teleological interpretation should be measured and restrained: it should not sweep away other canons of construction, but rather support and be supported by them. Third, and most importantly, it must be accompanied by contextual analysis that weighs non-consequentialist constraints, such as the deontic commitments we owe to individuals.

A1.3 "INTERNATIONAL" VERSUS "DOMESTIC" INFLUENCES

In a valuable addition to the conversation, James Stewart rightly emphasizes that not all of ICL's departures from principles flow from international reasoning (i.e. public international law, international human rights law, or international humanitarian law reasoning).[40] He notes that domestic legal systems often contain doctrines that arguably contradict fundamental liberal principles and that some problematic doctrines of ICL are drawn from domestic criminal law.

I completely agree with James' point. ICL, as a body of criminal law that draws on other criminal law systems for inspiration, would naturally tend to inherit many of the problems, conundrums, and questionable doctrines of other criminal law systems.

My very minor quibble is that James presents this point as being in opposition to, and refuting, a suggestion alleged to have been made by others (such as Danner, Martinez, Fletcher, Ohlin, Damaška, Greenawalt, and me). James refers to and refutes the "thesis that broad modes of liability are *necessarily* hatched internationally"[41] and the "assurance that unprincipled international rules *necessarily* reveal the triumph of international agenda over the restraining force of the criminal law."[42] However, in my view, the scholars whom he cites were not arguing that *all* problems in ICL arise from international law reasoning, but rather *some* problems. James kindly acknowledges that I emphasized this in "Identity Crisis," for which I am grateful.[43] My reading of the other scholars is that they too were not advancing any absolutist hypotheses; rather, they were investigating tendencies in ICL that were distinctive and therefore interesting. The point of these scholars was

---

[40] J Stewart, "The End of 'Modes of Liability' for International Crimes" (2012) 25 LJIJ 165.

[41] *Ibid* at 179 (emphasis added).

[42] *Ibid* at 203 (emphasis added). In the same vein, Stewart goes on to demonstrate that some departures are not "nefarious creations of an illiberal international system" (*ibid* at 198) or a "nefarious utilitarian agenda derived from [ICL's] international political status" (*ibid* at 182).

[43] *Ibid* at 168; Robinson, *supra* note 1, at 929 and 961 (national systems also depart from principles; not all departures are caused by these habits of reasoning).

that, *in addition* to the problems one would expect in any criminal law system, ICL has particular features that can generate further difficulties. My focus was on how, in ICL, the *discourse* is often different from that in domestic criminal law: it is not the typical clash (law-and-order versus liberal principles), but rather that jurists thought they were applying sound, appropriate, and *liberal* tools of reasoning, which were inaptly transplanted.

Nonetheless, I think James' point is a valuable complement and corrective to the observations that I and others made. In the wake of articles highlighting the distinct influences and challenges in ICL, many jurists may have formed a romanticized, halcyon impression of domestic criminal law, or an impression that ICL is irremediably flawed. I think that I myself have fallen into the trap of overestimating the quality of reasoning in national systems. I have subsequently worked more with contemporary domestic criminal law and have had more occasion to be disconcerted by examples of fairly crude reasoning that focuses only on "sending a message," failing to engage with individual fault and fairness. Thus ICL starts to look considerably better in a comparative light. Insofar as that kind of oversimplified picture may have been forming among ICL thinkers (including myself), James' point is a valuable complementary corrective. It rightly rounds out the picture.

A1.4 "IDENTITY CRISIS" DOES NOT OBJECT TO HUMAN RIGHTS ANALYSES PER SE

Another occasional reading is that I (along with others such as Danner, Fletcher, and Ohlin) have suggested that there is something problematic about human rights law or human rights reasoning itself, or that criminal law and human rights law are somehow antithetical. Thus it is sometimes thought that we "blame international human rights," or that we are "blinded" to the fact that human rights law can be a tool to constrain and liberalize criminal law.[44]

I seize this opportunity to clarify: I do not suggest there is any incompatibility with human rights and criminal law, when they are properly interpreted. Nor do I subscribe to any simplistic dichotomy in which human rights thinking is "bad" and criminal law thinking is "good."

My concern is with the *mis*application – or, more precisely, the *inapposite* application – of human rights assumptions and reasoning habits in ICL in a way that *does not fully appreciate the context shift* from human rights to criminal law.[45]

---

[44] Such comments have arisen in conference debates, online symposia, and a draft paper by Frédéric Mégret. I mention the paper with the caveat that it is a draft, not intended to be quoted, and that it may not reflect the author's later thoughts (although it is an impressive testament to Mégret's influence that this paper was cited many times even as a draft): F Mégret, "Prospects for 'Constitutional' Human Rights Scrutiny of Substantive International Criminal Law by the ICC," Paper presented at Washington University School of Law, February 2010.

[45] Robinson, *supra* note 1, at 927 and 929; see also Robinson, *supra* note 21, at 134.

The context shift is a shift in structure, scope, and consequences: from state or organizational liability to individual liability; from promoting better systems and practices to condemning the most serious crimes of international concern; and from declaratory and remedial relief to the sanctioning and punishment of individual human beings.[46] When we make arguments in an international human rights regime, we have a set of assumptions (interpretive, structural, and ideological) that are perfectly appropriate in that context: they are designed to foster the liberal aspiration of advancing the protection of persons from the state.[47] But if we are making arguments about criminal law, then many of those assumptions and reasoning habits become inapposite. The addressee of the prohibitions is no longer the state, and the remedy is no longer civil; hence we have to engage with a new set of deontic constraints. The liberal aspiration of protecting persons from improper exercises of authority, which puts wind in the sails of human rights law, now blows at least in part the other way – because the ICL machinery is itself an exercise of authority, and its exercise of power over individuals must be tested and constrained.

If I may temporarily oversimplify the point in order to convey it more vividly: a *criminal law system that thinks like an international human rights law system* will run into contradictions. That is the "identity crisis." My concern was that recurring forms of reasoning in ICL were giving inadequate attention to that particular shift.

I muddied the waters when I used the hazy and inadequately explained shorthand terms "human rights liberalism" and "criminal law liberalism."[48] What I intended to signify with these clumsy terms was the *mindsets* – the set of assumptions and heuristics associated with each of these liberal (individual-protecting) projects. I was trying to say that the familiar assumptions and heuristics appropriate and liberal in one context (i.e. international human rights law monitoring bodies), when transplanted into a different context (i.e. criminal tribunals) without adequately reflecting on the context shift, ironically have the effect of undermining the stated principles. But my unexplained terms may have given rise to impressions that I thought human rights and criminal law to be themselves somehow incompatible.

Thus I hasten to clarify: of course human rights law can properly inform the rights of accused persons. In that case, human rights law is being mindfully and appropriately applied. And liberal criminal principles aim to uphold human rights.

It is sometimes suggested that scholars who point out the problems of inappropriately transplanted human rights reasoning in ICL (e.g. Danner, Martinez, or myself)

---

[46] Robinson, *supra* note 1, at 946–47. In a remarkably similar vein, arguing that ICL may, of course, draw on human rights and humanitarian law, but must recall the different "telos" of these areas of law, see P P Soares, "Tangling Human Rights and International Criminal Law: The Practice of International Tribunals and the Call for Rationalized Legal Pluralism" (2012) 23 Crim L Forum 161.

[47] See Chapter 2.

[48] Robinson, *supra* note 1, at 931 and 932. I did this even more so in Robinson, *supra* note 20.

have overlooked that human rights law can also uphold human rights. I do not think that any of us failed to notice this point. On the contrary, that is the basic and assumed starting point that gives "Identity Crisis" its irony and poignancy. That was the irony that interested me: how the *mis*application of human rights reasoning may wind up undermining human rights.

There is no incompatibility between criminal law and human rights law when they are interpreted and applied thoughtfully.[49] But a given institution needs to sort out what it is. By avoiding inapposite transplants, a criminal law body can of course scrupulously respect the human rights of accused persons. And it can, through its criminal law work, also advance the human rights of victims and affected persons (security of the person, right to a remedy), while complying with fundamental principles.

A1.5 "IDENTITY CRISIS" IS MELIORATIVE, NOT PESSIMISTIC

Finally, the message of "Identity Crisis" is *meliorative* – that is, it asserts that problems it identifies can be studied and remedied. It is entirely understandable, however, to assume that an article with the word "crisis" in the title must be pessimistic or alarmist. As Elies van Sliedregt and Sergey Vasiliev, in a book on pluralism in ICL, write:

> Can an "identity crisis" be deemed a crisis if it is a congenital and permanent condition of ICL, which by its origin and nature juggles multiple normative identities? The "normative pluralism" perspective on ICL provides one with a better observational position from which sense can be made of its ideological underwater currents, more neutral than the alarming language of crisis used elsewhere. This does not mean that the noted conflict of identities and the incoherence which results should be accepted and tolerated. On the contrary, contemplation of the tensions at work in ICL and procedure as "normative pluralism" will help produce a coherent methodology for channelling those currents.[50]

I agree entirely with the pushback against alarmism. ICL now exists in an era of blog posts and tweets, and those media encourage sensationalist reactions to every decision and setback. There has rightly been a pushback against these kinds of crisis narrative.[51] However, an "identity crisis" is not a "crisis" in this common sense of the

---

[49] See discussion in F Tulkens, "The Paradoxical Relationship between Criminal Law and Human Rights" (2011) 9 JICJ 577. Human rights at times constrains criminal law and at times calls for criminal law (as part of the security rights and rights to a remedy of persons).

[50] E van Sliedregt & S Vasiliev, "Pluralism: A New Framework for International Criminal Justice," in E van Sliedregt & S Vasiliev, eds, *Pluralism in International Criminal Law* (Oxford University Press, 2014) at 34.

[51] D Robinson, "Take the Long View of International Justice" (24 October 2016) EJIL Talk (blog); J C Powderly, "International Criminal Justice in an Age of Perpetual Crisis" (2019) 32 LJIL 1;

word. It is not like a heart attack or an invasion or an existential threat. An identity crisis (or a mid-life crisis) is not a call for panic; it is a call for calm and careful reflection on one's role, values, and principles. I selected the title "Identity Crisis" because it succinctly conveys in an accessible way the main themes of the paper: a criminal law system using thinking habits of a human rights system.

The methodology I advocated is very much compatible with the thoughtful method van Sliedregt and Vasiliev recommend.[52] I emphasized in "Identity Crisis" that the noted problems are *not* a permanent condition – that they are "a contingent phenomenon and not an immutable fatal flaw."[53] Indeed, I noted that the phenomena I was describing were already diminishing at that time.[54] I also mapped out the steps to resolve the problem (sorting through the assumptions and commitments, shedding inapposite habits, unearthing contradictions, refining principles, and thereby building coherence).[55]

A1.6 CONCLUSION

One of the implications of the coherentist method (see Chapter 4) is that we can learn from conversation and thereby refine our ideas. The reactions of other scholars have helped me to reconsider, improve, and clarify my arguments. This survey of the conversation will, I hope, helpfully sharpen my points and facilitate future debates.

S Vasiliev, "The Crises and Critiques of International Criminal Justice," in K J Heller et al, *Oxford Handbook on International Criminal Law* (Oxford University Press, 2020).

[52] This method recommended by van Sliedregt and Vasiliev, *supra* note 50, at 34 dovetails with the coherentist method outlined in Chapters 4 and 5: "It is not only the plurality of professional cultures, values, and ideologies, but also the conversation, interpenetration, and dialectic tensions between them, that makes the ICL a pluralistic system and a dynamic field of law and practice."

[53] Robinson, *supra* note 1, at 932.

[54] *Ibid* at 932.

[55] *Ibid* at 932 and 962–63. These ideas are now developed in this book.

Annex 2 The Rise of Joint Criminal Enterprise: Lessons for Reasoning

In Chapter 2, I shortened one important illustration – namely, the joint criminal enterprise (JCE) doctrine and the reasoning that produced it (see §2.2.3). I did so because I wanted to maintain a brisk and readable pace, because I had already amply demonstrated my points about interpretive approaches, and because the issues with JCE are now widely known and recognized in the field. Nonetheless, for those who may be new to the subject or who are otherwise interested in the topic, I provide a slightly more detailed explanation here.

A2.1 COMMON CONCERNS ABOUT JCE

The JCE doctrine is a judicial innovation that grew to play a major role in the charges and convictions before the Tribunals.[1] As articulated in Tribunal jurisprudence, JCE requires a plurality of persons acting pursuant to a common plan, design, or purpose involving the commission of a crime and that the accused participate in the common purpose.[2] The contribution need not entail physical participation in any element of a crime.[3] The doctrine has three variations:

(1) the "basic" form (JCE-I) requires shared intent, and is comparable to "co-perpetration," or "common purpose," as known in many national systems;[4]

(2) the "systemic" form (JCE-II) includes a knowing contribution; and

---

[1] H van der Wilt, "JCE: Possibilities and Limitations" (2007) 5 JICJ 91 at 92; N Piacente, "Importance of the Joint Criminal Enterprise Doctrine for the ICTY Prosecutorial Policy" (2004) 2 JICJ 446; A M Danner & J S Martinez, "Guilty Associations: Joint Criminal Enterprise, Command Responsibility, and the Development of International Criminal Law" (2005) 93 Calif L Rev 75 esp at 107–09.

[2] *Prosecutor v Vasiljević*, Judgment, ICTY A.Ch, IT-98-32-A, 25 February 2004 ("*Vasiljević* Appeal Judgment") at para 100.

[3] *Ibid*; *Prosecutor v Kvočka*, Judgment, ICTY A.Ch, IT-98-30/1-A, 28 February 2005 ("*Kvočka* Appeal Judgment") at para 99; *Prosecutor v Brđanin*, Judgment, ICTY A.Ch, IT-99-36-A, 3 April 2007 ("*Brđanin* Appeal Judgment") at para 427.

[4] K Hamdorf, "The Concept of a Joint Criminal Enterprise and Domestic Modes of Liability for Parties to a Crime" (2007) 5 JICJ 208.

(3) the "extended" form (JCE-III) includes additional crimes that were foreseeable.[5]

The JCE doctrine was initially welcomed as a valuable tool in securing convictions, but as the doctrine continued to develop through generous judicial interpretation, commentators began to question its conformity with fundamental principles.[6] Some have argued that the expansiveness of the doctrine raises a prospect of "guilt by association,"[7] and the doctrine came to be wryly referred to as "Just Convict Everyone."[8] The concerns about JCE have been amply discussed in other scholarship;[9] my focus here is on *reasoning*, and hence I will simply recap the main substantive concerns about JCE.

First, there are no limits on the *scope* of JCE, so the resulting exposure to liability is vast.[10] Initial justifications of JCE typically drew on domestic analogies (a small group of criminals jointly robbing a bank),[11] but the doctrine grew to apply atrocities across an entire region,[12] or even to a "nationwide government-organized system,"[13] or a "vast criminal regime comprising thousands of participants,"[14] in which the persons actually committing crimes are "structurally or geographically remote from

---

[5] *Prosecutor v Tadić*, Judgment, ICTY A.Ch, IT-94-1-A, 15 July 1999 ("*Tadić* Appeal Judgment") at paras 202, 204, 220 and 228; *Vasiljević* Appeal Judgment, *supra* note 2, at paras 99–101.

[6] See, e.g., van der Wilt, *supra* note 1; Danner & Martinez, *supra* note 1; M Osiel, "The Banality of Good: Aligning Incentives Against Mass Atrocity" (2005) 105 Columbia L Rev 1751; M Osiel, "Modes of Participation in Mass Atrocities" (2005) 38 Cornell Int'l LJ 793; S Powles, "Joint Criminal Enterprise: Criminal Liability by Prosecutorial Ingenuity and Judicial Creativity?" (2004) 2 JICJ 606; V Haan, "The Development of the Concept of Joint Criminal Enterprise at the International Criminal Tribunal for the Former Yugoslavia" (2005) 5 Int'l Crim L Rev 167; D Nersessian, "Whoops, I Committed Genocide! The Anomaly of Constructive Liability for Serious International Crimes" (2006) 30 Fletcher F World Aff 81; J D Ohlin, "Three Conceptual Problems with the Doctrine of Joint Criminal Enterprise" (2006) 5 JICJ 69; K Ambos, "Joint Criminal Enterprise and Command Responsibility" (2007) 5 JICJ 159.

[7] Danner & Martinez, *supra* note 1; Osiel, "Banality of Good," *supra* note 6, at 1751.

[8] See, e.g., M E Badar, "Just Convict Everyone! Joint Perpetration from *Tadić* to *Stakić* and Back Again" (2006) 6 Int'l Crim L Rev 293.

[9] In addition to the works cited in preceding footnotes, see also E van Sliedregt, "Joint Criminal Enterprise as a Pathway to Convicting Individuals for Genocide" (2007) 5 JICJ 184; D Guilfoyle, "Responsibility for Collective Atrocities: Fair Labelling and Approaches to Commission in International Criminal Law" (2011) 64 Current Legal Problems 255; E van Sliedregt, *Individual Criminal Responsibility in International Law* (Oxford University Press, 2012) at 133–45; N Jain, *Perpetrators and Accessories in International Criminal Law* (Hart, 2014) at 29–65; N Perova, "Stretching the Joint Criminal Enterprise Doctrine to the Extreme: When Culpability and Liability Do not Match" (2016) 16 Int'l Crim L Rev 761.

[10] Danner & Martinez, *supra* note 1; Osiel, "Modes of Participation," *supra* note 6.

[11] *Tadić* Appeal Judgment, *supra* note 5, at para 199 n 243; *Prosecutor v Kvočka*, Judgment, ICTY T.Ch, IT-98-30/1-T, 2 November 2001 ("*Kvočka* Trial Judgment") at para 307.

[12] *Brđanin* Appeal Judgment, *supra* note 3, at para 422.

[13] *Prosecutor v Rwamakuba*, Decision on Interlocutory Appeal, ICTR A.Ch, ICTR-98-44-AR72.4, 22 October 2004, at para 25. See also *Prosecutor v Karemera*, Decision on Jurisdictional Appeals, ICTR A.Ch, ICTR-98-44-AR72.5, 12 April 2006 ("*Karemera* Decision on Jurisdictional Appeals") at paras 11–18, holding that JCE may be of "vast scope."

[14] *Kvočka* Trial Judgment, *supra* note 11, at para 307.

the accused."[5] This novel scale of criminal liability alone warrants a pause for deontic analysis of the proper outer limits of such a doctrine.

Second, the accused need not perform any part of the *actus reus* of any crime.[16] The accused's acts need only to contribute to a common design.[17] Thus a minor contribution can trigger massive criminal liability.

Third, although jurisprudence defended the elastic *actus reus* requirement by pointing to the rigorous *mens rea* requirement,[18] the *mens rea* requirement was also eroded through generous judicial interpretation. Under JCE-II, the "intent" requirement relaxes into a mere "knowledge" requirement.[19] The extended form of JCE-III can be satisfied by *dolus eventualis*, so that foresight of a "possibility" of suffices.[20]

Fourth, under JCE-III, a person can be convicted as a principal to crimes of special intent requirements without having the requisite intent.[21] In *Brđanin*, the Appeals Chamber confirmed that a person can be convicted of "committing" genocide via JCE-III, which requires only that it was *foreseeable* that others might commit genocide as a result of the common plan. The Appeals Chamber held that JCE "is no different from other forms of criminal liability which do not require proof of intent to commit a crime," such as aiding and abetting.[22] This argument overlooks that JCE *is* different from those other forms of liability,

---

[15] *Karemera* Decision on Jurisdictional Appeals, *supra* note 13, at paras 11–18. Haan, *supra* note 6, at 195–96, argues that while JCE was "originally designed for cases where persons actually – and not only hypothetically – reach a common understanding to pursue a common criminal plan," it has been "silently adjusted" to fit the cases before the Tribunals, and now encompasses far-flung individuals who are not linked through agreements but through hierarchical structures.

[16] *Brđanin* Appeal Judgment, *supra* note 3, at para 427; *Kvočka* Appeal Judgment, *supra* note 3, at para 99. Early cases seemed to suggest that the contribution need not even be "significant": *ibid* at para 187. More recent cases have held that the contribution must at least be "significant": *Prosecutor v Prlić*, Judgment, ICTY A.Ch, IT-04-74-A, 29 November 2017, vol II at para 2768; *Prosecutor v Krajišnik*, Judgment, ICTY A.Ch, IT-05-87/1-A, 27 January 2014, at para 675.

[17] *Vasiljević*, Appeal Judgment, *supra* note 2, at para 102; *Kvočka* Appeal Judgment, *supra* note 3, at 97 and 187.

[18] *Tadić* Appeal Judgment, *supra* note 5, at para 229; *Brđanin* Appeal Judgment, *supra* note 3, at para 429; *Vasiljević* Appeal Judgment, *supra* note 2, at para 102.

[19] The *Kvočka* case held that awareness of contribution to the "everyday functioning and maintenance" of a system is also sufficient to establish the needed *mens rea*: *Kvočka* Appeal Judgment, *supra* note 3, at paras 105–06. Evidence that a person sought to prevent colleagues from mistreating victims, feared the consequences of quitting, or was seen as a "traitor" because of sympathies for victims (*ibid* at paras 103, 224, 242–45), would not detract from "knowledge" of contribution to "everyday functioning and maintenance," and hence deemed "intent," and hence deemed "commission" of all crimes in the JCE. In this way, the intent requirement that justified the harshness of JCE in fact reduces to a knowledge requirement.

[20] See, e.g., *Prosecutor v Stakić*, Judgment, ICTY A.Ch, IT-97-24-A, 22 March 2006, at para 97.

[21] For example, as the Appeals Chamber has affirmed, "genocide is one of the worst crimes known to humankind, and its gravity is reflected in the stringent requirement of specific intent. Convictions for genocide can be entered only where that intent has been unequivocally established": *Prosecutor v Krstić*, Judgment, ICTY A.Ch, IT-98-33-A, 19 April 2004, at para 131. See also, e.g., Genocide Convention, Art 2; ICTY Statute, Art 4(2).

[22] *Prosecutor v Brđanin*, Decision on Interlocutory Appeal, ICTY A.Ch, IT-99-36-A, 19 March 2004 ("*Brđanin* Decision on Interlocutory Appeal") at paras 5–10.

because they are forms of *accessory* liability (an accessory need not have the paradigmatic *mens rea* of a principal), whereas JCE is purportedly a form of *committing* the crime.[23]

Fifth, one of the most problematic features of JCE doctrine is that it deems the accused to have "*committed*" the crimes and, indeed, deems all members to be "equally guilty of the crime regardless of the part played by each in its commission."[24] The claim that JCE, including JCE-III, constitutes "commission" was necessary because JCE is not listed among the modes of liability, and hence jurisprudence asserted that it was implicit in the term "committed." This means, however, that the Tribunals impose principal liability on persons who meet neither the objective nor subjective requirements normally considered necessary for principal liability. The culpability gap can be vast: the low-level individual making a minor contribution becomes liable as a *principal* to *every* crime in the JCE.[25]

A common counter-argument in defence of JCE is that prosecutorial discretion will avoid the most egregious abuses of the doctrine. However, adopting overly broad doctrines with sanguine reliance on prosecutorial or judicial discretion to avoid their excesses is problematic, because it allows a "rule of officials" rather than a "rule of law."[26] Another common counter-argument is that the problem of assigning equal culpability to different levels of participation can be "adequately dealt with at the sentencing stage."[27] However, such a solution contravenes fair labelling by lumping together radically different levels of blameworthiness under one label.[28] More importantly, it contradicts the principle of culpability to convict a person for committing thousands of murders, and then take into account at the sentencing stage that the person did not really do it.

---

[23] On this difference between accessories and principals, see §8.3.2.
[24] *Vasiljević* Appeal Judgment, *supra* note 2, at para 111. See also, e.g., *Prosecutor v Stakić*, Judgment, ICTY T.Ch, IT-97-24-T, 31 July 2003, at para. 435; *Prosecutor v Milutinović*, Decision on Dragoljub Ojdanić's Motion Challenging Jurisdiction – Joint Criminal Enterprise, ICTY A.Ch, IT-99-37-AR72, 21 May 2003, at para 20.
[25] The difference between principal and accessory is discussed at §8.3.2.
[26] *United States v Reese*, 92 U.S. 214 (1875) at 221: "It would certainly be dangerous if the legislature could set a net large enough to catch all possible offenders, and leave it to the courts to step inside and say who could rightfully be detained, and who should be set at large." D Husak, *Philosophy of Criminal Law: Selected Essays* (Oxford University Press, 1987) at 138 argues that "discretion is not a reliable substitute for getting the rule right in the first place." Paul Robinson warns that "[t]he criminal law theorist suffers a moral defect when he unnecessarily defers to administrative or judicial discretion to make the criminal law just": P H Robinson, *Criminal Law Defences, Vol I* (West, 1984) at ix. Henry Kissinger, a critic of ICL, was correct to argue that "[a]ny universal system should contain principles not only to punish the wicked but to constrain the righteous": H Kissinger, "The Pitfalls of Universal Jurisdiction" (2001) 80 Foreign Affairs 86 at 88.
[27] *Brđanin* Appeal Judgment, *supra* note 3, at para 432.
[28] On such reasoning one could replace all international crimes and forms of liability with one finding of "felony": Ohlin, *supra* note 6, at 87.

A2.2   EXUBERANT TELEOLOGICAL REASONING: A CAUTIONARY TALE

My focus in this annex, and in Chapter 2, is not on rehearsing those substantive issues, but on the *reasoning*. How did the JCE doctrine come about? It came about through a series of analytical steps, each of which was convincing to the relevant jurists at the time. The JCE doctrine was first advanced in the *Tadić* case,[29] where it was derived from victim-focused teleology and specifically from the "Statute includes all *x*" technique.

The "Statute includes all *x*" argument was a type of reductive teleological argument that recurred in Tribunal jurisprudence. For example, in interpreting the definition of crimes against humanity and war crimes, the ICTY has held that the aim of its Statute is to "make all crimes against humanity punishable,"[30] or "not to leave unpunished any person guilty of any [war crime]."[31] The problem is that this argument is a *non sequitur*: asserting that "the Statute includes all *x*" does not give guidance on the question of what "*x*" entails. That question that must be answered by examining the text and the legal authorities. Nonetheless, "the Statute includes all *x*" was often used to define that content broadly.

Interestingly, in the *Tadić* decision, the Appeals Chamber correctly pointed out the fallacy of the "Statute includes all *x*" technique, yet then applied it a few paragraphs later. When the prosecution invoked the technique to argue that there is no motive requirement for crimes against humanity, the Appeals Chamber correctly rejected the argument because it "begs the question … whether a crime committed for purely personal reasons *is* a crime against humanity."[32] Yet, a few paragraphs later, the Appeals Chamber employed the very same argument in the course of its analysis of whether crimes against humanity require a discriminatory animus: "[T]he interpretation of Article 5 [of the ICTY Statute] in the light of its object and purpose bears out the above propositions. The aim of those drafting the Statute was to make all crimes against humanity punishable."[33]

Returning to *Tadić* and the birth of JCE: in *Tadić*, there was a particular charge for which the evidence did not support a conviction for commission or for aiding and abetting under Article 7(1) of the ICTY Statute. After acknowledging that Article 7(1) "sets out the parameters of personal criminal responsibility under the Statute" and that it referred only to persons who "planned, instigated, ordered, committed or

---

[29]   *Tadić* Appeal Judgment, *supra* note 5.
[30]   *Ibid* at para 285.
[31]   *Prosecutor v Tadić*, Decision on the Defence Motion for Interlocutory Appeal on Jurisdiction, ICTY A. Ch, IT-94-1-A, 2 October 1995, at para 92; *Tadić* Appeals Judgment, *supra* note 5, at paras 189 and 253.
[32]   *Ibid* at para 253 (emphasis in original).
[33]   *Ibid* at para 285.

otherwise aided and abetted in the planning, preparation or execution of a crime," the Appeals Chamber nonetheless held that:

> An interpretation of the Statute based on its object and purpose leads to the conclusion that the Statute intends to extend the jurisdiction of the International Tribunal to *all* those "responsible for serious violations of international humanitarian law" committed in the former Yugoslavia (Article 1) . . . Thus, all those who have engaged in serious violations of international humanitarian law, whatever the manner in which they may have perpetrated, or participated in the perpetration of those violations, must be brought to justice. If this is so, it is fair to conclude that the Statute does not confine itself to providing for jurisdiction over those persons who plan, instigate, order, physically perpetrate a crime or otherwise aid and abet in its planning, preparation or execution. The Statute does not stop there.[34]

Notice these features of the reasoning: an invocation of object and purpose, coupled with the "Statute includes all X" technique ("all those responsible"; "all those who have engaged . . . whatever the manner . . . must be brought to justice"). The "Statute includes all X" technique was used to push beyond the modes actually listed in the Statute ("the Statute does not confine itself" to the modes of liability listed in the Statute).[35] The method of reasoning, while fully consistent with the *effet utile* doctrine of areas such as human rights law, is a bit too insouciant and cursory in a criminal law context.

The widespread objections to this discovery of JCE are not based on narrow textual approaches. The judges read in a new mode of liability *vastly broader* than any appearing in the listed modes of liability, which is especially problematic. The argument that JCE-III can be inferred within the term "commission" has met widespread doubt. As George Fletcher notes:

> [T]he attempt by the *Tadić* court to squeeze JCE in the framework of these words has no warrant in logic of criminal responsibility or of the legal tradition. If we can read the word "commission" and arrive at liability for the foreseeable consequences of a "common plan," then we have a legal free for all: anything could qualify as commission of the offence.[36]

Notice the stark internal contrast between the Tribunal's approach – reading in a mode of liability broader than any listed based on strained readings – and the promised

---

[34] *Ibid* at paras 189–90 (emphasis in original).

[35] The chamber also argued that the JCE doctrine was implicit in the term "committed." However, the incongruity between the plain meaning of the term "committed" and the extended JCE doctrine is so great that judges themselves occasionally forget this claim and lapse into describing "commission" as requiring physical commission. See, e.g., *Prosecutor v Vasiljević*, Judgment, ICTY T.Ch, IT-98-32-T, 29 November 2002, at para 62: "The Accused will only incur individual criminal responsibility for committing a crime under Article 7(1) where it is proved that he personally physically perpetrated the criminal act in question or personally omitted to do something in violation of international humanitarian law."

[36] G Fletcher, "New Court, Old *Dogmatik*" (2011) 9 JICJ 179 at 186. See also Powles, *supra* note 6, at 611.

approach of strict construction, requiring legislative intent to be clearly expressed and unambiguous, and rejecting doubtful inferences.[37] The adoption of "broad and liberal" teleological interpretation familiar from human rights law engendered a conflict with the legality principle as articulated by the system itself. This teleological enthusiasm strained not only the legality principle, but also other deontic constraints such as culpability and fair labelling. One of the many noted ironies of JCE is that JCE-III is less demanding than aiding and abetting, even though the former is a form of principal liability and the latter is merely accessory liability.[38]

The same victim-focused teleological reasoning was pursued in subsequent cases as, issue by issue, chambers opted for the more progressive option. Thus later decisions held that no agreement between participants is needed,[39] that the physical perpetrators need not be part of the JCE,[40] that *dolus eventualis* suffices for JCE-III,[41] that the doctrine is not limited in scale and may include participants remote from each other,[42] and that JCE-III can be used to circumvent the special intent required for conviction for "committing" genocide.[43] Through reliance on such reasoning techniques, a system that prided itself on its compliance with fundamental principles wound up amalgamating the most sweeping features of various national laws into a single all-encompassing doctrine that appears to strain culpability and fair labelling in various ways.

The problems with JCE are now fairly widely known. The ICC has declined to apply it; instead, it has charted its own path under its own Statute.[44] The Extraordinary Chambers in the Courts of Cambodia (ECCC) declared that JCE-III is not supported in customary international law and declined to apply it.[45] The Special Tribunal for Lebanon (STL) declared that JCE-III is at least not applicable to crimes of special intent, such as terrorism.[46] Each of these

---

[37] See §2.2.1.

[38] See, e.g., Jain, *supra* note 9, at 32 and 61.

[39] *Prosecutor v Krnojelać*, Judgment, ICTY A.Ch, IT-97-25-A, 17 September 2003, at para 97; *Kvočka* Appeal Judgment, *supra* note 3, at para 415.

[40] Although the language in *Tadić* suggested that physical perpetrators must be part of the JCE, it was held that they need not be in *Brđanin* Appeal Judgment, *supra* note 3, at para 410.

[41] *Kvočka* Appeal Judgment, *supra* note 3, at paras 105–06. More recently, see *Prosecutor v Đordević*, Judgment, ICTY A.Ch, IT-05-87/1-A, 27 January 2014, at paras 906–07 ("the *mens rea* standard for the third category of joint criminal enterprise liability does not require awareness of a 'probability' that a crime would be committed. Rather, liability under the third category of joint criminal enterprise may attach where an accused is aware that the perpetration of a crime is a *possible* consequence of the implementation of the common purpose"). See also, to the same effect, *Prosecutor v Mladić*, Judgment, ICTY T.Ch, IT-09-92-T, 22 November 2017, at para 1360.

[42] *Brđanin* Appeal Judgment, *supra* note 3, at paras 422–23.

[43] *Brđanin* Decision on Interlocutory Appeal, *supra* note 22, at paras 5–10.

[44] ICC Statute, Art 25.

[45] *Prosecutor v Chea, Sary, Thirith and Samphan*, Decision on the Applicability of Joint Criminal Enterprise, ECCC T.Ch Case No 002/19-09-2007-ECCC-TC, 12 September 2011.

[46] *Prosecutor v Ayyash*, Interlocutory Decision on the Applicable Law: Terrorism, Conspiracy, Homicide, Perpetration, Cumulative Charging, Case No STL-11-01/I, STL A.Ch, 16 February 2011, at paras 248–49.

moves are arguably part of the "deontic turn" in ICL.[47] In this annex, my interest is not in the assessment or future interpretation of JCE per se; my aim was to review this reasoning as a cautionary tale about the risk that exuberant teleological reasoning can lose sight of deontic constraints.

---

[47]   See §2.5.

Annex 3 *Bemba:* ICC Engagement with Deontic Analysis

In Chapters 6 and 7, I discussed the contribution requirement of the culpability principle and the implications for command responsibility. The ICC has engaged with exactly these issues in its first case on command responsibility, the *Bemba* case. There are many reasons to study the judges' analyses of deontic questions.

(1) On a discursive level (in which we study frames of analysis), it is laudable that they engage directly and thoughtfully with deontic questions, as it contrasts with the sometimes hasty reasoning in earlier eras of ICL.[1]

(2) The judges generally avoid both of the pitfalls I warn against: disregarding deontic constraints or adopting unsupported overly rigid conceptions.

(3) Their method is best explained as an instantiation of the coherentist method that I advocate.

(4) There are still a few subtle areas in which scholars can assist by drawing on criminal law theory and deontic analysis to further refine arguments.

(5) The upshot of these analyses will dramatically affect the future trajectory of command responsibility.

The *Bemba* Trial Judgment provided what I believe to be the most sophisticated judicial analysis to date of these questions. Both the Pre-Trial Chamber and the Trial Chamber avoided the types of error that had ensnarled Tribunal jurisprudence (discussed in Chapter 6). They engaged directly with deontic questions and with the constructs of criminal law theory, and they did so with sophistication.[2]

---

[1] In contrasting the careful deontic engagement by the ICC with early approaches, I am not criticizing the early efforts of the Tribunals. They worked in a pioneering phase, developing little-used provisions of international law, drawing on diverse legal systems, and needing to address numerous issues in rapid succession. Now, there is time for more careful reflection on the details, on the nuances of criminal law, and on broader principled coherence.

[2] *Prosecutor v Jean-Pierre Bemba Gombo*, Decision Pursuant to Article 61(7)(a) and (b) of the Rome Statute on the Charges of the Prosecutor against Jean-Pierre Bemba Gombo, ICC PTC-II, ICC-01/05–01/08, 15 June 2009 (*"Bemba* Confirmation Decision"); *Prosecutor v Jean-Pierre Bemba Gombo*, Judgment Pursuant to Article 74, ICC-01/05–01/08, Trial Chamber III 21 March 2016 (*"Bemba* Trial Judgment").

Despite a unanimous conviction by the Trial Chamber, the Appeals Chamber substituted an acquittal, by a 3–2 majority.[3] The Appeals Chamber majority decision did not revolve around or address the specific controversies discussed here (e.g. causal contribution); instead, the decision was based on the commander's duty to take measures. Thus questions about causal contribution and the nature of command responsibility remain somewhat open. However, if we count up the separate opinions, three out of five judges expressly recognized command responsibility as a mode of accessory liability, and they also expressly recognized the causal contribution requirement. This is consistent with the analysis advanced in this book.

The Appeal Judgment was intensely controversial for many reasons (I will discuss these separate issues and controversies in Annex 4), but, in terms of the issues discussed here, it can at least be said that the judges engaged diligently and directly with deontic questions, and that this attention is commendable.

The deepening deontic engagement is a sign of the maturation of ICL. There is still a long way to go, however. As the field enters this new phase, the jurisprudence (particularly at the ICC) is tending to lurch significantly in different directions, at times possibly overestimating deontic constraints. I will touch on this in Annex 4. I think a coherentist method can assist, because it helps to ground arguments in common points of reference.

A3.1 THE TRIAL JUDGMENT (AND PRE-TRIAL CONFIRMATION DECISION)

The *Bemba* Trial Chamber issued a unanimous judgment, accompanied by two separate opinions, one by Judge Steiner (the "Steiner Opinion") and one by Judge Ozaki (the "Ozaki Opinion"). The Trial Judgment was consistent with the Pre-Trial Chamber's Confirmation Decision, albeit with some more detailed and developed analysis.

A3.1.1 A Mode of Accessory Liability

First, the Trial Chamber, like the Pre-Trial Chamber before it, simply and straightforwardly recognized that command responsibility is a mode of liability.[4] This clear, forthright position is a welcome contrast to Tribunal jurisprudence, in which the nature of command responsibility was murky and controverted (there are still simmering disputes about whether it is a mode, offence, neither, both, or

---

[3] *Prosecutor v Jean-Pierre Bemba Gombo*, Judgment on the appeal of Mr Jean-Pierre Bemba Gombo against Trial Chamber III's Judgment Pursuant to Article 74 of the Statute, ICC A.Ch, ICC-01/05–01/08 A, 8 June 2018 ("*Bemba* Appeal Judgment").

[4] *Bemba* Trial Judgment, *supra* note 2, at para 171, concurring with *Bemba* Confirmation Decision, *supra* note 2, at para 341. See also Steiner Opinion at para 7 (accessory liability) and Ozaki Opinion at para 5 (mode of liability and not a separate crime).

a mysterious new *sui generis* construct).[5] The "mode of liability" interpretation respects the explicit language of the ICC Statute,[6] conforms to long-standing transnational precedents,[7] and acknowledges the reality that commanders are literally charged with the underlying offences.[8]

The *Bemba* Trial Judgment contains one faint echo of Tribunal jurisprudence, when it describes command responsibility as a *"sui generis"* mode of liability.[9] Fortunately, the *Bemba* Trial Judgment does not invoke the label *sui generis* in either of the two problematic ways it has been invoked in Tribunal jurisprudence – that is, to suggest that command responsibility is thereby exempt from the contribution requirement of the culpability principle, or to suggest that it is neither a mode nor an offence, but some entirely new and undefined category.[10] The *Bemba* Trial Judgment echoes the *sui generis* language, but only to note that command responsibility is "distinct" from the other modes.[11] This use of this term is unproblematic, albeit trivial, since every mode must of course be distinct in some respect from other modes; otherwise, it would be duplicative.

A3.1.2 Respecting the Contribution Requirement

Second, the *Bemba* Trial Chamber, like the Pre-Trial Chamber, affirmed the requirement of causal contribution.[12] This finding ought to be unsurprising, since the requirement is explicit in the ICC Statute: Article 28 expressly requires that the crimes be "a result of" the failure by the commander "to exercise control properly."[13] However, as a result of the convoluted debate emerging from Tribunal jurisprudence, the matter had been contested. For example, Amnesty International advanced a strained textual interpretation to circumvent the explicit causation element.[14] Amnesty International argued that the words "as a result of or her failure

---

[5] As discussed in Chapter 6, even though the ICTY Appeals Chamber has affirmed that command responsibility is a mode of liability, the nature of command responsibility remains persistently controverted. The judicial claims that it is a *"sui generis"* category further shroud the question.

[6] ICC Statute, Art 28, explicitly states that the commander is held "criminally responsible for crimes within the jurisdiction of the Court committed by [subordinates]." Thus the provision is explicit that the commander shares in liability for the crimes themselves.

[7] See §6.5.2.

[8] See §6.6.

[9] *Bemba* Trial Judgment, *supra* note 2, at para 174.

[10] See §6.7.1 and §6.7.2.

[11] *Bemba* Trial Judgment, *supra* note 2, at paras 173–74, and see also the Ozaki Opinion at para 6.

[12] *Bemba* Trial Judgment, *supra* note 2, at paras 210–13.

[13] The term "failure to exercise control properly" is not specifically defined in Art 28, but in a contextual reading it can only refer back to the types of failure mentioned previously in Art 28 (e.g. failures to prevent or punish or refer for punishment).

[14] The chapeau of Art 28(1) reads: "A military commander . . . shall be criminally responsible for crimes within the jurisdiction of the Court committed by forces under his or her effective command and control, or effective authority and control as the case may be, *as a result of his or her failure to exercise control properly* over such forces, . . ."

to exercise control properly" were not a result element referring to the immediately previously mentioned commission of crimes by subordinates; instead, the words were simply re-explaining that the commander is liable for breaching the provision as a result of breaching the provision. This proposed reading was well intentioned: it was a result-oriented reading to circumvent what was presumably perceived as an arbitrary limitation. However, I would argue that the contribution requirement is not an arbitrary limit. On the contrary, it is a principle of justice – a fundamental requirement for personal culpability.[15]

Commendably, the *Bemba* Trial Judgment upheld the contribution requirement not only for doctrinal reasons (the text, the precedents[16]), but also for *deontic* reasons: to respect the culpability principle. The Judgment held that it is a "core principle of criminal law that a person should not be found individually criminally responsible for a crime in the absence of some form of personal nexus to it."[17]

The separate opinions of Judges Steiner and Ozaki engage even more deeply with culpability, deontic analysis, and constructs of criminal law theory. Judge Steiner concludes that command responsibility is accessory liability, and that all forms of accessory liability require a connection between the accused's conduct and the unlawful result[18] – namely, "a contribution" to the commission of the crime.[19] Similarly, Judge Ozaki concludes that the culpability principle requires a form of nexus or contribution to the crimes.[20]

A3.1.3 Omissions Can Make a Difference

Third, in both the Pre-Trial and Trial Chamber, the judicial reasoning was conversant with criminal law theory and juridical practice on omissions and causation. In Chapter 7,[21] I discussed the "naturalistic" conception of causation, in which omissions can never be causes, and the "normative" conception, in which we compare the outcome of an omission with the projected outcome of acting legally. The judges

---

[15]   See Chapters 6 and 7.

[16]   Steiner Opinion at paras 4–7; Ozaki Opinion at paras 3–11. Amnesty International argued that none of the prior international legal instruments required a causal contribution. In response, Judge Steiner pointed out that there *is* precedent – namely, Art 86(1) of Additional Protocol I to the Geneva Conventions. This exchange illustrates a theme that I mentioned earlier (§6.5.2): even in doctrinal (source-based) analysis, what we notice may be influenced by what we are attuned to. In other words, sensitivity to fundamental constraints may help us to notice sources that reflect those constraints; otherwise, we might overlook those patterns of practice. Furthermore, the fact that unilaterally imposed instruments did not contain a contribution requirement, whereas multilaterally negotiated instruments do, is an example of the tendency discussed in §2.4: sometimes, unilaterally imposed rules are inadequately mindful of constraints of justice.

[17]   *Bemba* Trial Judgment, *supra* note 2, at para 211.

[18]   Steiner Opinion at para 7.

[19]   *Ibid*. Similarly, at para 17, Judge Steiner notes that required nexus entails an "element of causality."

[20]   Ozaki Opinion at para 9.

[21]   See §7.1.2.

adopted the normative conception, which is overwhelmingly supported in juridical practice and in scholarship on criminal law theory.[22]

A3.1.4 A Nuanced Account of the Requisite Extent of Contribution

Fourth, both the Trial Chamber and Pre-Trial Chamber explored the required *extent* of contribution in a nuanced and laudable way. Judges in both chambers embraced a "risk aggravation" approach, which is consistent with patterns of juridical practice and with normative theories, as discussed in Chapter 6.

Both the Pre-Trial Chamber and the Trial Chamber rejected a "but for" standard of causation (i.e. "but for the commander's dereliction, the crimes would not have happened"). A "but for" standard would indeed be inappropriately demanding, whether from a doctrinal, teleological, or deontic perspective. Doctrinally, a "but for" test is not required by precedents.[23] Teleologically, it would exceed the purpose of the element (to comply with the culpability principle), and it would pose a hopelessly stringent test, given the extreme difficulty or even impossibility of identifying the determinants of human behaviour with that degree of confidence.[24] Deontically, that stringent standard is not required by the culpability principle. Accessory liability, which concerns relatively indirect responsibility for crimes, does not require "but for" causation, but a more modest standard of "contribution."[25]

The Pre-Trial Chamber concluded that the requisite standard is simply that the commander's omission "increased the risk of the commission of the crimes charged."[26] As discussed in Chapter 7, "risk aggravation" is one of the most plausible articulations of the contribution requirement.[27]

The Trial Chamber agreed that "but for" causation is not required, but found it unnecessary on the facts to determine the precise applicable standard.[28] The reason was that, on the available evidence, even the unnecessarily stringent "but for" test

---

[22] *Bemba* Confirmation Decision, *supra* note 2, at paras 423–25; *Bemba* Trial Judgment, *supra* note 2, at para 212 ("hypothetical" causation); the Steiner Opinion at para 18 explicitly discusses the "naturalistic" versus the "normative" conception; the Ozaki Opinion at paras 19–23 engages with the normative considerations and juridical practice.

[23] See §6.5.2 and §7.1.3; V Nerlich "Superior Responsibility under Article 28 ICC Statute: For What Exactly Is the Superior Held Responsible?" (2007) 5 JICJ 665 at 672–73; K Ambos, "Superior Responsibility," in A Cassese, P Gaeta & J R W D Jones, eds, *The Rome Statute of the International Criminal Court: A Commentary, Vol 2* (Oxford University Press, 2002) at 823; M Osiel, "The Banality of Good: Aligning Incentives against Mass Atrocity" (2005) 105 Columbia L Rev 1751 at 1780–81.

[24] See §7.1.3. See also, along similar lines, Osiel, *supra* note 23, at 1780–81; Nerlich, *supra* note 23, at 673.

[25] For more detailed analysis, see §7.1.3.

[26] *Bemba* Confirmation Decision, *supra* note 2, at para 425.

[27] See §7.1.3. See also discussion in K Ambos, "Critical Issues in the *Bemba* Confirmation Decision" (2009) 22 LJIL 715.

[28] *Bemba* Trial Judgment, *supra* note 2, at paras 211–13.

would be met, and thus the contribution requirement was in any case clearly satisfied.[29]

Judges Steiner and Ozaki, in their separate opinions, provide impressive and well-reasoned elaborations on the requisite degree of contribution. Judge Ozaki rightly notes that different standards of causation have been applied in different systems in fulfillment of the culpability principle.[30] She rightly notes that "but for" causation is sometimes applied for principals,[31] whereas a lesser standard is typically applied for the indirect responsibility ascribed to accessories.[32] She also surveys examples of requisite standards from legal practice: to facilitate, to render easier, to increase the risk.[33] She helpfully surveys the *normative* reasons for these more inclusive standards: the presence of multiple causes, including the will of principals; the difficulty of assessing the impact of omissions; the scale and complexity of crimes, and the many intervening actors; and the fact that we are ascribing only indirect liability. She asserts that "the starting point for the inquiry is the principle of personal culpability."[34] One outer limit she mentions is the objective foreseeability of consequences not as a requirement of *mens rea*, but rather as a commonly recognized outer limit of fair normative attribution in causation.[35]

Similarly, Judge Steiner endorsed the Pre-Trial Chamber conclusion that risk aggravation is the appropriate standard.[36] Judge Steiner rightly rejected defence arguments that the subordinate crimes must be shown to be a "certain" consequence of the commander's derelictions,[37] because a requirement of "certainty" is unsupported, impractical, and plays no part in accessory liability.[38] Judge Steiner noted that different legal systems have proposed and applied different standards, particularly in relation to omissions.[39] Judge Steiner settles on a requirement of a "high probability" that the crimes would have been prevented or would not have been committed in the same manner.[40]

The "high probability" interpretation seems plausible, albeit ambiguous. One hopes that "probability" was not meant in the sense of "greater than 50% likelihood," because there would be precedential, consequentialist, deontic, and consistency

---

[29] *Ibid* at paras 213 and 735–41.
[30] Ozaki Opinion at para 19.
[31] Even for principals, the "but for" test is not used where there are multiple sufficient causes. See *ibid*.
[32] *Ibid.*
[33] *Ibid.*
[34] *Ibid* at para 23.
[35] *Ibid.*
[36] *Ibid.*
[37] *Ibid* at para 20.
[38] Judge Steiner also rejected "foreseeability," which belongs more to *mens rea*. However, she noted that there is room for a type of foreseeability in a causation assessment, in the sense of looking at "what is 'adequate' to produce a result of the relevant kind based on the rules of experience." See Steiner Opinion at para 22.
[39] *Ibid* at para 24.
[40] *Ibid.*

reasons against that conclusion.[41] Presumably, Judge Steiner meant "probability" in its normal mathematical sense (i.e. as referring to the chance of an event occurring), and hence "high probability" means a very substantial likelihood.[42] The reference to the crime not occurring "in the same manner" is consistent with jurisprudence on the culpability principle. For example, if derelictions helped the subordinates to commit the crime more easily or with less need for concealment, that satisfies the culpability principle.[43] The "high probability" test is actually more demanding than the culpability principle itself requires, because the culpability principle is satisfied simply by "significant" facilitation or encouragement.[44] Nonetheless, a standard along the lines of "high probability" (or substantial likelihood) is arguably a good synthesis between the Statute text (and its different language versions), the deontic underpinnings, prior case law, and consequentialist considerations.

A3.1.5 Liability for Failure to Punish[45]

The *Bemba* Trial Chamber (rightly, in my view) rejected the argument that the "failure to punish" branch cannot be reconciled with a contribution requirement.[46] This was the argument that first led Tribunal jurisprudence into contradiction with its own principles, engendering all of the subsequent confusion.[47] Judges Osaka and Steiner noted that the argument is not a sufficient basis to disregard the contribution requirement.[48] The provision can be read in a non-contradictory way: failures to punish previous crimes *can* facilitate or encourage *subsequent* crimes, giving rise to indirect liability for the latter.[49] This reading gives a role to the "failure to punish branch", avoids contradiction, and

---

[41] If "probability" is instead interpreted in the sense of "more likely than not" (i.e. probable), then "high probability" would be almost tantamount to the "but for" test, which was rightly rejected.

[42] And, of course, layered over the substantive test is the evidentiary threshold. Thus, with a test of "high probability," the finder of fact still must be convinced "beyond reasonable doubt" that there was a "high probability."

[43] See §7.1.3.

[44] See §7.1.3.

[45] As noted in Chapter 6, I use the term "failure to punish" for simplicity, but the Rome Statute rightly foresees that a commander can punish crimes directly or refer the matter to appropriate authorities. ICC Statute, Art 28(a)(ii).

[46] In contrast, the Pre-Trial Chamber was ambiguous about this argument in the Confirmation Decision. On the one hand, it seemed to adopt the argument, holding that is "illogical to conclude that a failure [to punish] can retroactively cause the crimes to be committed," and hence it suggested that the contribution requirement relates only to the commander's duty to prevent: *Bemba* Confirmation Decision, *supra* note 2, at para 424. But then the Pre-Trial Chamber went on to say that failures to punish prior crimes will increase the risk of later crimes and hence rightly support liability in those subsequent crimes, which would reconcile the provision with the culpability principle: *ibid* at para 424.

[47] See Chapter 6.

[48] Osaka Opinion at para 17; Steiner Opinion at para 14.

[49] Osaka Opinion at para 17 note 23.

complies with the culpability principle. Thus this reading should be preferred over one that violates the culpability principle.[50]

I have argued in Chapter 6 in favour of this conclusion.[51] In my view, the "incompatibility" argument far too insouciantly ignores an explicit element that is stated in the Statute and which is required by the culpability principle. Given that there is an available textual interpretation that complies with the culpability principle, it should be adopted. An admitted limitation of this approach is that we cannot convict the commander for prior crimes, merely by virtue of her failure to punish them, if she in no way contributed to those crimes. However, as I argued in Chapter 6, given that international courts should be focusing on the gravest crimes, this "problem" of non-contributory derelictions has consumed too much attention. Every possible interpretation has shortcomings and involves straining or ignoring some part of the text, or even breaching the culpability principle.[52] This is the best available reconciliation of the text, the precedents, and the culpability principle.

A3.1.6 A Minor Caveat: The Reason for the Risk Aggravation Standard

I strongly commend both chambers, because they engage in sophisticated deontic reasoning. They directly engage with the principled limitations on culpability, and, in doing so, they demonstrate a strong command of juridical practice and the normative debates in criminal law theory and ICL scholarship. Their method concords with the coherentist method I advocate in Chapter 4: they draw on the available clues, including patterns of practice and normative arguments.

I advance only one very minor refinement, by providing a different *reason* why risk aggravation is the appropriate standard. The reason given in both the Pre-Trial Chamber and the Trial Chamber is that assessing the impact of an omission is more difficult than assessing that of an act.[53] As I have argued in Chapter 7, this view overestimates the difference in difficulty in assessing the impacts of omissions versus

---

[50] As I have argued in Chapter 6, by failing to punish past crimes and thus failing to send a signal of disapproval and deterrence, the commander culpably elevates the risk of subsequent crimes (compared to the situation that would pertain if the duty were met) and thus joins in liability for any subsequent crimes falling within the ambit of the created risk.

[51] See §6.3.2.

[52] To punish commanders for past crimes to which they did not contribute, based on a later failure to punish, contradicts the culpability principle and hence is particularly untenable, unless a new convincing conception of culpability is developed. The "separate offence" characterization contradicts Statute text, applicable law, and the actual charges and convictions, and it fails to capture the commander's indirect responsibility for the core crimes themselves. The "variegated" approach (in which command responsibility is sometimes a mode and sometimes a separate offence) avoids all of these problems, but it seems unnecessarily complex, and it is somewhat implausible that the text contains a hidden separate offence.

[53] The Pre-Trial Chamber held that, "[c]ontrary to the visible and material effect of a positive act, the effect of an omission cannot be empirically determined with certainty. In other words, it would not be practical to predict exactly what would have happened if a commander had fulfilled his obligation to prevent crimes": *Bemba* Confirmation Decision, *supra* note 2, at para 425. Similarly, the Trial

the impacts of acts. Both types of analysis involve counterfactual, and hence hypothetical, analysis, and in criminal cases the impact of acts is often extremely difficult to assess.[54] I suggest that the *better* reason for the risk aggravation standard is that, in accessory liability, we are trying to discern impacts on *human behaviour* (see §7.1.3). This consideration applies to all accessory liability, not only command responsibility. The more inclusive contribution standard also reflects that we are ascribing only indirect liability, and we are not declaring the person liable as a principal.

A3.2 THE *BEMBA* APPEAL JUDGMENT

Many Court-watchers hoped and expected that the *Bemba* Appeal Judgment would bring finality and clarity on these issues (e.g. the nature of command responsibility, causal contribution). Instead, the Appeal Judgment, decided by a 3–2 majority, went in many unexpected directions and turned on entirely different issues.[55] I will touch lightly on the resulting controversies and criticisms in Annex 4. Here, I will maintain focus on the nature of command responsibility and the causal contribution requirement.

Interestingly, although President Eboe-Osuji joined with the majority on other issues, he adopted the same position as the dissenting judges (Judges Monageng and Hofmański) on these issues. Thus, on these issues, there is actually a majority of three judges supporting the same conclusions as the chambers below, which are consistent with the prescriptions in this book. Because of the fragmentation in the Appeal Chamber, it will be most effective to discuss the Appeal Judgment opinion by opinion, rather than issue by issue.

A3.2.1 Judges Monageng and Hofmański

Judges Monageng and Hofmański, dissenting from the propositions advanced by the majority on other issues (see Annex 4), reached the same conclusions as the chambers below on the issues canvassed here.

Chamber also suggests the need for a more inclusive test, given "the hypothetical assessment required in cases of omission": *Bemba* Trial Judgment, *supra* note 2, at para 212. I note, however, that Judge Ozaki rightly refers to the more important difficulty of identifying the determinants of human behaviour: Ozaki Opinion at paras 19–23.

[54] Often, criminal courts have to decide whether one particular blow among many produced a prohibited consequence, or assess the impact of words of encouragement, or assess whether a particular effort to facilitate did indeed facilitate. There is not a bright-line quantum difference in difficulty in assessing acts versus omissions per se.

[55] The *Bemba* Appeal Judgment, *supra* note 3, is accompanied by three separate opinions: the Concurring Separate Opinion of Judge Eboe-Osuji ("Eboe-Osuji Opinion"), the Separate Opinion Judge Christine Van den Wyngaert and Judge Howard Morrison ("Van den Wyngaert and Morrison Opinion"), and the Dissenting Opinion of Judge Sanji Mmasenono Monageng and Judge Piotr Hofmański ("Monageng and Hofmański Opinion").

Like both of the Chambers below, they held that command responsibility is a mode of liability and that therefore the contribution requirement must be respected.[56] Like the chambers below, they rejected Amnesty International's arguments that they should read out the contribution requirement.[57] They also rejected the argument that respecting the contribution requirement would make command responsibility "redundant" with aiding and abetting; they correctly pointed out that command responsibility is still distinct because of the special *mens rea*.[58]

Judges Monageng and Hofmański agreed with the Trial Chamber that, even for "failure to punish" derelictions, the contribution requirement must be respected. Thus such derelictions create accessory liability only when they facilitate or encourage later crimes.[59] The judges acknowledged that this does leave a gap with respect to the initial crimes,[60] but they held that liability without contribution would violate the culpability principle.[61]

With respect to causation, they adopt the "normative" conception. They note that, with omissions, we compare the resulting situation to the situation that would have pertained had the person carried out their duty.[62] They joined with the chambers below in rejecting the "but for" standard of causation and adopting a "risk aggravation" standard – namely, a "high probability" that the crime would not have been committed or would have been committed in a different manner.[63]

I would underscore that their deontic analysis is far more informed and careful than analyses in earlier days of ICL, which admittedly were hurried days. For example, the argument that respecting culpability would make command responsibility "redundant" with other modes carried the day in early Tribunal jurisprudence, despite being plainly fallacious.[64] I think this is a sign of the maturation of ICL: judges are now a little more rigorous and more careful with criminal law theory and with deontic constraints.

A3.2.2 Judge Eboe-Osuji

Although Judge Eboe-Osuji sided with Judges Van den Wyngaert and Morrison on the issues on which the *Bemba* Appeal Judgment turned, on the issues discussed here he sided with Judges Monageng and Hofmansi. Thus there is actually a majority of three judges in the Appeals Chamber on these issues. Judge Eboe-

---

[56] Monageng and Hofmański Opinion, *supra* note 55, at para 331.
[57] *Ibid.*
[58] *Ibid.* See also §6.5.3.
[59] *Ibid* at para 333.
[60] See Chapter 6.
[61] Monageng and Hofmański Opinion, *supra* note 55, at para 333.
[62] *Ibid* at para 337.
[63] *Ibid* at paras 337–39.
[64] See §6.5.3.

Osuji's inquiry into deontic questions is particularly detailed and draws on juridical practice, criminal law theory, and normative scholarship.

On the controversy between the "separate offence" and the "mode of liability" characterization, Judge Eboe-Osuji assesses the arguments on both sides in considerable detail.[65] For the same types of reason canvassed in Chapter 6 (text, applicable law, the actual charges),[66] his analysis "leaves accomplice liability standing as the remaining theory" and "the more credible theory" of command responsibility.[67] He also rejects the description of command responsibility as "*sui generis*" in the sense that it is some entirely new category; instead, it is more simply understood as accessory liability.[68]

Accordingly, Judge Eboe-Osuji concludes that the contribution requirement, which is necessary for accessory liability, must be respected. This is so even when the alleged dereliction is a "failure to punish." He rejects the argument that respecting the contribution requirement would render ineffective the "failure to punish" branch. It is "possible – indeed desirable – to give separate life" to that provision, because the prosecution can prove derelictions by proving failures to punish past crimes.[69] Such derelictions can render the commander liable as an accessory for later crimes that were facilitated by those derelictions, for example because they were seen as licence to commit crimes.[70] Like Judges Monageng and Hofmański, Judge Eboe-Osuji rejects the faulty prosecution argument that respecting the contribution requirement would make command responsibility redundant with aiding and abetting, by pointing out significant remaining differences.[71]

Judge Eboe-Osuji acknowledges that this approach means that not every instance of failure to punish is punishable before the ICC. For example, the commander cannot be punished for the early, prior crimes if she did not facilitate them.[72] Nonetheless, the contribution requirement is a "fair price" for compliance with

---

[65] Eboe-Osuji Opinion, *supra* note 55, at paras 187–231.
[66] See §6.6.
[67] Eboe-Osuji Opinion, *supra* note 55, at paras 208 and 209.
[68] *Ibid* at para 198.
[69] *Ibid* at para 206.
[70] *Ibid* at paras 210–13. I would add that a contribution exists not only where the failure to punish was known to subordinates and seen by them as licence to commit crimes. Recall that, based on a normative conception of causation, we are comparing the resulting situation to that which would have pertained if the commander had met her expected commitments (see §7.1.2). Had she made diligent efforts to punish, it would have sent out an affirmative deterrent message. Thus the inaction facilitates and encourages crimes in comparison to that baseline. Accordingly, there can be a positive contribution, where subordinates know of the inaction, or a negative contribution, in the failure to affirmatively send out the deterrent and expressive message that the commander is obliged to send.
[71] Eboe-Osuji Opinion, *supra* note 55, at paras 217–22. Judge Eboe-Osuji responds that, under aiding and abetting, bystanders are liable only if they actually encouraged or facilitated or if a specific duty to act can be found, whereas command responsibility stipulates clear duties to act. I would add to this another distinguishing feature: that command responsibility offers the "should have known" mental standard. See §6.5.3.
[72] Eboe-Osuji Opinion, *supra* note 55, at paras 210 and 212.

culpability.[73] All of these conclusions are consistent with the analyses I offered in Chapter 6.

As for the impact of omissions, Judge Eboe-Osuji acknowledges that some scholars argue that omissions cannot have results. He reviews juridical practice and legal theory and – like the other judges – finds that the normative conception is overwhelmingly supported in legal practice, in legal theory, and even in ordinary language.[74]

Finally, Judge Eboe-Osuji discusses an "endangerment rationale" for command responsibility. At first glance, reference to "endangerment" may seem puzzling, because the term often refers to inchoate liability (liability without producing a prohibited result),[75] whereas accessory liability requires that crimes do arise. On closer reading, however, Judge Eboe-Osuji's point is about the deontic justification for command responsibility, and it matches the arguments advanced in Chapter 8.[76] Namely, he argues that if one takes on a role as commander of forces who pose a great danger to civilians, then that danger creates an obligation to take great care to insulate strangers from resulting harms.[77] Judge Eboe-Osuji advances two additional arguments beyond those I outlined in Chapter 8. One is that the justificatory rationale is even stronger when the danger to innocent strangers is imposed without their consent and with no promise of benefit to them.[78] The other is to point out that amassing and deploying an armed group so that they may kill and destroy is ordinarily itself criminal behaviour; it is permitted only because of a special legal regime, and that legal regime comes with accompanying requirements of care and responsibility.[79]

A3.2.3 Judges Van den Wyngaert and Morrison

On the issues canvassed here (causal contribution), the separate opinion by Judge Van den Wyngaert and Judge Morrison is the sole outlier. All other judges agreed that command responsibility is a mode of accessory liability, that it requires causal contribution, and that the relevant standard is risk aggravation.

Unlike the Trial Chamber judges and the other Appeals Chamber judges, Van den Wyngaert and Morrison appeared to accept the "incompatibility" argument (i.e. that the "failure to punish" branch cannot be reconciled with a contribution requirement).[80] They note that if the contribution requirement is recognized, the commander can never be held responsible for a single crime or the first crime in

---

[73]   *Ibid* at para 216.
[74]   *Ibid* at paras 167–85.
[75]   *Ibid* at paras 234 and 237.
[76]   *Ibid* at para 2.
[77]   *Ibid* at paras 235–46.
[78]   *Ibid* at para 235.
[79]   *Ibid* at para 265.
[80]   Van den Wyngaert and Morrison Opinion, *supra* note 55, at para 53.

a series, based on a failure to punish. (This is correct, although the commander could be responsible for initial or isolated crimes if she previously breached her duties to *prevent* crimes.) They consider the argument that a failure to punish the initial crime increases the risk of subsequent crimes. Unfortunately, because of their view on causation (to be discussed in a moment), they consider this to be only "theoretically possible," or possible in "very exceptional circumstances." Accordingly, they reject the interpretation, because it would "fall foul of the principle of effectiveness" by making the "failure to punish" branch impossible to apply.[81]

This "incompatibility" argument hinges, however, on an unsupported narrow conception of causation. The judges reject the "theory of probabilistic causation" adopted by all of the other judges throughout the proceedings (Pre-Trial, Trial, and Appeal), because, in their view, it does not "withstand critical analysis."[82] They argue that a failure to take measures is a failure to "*reduce* an existing risk" and that a failure to act "does not *increase* the risk."[83] They assert that the commander's duty to is "decrease the risk" of subordinate crimes and that "failing to reduce a risk" can hardly be seen as contributing to the manifestation of that risk.[84]

The problem with that argument is that it is rooted in the "naturalistic" conception of causation.[85] The naturalistic conception insists that omissions cannot "cause" anything, because they have no "causal energy." This view is voiced by a few scholars, but is rejected in juridical practice and by a convincing preponderance of normative argumentation.[86] Legal systems, ordinary language, widely shared intuitions, and most of the literature converge in supporting the "normative" conception of causation.[87] By contrast, the "normative" conception compares the outcome of the omission with the projected outcome had one fulfilled one's duty.

---

[81] In addition to the two problems I note here (unsupported conception of causation and failure to address culpability principle), there is a third problem with this argument: there is a contradiction in invoking the principle of effectiveness – i.e. that a textual provision should not be ignored – as an argument for ignoring the explicit textual provision that requires contribution.

[82] Van den Wyngaert and Morrison Opinion, *supra* note 55, at para 55.

[83] *Ibid* (emphasis in original).

[84] *Ibid.*

[85] See, e.g., K Ambos, *Treatise on International Criminal Law, Vol I: Foundations and General Part* (Oxford University Press, 2012) at 215.

[86] One of the voices arguing for the naturalistic conception is M S Moore, *Causation and Responsibility: An Essay in Law, Morals and Metaphysics* (Oxford University Press, 2009) at 446. For some examples of responses to such arguments, see G Fletcher, *Basic Concepts of Criminal Law* (Oxford University Press, 1998) at 67–69; G Fletcher, *Rethinking Criminal Law*, 3rd ed (Oxford University Press, 2000) 585–625; A Ashworth, *Principles of Criminal Law*, 5th ed (Oxford University Press, 2006) at 418–20; H L A Hart & A M Honoré, *Causation in the Law*, 2nd ed (Clarendon Press, 1985) at 30–31, 40 and 447–49; C Sartoria, "Causation and Responsibility by Michael Moore" (2010) 119 Mind 475; J Schaffer, "Contrastive Causation in the Law" (2010) 16 Legal Theory 259; V Tadros, *Criminal Responsibility* (Oxford University Press, 2010) at ch 6; R W Wright, "Causation: Metaphysics or Intuition?," in K Ferzan & S Morse, eds, *Legal, Moral and Metaphysical Truths: The Philosophy of Michael Moore* (Oxford University Press, 2016) 171.

[87] See §7.1.2.

(In one of the examples I gave in Chapter 7, where a pilot chooses to "omit" to carry out a landing and the plane crashes, the naturalist account would insist that the crash was caused only by gravity. However, almost all jurists and laypersons will blame not only gravity, but also the pilot. We compare the outcome of the omission with the projected outcome of meeting the duty, i.e. attempting to land the plane. The pilot's refusal to do her job "contributed" to the crash.)[88] In the commander scenario, the commander's inaction aggravates the risk of crimes *in comparison to the legally required baseline* behaviour of acting diligently to prevent and punish crimes. We rightly regard departures from that baseline as "contributions" to harms within the risk generated. (Interestingly, even Michael Moore, who takes the relatively lonely position that omissions cannot be causes, would still recognize culpability for "counterfactual dependence" and thus would also join in the mainstream view: the commander's culpable failure to decrease the risk of crimes, given the obligation to try to do so, is a sufficient contribution to those crimes.[89])

There is a possible lesson here about the merits of the coherentist method. The assertions in the Van den Wyngaert opinion rejecting probabilistic causation are entirely without citation of any authority or support.[90] By contrast, the other judges refer to legal authorities and scholars, and ground their conclusions in common reference points. As I have argued in Chapter 4, even in relation to abstract ideas such as causation, it can be useful to touch base with juridical practice and normative argumentation as a "humility check" on our opinions. This is all the more so in legal analysis, where conformity to authority is a desiderata of legitimacy. Of course, one could still successfully argue that everyone else is wrong, but in such case one should offer at least *some* argumentation attempting to address the contrary weight of practice and argumentation.

The opinion offers no explanation of how circumventing the causal contribution requirement accords with the culpability principle. That oversight is uncharacteristic, especially given that the Van den Wyngaert and Morrison opinion otherwise generally adopts visions of deontic constraints and procedural rights that are far more stringent than those of other judges (see Annex 4). To be justifiable, an account

---

[88] To give another example, imagine that a guard had a duty to feed a person (e.g. a prisoner) and chose not to do so, and the prisoner died of starvation. On a naturalistic conception, one would claim that that guard's omission did not contribute to the starvation: Omissions cannot be causes; the person simply died from lack of food and the guard merely "failed to avert" that death. On a normative conception, we compare the situation to what would have pertained if the guard met the relevant legal duty: the prisoner would have had food and would not have died of starvation. The normative conception conforms to ordinary language and widely shared intuitions of justice. Our failures do have consequences. Likewise, the commander's failure to send a deterrent message does have consequences.

[89] In other words, even if one insists that a refusal to carry out a duty to reduce risks technically does not increase the existing risks (from a naturalistic perspective), the refusal to reduce risks, where there is a duty to do so, creates a responsibility for those risks sufficient for accessory liability.

[90] Van den Wyngaert and Morrison Opinion, *supra* note 55, at para 55.

rejecting the contribution requirement would have to offer a non-causal conception of culpability (see §7.2).

A3.3 CONCLUSION

As for the specific prescriptions in Chapters 6 and 7, almost every judge, at every stage in *Bemba* (with the exception of two judges), reached conclusions consistent with those prescriptions: Command responsibility is a mode of accessory liability; it requires causal contributions; and risk aggravation is the appropriate standard.

More broadly, in all three chambers, the analyses of every judge engaged not only with doctrinal and consequentialist arguments, but also with deontic arguments. This is laudable. Furthermore, almost all of the judges adopted a "coherentist" method: they drew on juridical practice, criminal law theory, and normative argumentation to inform their views. None adopted a "foundationalist" approach, attempting to root claims in a master theory. Most of the judges advanced sophisticated and nuanced accounts that neither ignore constraints nor adopt unsupported rigid conceptions. Deontic analysis not only highlights constraints, but also helps to avoid unnecessarily rigid conceptions (such as grafting an inappropriate "but for" standard into a mode of accessory liability). The goal is to fashion a criminal law that is both fair and workable. In Annex 4, I touch on a final possibility: the danger of potential "overcorrection" by advancing rigid conceptions of deontic principles that are unsupported by the available clues.

Annex 4 The Pendulum Swing? Possible Questions from the *Bemba* Appeal Judgment

At a few points in this book, I have suggested that there is an opposite danger to the usual problem of inadequate attentiveness to deontic principles. The opposite danger is to *overestimate* the principles – that is, to adopt excessively rigid conceptions that are not actually supported by careful deontic analysis.[1] In such cases, one undermines the social aims of the system for no normative reason.

Now that judges and scholars are more attentive to fundamental principles,[2] the danger of overcorrection is more present. In my view, there is arguably a tendency, observable in a few decisions at the ICC, for judges to announce new and stringent requirements,[3] based only on their impressions and without providing any authority for the claims. The absence of authority is somewhat understandable: the judges are simply expounding on what they perceive to be the obvious and incontrovertible implications of time-honoured principles of criminal law. However, the danger in these unadorned declarations is that one might, without realizing, be advancing idealized, exaggerated, or rarefied conceptions that are both contrary to past practice and normatively unsound.

Of course, judges do not always need precedent or authority for their pronouncements; sometimes, they must chart a path in new terrain, or even reject flawed past practice. But past practice is valuable at least as a touchstone, because it is a clue to conceptions of justice worked out by jurists over time with experience. It indicates some of the previously accepted reconciliations between the different components of a criminal justice system.[4] One could still argue for rejection of past practice, but ideally one does so with awareness that one is departing from practice, and one would show how the past practice was based on faulty arguments or otherwise

---

[1] In Chapter 8, I touched on one possible example of excessive caution: the move in early Tribunal jurisprudence to steer clear of criminal negligence. I argued that, although the caution was commendable, on a careful analysis that standard is deontically justified in the context of command responsibility.

[2] See §2.5 on the "deontic turn" in ICL.

[3] These can be definitional, evidentiary, or procedural requirements.

[4] See Chapter 4.

flawed. This is all the more important in legal argumentation, where one is supposed to be constrained by sources and methods that circumscribe the free rein of our own understandings.

It is possible to make the polar opposite error from that which I described in Chapter 2, which was single-issue reasoning that focuses only on victim protection and disregards all other considerations, such as deontic principles or rights of the accused. The diametric opposite of that reasoning is to focus only on protecting the accused, disregarding other considerations such as victim protection, procedural economy, and feasibility, and such reasoning is also problematically simplistic. Between those two extremes is a vast spectrum allowing for different plausible interpretations. Notice that I am not suggesting that expedience should defeat rights of the accused. I am saying that if one has an idea about deontic principles or procedural rights, and if that idea turns out to be unsupported in criminal justice practice, contradicted by normative arguments, and infeasible or devastating for procedural economy, then one's idea about the right or the principle might be wrong.

The coherentist method can guard against this by providing at least some common points of reference. The coherentist method considers patterns of past practice, the panoply of normative arguments, and countervailing considerations. The method requires at least some grounding for views and provides a frame of reference for a common conversation.

There are some aspects of the majority views of the *Bemba* Appeal Judgment that are, at least arguably, examples of "overcorrection." In the *Bemba* Appeal Judgment, a fractured Appeals Chamber, by a 3–2 majority, overturned the unanimous Trial Judgment and substituted an acquittal.[5] The majority judgment went in many directions that were unexpected for most Court-watchers, and its reasoning has met with intense criticism.[6] For example, Joseph Powderly notes, "the *Bemba* appeal judgement sits alongside *Gotovina* and *Perišić* as an appellate anomaly.

---

[5]   *Prosecutor v Jean-Pierre Bemba Gombo*, Judgment on the Appeal of Mr Jean-Pierre Bemba Gombo against Trial Chamber III's Judgment Pursuant to Article 74 of the Statute, ICC A.Ch, ICC-01/05–01/08 A, 8 June 2018 (*"Bemba* Appeal Judgment") is accompanied by three separate opinions: the Concurring Separate Opinion of Judge Eboe-Osuji ("Eboe-Osuji Opinion"), the Separate Opinion Judge Christine Van den Wyngaert and Judge Howard Morrison ("Van den Wyngaert and Morrison Opinion"), and the Dissenting Opinion of Judge Sanji Mmasenono Monageng and Judge Piotr Hofmański ("Monageng and Hofmański Opinion").

[6]   L N Sadat, "Fiddling While Rome Burns? The Appeals Chamber's Curious Decision in *Prosecutor v Jean-Pierre Bemba Gombo*" (12 June 2018) EJIL Talk (blog); D M Amann, "In *Bemba* and beyond, Crimes Adjudged to Commit Themselves" (13 June 2018) EJIL Talk (blog); M Jackson, "Commanders' Motivations in *Bemba*" (15 June 2018) EJIL Talk (blog); S SáCouto, "The Impact of the Appeals Chamber Decision in *Bemba*: Impunity for Sexual and Gender-Based Crimes?" (22 June 2018) IJ Monitor (blog); J Trahan, "Bemba Acquittal Rests on an Erroneous Application of Appellate Review Standard" (25 June 2018) Opinio Juris (blog); J Powderly & N Hayes, "The *Bemba* Appeal: A Fragmented Appeals Chamber Destabilises the Law and Practice of the ICC" (26 June 2018) Human Rights Doctorate (blog); A Whiting, "Appeal Judges Turn the ICC on Its Head with *Bemba* Decision" (14 June 2008) Just Security (blog); F F Taffo, "Analysis of Jean-Pierre Bemba's Acquittal by

The judgment aberrates from established jurisprudence, policy, and principle on a host of issues."[7]

I will not attempt any conclusive analyses here; instead, I am merely highlighting some possible examples of "overcorrection," and flagging important questions for future study.

A4.1 STANDARD OF REVIEW

One of the biggest surprises was that the Appeal Chamber majority announced a new standard of appellate review. As Joseph Powderly notes, "[f]ew would have predicted that the Chamber would depart from the well-established standard of appellate review for factual errors ... This deviation from precedent is not accompanied by supporting reasoning; it is entirely declarative."[8]

This particular controversy relates to procedure, rather than my current topic of substantive principles, but it warrants brief mention as a potential example of the "pendulum swing" (see §2.5). The previous approach in ICL was that appellate chambers correct errors of law, including errors about assessment of evidence or the standard of proof, but otherwise show significant deference to factual findings of trial chambers.[9] In *Bemba*, the majority announced a new standard to set aside factual findings – namely, "when a reasonable and objective person can articulate serious doubts about the accuracy of a given finding, and is able to support this view with specific arguments."[10] This standard has been met with a wave of concerns and criticisms: that the majority offered no legal authority or precedent for this new standard; that it goes against long-established practice and precedent; that it confuses the burden of proof with the burden of substantiating arguments on appeal; that it contradicts other parts of the ICC Statute; that it eliminates deference to findings of trial judges who sat through the presentation of the evidence and are, in principle, better placed to assess it;[11] that it is unworkable (it would at least require a *de novo*

---

the International Criminal Court" (13 December 2018) Conflict Trends (blog); J C Powderly, "Introductory Note to *Prosecutor v Jean-Pierre Bemba Gombo*" (2018) 57 Int'l Legal Materials 1031; S SáCouto & P Viseur Sellers, "The *Bemba* Appeals Chamber Judgment: Impunity for Sexual and Gender-Based Crimes" (2019) 27 Wm & Mary Bill Rts J 599.

7   Powderly, *supra* note 6, at 1031.
8   *Ibid* at 1032.
9   The traditional standard for interfering with a finding of fact is that no reasonable Trial Chamber could make that finding on the evidence.
10 *Bemba* Appeal Judgment, *supra* note 5, at paras 3 and 45–46. The majority also considered that factual findings must be "unassailable."
11 On this issue in particular, the dissenting judges convincingly argue that the proposed standard contradicts Art 83(2) of the ICC Statute, which requires a finding that the error "materially affected" the decision. In addition, they argue that the new standard does not cohere with Art 74(3) of the Statute, which allows trial decisions by majority. Where a judge dissents at trial, presumably this new standard (a reasonable person can articulate some doubts about findings and back it up with reasons) is *ipso facto* satisfied. Thus the fact that the Statute (and indeed transnational practice) allows dissents

review of the evidence to be properly applied); and that it disregards various other considerations such as predictability, finality, and institutional roles.[12]

The majority had commendable intentions: it perceived this standard as an obvious and basic corollary of the rights of the accused. And, indeed, the standard is the *ne plus ultra* for protection of rights. However, the majority did not suggest any authority or even human rights jurisprudence supporting its new approach. The rights of the accused have traditionally been considered to be adequately protected in a system that entrusts trial judges to oversee the trial and reach a verdict, with appellate supervision to carry out an error-correction function. While the goal was laudable, the absence of supporting authority or practice, the contrary weight of practice, and the absence of careful normative argumentation, as well as the numerous noted problems and inconsistencies with other features of the Statute,[13] all raise grave doubts about whether the majority's purported deductive reasoning was correct. Consulting common points of reference offers a helpful test of our beliefs about rights and principles. Doing so at least helps us to see how extraordinary our claims might be and what the corresponding burden of justification for our proposed new conception might be.

A4.2 FAILURE TO TAKE MEASURES

The *Bemba* Appeal Judgment hinged on the interpretation of the "failure to take measures" element, which is an important element of command responsibility, although it is not one of the specific issues in my case study in this book. I can commend all of the Appeals Chamber judges for approaching the provision with empathy for potential accused persons.[14] For example, the majority judgment notes that we cannot expect a person to take every possible measure, that we have to

means that the proposed new standard cannot be correct, because otherwise there would be a contradiction or incoherence. Monageng and Hofmański Opinion, *supra* note 5, at paras 11–15.

Given the complex and controverted nature of most or all ICL cases, it will almost always be the case that reasonable observers can at least "articulate some doubts" about some of the findings. For example, an observer could reasonably consider that certain witnesses were more or less credible than the trial judges thought. Accordingly, this test will almost always be met in complex cases, requiring acquittals in most ICL cases; this is another clue that the new standard may be anomalous and unsound. The previous standard allowed deference to trial judge findings of fact unless an identified error (e.g. in assessing evidence) was shown.

[12] See, e.g., Monageng and Hofmański Opinion, *supra* note 5, at paras 2–18; Sadat, *supra* note 6; Trahan, *supra* note 6; Powderly & Hayes, *supra* note 6; Whiting, *supra* note 6; SáCouto & Sellers, *supra* note 6.

In the view of the dissent, the majority used this new standard to enter its own findings of fact, after assessing a very limited part of the evidence, and without considering the totality of findings, reasoning, and evidence relied upon by the Trial Chamber. It accepted evidence that was contradicted by the rest of the evidentiary record and rejected by the Trial Chamber, and it did not follow the usual approach of attempting to apply corrected standards to the available evidence. See, e.g., Monageng and Hofmański Opinion, *supra* note 5, at paras 45–47, 54–55.

[13] On inconsistencies with the Statute, see *ibid* at paras 11–15.

[14] In Chapter 3, I spoke of the importance of empathy in deontic analysis.

consider what is possible at that time, that we should not assess measures taken with the benefit of superior information gained in hindsight, and that the provision should not create strict liability.[15] I heartily agree. Their reasoning avoided a "deterrence-focused" perspective and rightly considers the limits of what criminal law can properly require.

It is, however, at least arguable that the majority may have swung too far in declaring what cannot be expected of a person. Scholars have noted various problems and have highlighted the lack of authority offered by the majority for its new limitations.[16] On a closer study, precedential, teleological, and deontic considerations may all converge in less indulgent standards. To give a particularly striking illustration, one major concern raised by commentators is that, on the evidentiary record, Mr Bemba took *no measures* at all in relation to widespread rapes.[17] Thus, even if we assume (contrary to the Trial Chamber findings) that Mr Bemba's measures in relation to pillaging and killing were adequate, there still remains a clear failure to respond to sexual violence, which were the overwhelming majority of reported crimes.[18] The majority apparently did not differentiate and thus did not notice this gap. It is hard to see how taking *no measures at all* in relation to *most* of the crimes could, in any sense, qualify as taking "all necessary and reasonable measures."

A4.3 REMOTE COMMANDERS

Another controversy in the literature concerns the more indulgent standards suggested for "remote commanders."[19] Passages in the majority judgment about

---

[15] *Bemba* Appeal Judgment, *supra* note 5, at paras 169–70.
[16] Scholars have noted that the majority's assertion that commanders are allowed to make a cost–benefit analysis, taking into account impact on operational effectiveness, also needs some qualifications in light of the duty to safeguard civilians. See, e.g., T Weigend, "Mr Bemba's Acquittal: A Shortcut to Justice?" (25 June 2019) James G Stewart (blog); Powderly & Hayes, *supra* note 6. For several other aspects, see Sácouto & Sellers, *supra* note 6; Sadat, *supra* note 6.
　The most prominent concerns relate to the analysis of commanders' motivations. The majority held that the Trial Judgment erred by focusing on Bemba's motivations rather than his measures, claiming that the Trial Judgment was "preoccupied" with motives and took an "unreasonably strict approach." *Bemba* Appeal Judgment, *supra* note 5, at paras 176–79. The majority is correct to point out that a commander may have self-serving motives to preserve her reputation or that of her forces, and yet still comply sufficiently with her duties of prevention and punishment. This proposition is not disputed by the dissent, nor in the academic reactions to the decision. The problem however, as pointed out by the dissent and by even the kindest commentators, is that the Trial Judgment does not appear to actually make the reasoning errors that the majority believes that it did. Instead, the Trial Judgment analysis explains that the measures were, in fact, inadequate and then refers to the corroborated evidence of Mr Bemba's motives in explaining why he chose measures that were plainly inadequate: *Prosecutor v Jean-Pierre Bemba Gombo*, Judgment Pursuant to Article 74 of the Statute, ICC T.Ch, ICC-01/05-01/08, 21 March 2016, at paras 719–34 and 728. See Monageng and Hofmański Opinion, *supra* note 5, at paras 70–78; Jackson, *supra* note 6; Weigend, *supra* note 16.
[17] Sácouto & Sellers, *supra* note 6.
[18] *Ibid.*
[19] *Bemba* Appeal Judgment, *supra* note 5, at paras 171–73 and again at 189 and 192.

"remote commanders" gave rise to discussion among commentators about whether this is a new (and unsubstantiated) legal test or only a factual consideration. The more generous view is that it is merely a factual consideration.[20]

However, even as a purely factual consideration, the lowered expectations for "remote commanders" may warrant further reflection before they are entirely embraced. At first glance, it seems entirely right that we must expect less of a remote commander, because it is more difficult for them to get information and to exercise control. However, if a person *chooses* to assemble and launch an armed group into another country, in proximity to civilian populations, can the person then excuse him- or herself on the grounds that the force is now in another country and difficult to control? This brings us back to the deontic roots of command responsibility: a special burden to maintain close control of such an exceptionally dangerous enterprise, and the principle that one cannot create the conditions of one's own excuse.

I suspect that the majority is correct that allowance must be made, but, in determining the scope of the allowance, we have to consider the special duties of military command and the deontically justified expectations held of commanders (in addition, of course, to consequentialist considerations). An examination of military practice might show that it is in fact feasible and expected to maintain considerable control and reporting in relation to remote forces. I expect that the various legitimate considerations can be reconciled in an account that draws on legal precedent, military practice, consequentialist considerations, and the deontic rationale for the responsibility of commanders to safeguard civilians from the forces they train, equip, and oversee.[21]

A4.4 KNOWLEDGE OF "VIRTUALLY CERTAIN" GUILT

Some passages of the Van den Wyngaert and Morrison opinion may fall into the pitfall of what I have elsewhere called "specificationism."[22] This is the idea that criminal charges have to lay out the minutest details of each allegation with intricate specificity.[23] The motivation for this thinking is laudable: it is a desire to uphold the highest standards for rights of the accused. At times, however, this thirst for specificity has been applied by ICC judges with an enthusiasm that goes beyond any other legal system, which is not supported by legal sources, nor by human rights

---

[20] The Eboe-Osuji Opinion, *supra* note 5, at para 258 suggests as much. See also M Jackson, "Geographic Remoteness in *Bemba*" (30 July 2018) EJIL Talk (blog).

[21] See Chapter 8.

[22] D Robinson, "The Other Poisoned Chalice: Unprecedented Evidentiary Standards in the *Gbagbo* Case? (Part 2)" (6 November 2019) EJIL Talk (blog).

[23] See also the many concerns and criticisms about the majority's expected level of detail for charges, as well as restrictions on the ability to respond to new evidence, so that cases can only degrade and cannot be shored up: Sadat, *supra* note 6; Powderly & Hayes, *supra* note 6; Whiting, *supra* note 6.

jurisprudence, and which raises a host of problems for procedural economy and even elementary feasibility.[24]

A potential example of "specificationism" is the suggestion in the Van den Wyngaert and Morrison opinion about how specific information must be for the commander to have "knowledge" of subordinate crimes. They suggest that the commander must know the identity of soldiers or units about to commit crimes[25] and that the information must be proven to have rendered the commander *"virtually certain* of the guilt of his subordinates."[26] They declare that "awareness of allegations, even if substantiated with prima facie credible evidence" is insufficient.[27] Judge Eboe-Osuji did not embrace this passage, and thus it does not form part of the majority opinion.

There are reasons to doubt such a restrictive conception, and further analysis is likely warranted. It is not supported by precedents. Nor is it supported by teleological analysis. Indeed, even the Van den Wygaert and Morrison opinion starts by noting that, "[f]rom a policy point of view, it should suffice that he or she is aware that there are 'reasonable grounds to believe' that subordinates committed crimes."[28] They advance their narrower *"virtual certainty"* interpretation because of a belief that principles require it. But I think, on closer inspection, that it is not required by deontic principles. The opinion arrives at this standard by transplanting the "virtual certainty" test for indirect intent, but that is a test for *intent*, not awareness.[29] I think a more careful study of different approaches to knowledge will show that more practical and less implausibly rigid formulations are quite viable. The reasoning was well intentioned and was advanced in the name of rigour, but the tools of deontic criminal law theory are more sophisticated than some of these initial judicial forays assume.

A4.5 ADVANCE SPECIFICATION OF "KNEW" OR "SHOULD HAVE KNOWN"

Another example of "specificationism" is the argument advanced in the Van den Wyngaert and Morrison opinion that the charges must specify in advance which of two alternatives is alleged: that the commander knew, or that the commander should have known.[30] The dissent disagreed with this proposition, because it makes no

---

[24]   For a very initial discussion, see Robinson, *supra* note 22; Sadat, *supra* note 6; Powderly & Hayes, *supra* note 6; Whiting, *supra* note 6.

[25]   Van den Wyngaert and Morrison Opinion, *supra* note 5, at para 45.

[26]   *Ibid* at para 46 (emphasis added).

[27]   *Ibid.*

[28]   *Ibid.*

[29]   *Ibid.* For discussion of the virtual certainty test in ICC jurisprudence, see D Piragoff & D Robinson, "Article 30," in K Ambos, ed, *Commentary on the Rome Statute of the International Criminal Court: Observers' Notes, Article by Article*, 4th ed (Beck, 2020).

[30]   Van den Wyngaert and Morrison Opinion, *supra* note 5, at para 38.

difference to liability and because, in many fact situations, the two will be difficult to distinguish anyway.[31] The Van den Wyngaert and Morrison opinion argues that the two alternatives lead to different expectations: In a "knowledge" case, we look at what measures are expected of someone with that knowledge; in a "should have known" case, the commander will obviously not take any measures.[32] They argue that "no one would expect a doctor to prescribe a treatment before he or she has made a diagnosis of the disease."[33]

The argument is initially plausible, but it is problematic for multiple reasons. First, the point of command responsibility is that we often cannot know from the outside whether the commander knew or ought to have known, but the point is that either way she bears responsibility. Importantly, I am not making a 1990s-style "it's too difficult to prove, so let's not require proof" argument. On the contrary, I have developed in detail the deontic justification for the equivalent blameworthiness of "should have known" in command responsibility (see Chapter 8). The special insight of command responsibility is that either failure – whether the commander (i) knew and nonetheless failed to act, or (ii) showed criminally culpable disregard in failing even to meet the duty to *try* to acquire the information – creates sufficiently equal culpability. The very point of command responsibility is that it does not require proof of inner workings, and the doctrine is supported not only precedentially and teleologically, but also deontically.

Second, it is not true that the two alternatives affect what the prosecution must prove under other elements.[34] Either way, the prosecution must prove all of the other elements, including a failure to take adequate measures in response. Under either alternative, the failure to be proven is a failure compared to what would be expected of a commander with *knowledge* in those circumstances. Of course, the commander who does not have actual knowledge, because of her criminally negligent indifference, will not have that specific opportunity to take concrete actions. But she *chose* to deprive herself of that opportunity when she criminally departed from her duty to try to stay informed and thereby showed culpable indifference to the exact class of risks that materialized.[35] Turning to the doctor metaphor, if a doctor negligently fails to treat the patient, then it does not matter if that doctor (i) knew of the disease and did not care, or (ii) was criminally negligent in failing even to try to find out. Either way, it is criminally culpable, and the doctor can be convicted even if we are not certain which of the two scenarios was the case.[36]

---

[31] Monageng and Hofmański Opinion, *supra* note 5, at paras 264–66.
[32] Van den Wyngaert and Morrison Opinion, *supra* note 5, at paras 38–41.
[33] *Ibid* at para 38.
[34] *Ibid* at para 39.
[35] See Chapter 8.
[36] Or, if I drive into a market and hit people, and if it is unclear whether I was wearing a blindfold, the case does not fail if the prosecution cannot specify whether I could actually see the people I hit (knowledge) or not (culpable indifference encompassing the harm); there is no difference in my culpability. See Chapter 8.

Third, the proposed requirement cites no authority and, in fact, is contrary to all past practice. This is another clue about possible error in a normative assessment, and it is an even bigger problem for a legal argument.[37]

Fourth, when stipulating requirements, another clue to consider is absurd consequences. For example, if the prosecutor charges "should have known," and testimony at trial convincingly shows that the commander actually *knew* of the crimes and laughed about them, then, based on the proposed standard, the commander would be *acquitted*. The charge was "should have known," not "knew," and, based on the proposed standard, an amendment is not permissible.[38] That outcome is contradicted by doctrinal, teleological, and deontic considerations.[39] While the proposal for this level of specificity was made in the best of faith, all of these considerations converge in suggesting that the proposal – which was advanced without any legal support – may overestimate the relevant rights or fundamental principle.

A4.6 CONCLUSION

Each of these examples warrants more careful analysis and scrutiny. There is reason to believe that they are examples of "overcorrection": the adoption of excessively rigid conceptions that would not actually be supported by careful principled analysis.The Van den Wyngaert and Morrison opinion suggests that the difference between the majority and the dissent may be that "we attach more importance to the strict application of the burden and standard of proof. We also seem to put more emphasis on compliance with due process norms that are essential to protecting the rights of the accused in an adversarial trial setting."[40] This is an uncharitable understanding of the dissent position. The dissenting opinion is meticulously reasoned, shows great care for rights and deontic principles, and anchors its positions in legal practice and other established points of reference. The dissent argument is not that rights and principles do not matter, but rather that the majority has adopted unsupported and unsound conceptions. The dissent draws on considerable authority and argumentation to support these arguments.[41] The real dispute is about the best *understandings* of rights and principles. But the exchange reveals one of the

---

[37] Legally, judicial propositions should be consistent with past authority, and where there is a deviation, the judge should at least provide argumentation for the deviation.

[38] Van den Wyngaert and Morrison Opinion, *supra* note 5, at paras 40–41.

[39] Another clue is that it will often be impossible for the prosecution to specify "knew" or "should have known," given the contradictory legal standards from the ICC judges on what those tests mean. For example, even if the prosecutor knew exactly what knowledge the accused had – say, she knew of a very high probability of pending crimes – the prosecutor would still have to make alternative charges based on what legal interpretation the judges might later adopt. So the charge would say " 'should have known' if the standards of van den Wyngaert and Morrison prevail, and 'knew' if the standards of the other judges prevail." The complexity of this consequence is untenable.

[40] Van den Wyngaert and Morrison Opinion, *supra* note 5, at para 4.

[41] Monageng and Hofmański Opinion, *supra* note 5.

challenges for these types of conversation: those arguing for narrower conceptions can easily perceive others' disagreements as reflecting a lack of concern for rights and principles.

The topics of rights and fundamental principles can evoke passion, and those defending rights and principles can justifiably claim a high ground, but there must be a method to argue against idealized, romanticized, exaggerated, ungrounded, and excessively formalistic conceptions. A coherentist method can help us not only to uphold important deontic principles, but also to debate their limits. Criminal law is not a thought experiment taking place in a laboratory of the mind; it is a social practice that is supposed to work in earthly conditions, and thus an appropriate part of any analysis is to think about whether and how it would *work*. Reasoning about constructs of criminal law not only is analytical and cerebral, but also must be informed by practicality, humanity, and heart.

Glossary of Selected Terms

The following are a handful of the terms used in the book of which explanation may be helpful.

analytical Concerned with concepts and how they fit together.

anti-Cartesian Rejecting insistence on a guarantee of "certainty."

articulation of a fundamental principle A possible understanding about what a fundamental principle entails, for example that the legality principle requires written prohibitions or that the culpability principle requires a contribution to a crime.

casuistic Reasoning that reflects on concrete factual situations, including hypotheticals, to test ideas.

coherentism A method for justifying beliefs that does not require propositions to be grounded in an ultimate foundation of certainty; instead, one forms beliefs by reconciling all available clues to the best extent possible.

core crimes Genocide, crimes against humanity, and war crimes, and – unless the context requires otherwise – the relatively new crime of aggression.

deontic Pertaining to duties owed to others. In criminal law, a type of reasoning focused on principled constraints reflecting our commitment to the individual. As I argue, deontic principles may be rooted in deontological ethical theories or other ethical theories.

deontic principles Principles reflecting deontic constraints of criminal justice. For purposes of this book, these are the culpability principle, the legality principle, and (most likely) the fair labelling principle.

deontological Normative reasoning focused on rightness or wrongness in light of duties and obligations. It contrasts with, for example, consequentialist reasoning, which focuses on maximizing specified desiderata.

doctrinal I use this term as used in common law scholarship: It refers to the use of standard tools of legal reasoning, and it often implies a surface-level analysis rather than a deep conceptual or philosophical systematization. The connotation is, unfortunately, almost the opposite in some other traditions, where it refers to scholarly efforts to systematize the law.

doctrine A rule recognized in a legal system.

fallibilistic An approach that acknowledges the possibility of error. Instead of seeking guarantees of certainty, it seeks to do the best possible to detect and correct error.

foundationalism A method of justifying beliefs that requires each proposition to be supported by more basic propositions, ultimately rooted in foundations that are self-evident or accepted as axioms.

fundamental principles For the purposes of this book (which focuses primarily on deontic principles), this term is synonymous with deontic principles.

international criminal law (ICL) For the purposes of this book, the law for the investigation and prosecution of persons responsible for genocide, crimes against humanity, war crimes, and aggression, along with attendant principles such as modes of liability and defences.

liberal In this this book, I use the term "liberal" in a minimalist sense, meaning that the system is attentive to deontic constraints.

mid-level principle A principle arguably embodied within a body of practice, offering a best explanation for that practice. It should generally analytically fit and be normatively convincing; it can be used to explain, systematize, and critique practice.

naturalist fallacy The leap from an "is" to an "ought" – that is, the assumption that because things *are* a certain way, they *ought* to be that way.

naturalistic conception of causation An approach to causation that focuses only on sufficient causes of an outcome and hence holds that omissions cannot be causes.

normative Concerned with right or wrong, good or bad.

normative conception of causation An approach to causation that includes the differences that omissions make, by comparing outcomes to what people are legally required to do. For example, if I have a duty to drive off someone's foot, but refuse to do so, then my omission "causes" the person to remain trapped.

teleological Reasoning in light of the aims of a provision.

vicarious Holding a person liable for the acts of another, by virtue of their relationship, without considering objective and subjective culpability.

Bibliography

Akerson D & Knowlton N, "President Obama and the International Criminal Law of Successor Liability" (2009) 37 *Denver J Intl L & Pol'y* 615.

Aksenova M, van Sliedregt E & Parmentier S, eds, *Breaking the Cycle of Mass Atrocities: Criminological and Socio-legal Approaches in International Criminal Law* (Hart, 2019).

Alexander L & Kessler Ferzan K, *Crime and Culpability: A Theory of Criminal Law* (Cambridge University Press, 2011).

Alexy R & Peczenik A, "The Concept of Coherence and Its Significance for Discursive Rationality" (1990) 3 *Ratio Iuris* 130.

Amann D M, "In *Bemba* and beyond, Crimes Adjudged to Commit Themselves" (13 June 2018), online: www.ejiltalk.org/in-bemba-and-beyond-crimes-adjudged-to-commit-themselves/.

Amaya A, *The Tapestry of Reason: An Inquiry into the Nature of Coherence and Its Role in Legal Argument* (Hart, 2015).

Ambos K, *Der Allgemeine Teil des Völkerstrafrechts* (Duncker & Humblot, 2002).

Ambos K, "Superior Responsibility," in A Cassese, P Gaeta & J R W D Jones, eds, *The Rome Statute of the International Criminal Court: A Commentary, Vol 2* (Oxford University Press, 2002).

Ambos K, "Remarks on the General Part of International Criminal Law" (2006) 4 *JICJ* 660.

Ambos K, "Joint Criminal Enterprise and Command Responsibility" (2007) 5 *JICJ* 159.

Ambos K, "Article 25," in O Triffterer, ed, *Commentary on the Rome Statute of the International Criminal Court: Observers' Notes, Article by Article*, 2nd ed (Beck, 2008).

Ambos K, "Critical Issues in the *Bemba* Confirmation Decision" (2009) 22 *LJIL* 715.

Ambos K, "Toward a Universal System of Crime: Comments on George Fletcher's *Grammar of Criminal Law*" (2010) 28 *Cardozo L Rev* 2647.

Ambos K, *Treatise on International Criminal Law, Vol I: Foundations and General Part* (Oxford University Press, 2012).

Ambos K, "Punishment without a Sovereign? The *Ius Puniendi* Issue of International Criminal Law: A First Contribution towards a Consistent Theory of International Criminal Law" (2013) 33 *Oxf J L Stud* 293.

Ambos K, "The ICC and Common Purpose: What Contribution Is Required?," in C Stahn, ed, *The Law and Practice of the ICC: A Critical Account of Challenges and Achievements* (Oxford University Press, 2015).

Ambos K, "Article 25," in O Triffterer & K Ambos, eds, *The Rome Statute of the International Criminal Court: A Commentary*, 3rd ed (Beck, Hart, Nomos, 2016).

Ambos K, "Complicity in War Crimes through (Legal) Arms Supplies?" (20 January 2020), online: www.ejiltalk.org/complicity-in-war-crimes-through-legal-arms-supplies/.

Ambos K & Steiner C, "On the Rationale of Punishment at the Domestic and International Level," in M Henzelin & R Roth, eds, *Le Droit Pénale à l'Éprouve de l'Internationalisation* (LGDJ, 2002).

American Law Institute, *Model Penal Code: Official Draft and Explanatory Notes – Complete Text of Model Penal Code as Adopted at the 1962 Annual Meeting of the American Law Institute at Washington* (ALI, 1985).

Anonymous, "The New Rule of Lenity" (2006) 119 *Harvard L Rev* 2420.

Appiah K, *Cosmopolitanism: Ethics in a World of Strangers* (W W Norton & Co, 2006).

Archibugi D, "Immanuel Kant, Cosmopolitan Law and Peace" (1995) 1 *Eur J Int'l Rel* 429.

Archibugi D, Held D & Köhler M, *Re-imagining Political Community: Studies in Cosmopolitan Democracy* (Stanford University Press, 1998).

Aristotle, *Politics* (Clarendon Press, 1910).

Arnold R, "Command Responsibility: A Case Study of Alleged Violations of the Laws of War at Khiam Detention Centre" (2002) 7 *J Conflict & Sec L* 191.

Arnold R & Triffterer O, "Article 28: Responsibility of Commanders and Other Superiors," in O Triffterer, ed, *Commentary on the Rome Statute of the International Criminal Court: Observers' Notes, Article by Article*, 2nd ed (Beck, 2008).

Ashworth A, "The Elasticity of Mens Rea," in C F H Tapper, ed, *Crime, Proof and Punishment: Essays in Memory of Sir Rupert Cross* (Butterworths, 1981).

Ashworth A, *Principles of Criminal Law*, 5th ed (Oxford University Press, 2006).

Ashworth A & Horder J, *Principles of Criminal Law*, 7th ed (Oxford University Press, 2013).

Aukerman M J, "Extraordinary Evil, Extraordinary Crime: A Framework for Understanding Transitional Justice" (2002) 15 *Harvard HRJ* 39.

Badar M E, "Just Convict Everyone! Joint Perpetration from *Tadić* to *Stakić* and Back Again" (2006) 6 *Int'l Crim L Rev* 293.

Badar M E, *The Concept of Mens Rea in International Criminal Law: The Case for a Unified Approach* (Hart, 2013).

Badinter R, "International Criminal Justice: From Darkness to Light," in A Cassese, P Gaeta & J R W D Jones, eds, *The Rome Statute of the International Criminal Court: A Commentary* (Oxford University Press, 2002).

Bandura A, *Moral Disengagement: How People Do Harm and Live with Themselves* (Worth, 2016).

Bantekas I, "The Contemporary Law of Superior Responsibility" (1999) 93 *AJIL* 573.

Bantekas I, "On Stretching the Boundaries of Responsible Command" (2009) 7 *JICJ* 1197.

Bantekas I, "Legal Anthropology and the Construction of Complex Liabilities," in C Jalloh, ed, *The Sierra Leone Special Court and Its Legacy: The Impact for Africa and International Criminal Law* (Cambridge University Press, 2014).

Bassiouni M C, "The Normative Framework of International Humanitarian Law: Overlaps, Gaps and Ambiguities" (1998) 8 *Transnat'l L & Contemp Probs* 199.

Bassiouni M C, *The Shari'a and Islamic Criminal Justice in Time of War and Peace* (Oxford University Press, 2013).

Bayles M, "Mid-level Principles and Justification," in J R Pennock & J W Chapman, eds, *Justification* (New York University Press, 1986).

Bayles M, "Moral Theory and Application," in J Howie, ed, *Ethical Principles and Practice* (Southern Illinois University Press, 1987).

Beauchamp T & Childress J, *Principles of Biomedical Ethics*, 7th ed (Oxford University Press, 2012).

Bederman D J, "The Pirate Code" (2008) 22 *Emory Int'l L Rev* 707.

Beitz C R, *Political Theory and International Relations* (Princeton University Press, 1999).

Beitz C R, "Social and Cosmopolitan Liberalism" (1999) 75 *International Affairs* 515.

Benhabib S, *Another Cosmopolitanism* (Oxford University Press, 2006).

Bergsmo M, Buis E J & Bergsmo N H, "Setting a Discourse Space: Correlational Analysis, Foundational Concepts, and Legally Protected Interests in International Criminal Law," in M Bergsmo & E J Buis, eds, *Philosophical Foundations of International Criminal Law: Correlating Thinkers* (Torkel Opshal Academic, 2018).

Berman P S, *Global Legal Pluralism: A Jurisprudence of Law beyond Borders* (Cambridge University Press, 2012).

Blake W, "Auguries of Innocence," in D H S Nicholson & A H E Lee, eds, *The Oxford Book of English Mystical Verse* (Clarendon Press, 1917).

Bock S & Stark F, "Preparatory Offences," in K Ambos et al, eds, *Core Concepts in Criminal Law and Criminal Justice, Vol I* (Cambridge University Press, 2019).

Bohlander M, "Commentary," in A Klip & G Sluiter, eds, *The International Criminal Tribunal for the former Yugoslavia 2000–2001* (Intersentia, 2003).

Bohman J & Lutz-Bachmann M, eds, *Perpetual Peace: Essays on Kant's Cosmopolitan Ideal* (MIT Press, 1997).

Boister N & Cryer R, eds, *Documents on the Tokyo International Military Tribunal; Charter, Indictment and Judgments* (Oxford University Press, 2008).

BonJour L, "The Coherence Theory of Empirical Knowledge" (1976) 30 *Philosophical Studies* 281.

BonJour L, *The Structure of Empirical Knowledge* (Cambridge University Press, 1985).

Boot M, *Genocide, Crimes against Humanity and War Crimes: Nullum Crimen Sine Lege and the Subject Matter Jurisdiction of the International Criminal Court* (Intersentia, 2002).

Bourdieu P, "Participant Objectivation" (2003) 9 *Journal of the Royal Anthropology Institute* 281.

Brody B, "Quality of Scholarship in Bioethics" (1990) 15 *Journal of Medicine and Philosophy* 161.

Brooks R E, "Law in the Heart of Darkness: Atrocity and Duress" (2003) 43 *Virginia J Int'l L* 861.

Broomhall B, "Article 22, Nullum Crimen Sine Lege," in O Triffterer, ed, *Commentary on the Rome Statute of the International Criminal Court: Observers' Notes, Article by Article*, 2nd ed (Beck, 2008).

Brown D E, *Human Universals* (McGraw-Hill, 1991).

Brudner A, *Punishment and Freedom: A Liberal Theory of Penal Justice* (Oxford University Press, 2009).

Caldwell E, "Social Change and Written Law in Early Chinese Legal Thought" (2014) 32 *LHR* 1.

Calnan A, "Beyond Jurisprudence" (2017) 27 *S Cal Interdisc LJ* 1.

Capps P & Olsen H P, eds, *Legal Authority beyond the State* (Cambridge University Press, 2018).

Cassese A, "Current Trends towards Criminal Prosecution," in N Passas, ed, *International Crimes* (Ashgate/Dartmouth, 2003).

Cassese A, *International Criminal Law* (Oxford University Press, 2003).

Cassese A, "The Proper Limits of Individual Responsibility under the Doctrine of Joint Criminal Enterprise" (2007) 5 *JICJ* 109.

Cassese A, *International Criminal Law*, 2nd ed (Oxford University Press, 2008).

Cassese A, Gaeta P & Jones J, eds, *The Rome Statute of the International Criminal Court: A Commentary, Vol 2* (Oxford University Press, 2002).

Cavanagh E, "A Company with Sovereignty and Subjects of Its Own? The Case of the Hudson's Bay Company, 1670-1763" (2011) 26 *Can J L & Soc* 25.

Chiao V, "What Is the Criminal Law for?" (2016) 35 *L & Phil* 137.

Ching A, "Evolution of the Command Responsibility Doctrine in Light of the *Čelebići* Decision of the International Criminal Tribunal for the former Yugoslavia" (1999–2000) 25 *NC J Intl & Com Reg* 167.

Choi T H & Kim S, "Nationalized International Criminal Law: Genocidal Intent, Command Responsibility, and an Overview of the South Korean Implementing Legislation of the ICC Statute" (2011) 19 *Michigan State J Int'l L* 589.

Chouliaras A, "Bridging the Gap between Criminological Theory and Penal Theory within the International Criminal Justice System" (2014) 22 *Eur J Crime Cr L Cr J* 249.

Christie H, "The Poisoned Chalice: Imperial Justice, Moral Relativism, and the Origins of International Criminal Law" (2010) 72 *U Pittsburgh L Rev* 361.

Churchland P S, *Braintrust: What Neuroscience Tells Us about Morality* (Princeton University Press, 2011).

Cogan J K, "The Regulatory Turn in International Law" (2011) 52 *Harvard Int'l LJ* 322.

Coleman J, *The Practice of Principle: In Defence of a Pragmatist Approach to Legal Theory* (Oxford University Press, 2003).

Cryer R, "International Criminal Law vs State Sovereignty: Another Round?" (2005) 16 *EJIL* 979.

Cryer R, *Prosecuting International Crimes* (Cambridge: Cambridge University Press, 2005).

Cryer R, "Superior Orders and the International Criminal Court," in R Burchill, N White & J Morris, eds, *International Conflict and Security Law: Essays in Memory of Hilaire McCoubrey* (Cambridge University Press, 2005).

Cryer R, "The Ad Hoc Tribunals and the Law of Command Responsibility: A Quiet Earthquake," in S Darcy & J Powderly, eds, *Judicial Creativity at the International Criminal Tribunals* (Oxford University Press, 2010).

Cupido M, *Facts Matter: A Study into the Casuistry of Substantive International Criminal Law* (Eleven International, 2015).

Damaška M, "The Shadow Side of Command Responsibility" (2001) 49 *Am J Comp L* 455.

Dana S, "Beyond Retroactivity to Realizing Justice: A Theory on the Principle of Legality in International Criminal Law Sentencing" (2009) 99 *JCLC* 857.

Dan-Cohen M, "Responsibility and the Boundaries of the Self" (1992) 105 *Harvard L Rev* 959.

Daniels N, "Wide Reflective Equilibrium and Theory Acceptance in Ethics" (1979) 76 *J Phil* 256.

Danner A M, "When Courts Make Law: How the International Criminal Tribunals Recast the Laws of War" (2006) 59 *Vanderbilt L Rev* 1.

Danner A M & Martinez J S, "Guilty Associations: Joint Criminal Enterprise, Command Responsibility and the Development of International Criminal Law" (2005) 93 *Calif L Rev* 75.

Darcy S, "Imputed Criminal Liability and the Goals of International Justice" (2007) 20 *LJIL* 377.

Davidson C, "How to Read International Criminal Law: Strict Construction and the Rome Statute of the International Criminal Court" (2017) 91 *St John's L Rev* 37.

Davidson E, "Economic Oppression as an International Wrong and a Crime against Humanity" (2005) 23 *Neth Q Hum Rights* 173.

de Magt S, "Reflective Equilibrium and Moral Objective" (2017) 60 *Inquiry* 443.

DePaul M, "Two Conceptions of Coherence Methods in Ethics" (1987) 96 *Mind* 463.

DePaul M, "The Problem of the Criterion and Coherence Methods in Ethics" (1988) 18 *Canadian J Phil* 67.

DePaul M, *Balance and Refinement: Beyond Coherence Methods of Moral Inquiry* (Routledge, 1993).

Dewey J, *The Quest for Certainty: A Study of the Relation of Knowledge and Action* (Putnam, 1929).

Diaz P C, "The ICC in Northern Uganda: Peace First, Justice Later" (2005) 2 *Eyes on the ICC* 17.

Dickstein M, ed, *The Revival of Pragmatism: New Essays on Social Thought, Law, and Culture* (Duke University Press, 1998).

Diekmann S, "Moral Mid-level Principles in Modeling" (2013) 226 *Eur J Oper Res* 132.

Dorsett S & McVeigh S, "Jurisprudences of Jurisdiction: Matters of Public Authority" (2014) 23 *Griffith L Rev* 569.

Douzinas C, "Human Rights and Postmodern Utopia" (2000) 11 *L&C* 219.

Dressler J, "Reassessing the Theoretical Underpinnings of Accomplice Liability: New Solutions to an Old Problem" (1985) 37 *Hastings LJ* 91.

Dressler J, *Understanding Criminal Law*, 5th ed (LexisNexis, 2009).

Drumbl M, "Toward a Criminology of International Crime" (2003) 19 *Ohio St J on Disp Resol* 263.

Drumbl M, "Collective Violence and Individual Punishment: The Criminality of Mass Atrocity" (2005) 99 *Nw U L Rev* 539.

Drumbl M, "Pluralizing International Criminal Justice" (2005) 103 *Michigan L Rev* 1295.

Drumbl M, *Atrocity, Punishment and International Law* (Cambridge University Press, 2007).

Drumbl M, "Collective Responsibility and Postconflict Justice," in T Isaacs & R Vernon, eds, *Accountability of Collective Wrongdoing* (Cambridge University Press, 2011).

Drumbl M, "International Criminal Law and Moral Agency" (10 April 2013), online: http://opiniojuris.org/2013/04/10/ljil-symposium-international-criminal-law-and-moral-agency/.

Dubber M, "A Political Theory of Criminal Law: Autonomy and the Legitimacy of State Punishment" (15 March 2004), online: http://papers.ssrn.com/sol3/papers.cfm?abstract_id=529522.

Dubber M, "Theories of Crime and Punishment in German Criminal Law" (2005) 53 *Am J Comp L* 679.

Dubber M, *The Sense of Justice: Empathy in Law and Punishment* (Universal Law, 2006).

Dubber M, "Criminalizing Complicity: A Comparative Analysis" (2007) 5 *JICJ* 977.

Dubber M, "Common Civility: The Culture of Alegality in International Criminal Law" (2011) 24 *LJIL* 923.

Duff A, *Intention, Agency and Criminal Liability* (Blackwell, 1990).

Duff R A, *Answering for Crime: Responsibility and Liability in the Criminal Law* (Hart, 2007).

Dungel J & Ghadiri S, "The Temporal Scope of Command Responsibility Revisited: Why Commanders Have a Duty to Prevent Crimes Committed after the Cessation of Effective Control" (2010) 17 *U C Davis J Int'l L & Pol'y* 1.

Duttwiler M, "Liability for Omissions in International Criminal Law" (2006) 6 *Int'l Crim L Rev* 1.

Dworkin R, *Law's Empire* (Harvard University Press, 1986).

Ebertz R, "Is Reflective Equilibrium a Coherentist Model?" (1993) 23 *Canadian J Phil* 193.

Engel M Jr, "Coherentism and the Epistemic Justification of Moral Beliefs: A Case Study in How to Do Practical Ethics without Appeal to a Moral Theory" (2012) 50 *Southern J Phil* 50.

Epps V, "The Soldier's Obligation to Die When Ordered to Shoot Civilians or Face Death Himself" (2003) 37 *New England L Rev* 987.

Erskine T, "Kicking Bodies and Damning Souls: The Danger of Harming Innocent Individuals While Punishing Delinquent States," in T Isaacs & R Vernon, eds, *Accountability of Collective Wrongdoing* (Cambridge University Press, 2011).

Eser A, "Individual Criminal Responsibility," in A Cassese, P Gaeta & J R W D Jones, eds, *The Rome Statute of the International Criminal Court: A Commentary, Vol 2* (Oxford University Press, 2002).

Estreicher S & Stephan P B, "Foreword: Taking International Law Seriously" (2003) 44 *Virginia J Int'l L* 1.

Fanselow R, "Self-Evidence and Disagreement in Ethics" (2011) 5 *J Ethics Soc Philos* 1.

Fenrick W, "Some International Law Problems Related to Prosecutions before the International Criminal Tribunal for the former Yugoslavia" (1995) 6 *Duke J Comp & Int'l L* 103.

Fenrick W, "Article 8, War Crimes," in O Triffterer, ed, *Commentary on the Rome Statute of the International Criminal Court: Observers' Notes, Article by Article*, 2nd ed (Beck, 2008).

Fichtelberg A, "Liberal Values in International Criminal Law: A Critique of *Erdemović*" (2008) 6 *JICJ* 3.

Fisher K J, *Moral Accountability and International Criminal Law: Holding the Agents of Atrocity Accountable to the World* (Routledge, 2012).

Fletcher G, *Basic Concepts of Criminal Law* (Oxford University Press, 1998).

Fletcher G, *Rethinking Criminal Law*, 3rd ed (Oxford University Press, 2000).

Fletcher G, "Liberals and Romantics at War: The Problem of Collective Guilt" (2002) 111 *Yale LJ* 1499.

Fletcher G, "The Fault of Not Knowing" (2002) 3 *Theoretical Inq L* 265.

Fletcher G, "Collective Guilt and Collective Punishment" (2004) 5 *Theoretical Inq L* 163.

Fletcher G, *The Grammar of Criminal Law: American, Comparative and International, Vol 1* (Oxford University Press, 2007).

Fletcher G, "New Court, Old *Dogmatik*" (2011) 9 *JICJ* 179.

Fletcher G & Ohlin J D, "Reclaiming Fundamental Principles of Criminal Law in the *Darfur* Case" (2005) 3 *JICJ* 539.

Fletcher L, "From Indifference to Engagement: Bystanders and International Criminal Justice" (2005) 26 *Michigan J Int'l L* 1013.

Fletcher L & Weinstein H, "Violence and Social Repair: Rethinking the Contribution of Justice to Reconciliation" (2002) 24 *HRQ* 573.

Foka Taffo F, "Analysis of Jean-Pierre Bemba's Acquittal by the International Criminal Court" (13 December 2018), online: www.accord.org.za/conflict-trends/analysis-of-jean-pierre-bembas-acquittal-by-the-international-criminal-court.

Ford R T, "Law's Territory (A History of Jurisdiction)" (1998–99) 97 *Michigan L Rev* 843.

Fournet C, "When the Child Surpasses the Father: Admissible Defences in International Criminal Law" (2008) 8 *Int'l Crim L Rev* 509.

Fox C T, "Closing a Loophole in Accountability for War Crimes: Successor Commanders' Duty to Punish Known Past Offences" (2004) 55 *Case W Res L Rev* 443.

Frost R, "Centenary Reflections on *Prince's Case*" (1975) 91 *LQR* 540.

Fruehwald E, "A Biological Basis of Rights" (2009) 19 *S Cal Interdisc LJ* 195.

Frulli M, "Are Crimes against Humanity More Serious than War Crimes?" (2001) 12 *EJIL* 329.

Fuller L, *The Morality of Law*, 2nd ed (Yale University Press, 1969).

Gaeta P, "The Defence of Superior Orders: The Statute of the International Criminal Court versus Customary International Law" (1999) 10 *EJIL* 172.

Gallant K, *The Principle of Legality in International and Comparative Criminal Law* (Cambridge University Press, 2009).

Gardner J, "Complicity and Causality" (2007) 1 *Crim L & Philos* 127.

Gardner J, "Introduction," in H L A Hart, ed, *Punishment and Responsibility*, 2nd ed (Oxford University Press, 2008).

Gardner J, "Justifications under Authority" (2010) 23 *Can JL & Jur* 71.

Gardner J, *Law as Leap of Faith* (Oxford University Press, 2012).

Garraway C, "Command Responsibility: Victors' Justice or Just Deserts?," in R Burchill, N D White & J Morris, eds, *International Conflict and Security Law: Essays in Memory of Hilaire McCoubrey* (Cambridge University Press, 2005).

Grabert A, *Dynamic Interpretation in International Criminal Law: Striking a Balance between Stability and Change* (Herbert Utz Verlag, 2014).

Graham R, "Politics and Prices: Judicial Utility Maximization and Construction" (2007) 1 *Indian J Const L* 57.

Green L C, *The Contemporary Law of Armed Conflict* (Manchester University Press, 2000).

Green L C, *The Authority of the State* (Clarendon Press, 1988).

Greenawalt A K A, "The Pluralism of International Criminal Law" (2011) 86 *Indiana LJ* 1063.

Greenawalt A K A, "International Criminal Law for Retributivists" (2014) 35 *U Pa J Int'l L* 969.

Greenberg J & Sechler M J, "Constitutionalism Ancient and Early Modern: The Contributions of Roman Law, Cannon Law, and English Common Law" (2013) 34 *Cardozo L Rev* 1021.

Greenwood C, "Command Responsibility and the *Hadžihasanović* Decision" (2004) 2 *JICJ* 598.

Grover L, "A Call to Arms: Fundamental Dilemmas Confronting the Interpretation of Crimes in the Rome Statute of the International Criminal Court" (2010) 21 *EJIL* 543.

Grover L, *Interpreting Crimes in the Rome Statute of the International Criminal Court* (Cambridge University Press, 2014).

Guilfoyle D, "Responsibility for Collective Atrocities: Fair Labelling and Approaches to Commission in International Criminal Law" (2011) 64 *Current Legal Problems* 255.

Guilfoyle D, "Of Babies, Bathwater, and List B Judges at the International Criminal Court" (13 November 2019), online: www.ejiltalk.org/of-babies-bathwater-and-list-b-judges-at-the-international-criminal-court/.

Gustafson K, "ECCC Tackles JCE" (2010) 8 *JICJ* 1323.

Haan V, "The Development of the Concept of Joint Criminal Enterprise at the International Criminal Tribunal for the Former Yugoslavia" (2005) 5 *Int'l Crim L Rev* 167.

Habermas J, *Moral Consciousness and Communicative Action*, trans C Lenhart & S Weber Nicholson (MIT Press, 1990).

Habermas J, "Kant's Idea of Perpetual Peace, with the Benefit of Two Hundred Years' Hindsight," in J Bohman & M Lutz-Bachmann, eds, *Perpetual Peace: Essays on Kant's Cosmopolitan Ideal* (MIT Press, 1997).

Hakimi M, "Constructing an International Community" (2017) 111 *AJIL* 317.

Hall J, *General Principles of Criminal Law* (Bobbs Merrill, 1947).

Hall J, *General Principles of Criminal Law*, 2nd ed (Bobbs Merrill, 1960).

Hamdorf K, "The Concept of a Joint Criminal Enterprise and Domestic Modes of Liability for Parties to a Crime" (2007) 5 *JICJ* 208.

Hart H L A, *Punishment and Responsibility: Essays in the Philosophy of Law*, 2nd ed (Oxford University Press, 2008).

Hart H L A & Honoré A M, *Causation in the Law*, 2nd ed (Clarendon Press, 1985).

Hauser M D, *Moral Minds* (Harper Collins, 2006).

Hayden P, "Cosmopolitanism and the Need for Transnational Criminal Justice: The Case of the International Criminal Court" (2004) 104 *Theoria* 69.

Hegel G W F, *Elements of the Philosophy of Right*, ed A Wood (Cambridge University Press, 1991).

Held D, *Democracy and the Global Order: From the Modern State to Cosmopolitan Governance* (Polity, 1995).

Heller K J, *The Nuremberg Military Tribunals and the Origins of International Criminal Law* (Oxford University Press, 2011).

Heller K J, "Why the ICTY's 'Specifically Directed' Requirement Is Justified" (2 June 2013), online: http://opiniojuris.org/2013/06/02/why-the-ictys-specifically-directed-requirement-is-justified/.

Heller K J & Dubber M, *The Handbook of Comparative Criminal Law* (Stanford Law Books, 2011).

Hencaerts J M & Doswald-Beck L, *Customary International Law, Vol II: Practice* (Cambridge University Press, 2005).

Henley K, "Abstract Principles, Mid-level Principles and the Rule of Law" (1993) 12 *L & Phil* 121.

Hirsh D, *Law against Genocide: Cosmopolitan Trials* (Routledge, 2003).

Hobbes T, *Leviathan*, ed C B MacPherson (Penguin Books, 1985).

Horder J, "Gross Negligence and Criminal Culpability" (1997) 47 *U Toronto LJ* 495.

Horder J, *Ashworth's Principles of Criminal Law*, 8th ed (Oxford University Press, 2016).

Hunt D, "High Hopes, 'Creative Ambiguity' and an Unfortunate Mistrust in International Judges" (2004) 2 *JICJ* 56.

Hurley S, *Natural Reasons: Personality and Polity* (Oxford University Press, 1989).

Husak D, "Omissions, Causation and Liability" (1980) 30 *The Philosophical Quarterly* 318.

Husak D, *Philosophy of Criminal Law: Selected Essays* (Oxford University Press, 1987).

Hyland B, "The Impact of the *Bemba* Appellate Judgment on Future Prosecution of Crimes of Sexual and Gender-Based Violence at the ICC" (25 May 2019), online: https://iccforum.com/forum/permalink/116/31935.

International Commission of Jurists (ICJ), Corporate Complicity and Legal Accountability, *Report of the International Commission of Jurists Expert Legal Panel on Corporate Complicity in International Crimes* (ICJ, 2008).

International Committee of the Red Cross (ICRC), *Commentary on the Additional Protocols of 8 June 1977 to the Geneva Conventions of 12 August 1949* (Martinus Nijhoff, 1987).

Isaacs T, "Individual Responsibility for Collective Wrongs," in J Harrington, M Milde & R Vernon, eds, *Bringing Power to Justice? The Prospects of the International Criminal Court* (McGill-Queen's University Press, 2006).

Isser D, ed, *Customary Justice and the Rule of Law in War-Torn Societies* (USIP Press, 2011).

Jackson M, *Complicity in International Law* (Oxford University Press, 2015).

Jackson M, "The Attribution of Responsibility and Modes of Liability in International Criminal Law" (2016) 29 *LJIJ* 879.

Jackson M, "Commanders' Motivations in *Bemba*" (15 June 2018), online: www.ejiltalk.org/commanders-motivations-in-bemba/.

Jackson M, "Geographic Remoteness in *Bemba*" (30 July 2018), online: www.ejiltalk.org/geographical-remoteness-in-bemba/.

Jackson M, "Virtuous Accomplices in International Criminal Law" (2019) 68 *Int'l & Comp LQ* 818.

Jain N, "The Control Theory of Perpetration in International Criminal Law" (2011) 12 *Chicago J Int'l L* 159.

Jain N, *Perpetrators and Accessories in International Criminal Law* (Hart, 2014).

Jain N, *Principals and Accessories in International Criminal Law: Individual Modes of Responsibility for Collective Crimes* (Hart, 2014).

Jain N, "Judicial Lawmaking and General Principles of Law in International Criminal Law" (2016) 57 *Harvard Int'l LJ* 111.

James W, *Pragmatism* (Longman Green & Co, 1907).

Jaspers K, *The Question of German Guilt*, trans E B Ashton (Fordham University Press, 1947).

Jescheck H, "The General Principles of International Criminal Law Set out in Nuremberg, as Mirrored in the ICC Statute" (2004) 2 *JICJ* 38.

Jia B B, "The Doctrine of Command Responsibility Revisited" (2004) 3 *Chinese J Int'l L* 1.

Kadish S H, "Complicity, Cause and Blame: A Study in the Interpretation of Doctrine" (1985) 73 *Calif L Rev* 323.

Kagan S, *Normative Ethics* (Avalon, 1998).

Kahn P W, *Putting Liberalism in Its Place* (Princeton University Press, 2005).

Kahombo B, "Bemba's Acquittal by the Appeals Chamber of the International Criminal Court: Why Is It So Controversial?" (9 July 2018), online: www.icjafrica.com/single-post /2018/07/09/Bemba%E2%80%99s-acquittal-by-the-Appeals-Chamber-of-the-International-Criminal-Court-Why-is-it-so-controversial.

Kamel T, "The Principle of Legality and Its Application in Islamic Criminal Justice," in M C Bassiouni, ed, *The Islamic Criminal Justice System* (Oceana, 1982).

Kant I, *The Metaphysics of Morals*, trans M Gregor (Cambridge University Press, 1996).

Kant I, *Groundwork of the Metaphysics of Morals*, trans M Gregor (Cambridge University Press, 1998).

Kant I, "On a Supposed Right to Lie from Philanthropy," in *Practical Philosophy*, trans M J Gregor (Cambridge University Press, 1999).

Karnavas M G, "Forms of Perpetration," in P Behrens & R Henham, *Elements of Genocide* (Routledge, 2013).

Kelsen H, "Will the Judgment in the Nuremberg Trial Constitute a Precedent in International Law?" (1947) 1 *Int'l LQ* 153.

Kennedy D, "Strategizing Legal Behaviour in Legal Interpretation" (1996) 3 *Utah L Rev* 785.

Kissinger H, "The Pitfalls of Universal Jurisdiction" (2001) 80 *Foreign Affairs* 86.

Kiyani A G, "International Crime and the Politics of Criminal Theory: Voices and Conduct of Exclusion" (2015) 48 *NYU J Int'l L & Pol* 187.

Kloppenberg J T, "Pragmatism: An Old Name for Some New Ways of Thinking?," in M Dickstein, ed, *The Revival of Pragmatism: New Essays on Social Thought, Law, and Culture* (Duke University Press, 1998).

Knop K, "Statehood: Territory, People, Government," in J Crawford & M Koskenniemi, eds, *The Cambridge Companion to International Law* (Cambridge University Press, 2012).

Koch C Jr, "Judicial Dialogue for Legal Multiculturalism" (2004) 25 *Michigan J Int'l L* 879.

Kochenov D, "The Just World," in D Kochenov, G de Búrca & A Williams, *Europe's Justice Deficit?* (Hart, 2015).

Koller D, "The Faith of the International Criminal Lawyer" (2008) 40 *NYU J Int'l L & Pol* 1019.

Koskenniemi M, *From Apology to Utopia: The Structure of International Legal Argument* (Reissue with new epilogue) (Cambridge University Press, 2005).

Koskenniemi M, *"Humanity's Law, Ruti G. Teitel"* (2012) 26 *Ethics & International Affairs* 395.

Kreß C, "On the Outer Limits of Crimes against Humanity: The Concept of Organization within the Policy Requirement: Some Reflections on the March 2010 ICC Kenya Decision" (2010) 23 *LJIL* 855.

Kreß C, *Towards a Truly Universal Invisible College of International Criminal Lawyers* (Torkel Opsahl Academic, 2014).

Krieger H, "International Law and Governance by Armed Groups: Caught in the Legitimacy Trap?" (2018) 12 *Journal of Intervention and Statebuilding* 563.

Kuhn T, *The Structure of Scientific Revolutions* (University of Chicago Press, 1962).

Kutz C, "Causeless Complicity" (2007) 1 *Crim L & Philos* 289.

Lacey N, *State Punishment: Political Principles and Community Values* (Routledge, 1988).

Lamb S, "Nullum Crimen, Nullum Poena Sine Lege," in A Cassese, P Gaeta & J R W D Jones, eds, *The Rome Statute of the International Criminal Court: A Commentary* (Oxford University Press, 2002).

Lang A F, "Punishing Genocide: A Critical Reading of the International Court of Justice," in T Isaacs & R Vernon, eds, *Accountability of Collective Wrongdoing* (Cambridge University Press, 2011).

Langston E, "The Superior Responsibility Doctrine in International Law: Historical Continuities, Innovation and Criminality – Can East Timor's Special Panels Bring Militia Leaders to Justice?" (2004) 4 *Int'l Crim L Rev* 141.

Larcom S, "Accounting for Legal Pluralism: The Impact of Pre-colonial Institutions on Crime" (2013) 6 *LDR* 25.

Lehrer K, "Justification, Coherence and Knowledge" (1999) 50 *Erkenntnis* 243.

Liss R, "Crimes against the Sovereign Order: Rethinking International Criminal Justice" (2019) 113 *AJIL* 727.

Liu Y, *Origins of Chinese Law: Penal and Administrative Law in its Early Development* (Oxford University Press, 1998).

Lorton D, "The Treatment of Criminals in Ancient Egypt: Through the New Kingdom" (1977) 20 *Journal of Economic and Social History of the Orient* 2.

Lu C, "Cosmopolitan Liberalism and the Faces of Injustice in International Relations" (2005) 31 *Review of International Studies* 401.

Luban D, "Contrived Ignorance" (1999) 87 *Georgetown LJ* 957.

Luban D, "State Criminality and the Ambition of International Criminal Law," in T Isaacs & R Vernon, eds, *Accountability of Collective Wrongdoing* (Cambridge University Press, 2011).

Luban D, Strudler A & Wasserman D, "Moral Responsibility in the Age of Bureaucracy" (1992) 90 *Michigan L Rev* 2348.

Lucas J, Graif C & Lovaglia M, "Misconduct in the Prosecution of Severe Crimes: Theory and Experimental Test" (2006) 69 *Soc Psychol Q* 97.

MacCormack G, *Traditional Chinese Penal Law* (Edinburgh University Press, 1990).

MacCormack N, "Coherence in Legal Justification," in A Peczenik, L Lindahl & B van Roermund, eds, *Theory of Legal Science* (Reidel, 1984).

Maier-Katkin, D, Mears D P & Bernard T J, "Towards a Criminology of Crimes against Humanity" (2009) 13 *Theoretical Criminology* 227.

Malekian F, "The Homogeneity of the International Criminal Court with Islamic Jurisprudence" (2009) 9 *Int'l Crim L Rev* 607.

Mani R, *Beyond Retribution: Seeking Justice in the Shadows of War* (Wiley, 2002).

Manning J G, "The Representation of Justice in Ancient Egypt" (2012) 24 *Yale J L & Humanity* 111.

Martinez J S, "Understanding *Mens Rea* in Command Responsibility: From *Yamashita* to *Blaškić* and beyond" (2007) 5 *JICJ* 638.

May L, *Crimes against Humanity: A Normative Account* (Cambridge University Press, 2005).

May L, "Collective Punishment and Mass Confinement," in T Isaacs & R Vernon, eds, *Accountability of Collective Wrongdoing* (Cambridge University Press, 2011).

Mayr E, "International Criminal Law, Causation and Responsibility" (2014) 14 *Int'l Crim L Rev* 855.

McGonigle Leyh B, "Pragmatism over Principles: The International Criminal Court and a Human Rights-Based Approach to Judicial Interpretation" (2018) 41 *Fordham Int'l LJ* 697.

Mégret F, "Politics of International Criminal Justice" (2002) 13 *EJIL* 1261.

Mégret F, "Prospects for 'Constitutional' Human Rights Scrutiny of Substantive International Criminal Law by the ICC," Paper presented at Washington University School of Law, February 2010.

Mègret F, "Too Much of a Good Thing? ICC Implementation and the Uses of Complementarity," in C Stahn & M El-Zeidy, eds, *The International Criminal Court and Complementarity: From Theory to Practice* (Cambridge University Press, 2010).

Mégret F, "What Sort of Justice Is 'International Criminal Justice'?" (2015) 13 *JICJ* 77.

Meloni C, "Command Responsibility: Mode of Liability for the Crimes of Subordinates or Separate Offence of the Superior?" (2007) 5 *JICJ* 619.

Meloni C, *Command Responsibility in International Criminal Law* (TMC Asser, 2010).

Merges R, *Justifying Intellectual Property* (Harvard University Press, 2011).

Merges R, "Foundations and Principles Redux: A Reply to Professor Blankfein-Tabachnik" (2013) 101 *Calif L Rev* 1361.

Meron T, "Revival of Customary Humanitarian Law" (2005) 99 *AJIL* 817.

Mettraux G, "Crimes against Humanity in the Jurisprudence of the ICTY and ICTR" (2002) 43 *Harvard Int'l LJ* 237.

Mettraux G, *International Crimes and the Ad Hoc Tribunals* (Oxford University Press, 2005).

Mettraux G, *The Law of Command Responsibility* (Oxford University Press, 2009).

Mill J S, "Utilitarianism," in M Lerner, ed, *Essential Works of John Stuart Mill* (Bantam Books, 1961).

Mill J S, "Bentham," in A Ryan, ed, *Utilitarianism and Other Essays* (Penguin Random House, 1987).

Misak C, *The American Pragmatists* (Oxford University Press, 2013).

Mohamed S, "Of Monsters and Men: Perpetrator Trauma and Mass Atrocity" (2015) 115 *Columbia L Rev* 1157.

Mohamed S, "Leadership Crimes" (2017) 105 *Calif L Rev* 777.

Møllmann M, "Who Can Be Held Responsible for the Consequences of Aid and Loan Conditionalities? The Global Gag Rule in Peru and Its Criminal Consequences," Michigan State University's Women and International Development Program Working Paper #29 (2004).

Moloto B J, "Command Responsibility in International Criminal Tribunals" (2009) 3 *Publicist* 12.

Moore M S, *Placing Blame: A General Theory of Criminal Law* (Oxford University Press, 1997).

Moore M S, "Causing, Aiding, and the Superfluity of Accomplice Liability" (2007) 156 *U Pa L Rev* 395.

Moore M S, *Causation and Responsibility: An Essay in Law, Morals and Metaphysics* (Oxford University Press, 2009).

Morse S J, "The Moral Metaphysics of Causation and Results" (2000) 88 *Calif L Rev* 879.

Morss J R, "Saving Human Rights from Its Friends: A Critique of the Imaginary Justice of Costas Douzinas" (2003) 27 *Melbourne U L Rev* 889.

Nagel T, *Mortal Questions* (Cambridge University Press, 1979).

Napoleon V & Friedland H, "Indigenous Legal Traditions: Roots to Renaissance," in M D Dubber & T Hörnle, eds, *The Oxford Handbook of Criminal Law* (Oxford University Press, 2014).

Nerlich V, "Superior Responsibility under Article 28 *ICC Statute*: For What Exactly Is the Superior Held Responsible?" (2007) 5 *JICJ* 665.

Nersessian D, "Whoops, I Committed Genocide! The Anomaly of Constructive Liability for Serious International Crimes" (2006) 30 *Fletcher F World Aff* 81.

Neurath O, "Anti-Spengler," in M Neurath & R Cohen, eds, *Empiricism and Sociology* (D Reidel, 1973).

Nickel J W, "Are Human Rights Utopian?" (1982) 11 *Phil & Pub Aff* 246.

Nollkaemper A & van der Wilt H, eds, *System Criminality in International Law* (Cambridge University Press, 2009).

Nouwen S, "International Criminal Law: Theory All over the Place," in A Orford & F Hoffman, eds, *Oxford Handbook of the Theory of International Law* (Oxford University Press, 2016).

Nsereko D, *Criminal Law in Botswana* (Kluwer, 2011).

Nybondas M L, *Command Responsibility and Its Applicability to Civilian Superiors* (TMC Asser Press, 2010).

Ohlin J D, "Three Conceptual Problems with the Doctrine of Joint Criminal Enterprise" (2006) 5 *JICJ* 69.

Ohlin J D, "MJIL Symposium: A Response to Darryl Robinson by Jens Ohlin" (15 November 2012), online: http://opiniojuris.org/2012/11/15/mjil-symposium-a-response-to-darryl-robinson-by-jens-ohlin/.

Ohlin J D, "Second-Order Linking Principles: Combining Vertical and Horizontal Modes of Liability" (2012) 25 *LJIL* 771.

Ohlin J D, "Co-perpetration: German Dogmatik or German Invasion?," in C Stahn, ed, *The Law and Practice of the International Criminal Court: A Critical Account of Challenges and Achievements* (Oxford University Press, 2015).

Ohlin J D, "Specific Direction Again" (17 December 2015), online: http://opiniojuris.org/2015/12/17/specific-direction-again/.

Ohlin J D, van Sliedregt E & Weigend T, "Assessing the Control Theory" (2013) 26 *LJIL* 725.

Olásolo H, "Developments in the Distinction between Principal and Accessory Liability in Light of the First Case Law of the International Criminal Court," in C Stahn & G Sluiter, eds, *The Emerging Practice of the International Criminal Court* (Brill, 2009).

Olivelle P, *Dharmasutras: The Law Codes of Apastamba, Gautama, Baudhayana, and Vasistha* (Motilal Banarsidass, 2003).

O'Reilly A T, "Command Responsibility: A Call to Realign the Doctrine with Principles of Individual Accountability and Retributive Justice" (2004–05) 40 *Gonzaga L Rev* 127.

Orford A, "Jurisdiction without Territory: From the Holy Roman Empire to the Responsibility to Protect" (2008–09) 30 *Michigan J Int'l L* 981.

Orie A M M, "*Stare Decisis* in the ICTY Appeal System: Successor Responsibility in the *Hadžihasanović* Case" (2012) 10 *JICJ* 635.

Osiel M, *Obeying Orders: Atrocity, Military Discipline and the Law of War* (Routledge, 2002).

Osiel M, "Modes of Participation in Mass Atrocities" (2005) 38 *Cornell Int'l LJ* 793.

Osiel M, "The Banality of Good: Aligning Incentives against Mass Atrocity" (2005) 105 *Columbia L Rev* 1751.

Osiel M, *Making Sense of Mass Atrocity* (Cambridge University Press, 2009).

Parks W H, "Command Responsibility for War Crimes" (1973) 62 *Military L Rev* 1.

Paust J J, "Content and Contours of Genocide, Crimes against Humanity, and War Crimes," in S Yee & W Tieya, *International Law in the Post-Cold War World: Essays in Memory of Li Haopei* (Routledge, 2001).

Pejic J, "The International Criminal Court Statute: An Appraisal of the Rome Package" (2000) 34 *International Lawyer* 65.

Pellet A, "Applicable Law," in A Cassese, P Gaeta & J R W D Jones, eds, *The Rome Statute of the International Criminal Court: A Commentary* (Oxford University Press, 2002).

Perova N, "Stretching the Joint Criminal Enterprise Doctrine to the Extreme: When Culpability and Liability Do not Match" (2016) 16 *Int'l Crim L Rev* 761.

Piacente N, "Importance of the Joint Criminal Enterprise Doctrine for the ICTY Prosecutorial Policy" (2004) 2 *JICJ* 446.

Piragoff D & Robinson D, "Article 30," in K Ambos, ed, *Commentary on the Rome Statute of the International Criminal Court: Observers' Notes, Article by Article*, 4th ed (Beck, 2020).

Pogge T W, "Cosmopolitanism and Sovereignty" (1992) 103 *Ethics* 48.

Pollock F, *The Genius of the Common Law* (Columbia University Press, 1912).

Posner R, "What Do Judges and Justices Maximize? (The Same Thing Everyone Else Does)" (1993) 3 *SCER* 1.

Powderly J C, "Judicial Interpretation at the Ad Hoc Tribunals: Method from Chaos?," in J C Powderly & S Darcy, eds, *Judicial Creativity at the International Criminal Tribunals* (Oxford University Press, 2010).

Powderly J C, "The Rome Statute and the Attempted Corseting of the Interpretative Judicial Function: Reflections on Sources of Law and Interpretative Technique," in C Stahn, ed, *The Law and Practice of the International Criminal Court* (Oxford University Press, 2015).

Powderly J C, "Introductory Note to Prosecutor v Jean-Pierre Bemba Gombo" (2018) 57 *Int'l Legal Materials* 1031.

Powderly J C, "International Criminal Justice in an Age of Perpetual Crisis" (2019) 32 *LJIL* 1.

Powderly J C & Hayes N, "The *Bemba* Appeal: A Fragmented Appeals Chamber Destabilises the Law and Practice of the ICC" (26 June 2018), online: humanrightsdoctorate .blogspot.com/2018/06/the-bemba-appeal-fragmented-appeals.html.

Powles S, "Joint Criminal Enterprise: Criminal Liability by Prosecutorial Ingenuity and Judicial Creativity?" (2004) 2 *JICJ* 606.

Prost K & Robinson D, "Canada," in C Kress et al, eds, *The Rome Statute and Domestic Legal Orders, Vol 2* (Nomos, 2000–05).

Provost R, "Authority, Responsibility, and Witchcraft: From Tintin to the SCSL," in C Jalloh, ed, *The Sierra Leone Special Court and Its Legacy: The Impact for Africa and International Criminal Law* (Cambridge University Press, 2014).

Provost R, *Rebel Courts: The Administration of Justice by Armed Insurgents* (Oxford University Press, forthcoming).

Ramasastry A & Thompson R C, *Commerce, Crime and Conflict: Legal Remedies for Private Sector Liability for Grave Breaches of International Law – A Survey of Sixteen Countries* (FAFO, 2006).

Rauter T, *Judicial Practice, Customary International Criminal Law and Nullum Crimen Sine Lege* (Springer, 2017).

Rawls J, "Two Concepts of Rules" (1955) 64 *Philosophical Review* 3.

Rawls J, *A Theory of Justice* (Oxford University Press, 1999).

Rawls J, *Justice as Fairness: A Restatement*, ed E Kelly (Harvard University Press, 2001).

Reisman W M, "Legal Responses to Genocide and Other Massive Violations of Human Rights" (1996) 4 *Law & Contemp Probs* 75.

Richardson H, *Practical Reasoning about Final Ends* (Cambridge University Press, 1994).

Rittich K, "Enchantments of Reason/Coercions of Law" (2003) 57 *U Miami L Rev* 727.

Roach K, "Four Models of the Criminal Process" (1999) 89 *JCLC* 671.

Roach S C, *Politicizing the ICC: The Convergence of Ethics, Politics and Law* (Rowman & Littlefield, 2006).

Robbennolt J K, "Outcome Severity and Judgments of 'Responsibility': A Meta-Analytical Review" (2000) 30 *J Appl* 2575.

Roberts P & MacMillan N "For Criminology in International Criminal Justice" (2003) 1 *JICJ* 315.

Robertson G, *Crimes against Humanity: The Struggle for Global Justice* (The New Press, 2006).

Robinson D, "The Identity Crisis of International Criminal Law" (2008) 21 *LJIL* 925.

Robinson D, "Legality and Our Contradictory Commitments: Some Thoughts about the Way We Think" (2009) 103 *ASIL Proc* 104.

Robinson D, "The Two Liberalisms of International Criminal Law," in C Stahn & L van den Herik, eds, *Future Perspectives on International Criminal Justice* (TMC Asser Press, 2010).

Robinson D, "The Controversy over Territorial State Referrals and Reflections on ICL Discourse" (2011) 9 *JICJ* 355.

Robinson D, "How Command Responsibility Got So Complicated: A Culpability Contradiction, Its Obfuscation, and a Simple Solution" (2012) 13 *Melbourne J Int'l L* 1.

Robinson D, "Inescapable Dyads: Why the ICC Cannot Win" (2015) 28 *LJIL* 323.

Robinson D, "Take the Long View of International Justice" (24 October 2016), online: www .ejiltalk.org/take-the-long-view-of-international-justice/.

Robinson D, "A Justification of Command Responsibility" (2017) 28 *Crim L Forum* 633.

Robinson D, "The Other Poisoned Chalice: Unprecedented Evidentiary Standards in the *Gbagbo* Case?" (5 November 2019), online: www.ejiltalk.org/the-other-poisoned-chalice-unprecedented-evidentiary-standards-in-the-gbagbo-case-part-1/.

Robinson D, "The Strangest Debate in Complementarity and the Better Debate Ahead," in C Stahn & M El Zeidy, eds, *The International Criminal Court and Complementarity: From Theory to Practice*, 2nd ed (Cambridge University Press, 2020).

Robinson D & MacNeil G, "The Tribunals and the Renaissance of International Criminal Law: Three Themes" (2016) 110 *AJIL* 191.

Robinson P H, *Criminal Law Defences, Vol I* (West, 1984).

Robinson P H, "Imputed Criminal Liability" (1984) 93 *Yale LJ* 609.

Robinson P H, "Fair Notice and Fair Adjudication: Two Kinds of Legality" (2005) 154 *U Pa L Rev* 335.

Robinson P H, *Intuitions of Justice and the Utility of Desert* (Oxford University Press, 2013).

Robinson P H, "Natural Law and Lawlessness: Modern Lessons from Pirates, Lepers, Eskimos, and Survivors" [2013] *U Illinois L Rev* 433.

Robinson P H & Darley J M, "The Utility of Desert" (1997) 91 *Nw U L Rev* 453.

Robinson P H & Kurzban R, "Concordance and Conflict in Intuitions of Justice" (2006–07) 91 *Minnesota L Rev* 1829.

Root J, "Some Other *Mens Rea*? The Nature of Command Responsibility in the Rome Statute" (2013) 23 *Transnat'l L & Policy* 119.

Rorty R, *Consequences of Pragmatism: Essays: 1972–1980* (University of Minnesota Press, 1982).

Roth B, "Coming to Terms with Ruthlessness: Sovereign Equality, Global Pluralism, and the Limits of International Criminal Justice" (2010) 8 *Santa Clara J Int'l L* 231.

Rothe D L & Mullins C W, "Toward a Criminology of International Criminal Law: An Integrated Theory of International Criminal Violations" (2009) 33 *IJCACJ* 97.

Rundle K, *Forms Liberate: Reclaiming the Jurisprudence of Lon L Fuller* (Oxford University Press, 2012).

Russell-Brown S L, "The Last Line of Defense: The Doctrine of Command Responsibility and Gender Crimes in Armed Conflict" (2004) 22 *Wisconsin Int'l L J* 125.

Ryngaert C, "Territory in the Law of Jurisdiction: Imagining Alternatives" (2017) 47 NYIL 49.

SáCouto S, "The Impact of the Appeals Chamber Decision in *Bemba*: Impunity for Sexual and Gender-Based Crimes?" (22 June 2018), online: www.ijmonitor.org/2018/06/the-impact -of-the-appeals-chamber-decision-in-bemba-impunity-for-sexual-and-gender-based-crimes.

SáCouto S & Viseur Sellers P, "The *Bemba* Appeals Chamber Judgment: Impunity for Sexual and Gender-Based Crimes" (2019) 27 *Wm & Mary Bill Rts J* 599.

Sadat L N, *The ICC and the Transformation of International Law: Justice for the New Millennium* (Transnational Press, 2002).

Sadat L N, "Can the ICTY *Šainović* and *Perišić* Cases Be Reconciled?" (2014) 108 *AJIL* 475.

Sadat L N, "Fiddling While Rome Burns? The Appeals Chamber's Curious Decision in *Prosecutor v Jean-Pierre Bemba Gombo*" (12 June 2018), online: www.ejiltalk.org/fiddling-while-rome-burns-the-appeals-chambers-curious-decision-in-prosecutor-v-jean-pierre-bemba-gombo/.

Sadat L N, "Judicial Speculation Made Law: More Thoughts about the Acquittal of Jean-Pierre Bemba Gomba by the ICC Appeals Chamber and the Question of Superior Responsibility under the Rome Statute" (27 May 2019), online: https://iccforum.com /responsibility.

Sadat L N & Jolly J, "Seven Canons of ICC Treaty Interpretation: Making Sense of Article 25's Rorschach Blot" (2014) 27 *LJIL* 755.

Saland P, "International Criminal Law Principles," in R S Lee, ed, *The International Criminal Court: The Making of the Rome Statute* (Kluwer, 1999).

Sander B, "Unravelling the Confusion Concerning Successor Superior Responsibility in the ICTY Jurisprudence" (2010) 23 *LJIL* 105.

Sarch A, "Condoning the Crime: The Elusive *Mens Rea* for Complicity" (2015–16) 47 *Loy U Chi LJ* 131.

Sartoria C, "Causation and Responsibility by Michael Moore" (2010) 119 *Mind* 475.

Sayre F B, "Criminal Responsibility for the Acts of Another" (1930) 43 *Harvard L Rev* 689.

Sayre-McCord G, "Coherentism and the Justification of Moral Beliefs," in M Timmons & W S Armstrong, eds, *Moral Knowledge* (Oxford University Press, 1996).

Scanlon T M, *What We Owe to Each Other* (Harvard University Press, 1998).

Schabas W, "Sentencing by International Tribunals: A Human Rights Approach" (1997) 7 *Duke J Comp Int'l L* 461.

Schabas W, "General Principles of Criminal Law in the International Criminal Court (Part III)" (1998) 6 *Eur J Crime Cr L Cr J* 400.

Schabas W, *Genocide in International Law: The Crime of Crimes* (Cambridge University Press, 2000).

Schabas W, "Interpreting the Statutes of the Ad Hoc Tribunals," in L C Vohrah et al, eds, *Man's Inhumanity to Man* (Brill, 2003).

Schaffer J, "Contrastive Causation in the Law" (2010) 16 *Legal Theory* 259.

Schauer F, "Incentives, Reputation and the Inglorious Determinants of Judicial Behavior" (1999–2000) 68 *U Cincinnati L Rev* 615.

Schechter F, "Popular Law and Common Law in Medieval England" (1928) 28 *Columbia L Rev* 269.

Schmitt C, *The Concept of the Political* (Duncker & Humblot, 1932; trans and reprinted University of Chicago Press, 2006).

Sepinwall A J, "Failures to Punish: Command Responsibility in Domestic and International Law" (2009) 30 *Michigan J Int'l L* 251.

Sepinwall A J, "Citizen Responsibility and the Reactive Attitudes: Blaming Americans for War Crimes in Iraq," in T Isaacs & R Vernon, eds, *Accountability of Collective Wrongdoing* (Cambridge University Press, 2011).

Shahabuddeen M, "Does the Principle of Legality Stand in the Way of Progressive Development of the Law?" (2004) 2 *JICJ* 1007.

Shany T & Michaeli K R, "The Case against Ariel Sharon: Revisiting the Doctrine of Command Responsibility" (2001–02) 34 *NYU J Int'l L & Pol* 797.

Simester A P & Brookbanks W J, *Principles of Criminal Law* (Thomson Reuters, 2002).

Simester A P & Sullivan G R, *Criminal Law: Theory and Doctrine*, 3rd ed (Hart, 2007).

Simons K, "Culpability and Retributive Theory: The Problem of Criminal Negligence" (1994) 5 *J Contemp Legal Iss* 365.

Simpson G, "Politics, Sovereignty, Remembrance," in D McGoldrick, P Rowe & E Donnelly, eds, *The Permanent International Criminal Court: Legal and Policy Issues* (Hart, 2004).

Simpson G, *Law, War and Crime: War Crimes Trials and the Reinvention of International Law* (Polity, 2007).

Sivakumaran S, "Courts of Armed Opposition Groups: Fair Trials or Summary Justice?" (2009) 7 *JICJ* 489.

Sivakumaran S, "Ownership of International Humanitarian Law: Non-state Armed Groups and the Formation and Enforcement of IHL Rules," in B Perrin, ed, *Modern Warfare: Armed Groups, Private Militaries, Humanitarian Organizations, and the Law* (UBC Press, 2012).

Smandych R & Linden R, "Administering Justice without the State: A Study of the Private Justice System of the Hudson's Bay Company to 1800" (1996) 11 *Can J L & Soc* 21.

Smeulers A, "What Transforms Ordinary People into Gross Human Rights Violators?," in S C Carey & S C Poe, eds, *Understanding Human Rights Violations: New Systematic Studies* (Ashgate, 2004).

Smeulers A, "Why International Crimes Might Not Seem 'Manifestly Unlawful' to Low-Level Perpetrators" (2019) 17 *JICJ* 1.

Smeulers A, "A Criminological Approach to the ICC's Control Theory," in K J Helleret al, eds, *Oxford Handbook on International Criminal Law* (Oxford University Press, 2020).

Smeulers A & Grünfeld F, *International Crimes and Other Gross Human Rights Violations: A Multi- and Inter-disciplinary Textbook* (Martinus Nijhoff, 2011).

Smeulers A & Haveman R, eds, *Supranational Criminology: Towards a Criminology of International Crimes* (Intersentia, 2008).

Smeulers A, Weerdesteijn M & Hola B, "The Selection of Situations by the ICC: An Empirically Based Evaluation of the OTP's Performance" (2015) 15 *Int'l Crim L Rev* 1.

Smeulers A, Weerdesteijn M & Hola B, *Perpetrators of International Crimes: Theories, Methods, and Evidence* (Oxford University Press, 2019).

Smidt M, "*Yamashita, Medina,* and beyond: Command Responsibility in Contemporary Military Operations" (2000) 164 *Military L Rev* 155.

Soares P P, "Tangling Human Rights and International Criminal Law: The Practice of International Tribunals and the Call for Rationalized Legal Pluralism" (2012) 23 *Crim L Forum* 161.

Somer J, "Jungle Justice: Passing Sentence on the Equality of Belligerents in Non-international Armed Conflict" (2007) 89 *International Review of the Red Cross* 655.

Stahn C, "Between Faith and Facts: By What Standards Should We Assess International Criminal Justice?" (2012) 25 *LJIL* 251.

Stahn C, *A Critical Introduction to International Criminal Law* (Cambridge University Press, 2018).

Stahn C, *Justice as Message: Expressivist Foundations of International Criminal Justice* (Cambridge University Press, 2020).

Steer C, *Translating Guilt: Identifying Leadership Liability for Mass Atrocity Crimes* (TMC Asser Press, 2017).

Stern P J, " 'A Politie of Civill & Military Power': Political Thought and the Late Seventeenth-Century Foundations of the East India Company-State" (2008) 47 *Journal of British Studies* 253.

Stern R, "Coherence as a Test for Truth" (2004) 69 *PPR* 296.

Stewart J, "The End of 'Modes of Liability' for International Crimes" (2011) 25 *LJIL* 165.

Stewart J, "Overdetermined Atrocities" (2012) 10 *JICJ* 1189.

Stewart J, " 'Specific Direction' Is Indefensible: A Response to Heller on Complicity" (12 June 2013), online: http://opiniojuris.org/2013/06/12/specific-direction-is-indefensible-a-response-to-heller-on-complicity/.

Stewart J & Kiyani A, "The Ahistoricism of Legal Pluralism in International Criminal Law" (2017) 65 *Am J Comp L* 393.

Sullivan M & Solove D J, "Radical Pragmatism," in A Malachowski, ed, *The Cambridge Companion to Pragmatism* (Cambridge University Press, 2013).

Sunstein C, "Incompletely Theorized Agreements" (1995) 108 *Harvard L Rev* 1733.

Sunstein C, "Is Deontology a Heuristic? On Psychology, Neuroscience, Ethics and Law" (2014) 63 *Jerusalem Phil Q* 83.

Tadros V, *Criminal Responsibility* (Oxford University Press, 2010).

Tallgren I, "The Sensibility and Sense of International Criminal Law" (2002) 13 *EJIL* 561.

Tellenbach S, "Aspects of the Iranian Code of Islamic Punishment: The Principle of Legality" (2009) 9 *Int'l Crim L Rev* 691.

Thagard P & Verbeugt K, "Coherence as Constraint Satisfaction" (1998) 22 *Cognitive Science* 1.

Théodoridès A, "The Concept of Law in Ancient Egypt," in J R Harris, *The Legacy of Egypt*, 2nd ed (Clarendon Press, 1971).

Thorburn M, "Justifications, Power and Authority" (2008) 117 *Yale LJ* 1070.

Thorburn M, "The Criminal Law as Public Law," in R A Duff & S Green, eds, *The Philosophical Foundations of Criminal Law* (Oxford University Press, 2011).

Timmons M, "Foundationalism and the Structure of Ethical Justification" (1987) 97 *Ethics* 595.

Tooby J & Cosmides L, "The Psychological Foundations of Culture," in J H Barkow, L Cosmides & J Tooby, eds, *The Adapted Mind: Evolutionary Psychology and the Generation of Culture* (Oxford University Press, 1992).

Trahan J, "Bemba Acquittal Rests on Erroneous Application of Appellate Review Standard" (25 June 2018), online: http://opiniojuris.org/2018/06/25/bemba-acquittal-rests-on-erroneous-application-of-appellate-review-standard/.

Trechsel S, "Command Responsibility as a Separate Offence" (2009) 3 *Publicist* 26.

Tremblay P, "The New Casuistry" (1999) 12 *Geo J Legal Ethics* 489.

Triffterer O, "Causality, a Separate Element of the Doctrine of Superior Responsibility as Expressed in Article 28 Rome Statute?" (2002) 15 *LJIL* 179.

Triffterer O & Arnold R, "Article 28," in O Triffterer & K Ambos, eds, *The Rome Statute of the International Criminal Court: A Commentary*, 3rd ed (Beck, Hart, Nomos, 2016).

Tsagourias N, "Command Responsibility and the Principle of Individual Criminal Responsibility: A Critical Analysis of International Jurisprudence," in C Eboe-Osuji, ed,

Essays in International Law and Policy in Honour of Navanethem Pillay (Martinus Nijhoff, 2010).

Tulkens F, "The Paradoxical Relationship between Criminal Law and Human Rights" (2011) 9 *JICJ* 577.

Tyldesley J, *Judgement of the Pharaoh: Crime and Punishment in Ancient Egypt* (Weidenfeld & Nicolson, 2000).

Uhler O & Coursier H, *Commentary on the Geneva Conventions of 12 August 1949, Vol IV* (ICRC, 1958).

van der Wilt H, "Genocide, Complicity in Genocide and International v Domestic Jurisdiction: Reflections on the *van Anraat* Case" (2006) 4 *JICJ* 239.

van der Wilt H, "JCE: Possibilities and Limitations" (2007) 5 *JICJ* 91.

van der Wilt H, "Command Responsibility in the Jungle: Some Reflections on the Elements of Effective Command and Control," in C Jalloh, ed, *The Sierra Leone Special Court and Its Legacy; The Impact for Africa and International Criminal Law* (Cambridge University Press, 2014).

van Dyke J M, "The Fundamental Human Right to Prosecution and Compensation" (2001) 29 *Denver J Int'l L & Pol'y* 77.

van Hooft S, *Cosmopolitanism: A Philosophy for Global Ethics* (Cambridge University Press, 2009).

van Schaack B, "Command Responsibility: A Step Backwards" (1998), online: www .advocacynet.org/resource/369#Command_Responsibility:_A_Step_Backwards.

van Schaack B, "*Crimen Sine Lege*: Judicial Lawmaking at the Intersection of Law and Morals" (2008) 97 *Georgetown L Rev* 119.

van Sliedregt E, "Joint Criminal Enterprise as a Pathway to Convicting Individuals for Genocide" (2007) 5 *JICJ* 184.

van Sliedregt E, "Article 28 of the *ICC Statute*: Mode of Liability and/or Separate Offence?" (2009) 12 *New Crim L Rev* 420.

van Sliedregt E, "Command Responsibility at the ICTY: Three Generations of Case Law and Still Ambiguity," in A H Swart, A Zahar & G Sluiter, eds, *The Legacy of the ICTY* (Oxford University Press, 2011).

van Sliedregt E, *Individual Criminal Responsibility in International Law* (Oxford University Press, 2012).

van Sliedregt E, "Pluralism in International Criminal Law" (2012) 25 *LJIL* 847.

van Sliedregt E, "International Criminal Law," in M Dubber & T Hörnle, *The Oxford Handbook of Criminal Law* (Oxford University Press, 2014).

van Sliedregt E, "International Criminal Law: Over-Studied and Underachieving?" (2016) 29 *LJIL* 1.

van Sliedregt E & Vasiliev S, "Pluralism: A New Framework for International Criminal Justice," in E van Sliedregt & S Vasiliev, eds, *Pluralism in International Criminal Law* (Oxford University Press, 2014).

van Sliedregt E & Vasiliev S, eds, *Pluralism in International Criminal Law* (Oxford University Press, 2014).

Vanocore G, "Legality, Culpability and *Dogmatik*: A Dialogue between the ECtHR, Comparative and International Criminal Law" (2015) 15 *Int'l Crim L Rev* 823.

Vasiliev S, "On Trajectories and Destinations of International Criminal Law Scholarship" (2015) 28 *LJIL* 701.

Vasiliev S, "The Crises and Critiques of International Criminal Justice," in K J Heller et al, *Oxford Handbook on International Criminal Law* (Oxford University Press, 2020).

Vernon R, *Cosmopolitan Regard: Political Membership and Global Justice* (Cambridge University Press, 2010).

VerSteeg R, "The Machinery of Law in Pharaonic Egypt: Organization, Courts, and Judges on the Ancient Nile" (2001) 9 *Cardozo J of Int'l & Comp L* 105.

Vetter G, "Command Responsibility of Non-military Superiors in the International Criminal Court" (2000) 25 *Yale J Int'l L* 89.

Wall I, "Duress, International Criminal Law and Literature" (2006) 4 *JICJ* 724.

Walsh A, "Evolutionary Psychology and the Origins of Justice" (2000) 17 *Justice Quarterly* 841.

Weigend T, "Superior Responsibility: Complicity, Omission or Over-Extension of the Criminal Law?," in C Burchard, O Triffterer & J Vogel, eds, *The Review Conference and the Future of International Criminal Law* (Kluwer, 2010).

Weigend T, "Perpetration through an Organization: The Unexpected Career of a German Legal Concept" (2011) 9 *JICJ* 91.

Weigend T, "Mr Bemba's Acquittal: A Shortcut to Justice?" (25 June 2019), online http://jamesgstewart.com/mr-bembas-acquittal-a-shortcut-to-justice/.

Wells C, "Swatting the Subjectivist Bug" (1982) 1 *Crim L Rev* 209.

Werle G & Burghardt B, "Introductory Note" (2011) 9 *JICJ* 191.

Werle G & Jessberger F, " 'Unless Otherwise Provided': Article 30 of the ICC Statute and the Mental Element of Crimes under International Criminal Law" (2005) 3 *JICJ* 35.

Werle G & Jessberger F, *Principles of International Criminal Law*, 3rd ed (Oxford University Press, 2014).

Wessel J, "Judicial Policy-Making at the International Criminal Court: An Institutional Guide to Analyzing International Adjudication" (2006) 44 *Columbia J Transnat'l L* 377.

Whiting A, "Appeal Judges Turn the ICC on Its Head with *Bemba* Decision" (14 June 2008), online: www.justsecurity.org/57760/appeals-judges-turn-icc-head-bemba-decision/.

Williams G, *Criminal Law: The General Part*, 2nd ed (Stevens, 1961).

Williams G, "Conviction and Fair Labelling" (1983) 42 *Cambridge LJ* 85.

Williams G, *Textbook of Criminal Law* (Sweet & Maxwell, 1983).

Wilson R J, "Defences in Contemporary International Criminal Law" (2002) 96 *AJIL* 517.

Womack B, "The Development and Recent Application of the Doctrine of Command Responsibility, with Particular Reference to the Mens Rea Requirement," in S Yee, ed, *International Criminal Law and Punishment* (University Press of America, 2003).

Wright R W, "Causation: Metaphysics or Intuition?," in K Ferzan & S Morse, eds, *Legal, Moral and Metaphysical Truths: The Philosophy of Michael Moore* (Oxford University Press, 2016).

Wu T & Kang Y S, "Criminal Liability for the Actions of Subordinates: The Doctrine of Command Responsibility and Its Analogues in United States Law" (1997) 38 *Harvard Int'l LJ* 272.

Yahaya N, "Legal Pluralism and the English East India Company in the Straits of Malacca during the Early Nineteenth Century" (2015) 33 *Law & Hist Rev* 945.

Zahar A, "Command Responsibility of Civilian Superiors for Genocide" (2001) 14 *LJIJ* 591.

Zahar A, "Civilizing Civil War: Writing Morality as Law at the ICTY," in B Swart, G Sluiter & A Zahar, eds, *The Legacy of the International Criminal Tribunal for the Former Yugoslavia* (Oxford University Press, 2011).

Zimbardo P, *The Lucifer Effect: Understanding How Good People Turn Evil* (Random House, 2007).

Index

accessory after the fact, 185, 189
accessory versus principal distinction, 34, 89, 150, 182, 197, 209–13, 225
Additional Protocol I to the Geneva Conventions, 43
aiding and abetting, 197, 234
Ambos, Kai, 52, 184
anti-Cartesian, 103, 110–11, 225, 282
authority, 123, 125, 135, 233

Bemba, Prosecutor v
    Appeal Judgment, 6, 191, 236, 258, 265–71, 272–81
    Trial Judgment, 191, 257–65
bias, 83, 90
Blaškić, Prosecutor v, 44, 159, 161, 201
bloodguilt, 189

capacity. *See* criminal negligence
casuistic testing, 105, 106, 108, 225, 282
causation
    free will, 264
    naturalistic conception, 180, 269, 283
    normative conception, 180, 261, 266, 283
    omissions, 179–81, 225, 260, 266, 268
    ratification theory, 187–90
    risk aggravation, 181, 261, 264, 266
Čelebići case, 30, 43, 159, 160, 161, 200
China, criminal law of, 80
citizenship, 125
civilian superior. *See* command responsibility
coherentism, 85
    applied, 67, 69, 198, 224–27
    as best theory of criminal law theory, 100, 227–28
    conservative, 106–9
    definition, 13, 100–6, 282
    fallibilism, 110–11, 226
    humility check, 109, 114, 226, 270, 272, 273
    models, 102, 115

pragmatism, 103
    radical, 106–9
    structure of justification, 102, 228
    versus consistency, 14, 106–9
collective action, 74–76
colonialism, 90
command responsibility
    accessory after the fact, analogy to, 185
    accessory liability, 15, 148, 198, 220, 223, 258, 260, 266, 267
    benefit of studying, 139
    causal contribution, 15, 145, 259, 261–63, 267
    civilian superiors, 141, 221
    conflation with humanitarian law, 42, 158
    dangerous activity, 215–16, 268
    definition, 147
    due diligence, 202
    duty to inquire, 200, 202, 218
    duty to know everything, 202
    effective control, 232
    failure to punish, 145, 159, 175, 263, 266, 267, 268
    failure to take measures, 232, 275
    genius of, 197, 223
    had reason to know, 195, 203, 204, 205
    initial crime, 154, 155, 189, 190
    isolated crime, 155, 269
    non-contributory derelictions, 155, 172
    omission, 179–81
    possession test, 200, 203–5, 219
    reductive teleological reasoning, 31
    remote commanders, 276
    scope, 221
    separate offence, 143–69, 267
    should have known, 15, 194, 195, 199–205, 216–18, 219, 278–80
    successor commander, 155, 190
    sui generis characterization, 146, 169, 259, 267
    variegated approach, 172

For EU product safety concerns, contact us at Calle de José Abascal, 56–1°,
28003 Madrid, Spain or eugpsr@cambridge.org.

www.ingramcontent.com/pod-product-compliance
Ingram Content Group UK Ltd.
Pitfield, Milton Keynes, MK11 3LW, UK
UKHW020359140625
459647UK00020B/2556